D1187868

Phonetic
Lexicon

Phonetic Lexicon

of monosyllabic and some disyllabic words, with homophones, arranged according to their phonetic structure

Denyse Rockey M.A., L.C.S.T.

Formerly Audiologist to the Prince Henry and Prince of Wales Hospitals, Sydney, Australia

HEYDEN & SON LTD

London · New York · Rheine

Heyden & Son Ltd., Spectrum House, Alderton Crescent, London NW4 3XX
Heyden & Son Inc., 225 Park Avenue, New York 10017, U.S.A.
Heyden & Son GmbH, 4440 Rheine/Westf., Münsterstrasse 22, Germany

Library of Congress Catalog Card No. 72–88019

ISBN 0 85501 046 0

Printed in Great Britain by Alden & Mowbray Ltd at the Alden Press, Oxford

ERRATA

Page 6. In line 31 /ʒ/ should read /ɝ/.

Page 7. In the schema, just to the right of "/ɔ/ in words like": the group beginning *fall*, *saw* and the group beginning *sore*, *more* should be bracketed.

Page 8. *cne* should read *cue*.

Pages 56, 68, 72. Column 5 heading, /ɒ/ should read /ɑ/.

Page 72. Column 6 heading, /ɑ/ should read /ɒ/.

Page 78. Column 2, first entry, sh should read ish.

Page 91. In footnote line 2, page 223 should read page 233.

Page 206. Column 6 heading, ɒ(ɑ should read ɒ(ɑ.

Page 234. Group on final vz, line 10, initial gr should be gr.
Group on final nz, line 6, initial d should be dʒ.

Page 239. The word fo'c'sle, initial f, should be in the section on final ksl̩ not skl̩.

Page 241. Column 1, line 31, 223 should read 222.
Column 2, line 9, gn should read gn.

Page 242. Column 1, line 10, ks should read ŋks.
Column 1, line 13, gz should read gz.
Column 2, lines 1 and 2, 236 should read 235.
Column 2, line 22, kls should read ksl̩.

D. Rockey: PHONETIC LEXICON. Published by Heyden & Son, 1973

Contents

Preface

The *Phonetic Lexicon* developed from material compiled by the author during her years in speech and hearing clinics and, as such, has a practical rather than academic orientation. Consequently, while aiming to provide a multi-purpose reference, the main object has been to produce a book which is easy to use and convenient to handle in the teaching and therapeutic situation.

The *Phonetic Lexicon* may also be considered as a natural expansion of the many word lists which have appeared over the years in the literature of the various professions concerned with speech and language. These widely scattered lists, however, are not always practical. In addition, they are mostly insufficiently extensive and explicit and hence fail to manifest the similarities and contrasts of word-groups as a whole and the sound distribution features of the English language. Such lists, then, are often incommensurate with modern needs and the advance of scientific knowledge, which has provided teachers and therapists with a growing theoretical framework for their art and has opened the way for more systematically based programmes. Unfortunately, few therapists have the time to devise and organise extensive teaching materials and so it is hoped that this book will assist them in this aspect of their work.

The format of the *Phonetic Lexicon* has been selected so that words may be grouped according to the way they are said by those using the phonological system of British Received Pronunciation, or one similar to it. However, so that the book may have wider application, various symbols have been used to denote General American speech. Such a method has many shortcomings and one feels that any attempt to categorise such a dynamic phenomenon as speech must fail in some way. Nevertheless, the attempt has been made and if the book is of assistance to some of those concerned with the pronunciation of English it will have achieved its aim.

Acknowledgments

It is through association with others that our tasks are made easier, since we may thereby tap the extension of human learning and make it our own. I have done this many times over the past four years and have benefited from encouragement, criticism and guidance. As a consequence, the original concept of this book has undergone many changes and while the final manuscript is my own, some part of it must be credited to others.

Two colleagues, Bridget Pentland, M.SC., L.C.S.T. and Edwina Bryson, L.A.C.S.T. gave me much encouragement in the early stages of the project and without their belief in the clinical value of the book I might not have persevered with it. At this time I also received support from the Australian College of Speech Therapists for which I am most grateful.

Throughout the development of these lists the pronunciation of certain words has been problematical, especially those varying between accents. It has been my good fortune to have received guidance from two phoneticians: Professor Arthur Delbridge of the English Department at Macquarie University, Sydney and Dr. John Wells of the Phonetics Department at University College, London. Their suggestions have been invaluable and any phonetic weaknesses that persist are not of their making.

This manuscript was completed in Rome where I fortuitously met Professor Derrick Plant of the Instituto Inglese, Università di Roma. His advice and friendliness has been most welcome.

The typing and checking of a manuscript such as this is both time-consuming and demanding and I am indebted to Vicki Maggs for the thoroughness of her work.

The final acknowledgments go to members of my family. Special thanks is due to my brother Julian Roberts for introducing me to the publishers and acting on my behalf while I was out of the country. Part of the book was completed during a brief visit to England when my parents, Constance and Harry Lant, provided facilities which enabled me to work in ease and for this assistance I am most appreciative. Lastly, I should like to thank my husband John Rockey for the calm way in which he has tolerated disruptions to our personal life and for his suggestions at every stage of the project.

Rome
April 1971

ACKNOWLEDGMENTS FOR THE USE OF COPYRIGHT MATERIAL

Various extracts from copyright material are quoted in the *Phonetic Lexicon* by permission of the following publishers, authors and editors, to whom grateful thanks are extended:

ACADEMIC PRESS, INC.: 'The Measurement of Hearing in Children' by D. Frisina, in *Modern Developments in Audiology* (1963) Ed. J. Jerger.

APPLETON-CENTURY-CROFTS and PETER OWEN: 'Terminology and Nomenclature' by K. Wood, in *A Handbook of Speech Pathology* (1959) Ed. E. Travis.

EDWARD ARNOLD LTD.: *An Introduction to the Pronunciation of English* (1962) by A. Gimson.

BASIL BLACKWELL: *How to Learn a Language* (1948) by C. Duff.

CAMBRIDGE UNIVERSITY PRESS: 'Local Accents in England and Wales' by J. Wells, in: *Journal of Linguistics* (1970) Ed. F. Palmer.

W. & R. CHAMBERS LTD.: *Chambers's Twentieth Century Dictionary* (1952) Ed. W. Geddie.

J. M. DENT & SONS LTD. and E. P. DUTTON & CO. INC.: *English Pronouncing Dictionary* (1969) by D. Jones. Ed. A. Gimson.

GRUNE & STRATTON, INC.: *Learning Disabilities: Educational Principles and Practices* (1967) by D. Johnson and H. Myklebust.

W. HEFFER AND SONS LTD.: *English Pronunciation* (1950) by P. MacCarthy.

WILLIAM HEINEMANN MEDICAL BOOKS LTD.: *The Deaf Child* (1964) by E. Whetnall and D. B. Fry.

HOLT, RINEHART AND WINSTON, INC.: *Linguistics and Reading* (1962) by C. Fries.

LONGMAN GROUP LTD.: 'Phonetics' by D. Abercrombie, in: *English Teaching Extracts* (1969) Ed. D. Byrne.

Journal of the Acoustical Society of America and *The American Institute of Physics:* 'Diagnostic Rhyme Test for the Evaluation of Communications Systems' (1965) Vol. 37, by M. Cohen, J. Mickunas Jnr., J. Miller and W. Voiers.

Journal of the Australian College of Speech Therapists, Ed. E. Bryson

THE MACMILLAN COMPANY and ROUTLEDGE & KEGAN PAUL LTD.: *Origins* (1958) by E. Partridge.

G. & C. MERRIAM CO.: *A Pronouncing Dictionary of American English* (1953).

Medical World: 'The Young Deaf Child' by Mary Sheridan. (1955) Vol. 82.

METHUEN & CO.: 'Signs and Signals' by W. Haas, 'Linguistics and Speech Pathology' by J. Trim and 'Coding and Decoding in Speech' by D. Fry, in: *Signs, Signals and Symbols* (1963) Ed. S. Mason and *Speech and Voice* (1942) by L. Stein.

MOUTON & CO.: *Traumatic Aphasia* (1970) by A. R. Luria.

OXFORD UNIVERSITY PRESS: *Rules of Pronunciation for the English Language* (1966) by A. Wijk.

DR. J. M. PICKETT: 'Sound Patterns of Speech: An Introductory Sketch' *American Annals of the Deaf* (1968).

PRENTICE-HALL INC.: *Voice and Articulation* by C. Van Riper and J. Irwin (1958).

ST. MARTIN'S PRESS, INC.: *A Structural History of English* (1966) by J. Nist.

The Modern Language Journal: Ed. C. L. King, 'Auditory vs. Articulatory Training in Exotic Sounds' by J. Catford and D. Pisoni (1970).

THE UNIVERSITY OF CHICAGO PRESS: *The Sounds of English and Italian* (1965) by F. Agard and R. di Pietro.

THE UNIVERSITY OF MICHIGAN PRESS: *Teaching and Learning English as a Foreign Language* (1954) by C. Fries and *Linguistics across Cultures* (1957) by R. Lado.

UNIVERSITY OF MINNESOTA PRESS: *Differential Diagnosis of Aphasia with the Minnesota Test* (1965) by H. Schuell.

WADSWORTH PUBLISHING COMPANY, INC.: 'Disorders of Articulation: Dyslalia' by G. Arnold, in: *Voice–Speech–Language* (1965) by R. Luchsinger and G. Arnold.

DR. J. WEPMAN: *Auditory Discrimination Test Manual* (1958).

THE WORLD PUBLISHING COMPANY: *Webster's New Twentieth Century Dictionary* (1962).

Key to Symbols

Consonants			Vowels		
p	as in pea		i	as in beat
b	,, ,, be		ɪ	,, ,, bit
t	,, ,, tea		ɛ	,, ,, bet
d	,, ,, do		æ	,, ,, bat
k	,, ,, key		ɑ	,, ,, barn
g	,, ,, go		ɒ	,, ,, not
f	,, ,, four		ʊ	,, ,, put
v	,, ,, vow		u	,, ,, boot
θ	,, ,, thaw		ʌ	,, ,, but
ð	,, ,, they		ɜ	,, ,, bird
s	,, ,, see		eɪ	,, ,, bait
z	,, ,, zoo		oʊ	,, ,, boat
ʃ	,, ,, shoe		aɪ	,, ,, bite
ʒ	,, ,, rouge		aʊ	,, ,, out
h	,, ,, he		ɔɪ	,, ,, toy
tʃ	,, ,, chew		iə	,, ,, here
dʒ	,, ,, jaw		ɛə	,, ,, there
m	,, ,, mow		ju	,, ,, few
n	,, ,, no			
l	,, ,, low		ɒ	⎫ mainly found in
r	,, ,, row		iə	⎬ RP English
w	,, ,, woe		ɛə	⎭

Additional Markings

* indicates homophones

† ,, ,, obsolete, dialectal, technical words etc.

(,, ,, the following sound may replace the preceding one.

/ ,, ,, ,, ,, ,, ,, be added to the preceding one.

ˌ when placed below a consonant indicates it may be syllabic.

r ,, ,, at the head of a column indicates either the presence of some variety of /r/ or r-colouring in the previous vowel.

[] enclose words which have an alternate form both in spelling and pronunciation.

() ,, ,, ,, ,, ,, ,, pronunciation. This does not apply to words where the variation is indicated by additional symbols at the column head.

Italics are used in the Tables to indicate words which may be presented in picture form (see page 12).

CHAPTER 1
Explanatory Notes

A. PREAMBLES

B. THE ACCENTS

    I.   RP ENGLISH
    II. GENERAL AUSTRALIAN
    III. GENERAL AMERICAN

C. THE PHONETICS

    I.   DIFFERENCES BETWEEN THE ACCENTS
       1. RP and Australian
       2. RP and American
    II. ARRANGEMENT OF THE TABLES
       1. The Initial Consonants
       2. The Medial Vowels
       3. The Final Consonants
    III. CHOICE OF SYMBOLS
       1. Phonetic Symbols
       2. Qualifying Symbols
    IV. PRONUNCIATION OF SPECIFIC WORDS
       1. Foreign Words
       2. Dialectal Words
       3. Particular Words
       4. Disyllables
       5. Homophones

D. THE WORDS

    I.   WORDS INCLUDED IN THE LEXICON
       1. Proper Names
       2. Letters of the Alphabet
       3. Colloquialisms and Slang
       4. Common Abbreviations
       5. Common Contractions
       6. Acronyms
       7. Foreign Words
       8. Dialectal Words
       9. Obsolete and Archaic Words
     10. Technical Words
     11. Homophones
    II. WORDS OMITTED FROM THE LEXICON
       1. Foreign and Dialectal Words
       2. Words with /ʊə/ & /ɔə/
       3. Prefixes and Suffixes
       4. Possessive forms
       5. Inflected forms
    III. SPELLING

E. REFERENCES

A. PREAMBLES

These explanatory notes are not intended as a serious treatise on the subjects they cover: their purpose is to give a brief understanding of the way the book is organised and the reasons for the structure and pronunciation which has been adopted.

B. THE ACCENTS

In order to understand the terms of reference it is necessary from the outset to distinguish between *accent* and *dialect*. Nist (1966) defined the latter as:

> 'A variant version of a language distinguished by its peculiar idiom, vocabulary, phonology, and morphology. A dialect usually impedes speech communication, as in the Cockney of British English.'

In Wells' (1970a) words, *accent* is:

> '. . . the phonetic aspect of a dialect . . .'

This division conforms with that proposed by Abercrombie (1963, 1965) who points out in the earlier work that, notwithstanding some confusion on this subject, *dialect* is never a matter of sounds only and therefore, though diversity of dialect is accompanied by a change in accent, the converse is not necessarily true.

Dialects concern us here only to the extent that some words of dialectal origin are included in the book. Of more importance is *accent*, since the word-lists are arranged according to the pronunciation of a given group of speakers. This is not always easy to determine for speech is an historical process, in constant flux, and it is consequently often difficult to delineate and describe what is taking place. Changes, sometimes occurring within a lifetime, tend to follow three trends. First, there may be a general modification of sounds, e.g. the closer vowel in *saw* accompanied by stronger lip-rounding, noted by Gimson (1962), in younger speakers of the south of England. Then there is the swing from one phoneme to another, e.g. the RP move from /ɔ/ to /ɒ/ before /f/, /θ/, /s/ in words like *often, loss, cost* (Gimson, 1962; Wells, 1970a). Lastly, there may be changes involving isolated words, e.g. *retch*.

Obviously, such changes cannot be anticipated nor many variations recorded in a book intended primarily as a clinical tool for it would then become both confusing to the teacher and perplexing to the foreign student. We must content ourselves with recording one accent and indicating important departures from this by means which will be discussed later (Sections C.I,II,III). Received Pronunciation (RP) is the standard which has been adopted and the other accents recorded, namely Australian and American, will be discussed in relation to this.

B. I. Received Pronunciation

This is the speech of those upper and upper-middle class English, who share a similar educational background. It is a regionless accent often wrongly associated with southern England (Wells, 1970a). This author also states that Standard English is 'the standard DIALECT of English, while Received Pronunciation is – in England if not elsewhere – its standard ACCENT'. Despite this, RP English is not spoken by the majority of Englishmen though it is a 'widely understood pronunciation' both in England and English-speaking countries (Jones, 1969).

For this reason, and because the standard references on English pronunciation are concerned with the RP accent, it has been chosen as the basis for this book. In doing so, the regional accents of England have not been entirely ignored: many such variations are in line with American speech and are indicated accordingly (e.g. the *r*-colouring in the rhotic accents of south-west England and the northern vowel distinctions /æ/ and /ɑ/ in words like *glass* and *farm*).

B. II. General Australian

Fortunately Australian speech can be easily accommodated within the format of this book since it has the same phoneme system as RP English; such isomorphism means the two can have an identical phonetic transcription (Turner, 1966; Wells, 1970b). Although these accents sound quite distinct, their difference is in realisation only. Once again, Wells (1970a) puts the situation clearly:

> 'Australian English . . . has the same phoneme system as RP, with comparatively minor differences in distribution and incidence; yet it sounds quite different, and diverges from RP in the realisation of almost every vowel phoneme.'

The task is further simplified by the fact that Australia is linguistically unified; indeed, Mitchell and Delbridge (1965) note that it is remarkable for its comparative uniformity. Following Baker, they identify three major sub-groups: the Broad; the General, containing over half the population; and the Cultivated. This classification corresponds with Baker's types A_1, A_2 and A_3, as signified in the later edition of his book (1966). Though these groups are acoustically distinct, many of the differences are to be found in phoneme realisation, vocal quality and prosody, which do not concern us here.

B. III. General American

Uniformity is also found in the speech of Americans. Nist (1966) states that: 'the major characteristic of American English today is the general uniformity in its pronunciation throughout the United States'. Regional variations are more marked than in Australia but Nist, unlike Francis (1958), does not look upon them as dialectal since they are no impediment to communication. It seems that there is a general levelling of these variations, possibly under the influence of broadcasting, and a standard General American (GA) accent is now emerging, in all but the extreme eastern and southern areas (Nist).

Generally speaking, the American accent is more difficult to incorporate within the format of this book since its vowel system varies a good deal, in some respects, from RP English (see Section C.I.2). Fortunately, for those readers requiring greater accuracy than this book provides, there is a list of mono-syllables arranged according to American pronunciation (Moser, 1969).

As with the British dialects, American regional variations are catered for to the extent that they resemble one of the other two accents which are included. For example, some speakers in the Eastern United States distinguish between the vowels /æ/, /a/ and /ɒ/ in a way similar to RP speakers (Bronstein, 1960) in words like *cat*, *farm* and *pot*. These resemblances and differences will now be discussed more fully.

3

C. THE PHONETICS

In this section it is necessary to consider the phonetic differences between the accents and how these divergencies are recorded in the Tables; the arrangement of the Tables and the sound groups included; the symbols used, both phonetic and qualifying; and the pronunciation of certain words and homophones.

C. I. Differences between the Accents

As it is convenient to compare variations with some standard, the Australian and American accent will be considered in relation to Received Pronunciation, which has been adopted as the reference point of this book.

1. *RP and General Australian Speech*

It has already been pointed out in the previous Section that there is little distinction between the phoneme systems of these two accents. However, as regards the words recorded in the Tables, some noteworthy differences are to be found. For example, Australians have long been using the short /ɒ/ for /ɔ/ before the fricatives /f/, /θ/ and /s/, e.g. in *off* and, although RP speakers now appear to be following suit, it remains to be seen whether they will adopt the Australian pattern of using it consistently before /l/ as in *oral*, *salt*, and before /s/ + a consonant, e.g. *Austria*. Also of note is the Australian preference of /æ/ for /a/ before fricatives as in *grasp* and words derived from the Greek *aph* (Turner, 1966). Finally, differences are present in the pronunciation of specific words, e.g. the use of /ɪ/ in *bream*.

2. *RP and General American Speech*

In this book, General American speech should be taken to correspond with the 'cultivated colloquial' accent recorded by Kenyon and Knott (1953) in their dictionary as the standard form of spoken English in America. This varies a good deal from RP, especially in respect to the use of certain vowels and, as these are poorly stabilised in many regions of the United States, it is necessary to discuss them at some length. The main characteristics of GA speech, and the way these are indicated in the Tables, are listed below:

(a) The use of /æ/ before the voiceless fricatives /f/, /θ/, /sp/ etc., e.g. *bath, clasp* and when the vowel is followed by a cluster beginning with /m/ or /n/, e.g. *sample, branch*. Bronstein (1960), points out that until the eighteenth century /æ/ was the common form, but a change to /ɑ/ or /a/ took place in words having a final or preconsonantal *r*, e.g. *car, card*, and also those containing a silent *l*, e.g. *calm, psalm*. Words with such straightforward variant pronunciations are parenthesised and recorded in the two appropriate columns.

(b) The absence, or infrequent use, of /ɒ/ in words like *not* and *bomb*. This sound is heard in the speech of some Americans when it is usually, according to Thomas (1958), an allophone of either /ɑ/ or /ɔ/. Bronstein contends that it is one of the most unstable sounds of American English being heard inconsistently in a variety of words throughout the country, regardless of region. Kenyon and Knott, in their *Pronouncing Dictionary of American English* describe it as an historical sound not in universal use but found in the east and south and 'in certain kinds of words . . . in all parts of the country'. What, then, happens to words which for RP speakers contain the /ɒ/ phoneme?

(i) First, /ɑ/ is frequently heard in the 'short *o*' words giving rise to a similarity between *card-cod*; *sharp-shop*; *harp-hop*. However, these pairs may be distinguished by the addition of /ə/ or /r/, or an increase in vowel length, where an *r* occurs in the spelling (Bronstein). Excepting some *wa* words, the pronunciation of which is variable, Kenyon (1958) records the frequent use of /ɑ/ when the vowel is followed by: a plosive, e.g. *chop, watt, frog*; /ʃ/, e.g. *squash*; an affricate, e.g. *botch, lodge*; /l/, e.g. *doll* and the nasals /m/ and /n/, notable exceptions being *gone* and *shone*. In fact, the situation is not quite so clear cut, and opinions vary especially in regard to velar sounds. For instance, Kenyon himself gives a choice of /ɑ/ or /ɔ/ before final /g/ words; Bronstein says that *o* words followed by any velar consonant are generally /ɔ/ outside the eastern United States; while Thomas maintains that /ɑ/, /ɔ/ or /ɒ/ may be present not only in these situations but also before /l/, e.g. *doll*, and in miscellaneous words such as *on*.

(ii) Secondly, /ɔ/ is frequently heard both before /ŋ/ and the voiceless fricatives /f/, /θ/ and /s/, this latter pronunciation being retained in certain words by some RP speakers, e.g. *off*. Once again, opinions vary as to precisely when this sound is used. Thomas says it is heard when *o* precedes any nasal, and he ascribes /ɑ/, /ɔ/ or /ɒ/ to words with an intervocal *r*, e.g. *foreign, laurel*, where Kenyon says /ɔ/ is usually heard.

(iii) Thirdly, /ɑ/, /ɔ/ or /ɒ/ may be used. Thomas points to the complicated picture before velar consonants; similar inconsistencies are to be found with *wa* words, e.g. *wash*. In addition, we have seen that the position is unclear before /l/ as in *doll*, and in those words having an intervocal *r*. Regional differences alone do not seem to explain these occurrences.

It follows from the more frequent use of /æ/ and the absence of /ɒ/ in much GA speech, that differences will be evident in the distribution of certain other vowels, especially /ɑ/ and /ɔ/.

(c) The use of /ɑ/ varies from RP speech, as already noted, in being absent from words like *aunt* and present in certain 'short *o*' and *wa* words, e.g. *doll* and *watch*.

(d) The use of /ɔ/ varies a good deal except before final *r* or *r*+a consonant, e.g. *war, horse*. According to Kenyon and Knott, the variants /ɑ/ or /ɒ/ are commonly heard when the sound precedes /l/+a consonant, e.g. *salt*. The sound may be absent when *au* is followed by /n/+a consonant, e.g. *daunt*; conversely, it may be present in some 'short *o*' words, e.g. *dog*.

Due to the inconsistent use of /ɑ/, /ɔ/ and /ɒ/ in GA speech, words having these sounds are difficult to classify within the format of this book. Listing the words in several columns is not a satisfactory solution as it would be confusing to readers with RP speech and would result in the formation of numerous word-pairs which do not generally rank as homophones. Since /ɒ/ has definite phonemic status in England and, according to Bronstein, is more frequently used throughout the States than is usually thought, only the RP version of the words in question is recorded. Divergencies from this are indicated by suitable symbols at the head of the columns (Section C. III.1.b,c,d). Fortunately, the other distinctive features of American speech follow a more regular pattern.

5

(e) The use of /oʊ/ in words like *borne, cored, course, four, hoarse, mourn, ore, roar, sore, worn, wore* thereby distinguishing them from *born, cord, coarse, for, horse, morn, or, raw, saw* and *warn*. According to Kenyon, the /oʊ/ in these environments, while belonging to the same phoneme, differs from that of *note* in being lowered by the adjacent /r/. This historical distinction between /ɔ/ and /oʊ/ is preserved in some parts of the country but most authorities seem to agree that a swing to /ɔ/ in all these words is on the increase. However, provision for this variation has been made by adding /oʊ/ to the /ɔ/ column of the relevant Tables (Section C.III.d).

(f) The reduction of the RP diphthongs /iə/ and /ɛə/ to a variety of /i/ or /ɪ/ and /ɛ/ in some areas outside the northern United States (Kenyon and Knott, 1953). However, a diphthongal form is retained since the /ə/ is replaced by /r/ which, according to Bronstein, has a semi-vocal nature in American English. Thus the vowels in *fear* and *care* may be transcribed /iɚ/ and /ɛɚ/ or /ir/ and /ɛr/ (Section C.III.1.b). A similar feature is evident in the rhotic accents of the west of England but these differ from their American counterparts in preserving a contrast between such pairs as *spear it-spirit* and *fairy-ferry* (Wells, 1970a). Kenyon points to variations of /ir/ and /ɛr/ in GA speech resulting in a difference between *we're-weir* and *they're-there*. Such fine distinctions do not concern us here and these pairs are listed as homophones. It is interesting to note in passing that a reduced monothongal form of the phoneme may be heard in Australia (Mitchell and Delbridge 1965; Turner, 1966) and sometimes in New York City (Thomas, 1958). Since most American speakers differentiate such words as *ken* and *cairn*, whether by the addition of /ə/ or /r/ or by an increase in vowel length, it seems justifiable to keep the /iə/ and /ɛə/ columns separate from those of /i/, /ɪ/ and /ɛ/ and to use /iə/ rather than /ɪə/ to depict that length.

(g) The use of /r/ in final or pre-consonantal positions, e.g. *car, card, cared*, in many regions of the United States. Bronstein says that /r/ might rank as the most variable of the consonants in the language; indeed, it often loses its consonantal form and disappears entirely in the *r*-less territories, being then replaced by either a lengthened vowel, permitting a distinction between *dark* and *dock*, or the weak /ə/ as in *fear* and *horse*. In other cases, the vowel before the spelled *r* becomes retroflexed giving rise to the characteristic *r*-colouring, usually symbolised /ɚ/ or /ɜ/. In this book, such divergencies are signified solely by /r/ at the head of the relevant columns. Separate Tables have not been made for final /r/, /rb/, /rt/ etc. since this would mean duplication of a large number of words of little interest to those using the RP phonological system. Consequently for some American speakers, there is no strict rhyme between all the words in a given column, e.g. *saw, core*, even when the same vowel is used in both, nor are some words properly homophonous, e.g. *caw-core*. Readers will have to interpret these words according to their own need and usage. Fortunately the distinction is not of clinical importance.

(h) The use of /u/ for /ju/ after alveolar sounds and /θ/, e.g. *new, dune*. This phenomenon is also found in the speech of some Londoners (Wells, 1970a), and may be heard in RP speech after /s/, /θ/ and /l/, e.g. in *sue* and *lute* (Wells, 1970b). However, not all Americans adopt such pronunciation and many have an intermediary /iu/ form. Words having a /u/ and /ju/ pronunciation are recorded in both these columns.

General American speech is distinguished from Received Pronunciation in the use of several vowels and the /r/ sound. These differences are readily apparent in the following Schema.

RP ENGLISH USES:

- /ɑ/ in words like:
  - *laugh, bath, clasp, sample* before /f/,/θ/,/s/ and covered nasals /m/ and /n/ AND .... /æ/
  - *father, car, shah,* .... /ɑ/

- /ɒ/ in the following
  - 'short *o*' words before plosives, affricates, /m/,/n/, and /ʃ/ e.g. *shop, botch, bomb, don* and *squash*
  - *wa* and miscellaneous words, those with an intervocal /r/, and before velar consonants and /l/, e.g. *wash, honk, doll, foreign* .... /ɑ/,/ɔ/ or /ɒ/
  - 'short *o*' words before /f/,/θ/,/s/, e.g. *off, toss,* ....

- /ɔ/ in words like:
  - *fall, saw, caught, bought* and before final /r/ or /r/+a consonant, e.g. *for, form* .... /ɔ/
  - *sore, more* (i.e. *re* words) and others, e.g. *four, course, roar, worn* .... or /oʊ/

- No /r/ in final or preconsonantal positions .... /r/

- /ju/ after alveolar sounds, e.g. *tune, dune* .... /u/

- /iə/ and /ɛə/ in such words as *here* and *there* .... /ɪr/,/ɪɚ/ /ɛr/,/ɛɚ/

OFTEN USED BY GA SPEAKERS

SCHEMA SHOWING THE MAIN DIFFERENCES BETWEEN GA AND RP ENGLISH

C. II. Arrangement of the Tables

The size and organisation of this book has been determined largely by its intended use in a clinical or teaching situation, where limitations of space and the need for speed of reference are often of great importance.

Seventy-nine Tables are presented each containing nineteen columns and forty lines of words, positioned according to their initial, medial and final sound. This system facilitates a direct and quick comparison of the initial and vowel sounds of words, and gives an overall view of the distribution of these particular sound-groups in the English language. The format of every page remains constant but each contains words ending with a different consonant, indicated at the top right of the page. A comparison of final sounds may be made from one page to another.

1. *The Initial Consonants*

These are indicated by the symbols in the extreme left-hand column and follow the order from top to bottom: plosives, fricatives, affricates, nasals, liquids and semivowels. The single initial consonants are followed by clusters arranged in a similar order with such combinations as /tr/ and /dr/ being treated in this group rather than with the affricates.

7

Rare initial combinations, e.g. /dw/ have been excluded but the pertinent words are listed in the Appendix if there are more than four in number.

Allophonic variations are not shown, e.g. /ç/ for /hj/ in words like *hugh* and *human* neither has the coalescence of /tj/ and /dj/ to /tʃ/ and /dʒ/ as in *tube* and *dune*.

2. *The Medial Vowels*

There are nineteen columns each containing words having a different vowel. Hence words within any one column may rhyme for a given speaker, but not necessarily for all, e.g. *nude* and *rude* in the /u/ column rhyme for American but not RP speakers. As previously noted, there is no strict rhyme between words in those columns where the /r/ symbol is used to denote *r*-colouring (see Sections C.I.2.g and C.III.1.b).

The sequence of the vowel columns from left to right is: front and then back vowels, diphthongs and the /j+u/ combination. The following points should also be observed:

(a) The vowel /ə/ is omitted since its use is variable and it is not found in the strong form of monosyllables.

(b) /ju/ is placed in the vowel column for reasons of space and convenience of grouping. If, in such words as *cne*, *few* and *skew*, the /j/ were treated as a consonant, the clusters /kj/, /fj/, /skj/ etc. would be formed. This arrangement would increase the length of the book relative to its width and obscure the group of words having the distinctive /ju/ feature, for then they would find themselves in the /u/ column along with *food* and *rude*. The present arrangement means that duplication occurs between the extreme top right-hand slot /ju/ and the middle slot formed where the /j/ line and the /u/ columns meet. The selection of words for each position is discussed later (Section D.I.11.d and f).

(c) The /ɔə/ diphthong is omitted. The use of this diphthong seems to be losing ground to /ɔ/ in both America and Australia (Bronstein; Mitchell and Delbridge). The pattern in England is similar with /ɔ/ being increasingly heard in words spelled *ore*, *oor*, *oar*, *our*, e.g. *fore*, *door*, *soar*, *four* though Gimson says the latter form 'is retained in conservative RP and in many regional dialects'. He also notes that the /ə/ may be used to signify the orthographic *r* in a word like *horse*, which may be said /hɔrs/ or /hɔəs/. In this book all such words are to be found in the /ɔ/ column with the /r/ symbol indicating the possible presence of this sound.

Words like *poor*, *sure*, *your*, which for RP speakers may be said /ɔə/, /ʊə/ or /ɔ/, cannot be represented according to the first two diphthongs as these are not included in the book.

(d) The /ʊə/ diphthong is usually omitted since it is partially obsolete and is found in very few words, of which the most notable are: *poor*, *boor-boer*, *tour*, *dour*, *moor*, *lure*, *Ruhr* and *your-you're*. Some of these words are listed according to their alternate monophthongal forms. Recording of /ʊə/ occurs on the /rm̩/, /rn̩/ and /rl̩/ Tables.

(e) The triphthongs and the /jʊə/ combination are found chiefly in words with no final consonant. Therefore no separate columns have been given over to them and they are listed in the Appendix (see pages 230–231), except on the Tables noted above.

3. *The Final Consonants*

Seventy-nine final consonants and consonantal clusters are given in the Tables, two pages for each. Monosyllables are presented before disyllables and within these two groups the ordering of the sounds follows that of the initial consonants already mentioned: plosives, fricatives, affricates and liquids, with the voiceless sound of each pair coming first. Sounds are ordered from front to back within each group, e.g. /p/, /b/, /t/, /d/, /k/, /g/. This does not mean that all final endings, amongst the words chosen for this book, are represented on the Tables. To the contrary, numerous other combinations exist but are not included for one of the following reasons:

(a) There are less than a dozen words for that particular sound or sound combination, e.g. the /ʒ/ in *beige*. In this and similar cases the words in question are listed separately in the Appendix.

(b) The final cluster represents primarily an inflected form of a word already listed, e.g. /bz/ as in *tubs*. Thus a /bz/ Table would be merely the unnecessary repetition, in plural form, of words on the /b/ Table and /pt/ would be a repeat of the verbs on the /p/ page, e.g. *tapped*. A note at the bottom of each Table indicates the main clusters which readers can form from it.

However, if the final cluster is found in a fair number of uninflected words, then a Table is presented, e.g. /ks/ catering for words like *wax* and *six*; if it is found in only a few uninflected words, these are listed separately in the Appendix, e.g. /nz/ found in *bronze*.

C. III. Choice of Symbols

The symbols used within the Tables are of two kinds: first, there are the phonetic symbols for sounds and sound groups; and secondly, there are the markings used to qualify a particular feature of a word. Each of these will be discussed in detail.

1. *Phonetic Symbols*

Over the past few years a variety of books have appeared using various symbols to represent a given phoneme. Unfortunately, usage has not been uniform and the following inconsistencies are evident:

(i) The use of one symbol for more than one phoneme, e.g. /e/ for the vowels in *play* and *pen* (see Barber, 1964; Bronstein, 1960; Heffner, 1950; Jones, 1969; Kenyon and Knott, 1953; Tibbits, 1963; Thomas, 1958 among others).

(ii) The transcription of one phoneme by more than one symbol, e.g. the vowel in *pen* has been represented by both the /e/ and /ɛ/ symbols.

(iii) In addition, some modification to well-established practice is found, for example, the use of /əu/ for /oʊ/ in *toe* (Jones, 1969). While this symbol may more accurately describe the sound, to avoid confusion it is not used here since it is sometimes employed to denote an Australian vowel (Turner, 1966).

A chart of a limited number of these divergencies is given by Bronstein.

In this book the older narrow script is used, as outlined by Ward (1948), in the hope that this will be more generally understood. The vowel symbols at the head of each column indicate phonemic categories rather than exact phonetic realisations and should not be interpreted as depicting accurately the speech of a given person or group. For example, for Australians and some Americans, /a/would depict the vowel in *bath* more precisely than the /ɑ/ used, but such fine distinctions are not considered necessary, for they are neither convenient to record nor practically useful.

Three other points are to be noted about the phonetic symbols:

(a) The /w/ is used for both the voiced /w/ and the unvoiced /ʍ/ forms of the semi-vowel. This distinction between the sounds is of little clinical importance and is fast dying out in everyday speech (Barber, 1964).

(b) The /r/ symbol is used to indicate all varieties of initial *r*. In addition, it is placed at the head of some columns to show its influence in final and preconsonantal positions with some speakers (see Section C.I.2.g). In the diphthong columns /iə/ and /ɛə/, slant lines are used to indicate that the /ə/ vowel may be missing. Therefore, i/ə/r and ɛ/ə/r could read i/r and ɛ/r (see Section C.I.2.f). However, where *r* forms part of a final cluster, e.g. the /rṇ/ Table, a word may be placed in both the /ɛ/ and /ɛə/ columns, e.g. *Aaron*.

(c) The vowel symbols /ɑ/, /ɒ/ and /ɔ/ are added to some columns to indicate the alternative sound/s which may be used; for example, for some American speakers there is no distinction between *Shan, John* and *lawn*, i.e. when /ɑ/ is heard. More usually a differentiation is made and the symbols indicate that some speakers must:

  (i) Read the /ɑ/ and /ɒ/ columns as one, and adjacent words like *card* and *cod* as homophones.

 (ii) Read at least part of the /ɒ/ and /ɔ/ columns as one, and *bomb* and *balm* as homophones.

(iii) Read at least part of the /ɔ/ and /ɑ/ columns as one, and *gant* and *gaunt* as homophones (see Section C.I.2.b,c and d).

The more common homophonic pairs are listed separately. Those looking for greater accuracy and convenience than this method provides are referred to Moser (1969) who has organised American monosyllables in such a way that the /ɒ/ sound is completely omitted.

(d) The diphthong /oʊ/ is added to the /ɔ/ column where appropriate to indicate the distinction between such words as *four-for* in some American Speech (see Section C.I.2.e).

Symbols at the head of the columns indicate American pronunciation only; where Australian differs from RP, e.g. *auction*, the word is repeated in the appropriate slots.

2. *Qualifying Symbols*

Six different qualifying symbols are placed beside the words in the Tables, Homophone Lists and the Appendix. In addition, some words are printed in italics. Each of these features will be considered separately.

(a) *An asterisk* (*) indicates a homophone. The other word/s of a similar phonetic composition are to be found in the Homophone Lists placed after the Tables. This system does not apply in the Appendix, where homophones are placed alongside each other, e.g. lapse, laps, Lapps.

(b) *A dagger* (†) is used to indicate obscure, archaic, vulgar, heraldic, poetic, technical, dialectal, provincial, colloquial and foreign words, plus slang, interjections and some abbreviations. As many of these words will not be of use in the clinical situation the † provides a quick means for them to be by-passed.

Foreign words are considered to be those which are not fully part of the English language and where the dictionary reference is to its country of origin rather than some distant etymological foundation, e.g. *schuit* (Dutch). If there is any discrepancy between the American and English dictionaries as to whether a word falls into one of the above categories, generally the *Chambers's English Dictionary* is followed. It is not unusual, for example, to find *Webster's Dictionary* treating a word as obscure or dialectal but not *Chambers's* and vice versa.

The † is not used in the following instances:
  (i) Common contractions, e.g. *can't*.
 (ii) Abbreviations of proper names, e.g. *Gert, Nat, Marg, Pam* etc.
(iii) Inflected forms of a word.
 (iv) Acronyms, e.g. *Waacs*.
  (v) Words having more than one meaning, where one of these is not obscure etc. For example, *kedge* is listed as provincial when it means 'brisk, lively: pot-bellied' but falls into none of the above categories when it means 'a small anchor for keeping a ship steady, and for warping the ship' (Chambers).

(c) *Parentheses* ( ) surround those words which have an alternate pronunciation either between accents, e.g. *bath*, or within one accent, e.g. *off*. These words are listed twice and may be placed in slots on the same page, e.g. *bath* in the /æ/ and /ɑ/ columns of final /θ/; or they may be placed on different pages as *trait*, which is to be found in the /eɪ/ column of the 'no final' and /t/ pages. The following points should also be noted:
  (i) Words are parenthesised if both the variants occur reasonably often; if one of the alternatives appears to be in more frequent use, then only the more unusual form is parenthesised, e.g. *clique* said /klɪk/, as is often heard in America and Australia. Not every alternative pronunciation is listed and variations which appear to be dialectal or regional are generally omitted. In the case of infrequently used words not entered in a pronunciation dictionary, e.g. *zygon*, usually the first alternative given in the standard dictionary is listed. When two dictionaries agree on one pronunciation then this is recorded. Similarly, the first listing of a phonetic dictionary is generally adopted unless the second is in line with another accent, e.g. *pore* which can be said with an /ɔ/ vowel by both American and RP speakers.
 (ii) A parenthesised word may only be recorded once, if its pair does not fit within the format of the Tables, e.g. *bourbon* cannot be listed according to its /ʊə/ form.

Parentheses are not used in the following cases:
  (i) For words where there is a slight difference in meaning with a change of sound, e.g. *prayer* signifying either 'one who prays' or a 'supplication' (Jones).
 (ii) Homographs such as *tear* which is placed in the /ɪə/ and /ɛə/ columns. In these cases the meaning is quite diverse and should be apparent to the reader. Special care must be taken with these words when they are recorded according to a variant spelling (see Section D.III). An example of this would be *put* which, when said with an /ʌ/ sound becomes homophonous with *putt*. With such a pronunciation it can signify (a) a Scottish verb meaning to hurl; (b) a card game; and (c) a greenhorn (Chambers). Differences in the pronunciation of proper names can also be considered under this category, e.g. *Broome*.

(d) *Square brackets* [ ] surround words which have alternate forms both in spelling and pronunciation but whose meaning remains the same, e.g. *coven, covin*; they are not used for synonyms nor where there is a spelling variation only. When such words are obsolete, dialectal etc. the fact is indicated by the † symbol, e.g. [sic]† a Scottish form of *such kind*; [sark]† and [serk]†. If one of these forms is much rarer than the other, then only it is bracketed, e.g. *wizen* and [*weazen*] both meaning 'dried up, then shrivelled' (Chambers). [ ] frequently surround a variant (usually archaic) inflected forms of verbs, e.g. *wreaked* and [*wroke*]; and *wreaked* and [*wroken*], the first pair being the past tense and the second the past participle.

No brackets are used where one variant of a word also has an independent and diverse meaning. For example, *gant* said /æ/ and *gaunt* said /ɔ/ are both variants of a Scottish verb meaning 'to yawn'. However, the latter word also means 'thin and emaciated' and is treated as such, i.e. not obscure or dialectal etc. This particular word does, however, have ( ) parentheses for its less usual form.

Where words have variants both as regards their pronunciation, ( ), and as regards their form and pronunciation, [ ], both sets of symbols are not used as this is somewhat confusing to the eye and the information is of no great import. Therefore, the [()] combination is not found. The set of brackets chosen is determined by which factors appear to predominate.

(e) A single slant line (/) indicates that the following sounds may be heard in some speakers. Thus, the word *here* in the i/ə/r column means that it may be said with a monophthongal form /hi/, /hiə/, /hir/, or /hiə/ followed by some variety of /r/.

(f) A single bracket (indicates that the following sound may replace the preceding one. For example, *hop* in the column headed ɒ(ɑ means that RP speakers say this word as /hɒp/ but /hɑp/ is heard in some other accents.

(g) *Italics* are used to indicate words which can easily be presented in visual form, that is, through pictures or graphically, for example, simple nouns like *car*, numbers, and letters of the alphabet. These words are often very useful clinically and may be quickly selected by this method. Not all nouns are italicised, but chiefly those for which readily recognisable pictures can be made, e.g. *bird* but not *thrush*; *tree* but not *birch*. Italics are not used in the Homophone Lists, nor in the Appendix.

The Key to the foregoing symbols is given before Chapter 1, on page xii, where readers may find a synopsis of these points.

C. IV. Pronunciation of Specific Words

The three main accents recorded have already been discussed in some detail. No indication is given as to which accent is applicable when a word is placed within a column, but generally the reader will be able to tell through reference to his own speech and to the symbols at the head of each column. Foreign readers will have more trouble and are referred to the discussion on the major differences between the accents (Section C.I.1 and 2).

As has been previously stated, this book does not claim to be an authoritative statement on word pronunciation; it aims to strike a balance between phonetic accuracy and practical convenience. The lists should therefore be *read critically* and allowances made for the looseness which is sometimes forced by the simple format and the desirability of grouping as many similar sounding words as possible. These weaknesses are set out in more detail below. The purist may sift the words according to more rigid criteria.

This does not mean that accuracy has been cast to the wind. Great care has been taken to follow the appropriate authorities (Baker, 1947 and 1966; Bender, 1964; Delbridge, 1968; Gimson, 1962; Jones, 1969; Kenyon and Knott, 1953; Turner, 1966; Wells, 1970b) and when the phonetic dictionaries do not list a word, reference is made to the standard dictionaries. This often poses a problem as their phonetic system is not always clear, e.g. the distinction between the vowels of *got* and *watch* by the *Shorter Oxford English Dictionary* and Webster's distinction between the vowels in *carry* and *fast* for American speech. Where such divergencies occur the author has had to chose what appears to be most likely correct.

In addition to these general points, there are some specific factors which should be borne in mind when reading the Tables:

1. *Foreign words* are listed according to their anglicised pronunciation, when the use of this seems common. Rarely are both forms given.

2. *Dialectal words* are listed according to the nearest sound of RP or General American English, e.g. the Scottish *ir* in *kirk* and *kirn* and the *ur* in *curn* are interpreted as representing the /3/ phoneme. *Webster's Dictionary* treats both these sounds as identical.

3. *Particular word groups* need special consideration as their pronunciation appears to be variable:

(a) *colt, bolt, jolt* etc. are transcribed both by Jones (1969) and Kenyon and Knott (1953) . as /oʊ/.‡ However, the /ɒ/ vowel in these words is widely heard and has therefore been recorded. Similarly, in words spelled *olv* there appears to be a swing towards the use of the /ɒ/ vowel (Wells, 1970a) and this, too, is noted.

(b) *prints, mints* and *mince, since* etc. Wells (1970a) points out that in the south of England /mɪnts/ is the usual pronunciation for *mince*. Jones (1969) does not include this variant in the main body of his dictionary. In a contrary fashion, the /t/ may be dropped in *prints* etc. giving rise to the pronunciation /prɪns/. When this or the other variation occurs such words as *prince* and *prints* become homophonous. In this book, words like *prints* and *mints* are not included on the final /ns/ page. Readers who pronounce them in this way should put the final /nt/ words into their inflected form and then combine the /nt/ and /ns/ Tables.

(c) *tune, dune* etc. are treated as a /t+ju/ combination and not as /tʃ/ or /dʒ/.

(d) *towel, loyal* etc. are listed twice: once in the monosyllabic final /l/ Table and once in the Appendix, as a disyllable ending with final /əl/.

(e) *pore, sore, more* etc. which in General American speech are said either with /oʊr/‡ or /ɔr/ are listed according to the second variant which is in line with RP English.

(f) *four, poor, sure, your, tour* are omitted if they have a diphthongal form /ɔə/ or /ʊə/ (see Section C.II.2.c,d).

4. *Disyllables* listed are terminated either by the syllabic consonants /m̩/, /l̩/,/n̩/, or by these sounds preceded by one of the short vowels: /ə/, /ɪ/, /ʊ/ or /ɒ/; usually the former two. Francis speaks of this pair as a 'free variation' in America depending upon region. An example of a difference in RP and American usage is provided by the words *pistol* and *pistil*. Kenyon and Knott transcribe them identically while Jones inserts a /ə/ before the /l/ in the latter word. Not only does the pronunciation of these words vary a good deal between speakers but often changes for a given speaker with increased rate of utterance. Wells (1970a) notes that in southern England the /ə/ or /ʊ/ versions are common but the RP accent usually adheres to the syllabic consonant.

While some words certainly call more strongly for a vowel insertion than others, it seems reasonable to treat them as identical for the purposes of this book. There is little practical benefit to be gained from making fine distinctions of this kind; indeed Hill

‡ As the sound is symbolised in this book – see Key to Symbols.

(1967) makes an opposite appeal when he states that phonetic precision is not always helpful to the practising language teacher concerned with consonantal clusters difficult for the foreign student. He complains, in particular, over the omission of such a word as *bottles* from the cluster list /tlz/ since this is interpreted by some phoneticians as /tǝlz/.

5. *Homophones* also pose something of a problem, especially when there is a variation between accents. As stated earlier, the book does not aim to cover a wide range of variations and many words, which in some regions may be homophonous, are not included.

Generally, the major American homophones are listed, if Whitford (1966) is to be taken as a guide, but his system of rhymes is not used to identify the pronunciations, e.g. *way – day – weigh*, and readers must check with the Tables if they are in doubt.

The following points should also be noted:

(a) *Close phonetic similarity* is counted as sufficient for words to be considered as homophones, with the exception of *prince-prints* etc. mentioned earlier (Section C.IV.3.b). This applies especially to words ending with a syllabic consonant. The example of *pistol-pistil* has already been cited and a similar situation is found with *able-Abel*, and *griffon-griffin*. A less justifiable pair is *Saturn* and *satin* both claiming a place in the /æ/ column. Readers requiring more precision may ignore this infrequent type of grouping.

(b) *Inflected and uninflected* forms of the same word are not listed as homophones when their pronunciation is similar, e.g. *barmen, barman*. Usually the plural form is listed in the Tables.

(c) *r-words* have already been discussed, e.g. *ah* and *are; core* and *caw* (Sections C.I.2.g and C.III.1.b). Readers must interpret these words according to their own use and needs.

(d) *Variant Pronunciations* may be homophonous in one instance but not in another; or they may be homophonous in both cases but with different words as happens with *aunt, ant;* and *aunt, aren't*. When the same pair is repeated in two columns, e.g. *cask* and *casque* under /æ/ and /ɑ/, it is not repeated twice in the Homophone Lists, unless it forms part of a longer group, e.g. *past, passed* said with /æ/ and *passed, parsed, past* said with /ɑ/. The first word in each group is presented, from left to right, according to its order in the Tables.

D. THE WORDS

Over 7,500 words are listed in the Tables, and 1,500 groups in the Homophone Lists. In deciding which words should be included, several standard dictionaries have been taken as a guide. With the exception of proper names and a few colloquialisms, all the entries in this book may be found in at least one of the reference dictionaries listed in the References. This may not always be readily apparent as some words are not listed alphabetically, but under some other related word; or they may be an inflected form which is not recorded. It is assumed that all verbs are regular unless otherwise stated by the dictionaries.

Slang and contractions are included as these are often more frequently used than their more formal equivalents; obscure and technical words are also listed to give a fuller picture of the sound distribution of the English language, which may be of interest to the language student.

D. I. Words included in the Lexicon

Only monosyllables and disyllables ending with a syllabic consonant are listed since these can be most readily fitted within the format of the book. As has been explained previously, the consonant may be preceded by a short vowel; however, the first syllable always carries the stress. The inclusion of these words gives further information on sound distributions in the language and also expands its use for auditory training where length comparisons are required, e.g. *less-lesson*.

The expansion of the work to include all disyllables would be too lengthy a process at the present time; it also poses many problems. First, many combinations result in too few words to justify a separate table for each – the alternative is an Appendix of numerous rather uninformative lists. Secondly, further liberties would have to be taken with the phonetics as words ending with consonantal clusters tend to be more divergent, especially in their stress pattern.

The following is a list of the main groups of words included in the book:

1. *Proper Names.* These are words which are 'written with a capital initial letter' (Jones, 1969). The list is not complete, especially as regards place names, but is limited to those words which are well known to a majority of English-speaking people. Within this group the further points should be noted:

(a) When one of these names has more than one spelling, e.g. *Clair, Clare; Ann, Anne*, and their pronunciation is identical, only one word is given and they are not considered homophonous.

(b) Some foreign names are included. These may be familiar to the English reader either because they are common in their native country, e.g. *Carl*, or because of their association with a famous personage, e.g. *Haydn*. In the latter case, some may be listed in a dictionary as usually happens when they have given their name to something, e.g. *Titian*.

(c) Names of literary and mythical characters if these are listed in a dictionary, e.g. *Fagin* and *Timon*.

2. *Letters of the Alphabet.* When representing the actual letter, these are recorded by their symbol, e.g. *H, S, M*; but when indicating a meaning, even if very similar, they are listed by their names, e.g. *aitch, ess, en*, the former two signifying 'shaped like . . .' and *en* also being 'a unit of print' (Chambers). Following Whitford, plural forms of alphabetical letters are considered as homophones, e.g. *peas, P's*, but this does not apply to names of letters in a foreign alphabet, e.g. *pi*.

3. *Colloquialisms and Slang*, such as *gyp*. These may be listed in the dictionary as vulgar, e.g. *gosh*; and some may be of dialectal origin, e.g. the Australian words *zack* and *chook*.

4. *Common Abbreviations.* These are shortened forms of either ordinary words, e.g. *'plane, peke* or proper names, e.g. *Liz, Ted*. If the word is not obviously an abbreviation, the dagger symbol is used to indicate this.

5. *Common Contractions.* These are widely used in everyday speech and are formed from two words making one syllable, e.g. *you're, he'll, it's* etc. Many are negative forms, e.g. *can't, won't*. All may rank as homophones.

6. *Acronyms.* These are formed from either letters or sections of words combined to form a new word, e.g. *Raf*. When there is a difference in spelling between accents, the British usage is usually followed, e.g. *Waacs* not *Wacs*.

7. *Foreign Words* are included if they are listed in one of the dictionaries and are in common use, e.g. *née*.

8. *Dialectal Words*. A limited number of these have been recorded since it is likely that they are used in their region of origin, e.g. *kirk, brae*. These words usually derive from South Africa, America and Australia as well as areas in the British Isles.

9. *Obsolete and Archaic Words*. The inclusion of these words is perhaps less justified as they have no current pronunciation and are of little practical use. However, since they are listed by standard dictionaries some are recorded here. They are possibly of historical interest to some.

10. *Technical Words*. These come from the professions of medicine, architecture, anthropology, astronomy etc. and many are quite familiar to the general public. When this is not so they are recorded with the dagger symbol.

11. *Homophones*. These are words which have a similar phonetic composition but a diverse spelling and meaning, e.g. *nave, knave* both said /neɪv/. Details on the pronunciation of these words have already been given (Section C.IV.5). All words which fall into the above ten categories may rank as homophones, i.e. slang, acronyms, contractions etc. even if the spelling distinction is only the presence of a capital letter, e.g. *may, May*. Words of different spelling but identical meaning do not constitute a homophonous group, e.g. *gaol, jail; disc, disk*. However, very slight differences of meaning are accepted, e.g. *coin, coign, quoin*.

Excepting /ju/, the Tables provide only one slot for a given sound combination, and hence phonetically identical words are recorded elsewhere in the Homophone Lists. The following points have determined which word of a group is chosen to be placed in the Tables:

(a) Preference is given to familiar words, especially if they can be presented in visual form and as a consequence be of special use with children. Therefore, in the group *ball, bawl* the former is placed in the Tables.

(b) Generally, full forms are chosen over contractions or abbreviations unless the latter are very much more familiar. Hence *weave* is recorded in the Tables in preference to *we've*.

(c) Similarly, preference is given to words which are uninflected. Consequently, *find, tax* and *pause* take precedence over *fined, tacks* and *paws*. This applies especially to words on the final /z/, /nd/, /ld/ and /ks/ pages.

(d) Usually nouns are selected before adjectives and these before verbs, unless the latter are more familiar.

(e) In the case where one word of a homophonous pair can be inflected, this is often selected for the later page. For example, in the pair *weak-week*, the word *weeks* is recorded on the final /ks/ page; and in the pair *stare-stair*, *stairs* is put on the final /z/ page because the word can be more easily presented visually in its plural form.

(f) When a homophone exists for the /j + u/ and /ju/ columns, a different word is selected for each slot, e.g. *U* and *ewe* are each recorded on the 'no final' page. Both are also entered, together with the other words, e.g. *you*, in the Homophone Lists.

D. II. Words omitted from the Lexicon

Words have been omitted from this book primarily because they cannot be fitted into the format; they do not fully rank as words; or because their inclusion would give rise to unnecessary duplication. The following are the chief words excluded:

1. *Foreign* and *Dialectal* words containing non-English sounds, e.g. *piton*
2. *Words containing the* /ʊə/ *and* /ɔə/ *diphthongs* (see Section C.II.2.c and d).
3. *Possessive forms* of proper names, e.g. *May's*. These may be formed by adding /s/ to the final /k/ page and /z/ to the 'no final' page.
4. *Inflected forms* of words where the final cluster would be primarily a repetition of the page containing uninflected words (see Section C.II.3.b).

D. III. Spelling

Some departure from the more international or usual spelling of a word is made when the alternate form differentiates what would otherwise be a homograph. A simple example is provided by the word *kerb*. Although this spelling is not used in the United States, it is employed here for 'the edging of a pavement' (Chambers) which is thus differentiated from *curb* 'a chain or strap attached to the bit for restraining a horse . . .' and also for the verb of similar meaning (Chambers). Similarly, the British variant *waggon* is used to distinguish it more clearly from *Wagon* 'Ursa Major'.

Sometimes two words each have a variant, e.g. *kame* which itself is a homograph. To elaborate: *kame* and *kaim* are either a Scottish term for 'a comb: . . .' or '. . . a bank or ridge of gravel . . .'; *kame* and *came* can signify 'a lead rod for framing a pane . . .' (Chambers) and of course *came* is also the past tense of *come*. By selecting the spellings *came*, *kame* and *kaim* all three of the above meanings can be distinguished.

Not all the dictionaries give the same spelling variants and where there are discrepancies the words in this book are usually in line with the version given by *Chambers's Dictionary*.

E. REFERENCES

ABERCROMBIE, D. (1963) *Problems and Principles in Language Study*, (2nd edn.), Longmans, Green, London.
ABERCROMBIE, D. (1965) *Studies in Phonetics and Linguistics*, Oxford University Press, London.
BAKER, S. J. (1947) *Australian Pronunciation*, Angus and Robertson, Sydney.
BAKER, S. J. (1966) *The Australian Language*, (2nd edn.), Currawong Publishing, Sydney.
BARBER, C. (1964) *Linguistic Change in Present-Day English*, Oliver & Boyd, Edinburgh.
BENDER, J. N. (1964) *NBC Handbook of Pronunciation*, (3rd) edn.), (Rev. T. L. Crowell Jnr.) Thomas Y. Crowell, New York.
BRONSTEIN, A. (1960) *The Pronunciation of American English*, Appleton-Century-Crofts, New York.
CHAMBERS'S TWENTIETH CENTURY DICTIONARY (1952) (Ed. W. Geddie), W. & R. Chambers, Edinburgh.
DELBRIDGE, A. (1968) Personal Communication, Macquarie University, Sydney.
FRANCIS, W. (1958) *The Structure of American English*, The Ronald Press, New York.
GIMSON, A. (1962) *An Introduction to the Pronunciation of English*, Edward Arnold, London.
HEFFNER, R-M. (1950) *General Phonetics*, University of Wisconsin Press, Madison, U.S.A.
HILL, L. A. (1967) *Selected Articles on the Teaching of English as a Foreign Language*, Oxford University Press, London, Chap. 7.
JONES, D. (1969) *Everyman's English Pronouncing Dictionary* (13th edn.) (Ed. A. Gimson), J. M. Dent & Sons, London.
KENYON, J. S. (1958) *American Pronunciation*, (10th edn.), George Wahr Publishing, Ann Arbor, Michigan.
KENYON, J. and KNOTT, T. (1953) *A Pronouncing Dictionary of American English*, G. & C. Merriam Company, Springfield, Mass., U.S.A.
MITCHELL, A. G. and DELBRIDGE, A. (1965) *The Pronunciation of English in Australia*, (rev. edn.), Angus & Robertson, Sydney.

MOSER, H. (1969) *One-Syllable Words*, Merrill's International Speech Series, Columbus, Ohio.

NIST, J. (1966) *A Structural History of English*, St. Martin's Press, New York.

NUTTALL'S STANDARD DICTIONARY OF THE ENGLISH LANGAUGE (1951) (Ed. and Rev. Lawrence H. Dawson), (new edn.), London.

THE CONCISE OXFORD DICTIONARY (1964) (Ed. H. W. Fowler and F. G. Fowler), Oxford University Press, Oxford.

THE OXFORD ENGLISH DICTIONARY (1933) Material collected by the Philological Soc., Clarendon Press, Oxford.

THE SHORTER OXFORD DICTIONARY ON HISTORICAL PRINCIPLES (1947) (3rd edn.), W. Little, H. Fowler & J. Coulson. (Rev. and Ed. C. T. Onions), Clarendon Press, Oxford.

THOMAS, C. K. (1958) *An Introduction to the Phonetics of American English* (2nd edn.), The Ronald Press, New York.

TIBBITS, E. (1963) *Practice Material for the English Sounds*, W. Heffer & Sons, Cambridge.

TURNER, G. W. (1966) *The English Language in Australia and New Zealand*, Longmans, Green, London.

WARD, I. (1948) *The Phonetics of English* (4th edn.), W. Heffer & Sons, Cambridge.

WEBSTER'S NEW TWENTIETH CENTURY DICTIONARY OF THE ENGLISH LANGUAGE (1962) (2nd edn.) (Rev. J. McKechnie), World Publishing, Cleveland, U.S.A.

WELLS, J. (1970a) 'Local Accents in England and Wales', *J. Linguistics*, Vol. 6, pp. 231–252.

WELLS, J. (1970b) Personal Communication, London University.

WHITFORD, H. (1966) *A Dictionary of American Homophones and Homographs*, N. Y. Teachers College Press, Columbia University, New York.

CHAPTER 2
Uses of the Phonetic Lexicon

A. PREAMBLES

B. RECEPTIVE FUNCTIONS

    I.   HEARING
       1. Testing
       2. Therapy: Auditory Training
    II. AUDITORY PERCEPTION
       1. Phonemic Defects
       2. Rhyming Defects

C. EXPRESSIVE FUNCTIONS

    I.   PHONETIC DEFECTS
    II. PHONEMIC DEFECTS
    III. TESTING AND TREATMENT

D. SPELLING AND READING

    I.   SPELLING
    II. READING

E. LIP READING

F. FOREIGN ACCENT: BARBARALALIA

    I.   TERMINOLOGY AND ETYMOLOGY
    II. COMPONENTS OF FOREIGN ACCENT
    III. CAUSES OF FOREIGN ACCENT
    IV. AIMS FOR PRONUNCIATION
    V. THE TEACHER
    VI. TESTING
       1. Prediction of Student's Errors
       2. Testing for Errors
    VII. CORRECTION
       1. Ear-training
       2. Sound Production
       3. Differentiation of Homophones and Homographs

G. RESEARCH

H. CONCLUSION

I. REFERENCES

A. PREAMBLES

In this chapter the application of the Tables and Homophone Lists will be discussed in relation to the person learning English either as a first or second language.

Words which differ greatly in phonetic structure usually contrast sufficiently to pose no special problems to the learner. On the contrary, monosyllables, lacking a rhythm and often separated by fine distinctions, frequently prove troublesome and consequently must form the nucleus of much remedial activity.

The diagnostic groups for which activities are designed cannot be discussed in detail: each warrants a separate book in itself. They are considered only in so far as the *Phonetic Lexicon* has relevance to them. Some are dealt with in greater detail than others, not because they are more important or common, but because either the average therapist appears uncertain of the topic or because there is a lack of well-organised material on the subject.

B. RECEPTIVE FUNCTIONS

In this section we are primarily concerned with words at a pre-syntactic level, that is, as they enter the organism as organised *sound*, are crudely *discriminated* and proceed as some sort of *image* which is *judged, classified* and stored in the memory for later *recognition*. These functions are roughly twofold:

(a) those relating to *hearing per se*; and
(b) those relating to the various *perceptual* processes.

This distinction has often been obscured of late but is important if we are to fully understand the nature of the disorders we are treating. An explanation of the basis for this distinction has been given by this author (Roberts, 1968) elsewhere:

> 'Sensation must be said to occur when there is a direct, physical relationship between the sense organ and the impinging stimulus, to which it is specially attuned and proportioned. It "knows" the external thing in its physical state, that is: as it naturally is in itself.
> Perception and other higher mental processes share no such direct relationship with external reality, which they know only by means of representations "standing in" for things. . . . That is, the neurophysiological changes which occur are not themselves provoked directly by the external stimulus, nor are they physically proportionate to it. For this reason, they are said to have a "psychic" existence which is quite different from the "real" existence of the thing.'

These two functions, hearing and auditory perception, their defects and the ways in which they may be tested and treated will now be discussed.

B. I. Hearing

This is the physical basis for all the auditory perceptual operations which follow. However, except in the case of reflex responses, the sense does not stand alone but acts as one part of the total auditory system. Thus, to test and assist hearing we are necessarily involved with the perceptual system; this does not mean that we should identify the two systems nor treat them equally, for the underlying processes are fundamentally diverse.

1. *Testing*

The speech material presented in hearing tests aims to determine, through discrimination, the degree to which the ear is distorting sound. For this reason, words are selected which are acoustically similar to others and consequently easily confused and difficult to select accurately in the absence of good reproduction or contextual clues. The PB‡ words used widely for this purpose are well known to audiologists. More recently, revisions have been made to the standard American tests. Peterson and Lehiste (1962) have produced lists based on word frequency and Black, Hess and Haagen (1963) have proposed a multiple-choice test where the stimulus word (italicised) differs either by one feature from the other three in the group:

form	bubble
warm	stubble
swarm	trouble
storm	*double*

or by more than one feature:

pit	guard
kick	hearten
kit	*garden*
pitch	bargain

Groups of words having minimal differences are also advocated by Lafon (1960) for use in the diagnosis of retro-cochlear disorders.

The lists presently available have been standardised and are useful clinical tools. However, it is possible that further tests will be developed to probe some particular facet of hearing and it is then that the *Phonetic Lexicon* might prove a valuable source of material, especially to English researchers.

The children's tests are less well standardised and are difficult to construct due to the vocabulary limitations. Dale (1967) has reviewed the speech tests available. These are composed of monosyllabic words familiar to the average child, e.g. *ship*, *home*, *cup*, *made*, *egg*, as are the lists given by Ballantyne (1960).

Reed (1960), working on the assumption that, for any degree of hearing impairment consonants are more difficult to discriminate than vowels, produced words in visual form with four to a page, differing by their initial and/or final consonant, e.g. *door*, *horse*, *4, ball*.

This is a fruitful line of investigation as far as it goes but, since many deaf children do have difficulty with vowel discrimination, it seems desirable that this be evaluated. Words suitable for children are printed in italics in the Tables of the *Phonetic Lexicon* and could form the basis for such a test.

The question of the use of homophenes in the testing of malingering will be covered in the discussion on Lip-Reading (Section E).

2. *Therapy: Auditory Training*

The deaf child, like the normal, must become proficient in the skill of primary recognition. This involves the development of a 'Phoneme Inventory' (about 40 in English) and the assignment of the ongoing auditory stimuli to phonemic categories.

As there is no exact correspondence between a given portion of the sound wave and a

‡ Phonetically balanced.

certain phoneme, the listener must select from information contained in overlapping time segments of the wave; he must convert the incoming sound into discrete units.

Whetnall and Fry (1964) point out that the phonemes do not depend upon absolute physical quantities but on the relations between them. Hence phoneme discrimination is possible with all manner of speakers, whether male or female. The phonemic systems, then, are systems of relations which, no doubt, can be impaired if their physical basis is sufficiently distorted.

Fortunately, the number of physical cues available for the identification of any one phoneme is more than is necessary under normal circumstances and this redundancy is most helpful to the hard-of-hearing patient.

In order to interpret a phonemic code with facility, the listener must both categorise the phonemes and predict their occurrence. This ability comes through a knowledge of the linguistic structure of the language and results from learning. The deafened adult has this capacity: the child has not.

The aims of any therapeutic programme are therefore diverse, for the adult must learn to listen for minimal physical cues and interpret these in the light of his memory patterns: a task quite difficult if the incoming information is grossly distorted. This distortion is not so troublesome for the child who knows nothing better. He has, however, the added job of developing his phonemic inventory and categorising ability. This perceptual training, which is an integral part of auditory training, is not provoked by a perceptual problem *per se*; rather, the difficulties are secondary to and dependent upon the deafness. As Whetnall and Fry (1964) point out '. . . the ability of the brain to organise information is in principle unaffected', and since little can be done to modify the end organ, all efforts must be made to enable the patient to learn to organise the incoming information while he is most disposed to do so; namely during his first five years. The following points are essential, if a therapeutic programme is to be successful in assisting a child to realise his full potential.

(a) *Early stimulation.* The perceptual processes are thereby stimulated at an age when the child is peculiarly tuned to language reception. This point has been admirably stressed by Whetnall and Fry when they say that '. . . in the early years of life the young child has a facility for making discriminations between sounds which to the adult are impossible'. And they comment further: 'The infant can make use of sounds which to the adult with fixed habits of listening are almost impossible.'

The time for beginning auditory training is as soon as possible and certainly before two years of age. If the child is 'sound deprived' during the normal 'readiness to listen' period of early life, he will be unable to make the perceptions necessary for speech development. 'The least vestige of auditory control is of value for the infant because of his great facility for using it.'

This is tragically evident in the case of the child whose condition is diagnosed late and who receives his hearing aid after the critical period. He is upset by it and avoids using it whenever possible. 'He is past the age at which discrimination can be easily learnt and all sounds to him are noises . . .' (Whetnall and Fry). It is in this child that we see most clearly how a potentially normal perceptual system has become more or less permanently functionally deficient.

(b) *Adequate stimulation.* This means that the auditory stimuli reaching the child's ear must be loud enough. The physical defect of deafness may be partially compensated for by a hearing aid which should be worn continuously in the presence of speech, so that the hard-of-hearing child is exposed to a near normal auditory environment. The brain must be provided with as much information as possible and even though this may be less than normal it could be sufficient for learning if adequate and appropriate training is given.

(c) *Frequent stimulation* must be given to insure learning, and the more deficient the hearing the more frequent must be the training. Through such a programme the auditory memory patterns, so necessary for phoneme recognition, are built up. This has rightly been stressed by Sheridan (1955; also cited by Ballantyne) when she says that the child 'must listen to the same speech sounds being repeated over and over again before he can store them in his memory, first as phonetic units, then as words with meaning.' This results in the child being able to discriminate with ever-decreasing auditory clues, as Whetnall and Fry point out: 'As sounds become familiar they become easy to detect and interpret and therefore can be recognised and understood at fainter intensities and at greater distances than when first heard.'

(d) *Appropriate stimulation*. In its more formal aspect this occurs in auditory training, during which the patient's individual needs must be recognised and treated in a systematic fashion. Although one frequently hears that children have failed with an auditory approach, this usually stems from lack of a suitably geared therapeutic plan and rarely from a deficiency in the child himself, as Whetnall and Fry note: '. . . the human brain has a quite extraordinary capacity for organising information and although it can clearly do nothing if the ears never supply any information . . . provided the deaf child is exposed to sounds that are loud enough and occur often enough, his brain will learn to recognise them in the same way as the brain of the normally hearing child'.

Rationale for Auditory Training

As we have seen, in any given listening experience there is usually more acoustic information available than is actually necessary for perception to take place. Thus, though the deaf child fitted with a hearing aid misses much of a word there is a good chance that he will learn to discriminate on the basis of the cues still available. This is most evident and, despite opinions to the contrary, this writer is in full accord with Whetnall and Fry when they say that: 'Improvement in auditory perception is so consistent that even the rare child who has no response at all to sound at first testing should be given an adequate trial of auditory training.'

How is it that a child can discriminate on the basis of so little information and how can his potential be fairly estimated? It is clearly not worth wasting valuable time and frustrating the child with a project having little chance of success. The answer to the second part of this question is found after a certain amount of trial and error with each case and in the early stages little more than crude non-verbal discriminations can be expected. As the child matures, an audiogram may be available and then some sort of prediction can be made, though children with similar audiograms do not necessarily perform in a like manner.

The answer to the first part of the question is to be found in the acoustic properties of the sounds themselves and their influence on the adjacent sounds in a given phonetic enviroment. This information is, as Whetnall and Fry mention, '. . . directly relevant to the problem of training the deaf child' because he learns largely by discriminating the changes in vowel formants as they are affected by the neighbouring consonants. Pickett (1968) explains one way this may come about: 'If the shape of the cavity in front of the constriction is in transition from one position to another, then frequency transitions in the cavity resonances take place which furnish auditory cues as to the identity of the preceding and following sounds.'

These transitions and the consequent change in acoustic information cannot be considered here in detail; suffice it to say that for phoneme identification the patient must determine the manner and place of articulation plus the status of the vocal cords (e.g. the judgement stop, labial, voiceless leads to the categorisation /p/) and this information depends upon the intensity, time and frequency cues to be found in the sound wave.

An example of an intensity cue is found in fricative recognition, where the voiceless sounds may be distinguished on this basis, with /s/ and /ʃ/ being of high intensity and /f/ and /θ/ low. Such a differentiation may be impossible for the hard-of-hearing patient but fortunately, as we have seen, a plurality of cues is available and therefore the patient has other pointers to fall back on.

Duration cues may offer more information depending upon the degree of loss. The length of the 'vowel gap', for example, is one aid in determining whether a consonant between any two vowels is voiced or unvoiced. Obviously the vowel gap tends to be *short* for voiced consonants because the voicing conditions are maintained since the vocal cords are together during the consonantal constriction, as may be found in the phrase: *a big ape*. Conversely, the cords are not operative for unvoiced consonants, as in the articulation of *the top ace*, and the vowel gap tends to be *long* and is sometimes at least double the length.

From the point of view of the deaf patient, the most useful clues are to be found in the vowel formants. The ways in which these are affected by adjacent consonants is clearly manifested in a chart of spectrograms given by Fletcher (1953) where each vowel is combined separately with a different consonant. If the frequency of the neighbouring consonant is near that of the second vowel formant, then little change occurs but if the frequency is quite different due to considerable movement of the speech musculature, a change is found. This is exemplified in words like *she* and *shoe* whose spectrograms are significantly different indicating that the patient with a high frequency loss, though not hearing the /ʃ/ well, if at all, can learn to discriminate between words containing the sound, and it is this skill which must be developed in auditory training, as Whetnall and Fry note: '. . . a child who has hearing for frequencies in the vowel formant range only can learn to make these consonantal discriminations'.

The Auditory Training Programme

Auditory training has been considered as the systematic development of residual hearing potential in hard-of-hearing persons with the aim of improving their communication. The two important concepts here are *systematic* and *potential*.

To deal with the last first: it must be remembered that the patient's prognosis depends upon his degree and type of loss, the state of his perceptual system, his suitability for hearing aid fitting, intelligence, motivation and age. One might have to be content with gross vowel discriminations in a severely deafened child; and the geriatric patient may be quite unable to accept amplification and to categorise the distorted incoming sounds. Obviously a training programme must take these factors into account.

Once treatment is begun it should be *systematic* and proceed step by step from easy to less easy discriminations. Much of the haphazard approach, and consequent failure, which is found in some training centres stems from the fact that the therapist or teacher does not understand the acoustic basis of the speech material he is using. For this reason, the foregoing discussion has been included in this book as it is essential if the words in the *Phonetic Lexicon* are to be presented with advantage.

The fact that the perceptual system is potentially normal in the deaf child and actually normal in the deafened adult has been stressed and it is assumed that, given well-graded acoustic material, the listener will have little difficulty with primary recognition. When he becomes proficient at differentiating non-verbal sounds and then words varying greatly in phonetic structure and rhythm, e.g. *elephant* and *top*, he will be ready for finer discriminatory tasks. For the purposes of discussion these may be considered as twofold: those involving vowel changes and those involving consonants.

(a) *Vowel differences*. These are easier to detect than consonantal changes and consequently are useful with the less advanced or more severely deaf patient. However, as the vowels are affected by the adjacent consonants it could be that when their position in any two words is similar (e.g. back or front) and the formant contrast is therefore reduced, they are more difficult to discriminate than some consonantal changes. This part of the programme might include:

(i) Discrimination of monosyllables varying both in vowels and consonants, e.g. *shark-pin; spoon-light.*

(ii) Discrimination between long and short vowels, e.g. *each-itch; shot-short; pull-pool.* Gimson suggests it is quality rather than length which is often contrastive in these cases.

(iii) Discrimination between long vowels, e.g. *tart-taught-toot.*

(iv) Discrimination between short vowels, e.g. *pit-pet-pat.*

(v) Discrimination between open and closed, and back and front vowels might be incorporated in the exercises of (iii) and (iv) above. Research (Pickett *et al.*, in press) indicates that back vowels are easier to discriminate than front ones.

(b) *Consonantal Differences*. This book contains some disyllables and a comparison of these with monosyllables, e.g. *less-lesson*, should be easier than between monosyllables alone because of the rhythm-length cue available. Later, a cluster differentiation could be added, e.g. *net-nettle-nettles.*

The consonants drilled in monosyllabic words may be varied according to their initial and final position but, in order to assist the patient in the three facets of phoneme recognition, they should be selected for:

(i) Discrimination of the manner of articulation, e.g. *rag-nag-lag; bin-bid-bill.*

(ii) Discrimination of place of articulation, e.g. *nip-knit-Nick; bill-dill-gill.*

(iii) Discrimination of the voice-voiceless distinction, e.g. *tip-dip; thief-thieve; cot-got.* Voiced and nasal consonants are more easily discriminated (Pickett *et al.*).

Later a more difficult task could be introduced:

(iv) Discrimination of clusters, e.g. *nets-nest; lots-lost; spear-stear; wisp-wist-whisk;*

Obviously the exercises should be organised in such a way that those involving easier discriminatory tasks may be tackled first. Haspiel and Bloomer (1961) point to the paucity of material on this subject and they provide a practical word list for use with the child in the more advanced stages of auditory training. The words are sequenced according to the developmental order and frequency of occurrence of their constituent sounds, thus facilitating a systematic approach to the remedial programme. The therapists' tasks are also aided by the research now available on the perceptual ability of deaf patients. A succinct review of the findings to date is given by Pickett *et al.*, together with a report on their own work.

The presentation of this material will depend upon the age and interests of the patient. Visual presentation is the easiest with children and could be incorporated in a picture lotto or 'fishing' game. Newby (1965) suggests that adults be given a written list of paired words which they check according to which they think has been said. Pointing or spoken responses could be substituted.

The words may be introduced with or without lip-reading, in isolation or in context. One useful method of presenting material in a natural and meaningful way is through the use of homophenes. The patient may then watch the speaker without getting information through lip-reading. The following sentence/s provides an example:

There is the *patch*
batch
match

As the patient progresses it is well to reduce all additional stimuli and present the material without lip-reading in the presence of background noise. Excluding secondary handicaps, a good performance can be expected from a child with an 80 db (I.S.O.) loss who has received constant and early therapy.

In the clinical situation it is not always easy to find the required combination of words at the right moment and delays result in loss of attention by the patient. It is envisaged that the *Phonetic Lexicon* will save considerable time in the auditory training process and enable it to be approached in a more systematic fashion.

B. II. Auditory Perception

Perception is a more abstract mode of knowing than sensation, for the physical dimensions of the stimulus have become transformed in order that they may be handled by the brain. As Fry (1963) says: 'The acoustic signals which arrive at the ear of the listener and are converted into neural signals give rise in the brain to patterns which correspond to percepts.'

Percepts, as the term is used here, are derived from those lower psychic functions of sense discrimination; imagination, as this pertains to sense imagery; estimative power, which is a primitive form of judgement; and memory. These will be briefly considered in turn:

(a) *Discrimination* occurs when the stimulus is *present*. It involves the sifting of incoming information, usually subconsciously, into background and foreground material and it is probably at this stage that the physical parameters of the stimulus are converted into their psychic equivalents, for example, the frequency, intensity and duration of the speech sound-waves are replaced by the dimensions of quality, pitch, loudness and length. The power also unifies the diverse incoming sensations in such a way that the animal may relate one sense to another and thus be able to function as an integral being. If this faculty is faulty not only will the organism be disoriented, inattentive and stimulus-bound, but his images will be blurred, his memory weak and his judgement unable to function satisfactorily.

(b) *Imagination* is formed of sense images derived from incoming impressions. It is, however, indifferent to the *presence* or *absence* of the causative stimulus. This is the faculty which is used when we produce in the mind an image as abstracted from real time and place, e.g. the words *hair* or *bear*, the visual image of a *jug*, and dreams. It is likely that a breakdown in this area is at the basis of many aphasic disturbances since the patient can no longer imagine the word in its printed or auditory form.

(c) *Estimative power* is concerned with the judgement of contrasts, of phenomena as they are in opposition and it is therefore responsible for distinguishing the like from the unlike. It scans incoming information, often subconsciously, in order that it may be categorised. Obviously some stimulus must be *present* for this to occur but it need not be an external stimulus since judgements can be made about something imagined. For example, one can imagine the words *bear* and *pear* and from this alone judge whether or not they rhyme. This faculty is required for the development of a phonemic system.

(d) *Memory* involves images and for this reason is similar to imagination and this likeness has been noted by Johnson and Myklebust (1967). However, these images relate specifically to *past* time and to phenomena as ordered in succession, e.g. the recall of a word said in a certain place at a certain time by a specific person; the recollection of a specific *jug* once experienced with a certain colour and shape in a given place; the sequence of events on a car trip or in a dream.

It can readily be seen that all these powers are operative in the development of language. However, as this book is primarily of use with the patient having difficulty in developing or using his phonemic system and in being able to rhyme, only these two facets of language acquisition will be discussed.

1. *Phonemic Defects*

The patient with an auditory phonemic defect receives the incoming impressions loudly and clearly, if his discriminative faculty is functioning normally, but he is unable to categorise them possibly because either the pattern-image against which the incoming information must be matched is inadequate, or because he is unable to make a correct judgement. He is in an analogous position to the adult learning a second language: he has difficulty sorting the relevant from the irrelevant auditory clues and as a consequence is unable to circumscribe the phonemes of his mother tongue. If the discriminative power is not sifting the arriving physical phenomena and converting them correctly into their psychic equivalents, then categorisation will be difficult even in the presence of good imaging and estimative powers.

In acquiring our mother tongue Fry (1963) notes that '. . . our perceptions are so trained and modified as to facilitate the phonemic grouping of incoming speech sounds.' This involves the overlooking of some information, as Fries (in Lado, 1957) explains: 'A child in learning his native language has learned not only to attend to (receptively and productively) the particular contrasts that function as signals in that language; he has learned to *ignore* all those features that do not so function. He has developed a special set of "blind spots" that prevent him from responding to features that do not constitute the contrastive signals of his native language.' For example, as the doubling of consonants is not significant in English we are unaware of this length factor when learning Italian. In this language the meaning is altered by a double consonant which must be sounded, e.g. *capelli* (hair) and *cappelli* (hats); not only is this distinction hard to notice at first, but even when it is recognised it is difficult to tell which of the two words is which.

It seems probable that many speech defectives are in a similar position, the severity of the disorder varying along the lines mentioned by Haas (1963): 'Failure to discriminate between phonemic features and phonemes is a serious error, especially if their contrasts carry a heavy functional load. Failure to discriminate conditioned features and allophones comes next, and free variants hardly matter; . . . .'

'Although two phonemes by definition differ by at least one articulatory feature, they may share some other feature or features' (Agard and di Pietro, 1965) and therefore the more similar the words the more difficult they are to identify, with monosyllables being the most difficult as there are no rhythmic clues available. Therefore, these words are particularly useful in testing and treating phonemic disorders.

(a) *Testing*

Tests for phoneme recognition should be designed with the aim of determining whether the patient has grasped the phonotactic rules of the language, that is, whether he knows the phonemes and their combinations. Haas (1963) notes that the patients' deviations are 'rarely capricious' and 'In order to see this, we require an exact diagnosis of the defects; and the subtler organisation that has been brought into phonetic analysis permits such diagnosis'.

From the information given by Haas it appears that three major lines of enquiry are called for. Does the problem relate to:

(i) *distinctive features*, e.g. does the patient fail to discern velarity (/k/, /g/, /ŋ/) or a voiceless stop (/p/, /t/, /k/)? Alveolar substitutions for velar consonants and cognate confusion are both seen quite frequently in infantile articulatory disorders. This defect may be assessed through analysis by contrastive substitution. This is demonstrated by Haas with his example of /p/ in the word *pin* where he shows that /b/, /t/, /d/, /k/, /f/, /θ/, /s/, /ʃ/, /w/ may all be substituted for this sound, in each case causing a change in meaning. These sounds are therefore said to be distinctive in English and form a substitution class or paradigm.

(ii) *allophonic variants*, e.g. does the patient recognise the unaspirated form of /p/ for example, in words like *play*, *spoon* and *apt*? Does he confuse it with /b/ in the first two instances?

(iii) *neutralisation* of the phonetic contrasts in some positions, i.e. does the patient miss, for example, the voice-voiceless distinction is some environments? Are /t/ and /d/ distinguished initially in *tip* and *dip* but not finally in *pot* and *pod*? Such a patient is reducing the importance of the opposition probably due to lack of generalisation.

There are two further points of interest in this connection:

(i) Does the patient err on some sounds which he can differentiate well, e.g. does he say /tæt/ for /kæt/ although he can recognise a difference?

(ii) Does the patient have greater or lesser trouble differentiating errors when spoken by himself or the therapist? Has he reached the stage, noted by Trim (1963) where, like most adults, he equates what he hears with what he says and has become insensitive to the differences he does not employ? Van Riper and Irwin (1958) make a valid point when they say 'Perhaps a discrimination test will yet be devised which will match the speaker's *own error* against the standard sound presented simultaneously or successively. We would anticipate that such a test would show marked deficiencies in auditory discrimination in speakers with defective articulation.'

The auditory diagnostic tests available for children at present include: (i) those investigating memory span (Beebe, 1944; Metraux, 1944); and (ii) those investigating discrimination either with nonsense syllables (Travis and Rasmus, 1931; Templin, 1943) or with words. It is the latter which interest us here.

The Travis-Rasmus test was adopted for use in picture form: twenty word-pairs presented on a card, the paired words were opposed to each other in each quadrant of the card, for example, *pole-bowl* and *pole-pole* occupied the top half, with *bowl-pole* and *bowl-bowl* in the lower half. The child was required to point to the stimulus pair. This test was revised by Pronovost and Dumbleton (1953), who presented the paired words on a card, e.g. *cat-cat*, *cat-bat*, *bat-bat*. Pointing responses were called for. Vowels, semi-vowels, plosives, fricatives and clusters were all tested but the authors point to the difficulty of finding enough words suitable for visual presentation.

Pictures were also used by Renfrew (1964) and the child was required to select the picture according to the stimulus word. No scoring system is given, in contrast to the Pronovost-Dumbleton test, and Renfrew recommends use of the Crichton Vocabulary test when patients fail with her pictures.

Wepman (1958) also presented paired words but not in picture form. The child was expected to indicate whether the words were same or different. Phonemes were compared within 'phonetic categories' but no 'cross phonetic category matching was done. This avoids the possibility of discrimination being based on differences in articulatory position rather than on the auditory basis being tested'. Wepman is explicit in his aims; the test has been standardised on school-aged children, and is said to be of some value with reading disorders. We shall see later (Section D.II) that these are often associated with auditory imperception.

The *Phonetic Lexicon* provides a source for much test material and would be most helpful to the therapist unfamiliar or unsatisfied with the evaluation procedures currently available. The Homophone Lists could be used to determine a child's grasp of similar sounding words. For example, the stimulus sound could be /pi/ and the school-age child who knows the letters of the alphabet by name could be required to select from a card containing: *P*, *B*, *pea*, *bee*, *T*, *D* in picture or graphic form. If he makes only one selection he could be asked whether there is another picture with the same sound. This procedure could be of benefit in some cases of reading disorder.

Phoneme discrimination in adults may be evaluated by one of the Aphasia tests. Schuell (1965) uses paired words while Luria's (1970) approach is through sounds in isolation and nonsense syllables. His thesis is that: 'Investigation of phonemic hearing must reveal the degree of preservation of auditory processes involving systemisations appropriate to the phonetic system of a given language.' He describes how some patients treat diverse phonemes as variants of the same phoneme and his testing procedures involve evaluation of both phonemic and non-phonemic features of sounds.

Luria notes that the more severe deficiencies of this type result from temporal lobe damage, while lesser forms of the disorder manifest themselves when there has been a loss of the articulatory schemata such as occurs in afferent motor aphasia.

Problems with phoneme identification are also found amongst foreigners learning a second language and more specific tests for this will be discussed later. (Section F.VI.2).

(b) *Therapy: Ear-training*

Ear-training, the process of acquiring the phonotactic rules of a language through systematic instruction, is a widely used therapeutic technique well known to all speech pathologists. The fact that, alone, it can successfully bring about the elimination of an articulation disorder reflects the degree to which such disturbances are receptively based.

The phonemes to be distinguished in ear-training will depend upon the patient's individual difficulties as revealed by testing. With children it is usually desirable to present the stimulus words in both auditory and visual form such as is found in the 'Sound Discrimination Game' devised by Berry and Eisenson (1956). Pictures are presented on either side of a page, for example, *cat*, *bat*, *rat* on the left side and *rat*, *cat*, *bat*, *hat* on the right. Strings are attached to the pictures on the left and the child must place the string on the stimulus word represented in the right-hand column. Numerous such games can be invented and there is no reason why some of the material used for testing could not be incorporated in the therapeutic programme.

There is no need for a detailed discussion of ear-training in children here and readers are referred to Van Riper (1954) and Van Riper and Irwin (1958) for a more thorough coverage of this important subject. The question of the use of ear-training with foreign accent will be considered later (Section F.VII.1).

The use of ear-training with aphasic adults presents a more complicated problem. The patient who is unable to recognise and recall words has, according to Luria (1970), a defect in the 'phonemic organisation of hearing'. Like the speech-defective child already discussed, the adult with such a loss is unable to discern the distinctive features of a sound. This results in an instability of the word schemata which are necessary for word constancy and comprehension. In addition, lack of adequate auditory feedback interferes with proper articulatory monitoring and errors result. Luria has found that the only answer to the recovery of 'phonemic hearing' is the association of sounds with meaning. Thus the patient may be able to discriminate /p/ and /b/ but be unable to recognise a difference between *pad* and *bad*.

The aim of his therapeutic programme is to re-establish the 'phonemic generalisations' which the patient has lost, through the use of words with minimal contrasts. His techniques go beyond simple ear-training to include a description and demonstration of the differences between similar sounding words, e.g. *man*, *fan*. A sound may be taught first, e.g. /t/, then placed in monosyllabic words, e.g. *Tim*, *time*, and finally contrasted with *dim* and *dime*. Luria contends that: 'By working with such words the patient becomes aware of the fact that a given phoneme retains certain constant features even though it seems to change in specific contexts. In working through the variants of a given phoneme it is imperative to represent it always by one and the same letter. The patient does exercises which involve filling in the letters in words printed under the pictures of objects.'

Once again, it is apparent that the *Phonetic Lexicon* can be a valuable clinical tool both with children and adults; an elaboration of the way the words could be used is quite unnecessary.

2. *Rhyming Defects*

There is a paucity of information regarding the normal and abnormal manifestations of rhyming behaviour. It is obviously a more difficult task than phoneme discrimination and appears to take place when the phoneme inventory is near complete. Frisina (1963), referring to the work of Spencer, states that: 'The ability to rhyme words proved to be quite difficult for children below $5\frac{1}{2}$ years of age. Thereafter, a sudden increment was noticed.' According to Schuell (1965) this ability correlates highly with other language tests.

Rhyming problems are evident in many Rh children whose handicaps appear similar to those found in a group of children described by Greene (1963) as having 'language learning difficulties'. One of the features she notes about these children is their inability to rhyme.

Similar deficits are evident in adult aphasic patients. Indeed, Schuell (1965) observed that few such patients could rhyme and those who could generally had only mild or minimal disturbances. In this work, Schuell also cites the unpublished findings of Biondo, who noted the presence of this defect in deaf children. Rhyming difficulties have also been found in non-aphasics and Schuell speculates: 'It is possible that the inability of non aphasics to rhyme represents the lower end of a continuum, the upper end of which is probably represented by the sensitivity of poets to the sound of words, and which is analogous to the range between individuals who are tone-deaf and those who have perfect pitch.'

The research edition of the *Minnesota Test* included a rhyming section. In this test the examiner was required to give the key word, e.g. *go* and the patient had to find a word which rhymed with it. Schuell's (1965) findings were that: 'Subjects consistently made no response or produced words associated with the given word by meaning rather than by sound . . . .' She also noted that patients with auditory imperception appeared to produce rhymes inadvertently. For example, one patient who was unable to rhyme voluntarily said *how*, *pow* and *tow* while trying to name *cow*. She rejects the notion that this is a true rhyming situation and suggests that the patient is, in fact, 'groping for an auditory pattern . . . recalled only in part.'

It is interesting to reflect on precisely what is involved in the rhyming process. Clearly an ability to discriminate and match sounds is required plus a good auditory memory and sufficient intellective power to understand what is required to select a word differing by the initial phoneme only. It is probably easier to determine whether two paired words spoken in sequence rhyme, e.g. *pea*, *bee*, than it is to decide whether to do two diversely spelled words, e.g. *hair*, *mare*, when no auditory cues are available. It is not surprising that patients receiving phonemic discrimination therapy for reading defects tend to depend more upon visual than auditory cues and are consequently mislead into grouping together as sounding alike such words as *shave*, *have* and *bead*, *dead* (Schuell, 1965). Possibly of equal difficulty for them is the finding of a rhyme in reply to a key word presented aurally.

The rhyming section was eliminated from the final version of the *Minnesota Test* partly because such deficits are not specific to aphasia, but mainly because it added little information above that supplied by the other language tests. Schuell suggests that it is a good supplementary test which should be employed when more exploration is required.

Hearing test investigating phoneme differentiation are best composed of rhymed words since minimal pairs readily reveal confusions in discriminating the place, manner and voicing of phonemes. Fairbanks (1958) devised a test using groups of five words, one being the test word e.g. hot-got-*not*-pot-lot. This was modified by House *et al.* (1963) and used to evaluate communications systems but the authors felt it also had potential as a diagnostic tool. A special version adapted to deaf subjects has been used by Pickett *et al.*

Rhymed words have also been used by Cohen *et al.* (1965) to investigate communications systems and Voiers (1968) studied the effects of masking speech on elementary consonant attributes. These authors developed the *Diagnostic Rhyme Test* (DRT) for use in their investigations. This test 'utilises a pool of 128 rhyming-word pairs, each designed to test for the transmission of a specific feature' (1965). The listener is simply asked to identify which member of a pair has been spoken.

Although little clinical use has been made of such material, there is no reason why it could not be fruitfully adapted to clinical audiology and various therapeutic programs, in addition to use with foreign students (see Section F.VI.1 and 2). Therapists wishing to investigate this function further for themselves will find a large source of rhyming words in the *Phonetic Lexicon*, though the exclusion of many polysyllabic words limits its usefulness as a rhyming dictionary.

C. EXPRESSIVE FUNCTIONS

In this section we are concerned only with that part of the expressive act known as *speech* (College of Speech Therapists, 1960). This is the encoding equivalent of the primary decoding act performed by the receptive powers. For the purpose of convenience, articulation breakdown will be considered under two heads: those of phonetic origin and those of phonemic origin. This division is not new as it would appear to be in line with that proposed by Stein (1942), who used a somewhat different terminology. He spoke of 'Disorders of Articulation', which arise from a defect in the formation of the sounds themselves; and 'Disorders of Articulate Speech', which occur when the defect is not in the sounds but in their 'articulation basis'. The latter he describes as a phonetic tendency which 'does not simply affect some sounds at random. There is always a certain conformity between the sounds of a group, so that it is generally a whole group of speech sounds which is changed.' He attributes this to the mutual influence of neighbouring sounds. This is in accord with the view of Haas, already mentioned, that such defects are 'rarely capricious'.

C. I. Phonetic Defects

These are conditions in which the child or adult is unable to make the appropriate phonetic realisation of the sound in question. They result from some disturbance in the executive mechanism itself and may be expressed by such diagnostic terms as *dysarthria* and *cleft palate*. Also in this category would fall some forms of *immaturity*, in so far as the patient has not acquired the neuromuscular skills necessary for fine co-ordination, as occurs with the child who has acquired the phonemes of English in the normal developmental order, but at a delayed rate.

As a consequence of *deafness*, secondary phonetic defects may be evident in the child who has poor neuromuscular control of breathing and the articulatory mechanism due to lack of practice with these skills. This patient knows, within the limits of his articulatory maturity, what phoneme is required in any position of a word but is unable to manipulate his speech musculature in such a way as to produce it.

C. II. Phonemic Defects

Fries (1962) points out that the habits of pronunciation learned during the acquisition of one's native tongue are not those of 'producing and hearing the separate sounds as isolatable items in individual words but rather habits of patterns of functioning contrasts in the unique structured system of a particular language'. It is the 'patterns of functioning contrasts' which are weak in phonemic defects. Most of the articulatory disorders in children and some of the adult aphasias are based in this deficiency; however, it seems probable that defects of willed movement should be considered separately.

In the previous section we have seen that many phonemic errors stem from a receptive problem. Nevertheless, since the manifest symptom is expressive, the disorder can be considered from two points of view, especially when habit factors take root.

In all cases the patient shows at least one of the following defects:

(i) failure to develop a complete phonetic inventory, which is usually the case with the child who has many *omissions*,

(ii) inappropriate use of the phonemes which have been acquired, which is often reflected in *substitutions*,

(iii) failure to use the phonemes which have been acquired, in certain phonetic environments. This lack of generalisation results in *omissions*,

(iv) inability to sequence clusters which results in *transpositions*,

(v) inability to combine consonantal phonemes to form clusters which may result in *omission*, *substitution* or *transposition* of at least one phoneme in the group,

(vi) misplacement of conditioned variants, or the use of a variant not normally found in English, which is heard as a *distortion*.

Omissions, substitutions, transpositions and distortions are, of course, found in phonetic defects but these arise purely through a failure of the speech musculature to position itself correctly for the required phoneme production.

Some children with a primary phonemic defect may have a secondary phonetic defect if skill has not been acquired with certain neuromuscular movements. For example, the child using tongue tip substitutions may not have learned, and will certainly not have practised, velar elevation and consequently may find this movement difficult. Ear-training may not be sufficient therapy for such a child.

Once again, the problem is more complicated in the adult aphasic who may also have articulatory problems of a receptive as well as an expressive nature. In the latter case, Luria (1970) contends that the problem results from a 'loss of the inner schemata of articulatory movement'. In severe cases the patient may be unable to find the requisite 'articuleme', while in less severe or recovering conditions he may confuse sounds with similar articulatory patterns, i.e. the labials /p/, /b/ and /m/.

C. III. Testing and Treatment

There is no need to dwell on these topics at length as speech therapists are familiar with the standard testing and treatment procedures, especially those used with children. Word lists and techniques have been proposed by Berry and Eisenson (1956), Fairbanks (1960), Fisher (1966), Morley (1957), Van Riper (1954) and Van Riper and Irwin (1958) amongst others. Luria is most explicit in his description of the testing and treatment of aphasic adults.

Speech (sound) testing is a routine procedure in most clinics when analysis is made of the patients' speech through a stimulus designed to elicit the required response. This may be achieved by means of a printed test such as provided by Templin and Darley, or therapists may use their own material and adapt it to the capabilities of the patient. In the latter event alternate words may be selected quickly from the *Phonetic Lexicon*.

In articulation therapy the target sounds are drilled in varying positions of a word. For example, the child who says /t/ for /s/, but has mastered this sound in isolation, is given the opportunity to practise it in such words as *soap, soup, sun, sum* etc. and later in simple sentences. Through imaginative games, these drills can be made most enjoyable.

When the patient has some confusion with spelling it may be useful to present him with words containing letters which may be said in several ways. For example, depending upon his vocabulary, he could be asked to decide which of the following words contain the /k/ sound: *kite, coat, cease, cup, C, Q, queue, cheque, quay, church, cell, sun, scent, chyle, king.*

Difficulty in generalising the linguistic rules of a language is also found in those cases who are, for instance, confused by the *ed* spelling in the regular past tense, e.g. *walked, robbed, hopped* etc. The patient, like the foreign student, may have great difficulty in deciding whether the /t/ or /d/ sound applies. Therapy must be directed to enable him to determine which sound is preceded by a voiced and which by a voiceless phoneme. This can be done through ear-training and some attention to spelling without explicit reference to the phonetic aspects of the sounds.

The *Phonetic Lexicon* provides a wide variety of words suitable for drills in articulation therapy.

D. SPELLING AND READING

In those languages using an alphabet for their written form, spelling and reading are closely linked with the former subserving the latter. It is said that normal English children take longer to learn to read than, say, Italian whose writing is more phonetically based. How much longer will it then take the child with a dysfunction in this area? Spelling and reading problems are much more common than was once thought and are the root cause of much learning retardation; often they are intimately linked with speech and language deficits.

In adults, breakdown to a lesser or greater extent is seen in *dysgraphia* and *dyslexia* usually associated with *aphasia*. The foreign student also has difficulty with written English.

Although spelling and reading are found together, they will be discussed separately as there is some distinction. The former involves the arrangement of alphabetic letters in a conventional form; the latter, which may be said to be the receptive equivalent, involves the interpretation of this form. It is not uncommon for even a normal person to be unsure of the spelling of a word but be quite capable of reading that same word, i.e. interpreting its meaning, although he might still not know whether it was correctly spelled, e.g. *determin.*

D. I. Spelling

English is one of the more irregularly spelled languages since it has failed to anglicise the many words of non-Anglo-Saxon origin. According to Wijk (1966), combinations of letters can have as many as half-a-dozen to a dozen different pronunciations. This fact has led many to suppose that there is little underlying order to our spelling system. This view he vigorously denies: '. . . for the vast majority of English words, about 90 to 95 per cent of the total vocabulary, do in fact follow certain regular patterns in regard to their spelling and pronunciation'. In a similar vein Fries (1962) writes: '. . . the view that English spelling is completely erratic or that it is so erratic that we must forego all the advantage of an alphabetic system is entirely without foundation.'

Fries (1962) used this inherent, though superficially obscure, regularity as the basis of his theory on teaching reading. His contention is that although single letters have never matched single sound features in English, nevertheless the spelling system is phonemically based. 'English spelling today cannot be satisfactorily dealt with by trying to match individual letters with individual sounds. To say this, however, does not deny the basic relation that does exist between sounds and spellings. To grasp that relation, the beginning reader must learn to respond to the significant features of the major patterns of spelling rather than try to learn the many various sounds that each letter can be said to represent.'

These patterns of spelling – the sequences of letters – are the foundation of written English; they represent word-patterns which, in spoken English, consist of phoneme sequences. However, the spelling patterns are not a facsimile of the phoneme-patterns.

Fries, speaking of one set of spelling-patterns, makes the important point that 'each of the five vowel letters represents a single vowel phoneme. The word-patterns represented by this very large set of spelling patterns are all single syllable words. But these syllables occur very frequently as parts of multisyllable words. . . . This set of spelling-patterns is basic for all English spelling and must be responded to at high speed with practically no errors by those who would read with high efficiency.'

He points out that the spelling-patterns, like the word-patterns of speech, 'acquire significance through contrast' and that probably the fundamental set are those for monosyllabic words formed of (consonant)-vowel-consonant. He shows how hundreds of words can be fitted into a pattern such as:

at	it	(et)	—	—	
bat	bit	bet	—	but	
cat	—	—	cot	cut	
—	—	—	dot	—	
fat	fit	—	—	—	etc.

Notice how *debt* is excluded from this pattern.

Contrasts can be made of final letters by comparing:

| | *bat* | with | bad, | bag, | ban | |
| and | *fat* | with | fad, | fag, | fan | etc. |

or with diagraphs e.g.:

| | bath | hath | lath | path | pith | with |
| and | ash | bash | dash | gash | lash | mash |

Patterns exist for initial and final consonantal clusters of which only /sp/, /st/ and /sk/ are found in both positions. The doubled consonants are also important, e.g. *ff*, *ss* and *ll* as are words with the final *e* unsounded, e.g. *bade*, *fade*, *made* etc. These can be usefully compared with *bad*, *fad*, *mad* etc.

It is not difficult to see the importance of monosyllabic words in the acquisition of spelling habits, nor the application of the *Phonetic Lexicon* to their development. The arrangement of the Tables is such that the relation between the phoneme and the written form is immediately evident. One has only to glance down the /aɪ/ column of the first Table to see the variety of ways this sound may be spelled: *eye, pie, by, chi, guy, thigh* and *chai*. However, the spelling patterns are also quickly discernible, e.g. *pie, tie, die, fie, vie, lie; by, my; thy, shy, why; sigh, high, nigh* etc. This should be of great practical value to the speech and reading therapist.

D. II. Reading

For many years reading theories have been polarised between two extremes – the phonic method and the so-called 'Look-and-Say' – with numerous books and articles proclaiming the merits of each. The recent advances in linguistic science have made it possible to investigate the reading process in a new light and to review the teaching techniques which have served in the past.

Fries (1962), looks upon learning to read as the '*process of transfer* from the auditory signs for language signals, which the child has already learned, to the new visual signs for the same signals'. This description needs some modification, it being too general in one respect and too limited in another. The deafened adult is involved in the transfer of learned auditory cues to visual ones in the lip-reading process – maybe aptly so named. The blind person reads through the transfer of auditory signs to tactile ones; the profoundly deaf child has to transfer one set of visual signs (oro-facial or manual) to another or he may learn the written word through direct association with the object; the deaf-blind child may sometimes make a similar direct association in identifying the thing with its braille representation.

It might be said that the learning of braille is not reading properly so called but an analogous process; if this is accepted then any definition of reading would necessarily include something about sight. Alternatively, it could be argued that reading relates to material which is sufficiently abstract that it can be preserved in time independently of the sender's 'presence'. This question is far too lengthy to consider here but the important point is that the reading process, considered from the visual standpoint, involves the representation of a 'thing', act or relation by a conventional written form, either graphic or pictographic, which is understood by the reader. When this occurs he may be said to know the 'meaning' of the visual symbol.

The parallel auditory memories similarly signifying the 'thing' are present in the normal individual and may assist in the reading process: at times they appear to interfere. What is of note is that, for the majority of those with good auditory word-memories, reading is best taught through the association of spelling-patterns with their heard counterpart. To what extent this applies with the acoustically deprived or confused child is difficult to say.

In the structural approach of Fries the alphabet must be learned so well that the recognition-responses become rapid and correct, i.e. *b* and *d* are clearly differentiated. Also at the pre-reading stage the child must learn to recognise identity and difference, indicated by same-different responses, in such pairs as A-AT, AT-AT, AT-HAT, HAT-BAT, PAN-PAD, PAN-NAP etc. When this is mastered a sequence of three is introduced e.g. MAT-MAP-NAP.

Fries completely abandons the approach of matching individual letters with sound units but encourages the development of automatic habits of responding to the contrastive features in the spelling-patterns. For instance, the three vowels /æ/, /eɪ/ and /i/ may be represented and contrasted in the following words:

man	mane	mean
dan	dane	dean
ban	bane	bean
hat	hate	heat

and so forth. He advocates the use of capital letters to start with.

This differs from the 'word method' because a different kind of identification is required, as Fries (1962) explains: 'The spelling-pattern approach here employed does develop the connections between alphabetic signs of reading and the sound-patterns of talk. This spelling-pattern approach also does treat the "words" as wholes. The significant identifying criteria used . . . differ greatly from those used by any common "phonics" method or by any common "word" method.' He advocates that materials be presented in a systematic way so as to facilitate the development of habits which are so automatic they leave no uncertainty in the mind of the identifying characteristics that mark off one written word from another.

The material must be programmed in such a way that each new item, always a whole word-pattern, is contrasted with one already well known. A recognition inventory is thereby acquired, e.g.: AT-CAT; CAT-RAT; A CAT-A RAT; AT-CAT-RAT-PAT; PAT A CAT; PAT A RAT; RAT-PAT-FAT; A FAT CAT; A FAT RAT; etc.

The difference that a particular letter, in a given spelling-pattern, makes to the sound of the word is learned through pronouncing a variety of minimally paired words e.g. CAT-AT; CAT-RAT; CAT-PAT. One must assume here that Fries is referring to the normally speaking child.

Once the basic spelling-patterns have been mastered, the child passes from the 'transfer' to the 'productive' stage of reading when the process of pattern recognition becomes so habitual that most of the stimulating clues sink below the threshold of attention 'leaving only the cumulative comprehension of the meaning'.

Speech is presented in time and this sequence is represented in writing through the direction of the letters in space. Fries (1962) maintains that: 'In most instances, the troubles pupils have in reversing the elements of letters or numbers . . . or the syllables of words . . . arise not from faulty seeing, or left-handedness, or any physical or psychological defect, but rather from insufficient learning of the significant features that depend upon the space-direction sequence of the written forms.' He does not explain why some children, exposed to the same teaching methods as others, show 'insufficient learning'.

Evidence seems to suggest that more than one factor underlies difficulty in reading. Goetzinger, Dirks and Baer (1960) show that some poor readers have auditory, rather than visual, perceptual difficulties. Both Myklebust (in Johnson and Myklebust, 1967) and Greene (1963) describe two different types of reading problems, though there does not seem to be close correspondence between their two groups. Myklebust speaks of *visual dyslexia* and *auditory dyslexia*. He says that patients with the former show confusion of similar appearing words, reversal and inversion tendencies and have difficulty with visual sequences. The auditory dyslexic, because of his perceptual difficulties 'cannot synthesise sounds into words or analyse words into parts; consequently, he does not learn with an alphabetic or phonic approach.' Such a child is unable to discern the similarity and difference in pairs like *cat* and *mat*; he may overlook one element of a cluster, e.g. *bent* is heard as *bet*; he cannot re-auditorise, i.e. when he sees a letter he cannot remember its sound and when he looks at a word he may be unable to say it although he knows its meaning.

Many poor readers are reported to show irregular non-rhythmic eye movements and one elaborate remedial approach has been to develop the control and speed of eye movements through visual aids like those used in the fast reading courses for adults. Fries looks upon such muscular irregularities as a symptom rather than a cause of poor reading.

To what extent the Fries correction method is successful with all forms of reading disorder is not clear. What he does say is that he has been able to teach children of three and four to read 'as well as "retarded" children of eleven and twelve of very low intelligence quotients'.

E. LIP-READING

As in most fields, theories of teaching lip-reading are spread between two extremes, from the analytic Müller-Walle method to the synthetic approach of Nitche. Whatever the method, certain words are going to be more difficult to comprehend than others; namely, those which are formed in the back of the mouth, e.g. *cook, creek*; those which have no rhythmic cues, including all the monosyllables; and those which are identical with others, i.e. the homophones. A wide selection of all these words is to be found in the *Phonetic Lexicon* which should help the therapist or teacher to exemplify the point to be learned. For example, it could be pointed out to the learner that some words look exactly alike on the lips and therefore it is necessary for him to guess the word from the context. The following sentences may serve as an illustration:

> *B* is a letter of the alphabet.
> *Be* is a frequently used verb.
> A *bee* makes honey.

If the patient has some useful hearing it could be pointed out that in certain words which look alike – the homophenes – a difference can be heard, e.g. *tug, tuck* and *tongue*. Lip-reading and auditory training practice in exercises using these words could be combined.

Homophenes have also been used by Falconer (1966) in his 'lip-reading' test for malingerers claiming deafness. These patients usually explain their ability to communicate well by a high degree of proficiency at lip-reading. It is not, therefore, difficult to get their co-operation with a 'lip-reading' test as they are usually most anxious to prove their skill. Falconer's lists are composed of twenty words and a good score can only reflect hearing since it is beyond probability that someone could do well through chance alone.

In the *Phonetic Lexicon* homophenes with the same final sound may be found on one Table by selecting the lines which contain initial phonemes formed in the same place, e.g. /p/, /b/ and /m/. Homophenes with different final sounds may be found by turning to the pages containing the sounds made in the same place, e.g. /t/, /d/, /l/ and /n/.

F. FOREIGN ACCENT – BARBARALALIA

Many of the problems found in the foreign student are similar to those of speech defectives; for example, difficulty with phonemic discriminations, articulation and reading etc. However, strictly, these cannot be considered pathological, since they are present in all foreigners, to a lesser or greater degree, learning a second language after the age of about twelve years. Therefore it seems justifiable to treat the question of foreign accent as a separate subject.

F. I. Terminology and Etymology

The acquisition of a second language is usually a long and troublesome task and the learner exhibits difficulties in all aspects of the linguistic process. Van Riper's (1954) term *foreign dialect* is consequently an apt description of the condition. To designate the more limited problems of pronunciation, many authors legitimately speak of *foreign accent*. The distinction between *dialect* and *accent* has already been discussed (Chapter 1; Section B).

Among some speech pathologists, particularly the early ones, the term *barbaralalia* is found to describe the speech of foreigners. Bender and Kleinfeld (1938) extend the term also to 'outlandish dialect'.

Barbaralalia appears to derive ultimately from the sanskrit *barbaras* meaning *stammering*. This is the root of the Greek *barbaros* and *hoi barbaroi* who were the non-Greeks or literally 'the Unintelligibles, The Stammerers' (Partridge, 1958). The origin of *stammering* is said to be echoic and Webster (1962) states that to the Greeks 'the talk of a foreigner sounded like *bar-bar*'. The word *barbarismos* is also noteworthy, meaning 'use of a foreign or misuse of one's own language' (Partridge).

From the Greek *barbaros* and *barbarikos* came the Latin *barbaricus* meaning foreign, outlandish, as opposed to Greek and Roman; *balbus* meaning *stammering*; and *barbarus* meaning strange, foreign or after the manner of a foreigner (Smith, 1933) whence comes the English word *barbarism*, 'the use of words and expressions not standard in a language . . .' (Webster).

Some modern languages retain similar words for *stammering*; for example, the French *balbutier, balbutiement*; the Spanish *balbucear, balbucencia*; and the Italian *balbettare, balbettio* etc. Interestingly enough English, too, has an equivalent form in the words *balbutiate, balbutient* and *balbuties*, the latter being defined as 'stammering, also, a kind of defective pronunciation' (Webster).

In pre-scientific days when speech symptoms were inadequately described, it is not difficult to see how the hesitancies and malpronunciation of foreigners came to be equated with stammering. This view is explicated by Green and Wells (1927), who argue that since *foreign accent* results from faulty articulation it should be classified, therapeutically, as 'stammering speech'. Others of the period concurred. Indeed, it is only relatively recently, in Anglo-Saxon countries, that *stammering* has become synonymous with *stuttering* and disordered rhythm. Arnold (1965) quotes Gutzmann's use in 1924 of *stuttering* for a disorder of diction and *stammering* for a disorder of pronunciation and this distinction is found still later in a publication by McAllister (1937). Arnold states that the distinction between the two ideas did not come until 1830 with the writings of Schulthess and he continues: 'The general public ignores this scientific distinction till this day.'

F. II. Components of Foreign Accent

According to the speech pathologist Wood (1959), *foreign accent* is 'the influence of speech sounds of a native language on those of a later learned second language'; he considers it synonymous with *barbaralalia* which he defines as the 'habitual use of the speech sounds and rhythmo-melody of a native language when learning to speak another'.

Using a somewhat complicated terminology and classification system, Stinchfield (1933) equates *barbaralalia* with *foreign dialect* and a defect of articulation; and *foreign accent* with *dysrhythmia*, the latter being a defect of breathing, stress or 'inflection'. A similar division is made by Robbins (1951), but he uses *barbaralalia* to denote defects of articulation and *barbararhythmia* to denote disordered rhythm.

While language teachers and phoneticians are not prone to define *foreign accent*, it is evident from the literature that their views are substantially the same, nor is there any reason to expect otherwise for the phenomenon is quite straightforward and clearly a problem of *pronunciation*.

Before proceeding further it is well to reflect on the components of pronunciation, so that the aims for correction are clearly seen from the start. Pronunciation is an action with many facets, which can best be shown in diagrammatic form.

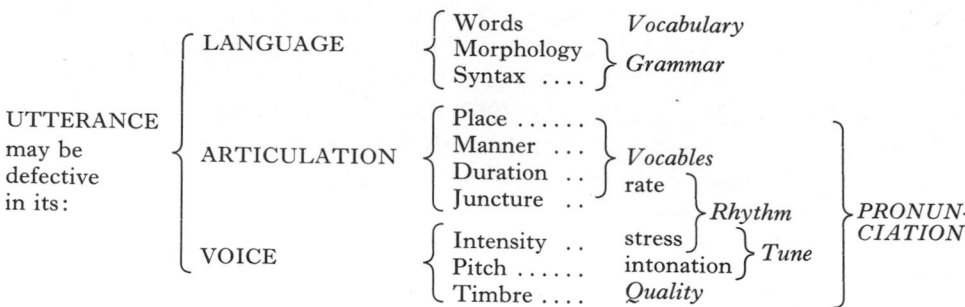

SCHEMA SHOWING THE FACTORS INVOLVED IN PRONUNCIATION

The inclusion of Quality in pronunciation, even though unimportant, in English, seems to be justified since in some languages it is a necessary feature. Trim (1963), referring to a certain word in Burmese, states that 'falling tone, nasalised vowel and breathy voice are all inherent distinctive features, present whenever the word is pronounced.... Questions of comparative efficiency, economy, beauty, social acceptability, of the differing voice qualities do not arise. Instead, they are meaningful, distinctive sound-features which must all be acquired and kept as distinct as possible'.

From the foregoing schema it is evident that speech sounds, rhythm, tune and quality all go to make up what is commonly called *pronunciation* and probably all will need to be corrected in any remedial programme. However, from the viewpoint of this book, we are only concerned with *articulation*.

F. III. Causes of Foreign Accent

The definition of *foreign accent* by Wood, already cited, is partly a statement about cause. His view is in agreement with many of the numerous others on the subject, which are usually expressed in a more explicit manner. Lado (1957), for one, states of learning a foreign language: ' . . . we tend to transfer our entire native language system . . . to that language, our phonemes and their variants, our stress and rhythm patterns, our transitions, our intonation patterns and their interaction with other phonemes.'

MacCarthy (1950) is looking at the matter from the receptive side when he says ' . . . sounds which to the native ear are different sounds belong to separate phonemes *however similar they may seem to the foreigner*, whereas the variants within a phoneme are generally not thought of by the native speaker as constituting separate sounds . . . not usually noticed . . . as being different . . . *however different their acoustic quality and organic foundation* . . . '.

As Harding (1967) points out, adult minds 'can never be a *tabula rasa*' and consequently the acquisition of a second language is quite a different task from learning the first. 'The basic problems arise not out of any essential difficulty in the features of the new language themselves but primarily out of the special "set" created by the first language habits' (Fries, in Lado, 1957).

The problem is clearly both receptive and expressive. On the receptive side, the student has the phonemic code of his mother tongue well established in his mind and, as a consequence, has difficulty in differentiating unfamiliar sounds. The Japanese problem with /l/ and /r/, which are allophones of the same phoneme in that language, is a good example. Fries (1962) lists the following sentences as sounding sufficiently similar to a Japanese that he would be hard put to determine whether there was a difference in meaning:

> They took the long road home
> They took the wrong road home
> They took the wrong load home

For every phonemic code there is a corresponding articulatory code and, as Fry (1963) points out, since the former vary between languages it follows that the latter must also vary. This articulatory code has become well canalised in the adult and the neuro-muscular habits so necessary for fluency and speed are not easily lost or adapted, which is noted by Agard and di Pietro (1965): '. . . the student reacts to the learning of a new language largely in terms of behavioural patterns imposed by his own language. In other words, he sees the structure of the foreign language through the filter of his in-built native habits; . . .'

This, then, is the reason why a second language is so difficult to learn for the majority of people and if their difficulty is to be fully understood by the teacher, it is well that he knows something of the structure of his student's native language.

F. IV. Aims for Pronunciation

The question now arises as to what standard of pronunciation should be expected from the foreign student. Obviously this will vary considerably depending upon his gifts, motivation and requirements: he may need to speak near perfectly or he may just want to make himself understood.

Some writers stress the importance of pronunciation more than others. Duff (1948) for instance claims that it is 'of at least twice as much importance as grammar!' and later in his book he elaborates why it stands before all other considerations: 'Without at least a passable pronunciation, *speech* – the soul of language – must be either imperfect, clumsy or agonising to the listener, or ineffective for its purpose or, as sometimes happens, just so much meaningless noise'.

We see here that although Duff is emphasising the need for instruction in pronunciation he is not advocating a high standard but speech which is 'passable'. Presumably this means reasonably easily understandable.

With the variety of accents to be found in the English-speaking communities it is necessary to consider which accent should be taught. Hill (1967) points out that a teacher cannot impart an accent 'better' than his own but this does not necessarily mean it should be RP: an Indian accent is quite acceptable in India and a Jamaican in Jamaica. His general criterion is that the speech have 'international intelligibility' and this would seem to be a desirable and realistic aim.

F. V. The Teacher

Of late, there has been a great upsurge in the number of foreigners wanting to learn English, which is becoming an international language in commercial circles. This increase in student population has led to a corresponding increase in the number of teachers required. Many of these are well qualified but there are numerous others whose sole qualification is that their mother tongue is English. This serves them adequately, especially if the students' aspirations are not high, but it often gives rise to a belief that an understanding of grammar and phonetics is quite unnecessary.

If the teacher is to be economical in the use of time, some knowledge of phonetics is desirable. Abercrombie (1969) states that it is 'misleading to ask whether phonetics is necessary for language teachers; it is merely a question of how efficient their Phonetics is to be'. He advocates a general understanding of the speech mechanisms, sound analysis and a knowledge of the phonetic structure of English and the student's native tongue. In addition, sensory training is useful to enable him to imitate the student's errors.

Ordinary people cannot give accurate information about the pronunciation of their own language unless they have been specially trained for the purpose according to MacCarthy (1950) and Catford and Pisoni (1970) say that 'The possession of a scientific knowledge of articulatory phonetics by the *teacher* was shown to be extremely successful in leading students to the correct pronunciation. . . .'

Like Abercrombie, Lado (1957) believes that the teacher should have an understanding of his own language and that of the student he is teaching. He quotes Fries (1945): 'The most efficient materials are those that are based upon a scientific description of the language to be learned, carefully compared with a parallel description of the native language of the learner.' Lado contends that in diagnosing difficulties the teacher 'should notice not only a "foreign" accent or an "incorrect" form but a clear-cut, specific distortion of a sound . . .'

This question has been raised here because it is felt to be important if the *Phonetic Lexicon* is to be used effectively and to be of maximum value to the teacher.

F. VI. Testing

If the student aims for a high level in pronunciation a fairly detailed programme must be embarked upon, part of which will involve evaluation procedures. The extent of the testing will probably vary from case to case.

1. *Prediction of Student's Errors*

This is an important, though not essential, step in a correction programme for it facilitates quick diagnosis and efficacious treatment. If the teacher knows something of the phonemic system of the student's native tongue he will know where the two languages diverge and what errors to expect. If a wide variety of nationals is being taught in one class it may not be easy, but this information is available for some languages in such lists as those provided by O'Connor (1967). Reference may also be made to longer comparative studies such as those of Agard and di Pietro (1965).

2. *Testing for Errors*

We have seen that students interpret the target language in terms of their own linguistic habits and are consequently oblivious to some important aspects of that language. Testing should aim to assess the extent of this phenomenon (Chreist, 1964).

(a) *Auditory Tests*. Words should be presented to determine whether the student can discern phonemes likely to be of particular difficulty to him. These will probably be the sounds which either do not exist in his language or which are variant forms of the one phoneme. Phonemes may be identified through minimal pairs and therefore these form good material for testing. For example, the groups *lim-rim; low-row* etc. could be used to assess a Japanese' ability to grasp the /l/-/r/ distinction. The position of the sounds may affect his discrimination and this calls for a greater knowledge of the distribution of these allophones in that language.

Same-different responses can be given or sentences could be written on the board and the students asked to select the appropriate one. A useful sentence for students having problems with /s/-/ʃ/, such as Spanish, would be:

The girl is washing the *sheet*
seat

Rhymes are also helpful. Many foreigners have difficulty with the /i/-/ɪ/ distinction in English. To avoid written clues, the following words could be drawn and the student asked to say which ones rhyme: *lip, whip, jeep, ship, zip.*

(b) *Expressive Tests*. The aim of these is similar to the 'Sound Tests' carried out routinely in speech clinics with patients having articulatory disorders (Section C.III). However, it is not necessary to evaluate every phoneme of English in an initial, medial and final position. Rather, one wants to know:

(i) Whether the student can make sounds not present in his own language, e.g. the English /r/.

(ii) Whether he can say them correctly in all the positions in which they are found in English. As Lado (1957) says: '. . . we must consider the distributional positions of sound clusters in order to analyse adequately the pronunciation problems involved . . .'

(iii) Whether he can form clusters or sequences. To quote Lado again: 'When the native language does not have a sequence, or when a sequence does not occur in a position in which it does occur in the foreign language, we will have located a problem.' He shows that Spanish permits no clusters before final pause and open juncture; therefore these students tend to hear *card, cart, carl, carp, cars* as *car*. Another example relates to /sp/, /sk/ and /st/ which, in Spanish, are always preceded by a vowel and are in two syllables. Therefore it is difficult for them to use these initially in one syllable.

It would be difficult for the average teacher to have enough word lists suitable for assessment of the manifold problems found amongst different nationals. The organisation of the material in the *Phonetic Lexicon* is such that it permits a quick selection of the words needed for a particular line of investigation.

F. VII. Correction

The lines of approach for the correction of faulty pronunciation are twofold: one aims to improve the patient's discriminative ability through ear-training and the other aims to correct the errors through instruction in correct phonetic placement. Usually a combina-

43

tion of the two is used. In addition the student must learn to differentiate between homophones, both conceptually and in their spelling.

1. *Ear-Training*

We have seen that the foreign adult cannot easily discern unusual phonemic differences. Little is understood of this phenomenon but Lado (1957) suggests that the learner '... does not actually hear the foreign language sound units – the phonemes. He hears his own. Phonemic differences in the foreign language will be consistently missed by him if there is no similar phonemic difference in his native language.' These differences must be taught.

One advocate of ear-training is MacCarthy (1950) who states that: 'Given the right kind of training, every ear can be very considerably improved.' He contends that it is the basis of all work on the spoken language and a most effective method for such training is the systematic practice in listening. This point has been emphasised already in relation to other disorders (Section B.I.2 and B.II.1b).

MacCarthy also suggests that training should stress differences rather than similarities in the two languages. He points out that, through 'identification', the foreign ear becomes dulled to the phonemic differences and no further attempt is made to distinguish them in pronunciation. To avoid this some training should be introduced fairly early on.

The first part of the ear-training process is *phonemetisation* according to Morton (cited by Harding, 1967), during which the student says nothing. He maintains that it may require 50 hours of listening for the student to develop an instinctive response to foreign sounds; only then is he ready to detect his own errors when these are played back. This is rather a long time for the student to remain passive and some people can certainly hear their errors at a fairly early stage.

Varying activities are available for ear-training practice. For example:

(i) Minimal pairs are presented differing only in the sound being drilled and students have to say which are the same and which different, e.g.

> *cot* - *cot*
> *cot* - *caught*
> *don* - *dawn*
> *cock* - *cork*

(ii) Numbers can be assigned to a vowel, e.g. 1-$/i/$ and 2-$/ɪ/$ and students must say which one they hear in the following words, e.g. *beat, sit, feet, meat, lit, mit* etc.
(iii) When there is some spelling confusion, it might be useful to write a selection of words on the board, e.g. *ache, king, cat, pique, church, cent* etc. and ask the student which words contain the $/k/$ sound. This can be done with or without listening.
(iv) The discrimination of clusters can be facilitated by the comparison of words in an increasingly complex group, e.g. *ring, wrinkle, wrinkles*.

Key words may be put into sentences and the students requested either:

(i) to point to the correct word, e.g.

> Can you see the *pen*
> *hen*
> *men*

44

(ii) to select the appropriate sentence, e.g.

The *guest eats* the breakfast
guests eat

or:

He's packed his bag. Is he going to *leave*
live

(iii) to select the word which rhymes, e.g.

At the top of a *heap*
They saw a *sheep*
ship

Numerous such activities can be devised and these can be presented with live voice by the teacher and, later, the students; alternatively, a tape recorder or record player may be used.

2. *Sound Production*

The relative importance of instruction in sound production compared with ear-training must be considered. For many years opinions have been divided as to whether there was an automatic capacity to form the correct sounds once these were clearly discriminated, or whether foreign phonemes can best be learned through conscious control of the articulatory mechanisms aided by a scientific understanding of phonetics.

Catford and Pisoni (1970) take the view that articulation practice is more efficacious than ear-training, providing it is *systematic*, i.e. it proceeds step by step. They experimented with two groups, one of which was given explicit instructions in how to produce 'exotic' sounds while the other group was given ear-training alone. The former group performed significantly better not only in articulation of the 'exotic' sounds but, most interesting from the viewpoint of the motor theory of speech production, in discrimination also.

Catford and Pisoni condemn the opinion that people can learn to produce sounds merely by being asked to listen and imitate them. They are not alone with this view. Duff (1948) describes 'imitated pronunciation' as a 'snare and a delusion'; MacCarthy (1950) maintains that, with few exceptions, 'such methods only produce rather bad approximations to the correct sounds, which are generally far from acceptable to the native ear'; and Barrutia (1970) says that if good pronunciation rested solely on imitation, then such methods as phonetic placement could be discarded.

The merits of these views depend on what is meant by imitation or mimicry. Consequently, the distinction made by Pike (1947) is useful since he distinguishes two kinds of mimicry which he calls 'blind' and experimental. The former relies on trial and error, is lengthy and often unfruitful while the latter involves deliberate placement of the articulators and is more efficacious. Obviously, it is the former variety which is to be avoided.

(a) *Sounds in Isolation*. There are a variety of techniques for eliciting specific sounds, but these do not concern us here. Usually, the student must work from an easy to a more difficult sound and suggestions as to how this may be achieved can be found in Barrutia (1970); Catford and Pisoni (1970); Chreist (1964); Gimson (1962); Hill (1967); Lado (1957 and 1964); Mackey (1965); O'Connor (1967); Van Riper (1954) among others. Some advocate the use of charts and the International Phonetic Alphabet.

In general, what is effective in the teaching of sound production is, in the words of Catford and Pisoni '. . . the systematic development by small steps from known articulatory postures and movements to new and unknown ones'.

45

Pike recognises three types of drills: *Production* drills for the actual learning of a sound; *Differential* drills for learning to tell the sounds apart; and *Skill* drills for learning to hear and make them in different sound sequences. The latter often involves combinations to be dicussed below.

(b) *Sounds in Words.* Obviously it is the aim of any remedial programme to use newly acquired sounds in words; indeed, the view is sometimes expressed (Stott, 1946) that sounds can only be produced naturally in words. The sound is certainly modified in a given phonetic environment but it may, nevertheless, be necessary to acquire it in isolation.

The approach to sound production will be along the lines outlined for ear-training and testing. The student will be required to practise:

(i) sounds he does not use in his native language, e.g. /θ/. O'Connor states that such sounds may need practice in all positions,

(ii) sounds in positions in which they do not occur in his native tongue,

(iii) clusters. Hill points out that the transition between clusters is very close in English and there is a tendency for some students to insert the weak vowel /ə/ in a word like *screws*, which may be said /səkəruz/. Special attention may also have to be given to syllabic consonants e.g. in *bubble*, *double*,

(iv) disjuncture. This feature of English is often difficult for foreigners. Drills are given by Fairbanks (1960) and Trim (1965), e.g. *an Asian, a nation;* and *be at, be fat, beef at, beef fat.*

It is usually not possible to teach all the sound features of English, for example all the allophonic variations, and Abercrombie (1969) suggests that a realistic goal for intelligibility is to present the student with carefully chosen features of the language and to avoid fine distinctions, such as the difference between the clear and dark /l/.

Even when the student has acquired the ability to pronounce a certain phoneme correctly, there is no certainty that he knows when to use it. That is, he may still not know how to say a given word. Lado (1957) holds that this is a vocabulary problem. Often it is related to a difficulty with spelling. In these cases, the following instruction may be helpful:

(i) the phonemic basis of the major spelling patterns of English could be brought to the student's attention (see Section D.I)

(ii) certain exceptions could be listed, e.g. the use of /h/ in *house, hot* and *head* but its omission in *hour,*

(iii) the use of /t/ and /s/ in inflected forms following a voiceless sound, e.g. *walked, talked, socks, bikes,* and the use of /d/ or /z/ following a voiced sound, e.g. *jogged, ribbed, digs, dogs.* When the same sound follows the use of the /ɪ/ or /ə/ vowel should be noted, e.g. *wanted, roses,*

(iv) words with similar spelling forms could be listed and the student be required to select which vowel was correct, e.g. the letters *oo* and the sounds /u/ and /ʊ/ in the sentences:

> The children st——d by the door
> Jane prepared the f——d for the picnic
> The children collected w——d for the fire

It is not necessary to give a detailed account of the types of words which should be compared nor how these may be drilled and incorporated into sentences; this will be obvious to most teachers, who doubtless have many ingenious techniques of their own. Beginners are referred to the writings of Amato (1970), Arnold and Gimson (1965), Lado (1957 and 1964), Lado and Fries (1954), MacCarthy (1965), O'Connor (1967) and Trim (1965) all of whom give many practical suggestions.

3. *Differentiation of Homophones and Homographs*

This task pertains to language rather than articulation but it will be discussed here as exercises for the two activities can often be combined.

Spelling and pronunciation is an aspect of the English language which is particularly troublesome to foreigners and it is important that they be assisted to distinguish both conceptually and orthographically between the many words which sound or are spelled alike. Activities with the student could include:

(a) *Reading aloud* with the view to:
- (i) deciding which is the appropriate pronunciation of a homograph, e.g.

    There is a *tear* in his shirt
- (ii) determining the meaning of a passage, which must then be re-written with the correct words, e.g.

    Wear did *ewe plaice* the *peace* of *would*

    or:

    determining which of a group of homophones is the correct one in the context, e.g.

    Aisle see yore teacher

(b) *Matching, Selecting, Correcting or Finding a Homophone* without the assistance of auditory cues:
- (i) matching the key word with a definition or word of similar meaning, e.g.

    queue –

    a letter of the alphabet

    cue –

    a line of people

    Q   –

    or:

    I met her in *Greece* (holiday, country, oil, room)
- (ii) selecting the appropriate word, e.g.

    Things aren't what they——(seam, seem)
- (iii) selecting the pairs which rhyme, e.g.

    Dane-pane; here-where; neigh-weigh;

    deign-pain; hear-wear; nay-way
- (iv) correcting the error e.g.

    The *reign* in Spain falls mainly *inn* the *plane*
- (v) finding the pair, e.g.

    I *hear* that apples are delicious——in England.

Although these exercises are often difficult, they can be presented in an interesting way and consequently they could be adapted for use with the linguistically handicapped, especially the less severely involved aphasic patient.

G. RESEARCH

It is not intended to discuss the various research projects which might be undertaken using monosyllabic words: the possibilities are too numerous to mention, not only for the speech and hearing sciences, but also in linguistics, psychology and education. The *Phonetic Lexicon* could serve as a useful reference for such investigations.

H. CONCLUSION

In the foregoing pages we have seen the trend towards a more systematic approach to the testing and remedy of communication problems. Some of these have been discussed in detail because the necessity of a systematic method is more obvious once the underlying theory is understood. It is hoped that the organisation of words in the *Phonetic Lexicon* will facilitate this approach to correction programmes.

I. REFERENCES

ABERCROMBIE, D. (1969) in *English Teaching Extracts* (Ed. Donn Byrne), Longmans, Green, London, Chaps. 13, 22.

AGARD, F. and DI PIETRO, R. (1965) *The Sounds of English and Italian*, The University of Chicago Press, Chicago.

AMATO, A. (1970) *English Phonetic Drills for Speakers of the Italian Language*, Angelo Signorelli Editore, Roma.

ARNOLD, G. and GIMSON, A. (1965) *English Pronunciation Practice*, University of London Press, London.

ARNOLD, G. (1965) 'Disorders of Articulation: Dyslalia' in *Voice—Speech—Language*, R. Luchsinger and G. E. Arnold, Wadsworth, Belmont, California, Section 2B.

BALLANTYNE, J. (1960) *Deafness*, J. & A. Churchill, London.

BARRUTIA, R. (1970) 'Visual Phonetics', *The Modern Language Journal*, Vol. LIV, No. 7, p. 482.

BEEBE, H. (1944) 'Auditory Memory Span for Meaningless Syllables', *J. Speech & Hearing Disorders*, Vol. 9, p. 273.

BENDER, J. and KLEINFELD, V. (1938) *Principles and Practices of Speech Correction*, Isaac Pitman & Sons, London.

BERRY, M. and EISENSON, J. (1956) *Speech Disorders—Principles and Practices of Therapy*. Appleton-Century-Crofts, New York.

BLACK, J. and HESS HAAGEN, C. (1963) 'Multiple-Choice Intelligibility Tests, Forms A and B', *J. Speech & Hearing Disorders*, Vol. 28, p. 77.

CATFORD, J. and PISONI, D. (1970) 'Auditory vs. Articulatory Training in Exotic Sounds', *The Modern Language Journal*, Vol. LIV, p. 477.

CHREIST, F. M. (1964) *Foreign Accent*, Prentice-Hall, Englewood Cliffs, N.J.

COHEN, M., MICKUNAS, J., MILLER, J. and VOIERS, W. F. (1965) 'Diagnostic Rhyme Test for the Evaluation of Communications Systems', *J. Acous. Soc. Amer.* Vol. 37, No. 6, p. 1206.

COLLEGE OF SPEECH THERAPISTS, LONDON. (1960) 'Terminology for Speech Pathology', *Speech Pathology & Therapy*, Vol. 3, p. 36.

DALE, D. (1967) *Applied Audiology for Children* (2nd edn.), Charles C. Thomas, Springfield, Illinois.

DUFF, C. (1948) *How to Learn a Language*, Basil Blackwell, Oxford.

FAIRBANKS, G. (1958) 'Test of Phoneme Differentiation: The Rhyme Test' *J. Acous. Soc. Amer.*, Vol. 30, No. 7, p. 596.

FAIRBANKS, G. (1960) *Voice and Articulation Drillbook* (2nd edn) Harper Bros., New York.

FALCONER, G. (1966) 'A Lip-Reading Test for Nonorganic Deafness', *J. Speech & Hearing Disorders*, Vol. 31, p. 241.

FISHER, H. (1966) *Improving Voice and Articulation*, Houghton Mifflin, Boston.

FLETCHER, H. (1953) *Speech and Hearing in Communication*, van Nostrand, Princeton, N.J.

FRIES, C. (1945) *Teaching and Learning English as a Foreign Language*, University of Michigan Press, Ann Arbor.

FRIES, C. (1962) *Linguistics and Reading*, Holt, Rinehart & Winston, New York.

FRISINA, D. R. (1963) 'The Measurement of Hearing in Children', Chap. 4, in *Modern Developments in Audiology*, (Ed. J. Jerger), Academic Press, New York & London.

FRY, D. (1963) 'Coding and Decoding in Speech' in *Signs, Signals and Symbols* (Ed. S. Mason), Methuen, London.

GIMSON, A. (1962) *An Introduction to the Pronunciation of English*, Edward Arnold, London.

GOETZINGER, C., DIRKS, D. and BAER, C. (1960) 'Auditory Discrimination and Visual Perception in Good and Poor Readers', *Annals of Otology, Rhinology & Laryngology*, Vol. 69, p. 121.

GREEN, M. (1963) 'Comparison of Children with Delayed Speech due to Co-ordination Disorder of Language Learning Difficulty', *Speech Pathology & Therapy*, Vol. 6, p. 69.

GREENE, J. S. & WELLS, J. (1927) *The Cause and Cure of Speech Disorders*, Macmillan.

HAAS, W. (1963) 'Signs and Signals', in *Signs, Signals and Symbols*, (Ed. S. Mason), Methuen, London.

HASPIEL, G. S. & BLOOMER, R. H. (1961) 'Maximum Auditory Perception (MAP) Word List', *J. Speech & Hearing Disorders*, Vol. 26, No. 2, p. 156.

HARDING, D. (1967) *The New Pattern of Language Teaching*, Longmans, London.

HILL, L. A. (1967) *Selected Articles on the Teaching of English as a Foreign Language*, Oxford University Press, London, Chap. 7.

HOUSE, A. S., WILLIAMS, C., HECKER, M. & KRYTER, K. (1963) 'Psychoacoustic Speech Tests: A Modified Rhyme Test'. *J. Acous. Soc. Amer.*, Vol. 35, No. 11, p. 1899.

JOHNSON, D. and MYKLEBUST, H. (1967) *Learning Disabilities*, Grune & Stratton, New York.

LADO, R. (1957) *Linguistics Across Cultures*, University of Michigan Press, Ann Arbor.

LADO, R. (1964) *Language Teaching: A Scientific Approach*, McGraw-Hill, New York.

LADO, R. and FRIES, C. (1954) *English Pronunciation*, University of Michigan Press, Ann Arbor.

LAFON, J-C. (1960) 'Contribution to the Diagnosis of Central Auditory Disorders by the Study of Phonetic Perception' (Extract from papers presented to the 5th Bonn Conference), *International Society of Audiology*.

LURIA, A. R. (1970) *Traumatic Aphasia*, Mouton, The Hague.

MACCARTHY, P. (1950) *English Pronunciation*, (4th edn.), W. Heffer & Sons, Cambridge.

MACCARTHY, P. (1965) *A Practice Book of English Speech*, Oxford University Press, London.

MACKEY, W. (1965) *Language Teaching Analysis*, Longmans, Green, London.

MCALLISTER, A. H. (1937) *Clinical Studies in Speech Therapy*, University of London Press, London.

METRAUX, R. (1944) 'Auditory Memory Span for Speech Sounds: Norms for Children', *J. Speech & Hearing Disorders*, Vol. 9, p. 31.

MORLEY, M. (1957) *Development and Disorders of Speech in Childhood*, Livingstone, London.

NEWBY, H. (1965) *Audiology: Principles and Practice* (2nd edn.), Vision Press, London.

O'CONNOR, J. (1967) *Better English Pronunciation*, Cambridge University Press, Cambridge.

PARTRIDGE, E. (1958) *Origins*, (A short Etymological Dictionary of Modern English), Routledge & Kegan Paul, London.

PETERSON, G. and LEHISTE, I. (1962) 'Revised CNC Lists for Auditory Tests', *J. Speech & Hearing Disorders*, Vol. 27, p. 62.

PICKETT, J. (1968) 'Sound Patterns of Speech: an Introductory Sketch', *Amer. Annals of the Deaf*, Vol. 113, p. 120.

PICKETT, J., MARTIN, E. S., JOHNSON, D., SMITH, S., DANIEL, Z., WILLIS, D. and OTIS, W. (in press) 'On Patterns of Speech Feature Reception by Deaf Listeners' *Proc. Int. Symposium on Speech Communication Ability and Profound Deafness, Stockholm 1970*, (Ed. G. Fant).

PIKE, K. L. (1947) *Phonemics*, University of Michigan Press, Ann Arbor.

PRONOVOST, W. & DUMBLETON, C. (1953) 'A Picture-Type Speech Sound Discrimination Test', *J. Speech & Hearing Disorders*, Vol. 18, p. 266.

REED, M. (1960) *Hearing Test Cards*, Royal National Institute for the Deaf, London.

RENFREW, C. (1964) 'Assessment of the Late or Poor Talker', in *The Child Who Does not Talk* (Ed. C. Renfrew and K. Murphy), The Spastics Soc. Med. Ed. & Inform. Unit.

ROBBINS, A. (1951) *Dictionary of Speech Pathology and Therapy*, Peter Owen, London.

ROBERTS, D. (1968) 'An Evaluation of the term "Central Deafness" ' *J. Australian Coll. of Sp. Therapists*, Vol. 18, p. 6.

SCHUELL, H. (1965) *Differential Diagnosis of Aphasia with the Minnesota Test*, University of Minnesota Press, Minnesota.

SHERIDAN, M. D. (1955) ' The Young Deaf Child', *Medical World (London)*, Vol. 82, No. 2, p. 146.

SMITH, W. (1933) *A Smaller Latin-English Dictionary*, John Murray, London.

STEIN, L. (1942) *Speech and Voice*, Methuen, London.

STINCHFIELD, S. (1933) *Speech Disorders*, Kegan Paul, Trench, Trubner, London.

STOTT, D. (1946) *Language Teaching in the New Education*, University of London Press, London.

TEMPLIN, M. (1943) 'Study of Sound Discrimination Ability of Elementary School Pupils', *J. Speech Disorders*, Vol. 8, p. 132.

TRAVIS, L. and RASMUS, B. (1931) 'The Speech-Sound Discrimination Ability of Cases with Functional Disorders of Articulation', *Quart. J. Speech*, Vol. 17, p. 217.

TRIM, J. (1963) 'Linguistics and Speech Pathology' in *Signs, Signals and Symbols* (Ed. S. Mason), Methuen, London.

TRIM, J. (1965) *English Pronunciation Illustrated*, Cambridge University Press, Cambridge.

VAN RIPER, C. (1954 and 1963) *Speech Correction: Principles and Methods* (3rd and 4th edns.), Prentice-Hall, Englewood Cliffs, N.J. Chaps. 7 & 11.

VAN RIPER, C. and IRWIN, J. (1958) *Voice and Articulation*, Prentice-Hall, Englewood Cliffs, N.J.

VOIERS, W. (1968) 'Effects of Masking Speech on the Discriminability of Elementary Consonant Attributes', *J. Acous. Soc. Amer.*, Vol. 44, p. 397.

WEBSTER'S NEW TWENTIETH CENTURY DICTIONARY OF THE ENGLISH LANGUAGE (1962) The World Publishing, Cleveland.

WEPMAN, J. (1958) *Auditory Discrimination Test*, University of Chicago.

WHETNALL, E. and FRY, D. (1964) *The Deaf Child*, Heinemann Medical Books, London.

WIJK, A. (1966) *Rules of Pronunciation for the English Language*, Oxford University Press, London.

WOOD, K. (1959) 'Terminology and Nomenclature' in *Handbook of Speech Pathology* (Ed. E. L. Travis), Peter Owen, London.

Tables

The following Tables are arranged according to the initial, medial and final sound/s of the words listed (Chapter 1: Section C.II, 1, 2, 3)

The pronunciation of the various accents has already been discussed (Chapter 1: Section A; B, I, IV) as has the choice of symbols (Chapter 1: C.III, 1, 2). Readers are also referred to the KEY TO SYMBOLS on page xii.

A footnote at the bottom left of each Table indicates the number of slots filled on that Table and *not* the actual number of words i.e. diverse meanings. More precisely, where there is an alternate spelling and/or pronunciation of a given word this may be repeated at least once. Homographs also have more than one listing. In addition, words containing /ju/, but having no homophonic pair, are duplicated in the top right and central slot. These points have already been fully explained (Chapter 1: C.II.2.b; III.2.c,d). The word count is further somewhat misleading because it does not represent the number of meaningful phonetic groupings in English either; many American variations, being indicated only by a symbol at the column head, do not appear in the count. Thus, the number of words recorded on each Table is only a rough guide to the distribution of the meaningful phonetic combinations in question.

	i	ɪ	ɛ	æ	ɑ/r	ɒ	ɔ(oʊ)/r	ʊ	u
–	*E**	·	·	·	are*	·	or*	·	[ou
p	*P**	·	·	·	par*	·	paw*	(pooh)	(po
b	*bee**	·	·	·	bar*	·	boar*	·	boo
t	tea*	·	·	·	tar*	·	tore*	·	*two
d	*D**	·	·	·	[darre]†		*door**	·	do*
k	*key**	·	·	·	*car**	[quo']†	core*	·	coo
g	[ghee]*	·	·	·	gar†	·	gore*	·	goo
f	fee*	·	·	·	far*	(foh)†	*four**	·	fou
v	*V*	·	·	·	·	·	vor†	·	·
θ	ye	(ye)†	·	·	·	·	thaw*	·	·
ð	thee*	·	·	·	·	·	·	·	·
s	*sea**	·	·	·	sar	·	saw*	·	(sue
z	(Z)†	·	·	·	tsar	·	·	·	zoo
ʃ	she*	·	·	·	shah	·	shore*	·	*shoe
ʒ	·	·	·	·	·	·	·	·	·
h	he	·	·	·	ha	·	haw*	·	who
tʃ	Tshi	·	·	·	char*	·	chore*	·	che
dʒ	*G**	·	·	·	*jar**	·	jaw	·	Jew
m	me*	·	·	·	mar*	·	more*	·	moo
n	knee*	·	·	·	knar*	·	nor*	·	(gnu
l	lea*	·	·	·	la*†	·	law*	·	loo*
r	re*	·	·	·	Ra*	·	raw*	·	rue
w	we*	·	·	·	·	·	wore*	·	woo
j	yet†	·	·	·	yarr*†	·	your*	·	ewe
pl	plea	·	·	·	·	·	·	·	[ple
pr	pree†	·	·	·	·	·	prore†	·	[pro
bl	bleet†	·	·	·	blah†	·	·	·	*blue
br	bree	·	·	·	·	·	braw	·	bre
tr	*tree*	·	·	·	tra	·	·	·	true
tw	·	·	·	·	(twa)†	·	(twa)†	·	·
dr	dree†	·	·	·	·	·	draw	·	dre
kl	·	·	·	·	·	·	claw	·	clue
kr	cree*	·	·	·	·	·	crore*	·	crew
kw	·	·	·	·	(qua)	·	·	·	·
gl	glee*	·	·	·	·	·	glaur	·	glu
gr	gree	·	·	·	·	·	·	·	grew
fl	flee*	·	·	·	·	·	floor*	·	flew
fr	free	·	·	·	·	·	[frore]	·	·
θr	*three*	·	·	·	·	·	thraw†	·	thr
sp	·	·	·	·	spa*	·	spore*	·	·
st	·	·	·	·	*star**	·	store*	·	stow
sk	ski	·	·	·	scar	·	score*	·	·
sm	[smee]	·	·	·	·	·	(smore)†	·	·
sn	·	·	·	·	snar†	·	snore	·	·
sl	[slee]†	·	·	·	·	·	slaw	·	slev
sw	[swee]†	·	·	·	·	·	swore	·	·
ʃr	·	·	·	·	·	·	·	·	shre
spl	·	·	·	·	·	·	splore†	·	·
spr	spree	·	·	·	·	·	·	·	spru
str	·	·	·	·	·	·	straw	·	stre
skr	scree	·	·	·	·	·	scraw	·	*scre
skw	·	·	·	·	·	·	squaw	·	·

* homophones—see pages 210–211
  Total number of words—426

ʌ	ɜ/r	eɪ	oʊ	aɪ	aʊ	ɔɪ	i/ə/r	ɛ/ə/r	ju
•	err*	A*	O*	eye*	(ow)	oy	ear	air*	U*
•	purr*	pay*	poh*†	pie*	pow	poy†	pier*	pear*	pew
•	burr*	bay*	bow*	by*	bough*	boy*	beer*	bear*	
•	.	[tae]	toe*	tie*	tau	toy	tear*	tare*	tew
•	.	day*	doe*	die*	dhow*	.	deer*	dare	(dew)*
•	cur*	K*	co	chi*	cow*	coy	kier	care	queue*
•	.	gay*	go	guy*	gau	goy	gear	gare	[gju]
•	fur*	fay*	foe	fie*†	.	foy	fear*	fair*	few*
•	.	[vae]	voe	vie	vow	.	veer	vare*	view
•	.	.	.	thigh	thou	.	Thea	.	thew
•	.	they*	though*	thy	thou†	.	.	there*	.
•	sir*	say*	sew*	sigh*	sow*	soy	cere*	[sair]	(sue)
•	.	.	[zo]	(xi)	.	.	.	.	.
•	shirr	shay*	show	shy	.	.	sheer*	share	.
•	.	.	[zho]	.	.	.	.	.	.
•	her*	hay*	hoe*	high*	how*	hoy	here*	hair*	hew*
•	chirr*	(chay)	.	chai*	chow*	.	cheer	chair*	.
•	.	jay*	joe*†	.	jow†	joy*	jeer	.	.
•	myrrh	may*	mow*	my	mow	moy†	mere*	mare	mew*
•	knurr	neigh*	no*	nigh*	now	noy	near*	nare*	(knew)*
•	.	lay*	low*	lie*	.	loy	leer*	lair*	(lieu)*
•	.	ray*	row*	rye*	row	Roy	rear	rare	.
•	were*	way*	woe*	why*	whow*†	.	weir*	wear*	.
•	(year)	yea*	yo	.	[yowe]*†	.	(year)	yare	.
•	.	play	.	ply	plough*	ploy	.	(player)	.
•	.	pray*	pro	pry	prow	.	.	(prayer)	.
•	blur	blay*	blow	.	.	.	blear	blare	.
•	Brer	bray*	.	.	brow	.	[breare]*†	brer	.
•	.	tray*	trow	try	[trow]†	troy*	.	.	.
•	'twere†	[tway]*†	.	.	.	.	[tweer]	.	.
•	.	dray*	.	dry	drow	.	drear	.	.
•	.	clay	.	cly†	(clough)*	cloy*†	clear	Clair	.
•	.	.	crow	cry	.	.	.	crare	.
•	.	(quey)*†	quo	.	.	.	queer	[quair]	.
•	.	.	glow	(gley)	.	.	.	glare*	.
•	.	grey*	grow	.	.	.	.	.	.
•	flurr	flay	flow*	fly	.	.	fleer	flair*	.
•	.	fray	fro	fry	frow	.	freer	.	.
•	.	thrae†	throw*	.	.	.	.	.	.
•	spur*	spay*	.	spy	.	.	spear*	spare	spew
•	stir	stay	stow	sty*	.	.	steer*	stare*	stew
•	skirr†	.	.	sky*	scow	.	skier	scare	skew
•	smur†	.	.	.	.	.	smear	.	smew
•	.	.	snow	.	.	.	sneer	snare	.
•	slur	sleigh*	slow*	sly	slough	.	.	.	.
•	.	sway	.	.	.	.	[sweer]	swear	.
•	.	.	[shrow]	.	.	.	.	.	.
•	.	splay	.	.	.	.	.	.	.
•	.	spray	.	spry	.	.	.	.	.
•	.	stray*	[strow]†	.	.	stroy†	stria	.	.
•	.	scray*	scrow	scry†	.	.	.	.	.
•	[squirr]†	.	.	.	.	.	.	square	.

For—/aɪə/, /aʊə/, /eɪə/, /oʊə/ and /jʊə/, see pages 230–231.
—/ɔə/, see page 8.
—/ʊə/, see page 8.

	i	ɪ	ɛ	æ	ɑ/r	ɒ(ɑ	ɔ(ɑ/ɒ)ɔ	ʊ	u
–	.	.	.	.	.	.	.	.	[ou...
p	peep*	pip	pep†	pap	.	pop	.	.	poo...
b	beep	.	.	bap	.	.	.	.	.
t	.	tip	.	*tap*	tap†	*top*	.	.	.
d	deep	dip	.	dap	.	dop	dorp	.	(du...
k	keep	kip*	kep	*cap**	carp*	cop*	[caup]†	.	coo...
g	.	.	.	gap	.	.	gaup	.	goo...
f	.	.	.	fap†	.	fop	.	.	.
v	.	.	.	.	.	.	.	.	.
θ	.	.	.	.	.	.	thorp	.	.
ð	.	.	.	.	.	.	.	.	.
s	seep	sip	.	sap	.	sop	.	.	sou...
z	.	*zip*	.	.	.	.	.	.	.
ʃ	*sheep*	*ship*	.	.	sharp	*shop*	.	.	.
ʒ	.	.	.	.	.	.	.	.	.
h	heap	hip*	[hep]	hap	harp	hop	.	(hoop)	hoo...
tʃ	cheap*	chip	.	chap	.	chop	.	.	.
dʒ	jeep	gyp†	.	Jap	(jaup)	.	(jaup)	.	.
m	.	.	.	*map*	.	*mop*	.	.	mo...
n	neap	nip*	nep	nap*	.	knop	.	noop*†	(no...
l	leap	*lip*	lep†	lap*	.	lop	.	.	loo...
r	reap	rip*	repp*	wrap*	.	.	.	.	roo...
w	weep	*whip*	.	[wapp]†	.	whop*	warp*	.	.
j	.	yip†	[yep]	yapp*	.	.	yaup	.	yoo...
pl	.	.	.	plap	.	plop	.	.	.
pr	.	.	prep	.	.	prop	.	.	.
bl	.	blip	.	.	.	.	.	.	.
br	.	.	.	.	.	.	.	.	.
tr	.	trip	.	trap	.	.	.	.	troo...
tw	.	.	.	.	.	.	.	.	.
dr	.	drip	.	.	[drap]†	drop	.	.	dro...
kl	cleep	clip	.	clap	.	clop	.	.	cloo...
kr	creep	.	(crepe)	.	[crap]†	crop	.	.	cro...
kw	.	quip	quep	.	.	quop	.	.	.
gl	Gleep	.	.	.	.	.	.	.	.
gr	(grippe)	grip*	.	.	.	.	.	.	gro...
fl	.	flip	.	flap	.	flop	.	.	.
fr	.	.	.	frap	.	frop	.	.	.
θr	threep	.	.	.	.	.	.	.	.
sp	.	.	.	.	.	.	.	.	.
st	steep	.	*step**	[stap]	[stap]	stop	.	.	stoc...
sk	.	skip	skep	.	scarp	.	scaup	.	scoo...
sm	.	.	.	.	.	.	..	.	.
sn	sneap	snip	.	snap	.	.	.	.	sno...
sl	sleep	slip	.	slap	.	slop	.	.	sloo...
sw	sweep	.	.	.	.	swop	.	.	swo...
ʃr	.	.	.	.	.	.	.	.	.
spl	.	.	.	.	.	.	.	.	.
spr	.	.	.	.	.	.	.	.	.
str	.	strip	.	strap	.	strop	.	.	stro...
skr	.	scrip	.	scrap	.	.	.	.	scro...
skw	.	.	.	.	.	.	.	.	.

* homophones—see page 211.
  Total number of words—223

ʌ	ɜ/r	eɪ	oʊ	aɪ	aʊ	ɔɪ	i/ə/r	ɛ/ə/r	ju
up	.	*ape*	ope†	.	.	.	.	.	.
pup	.	pape†	pope*	*pipe*	.	.	.	.	.
.	burp	.	.	.	.	.	.	.	.
tup	.	tape	tope*	type	.	.	.	.	.
dup	.	.	dope	.	doup	.	.	.	(dupe)
cup	.	cape	cope	kipe†	coup*†	.	.	.	.
gup	.	gape	.	.	.	.	.	.	.
.	.	.	.	.	.	.	.	.	.
.	.	.	.	.	.	.	.	.	.
.	.	.	.	.	.	.	.	.	.
sup	.	.	*soap*	sipe†	sowp†	.	.	.	.
.	.	.	.	.	.	.	.	.	.
.	.	shape	shope†	.	.	.	.	.	.
.	.	.	.	.	.	.	.	.	.
hup†	.	.	hope	.	.	.	.	.	.
.	chirp	chape	.	.	.	.	.	.	.
.	.	jape	.	.	.	.	.	.	.
.	.	.	mope	.	.	.	.	.	.
.	.	nape	nope	.	.	.	.	.	.
.	.	.	lope	.	loup†	.	.	.	.
.	.	rape	*rope*	ripe	.	.	.	.	.
.	.	.	.	wipe	.	.	.	.	.
.	.	.	.	yipe†	.	.	.	.	.
.	.	.	.	.	.	.	.	.	.
.	.	.	.	.	.	.	.	.	.
.	.	.	.	.	.	.	.	.	.
.	.	trape	trope	tripe	.	.	.	.	.
.	twerp	.	.	.	.	.	.	.	.
.	.	drape	.	.	.	.	.	.	.
.	.	(crepe)*	.	.	.	.	.	.	.
.	.	.	.	.	.	.	.	.	.
.	.	grape*	grope	gripe	.	.	.	.	.
.	.	.	.	flype	.	.	.	.	.
.	.	.	.	.	.	.	.	.	.
.	.	.	stope	stipe	.	.	.	.	(stupe)
scup	.	scape	scope	.	scoup†	.	.	.	.
.	.	.	.	snipe	.	.	.	.	.
.	.	.	slope	slipe*	.	.	.	.	.
.	.	.	.	swipe	.	.	.	.	.
.	.	.	.	.	.	.	.	.	.
.	.	.	.	.	.	.	.	.	.
.	.	.	.	stripe	.	.	.	.	.
.	.	scrape	.	.	.	.	.	.	.
.	.	.	.	.	.	.	.	.	.

Final—/pt/ . For inflected forms add /t/ to appropriate words, e.g. hopped.
. For uninflected forms, see page 231.
—/ps/ . For inflected forms add /s/ to appropriate words, e.g. hops.
. For uninflected forms, see pages 232–233.

	i	ɪ	ɛ	æ	ɒ/r	ɒ(ɑ	ɔ/r	ʊ	u
–	.	.	ebb	abb	.	ob	orb	.	.
p	.	.	.	.	.	.	.	.	.
b	.	bib*	.	.	barb*	bob*	.	.	.
t	.	Tib†	.	tab	.	.	.	.	(tu
d	dieb	dib	debt†	dab*	.	Dob†	daub	.	doo
k	.	.	keb†	cab	.	cob*	corbet†	.	.
f	.	gib	.	gab†	garb	gob	gaub	.	.
g	.	fib	.	.	.	fob	.	.	.
v	.	.	.	.	.	.	.	.	.
θ	.	.	.	.	.	.	.	.	.
ð	.	.	.	.	.	.	.	.	.
s	.	sib†	.	.	sab†	sob	sorb*	.	.
z	.	.	.	.	.	.	.	.	.
ʃ	.	.	.	.	.	.	.	.	.
ʒ	.	.	.	.	.	.	.	.	.
h	.	.	.	.	.	hob	.	.	.
tʃ	.	.	.	.	.	.	.	.	.
dʒ	.	jib*	.	jab	.	job	.	.	.
m	.	.	.	Mab*	.	mob	.	.	.
n	.	nib	neb	nab*	.	knob*	.	.	.
l	.	lib†	.	lab†	.	lob	.	.	loo
r	.	rib	.	.	.	rob*	.	.	.
w	.	.	*web**	.	.	.	.	.	.
j	.	.	.	.	.	.	.	.	.
pl	plebet†	.	plebt†	.	.	.	.	.	.
pr	.	.	.	.	.	.	.	.	.
bl	.	.	bleb	blabt†	.	blob	.	.	.
br	.	.	.	.	.	.	.	.	.
tr	.	.	.	.	.	.	.	.	.
tw	.	.	.	.	.	.	.	.	.
dr	.	drib†	.	drab	.	.	.	.	.
kl	.	.	.	.	.	.	.	.	.
kr	.	crib	.	*crab*	.	.	.	.	.
kw	.	quibt†	.	.	quab	quobt†	.	.	.
gl	glebet†	glib	.	.	.	.	.	.	.
gr	grebe	.	.	grab	.	.	.	.	.
fl	.	.	.	.	.	.	.	.	.
fr	.	.	.	frabt†	.	.	.	.	.
θr	.	.	.	.	.	throb	.	.	.
sp	.	.	.	.	.	.	.	.	.
st	.	.	.	stab	.	stobt†	.	.	.
sk	.	.	.	scab	.	.	.	.	.
sm	.	.	.	.	.	.	.	.	.
sn	.	snibt†	snebt†	.	.	snob	.	.	.
sl	.	.	.	slab	.	.	.	.	.
sw	.	.	.	.	.	swob	.	.	.
ʃr	.	.	.	.	.	.	.	.	.
spl	.	.	.	.	.	.	.	.	.
spr	.	.	.	.	.	.	.	.	.
str	.	.	.	.	.	.	.	.	.
skr	.	.	.	scrab	.	.	.	.	.
skw	.	squib	.	.	.	squab	.	.	.

* homophones—see page 211.
   Total number of words—117

ʌ	ɜ/r	eɪ	oʊ	aɪ	aʊ	ɔɪ	i/ə/r	ɛ/ə/r	ju
pub†									
bub		babe							
tub									(tube)
dub									
cub	curb*			kibe					cube
fub†									
	verb								
	Serb								
hub	herb								
chub*									
	gerbe		Job*	jibe*					
knub*									
			lobe						
rub			robe						
			probe						
blub†	blurb								
				bribe					
				tribe					
drub									
club									
			globe						
grub									
stub									
snub									
slub*									
shrub									
scrub			scrobe	scribe					

Final—/bd/ . For inflected forms add /d/ to appropriate words, e.g. robbed.
—/bz/ . For inflected forms add /z/ to appropriate words, e.g. robs.
. For uninflected forms, see page 233.

	i	ɪ	ɛ	æ	ɑ/r	ɒ(ɑ	ɔ(oʊ/r	ʊ	u
—	eat	it	(ate)	at	art	.	ought*	.	ut
p	peat*	pit*	pet	pat*	part*	pot	port*	put	.
b	beat*	bit*	bet*	*bat*	.	bot	bought*	.	*boot*
t	teat	tit	tete†	tatt*	*tart*	tot	taut*	.	toot
d	.	dit*†	debt	.	dart	dot	daut*†	.	.
k	.	kit	kett†	*cat*	cart*	*cot*	court*	.	coot
g	.	.	get	gat	.	got	ghat	.	.
f	*feet*	fit*	fet	fat	fart	[phot]	fort*	*foot*	.
v	vite	.	vet	vat	.	.	(vault)†	.	.
θ	thete	.	.	.	.	.	thought	.	.
ð	.	.	.	that	.	.	.	.	.
s	seat	sit*	set	sat	.	sot	sort*	soot	(suit)
z	.	.	.	.	.	.	.	.	.
ʃ	sheet	.	[shet]	.	sceat†	shot	short	.	shoot
ʒ	gite	.	.	.	.	.	.	.	.
h	heat*	hit	het†	*hat*	*heart*	hot	haut†	.	hoot
tʃ	cheat	chit	.	chat	chart	.	.	.	.
dʒ	geat	git†	*jet*	.	.	jot	.	.	jute
m	*meat*	*mitt*	met	*mat*	mart	mot*†	mort†	.	moot
n	neat	knit*	*net*	*gnat*	.	*knot*	nought*	.	(new•
l	leet*	lit*	let*	lat	.	lot	.	(loot)†	loot*
r	reate	writ*	ret	*rat*	.	rot	wrought*	.	root*
w	wheat*	wit*	wet*	.	.	what*	wart*	woot	.
j	.	.	yet*	.	*yacht*	.	.	.	.
pl	pleat	.	.	(plait)*	.	plot	.	.	.
pr	.	.	.	prat	.	.	.	.	.
bl	bleat	.	blet	.	.	blot	.	.	.
br	.	brit	.	brat	.	.	brought	.	brute
tr	treat	.	tret	.	.	trot	.	.	.
tw	tweet	twit	.	.	.	twot	.	.	.
dr	.	.	.	drat	.	.	.	.	.
kl	cleat	.	.	.	[clat]*†	clot	[claut]†	cloot	.
kr	Crete	.	.	.	.	.	.	.	crout•
kw	.	quit	.	.	.	quat	quart	.	.
gl	gleet	glit	.	.	.	.	.	.	.
gr	greet	grit	.	.	.	grot	.	.	.
fl	fleet	flit*	.	flat	.	.	flaught	.	flute
fr	freit†	frit	fret	.	.	.	fraught	.	*fruit*
θr	.	.	threat	.	.	.	.	.	.
sp	.	spit	[spet]	spat	spart	spot	sport	.	.
st	.	.	stet	.	start	stot	.	.	.
sk	skeet	skit	.	scat*†	skat*	scot*	.	.	scoot
sm	.	smit	.	.	smart	.	.	.	smoo•
sn	.	.	.	.	.	snot	snort	.	.
sl	sleet	slit	.	slat	.	slot	.	.	(sluit•
sw	sweet*	.	sweat	.	.	swat*	[swart]	.	.
ʃr	.	.	.	.	.	.	.	.	.
spl	.	split	.	splat	.	.	.	.	.
spr	.	sprit	.	sprat	.	.	.	.	.
str	street	.	.	.	.	.	straught†	.	.
skr	.	.	.	scrat	.	.	.	.	.
skw	.	squit	.	.	.	squat	.	.	.

* homophones—see page 212.
Total number of words—376

ʌ	ɜ/r	eɪ	oʊ	aɪ	aʊ	ɔɪ	i/ə/r	ɛ/ə/r	ju
.	.	*eight**	oat	.	out	.	.	airt†	.
putt*	pert	pate	pote†	[pight]†	pout	.	peart	.	.
but*	Bert	bait*	*boat*	bite*	bout*	.	.	.	butte*
tut	.	tait*	tote	tight*	tout*	.	.	.	.
.	dirt	date	dote	dight*†	doubt*	doit	.	.	.
cut	curt	cate*	*coat**	*kite**	.	quoit	.	.	cute
gut	girt*	*gate**	goat	gyte†	gout	.	.	.	.
phut	.	fate*	[phot]	fight	.	.	.	.	.
.	vert	.	vote	.	.	.	.	.	.
.	.	.	.	.	.	.	.	.	.
.	.	.	.	.	.	.	.	.	.
.	syrt*	sate*	.	sight*	.	.	.	.	(suit)
.	.	.	.	.	.	.	.	.	.
shut	*shirt*	.	shoat†	.	shout	.	.	.	.
.	.	.	.	gite†	.	.	.	.	.
hut	hurt	hate*	[hote]†	height*	.	hoit†	.	.	.
chut†	chert*	.	.	.	chout	.	.	.	.
jut	.	.	.	.	.	.	.	.	.
.	.	mate	moat*	might*	(mought).	.	.	.	mute
nut	.	.	note	night*	knout*	.	.	.	(newt)
.	.	late	[lote]	*light**	lout*	.	.	.	(lute)
rut	.	rate	wrote*	right*	(route)*	.	.	.	.
.	wort*	wait*	.	*white**	.	.	.	.	.
.	.	yate†	.	yite†	.	.	.	.	.
.	.	*plate**	.	plight	.	.	.	.	.
.	.	prate	.	.	.	.	.	.	.
.	blurt	blate	bloat	blight*	.	.	.	.	.
brut†	.	brait	.	bright	.	.	.	.	.
.	.	(trait)	troat	trite	trout	.	.	.	.
.	.	twaite	.	twite*	.	.	.	.	.
.	.	.	.	.	drought	droit	.	.	.
.	.	.	clote	.	clout	.	.	.	.
.	.	crate	.	krait	crout	.	.	.	.
.	quirt	.	quote	quite	.	.	.	.	.
glut	.	.	gloat	.	glout	.	.	.	.
.	.	great*	groat	.	grout	.	.	.	.
.	flirt	.	float*	flight*	flout	.	.	.	.
.	.	freight	.	fright	.	.	.	.	.
.	.	.	throat	.	.	.	.	.	.
.	spurt	spate	.	spite	spout	.	.	.	.
.	sturt	state	stoat	.	stout	stoit	.	.	.
scut	*skirt*	skate	scote†	.	scout*	schuit	.	.	.
smut	.	.	smote	smite	[smout]*†	.	.	.	.
.	snirt†	.	.	.	snout	.	.	.	.
slut	.	slate	sloat	slight*	.	.	.	.	.
.	.	.	.	.	.	.	.	.	.
.	.	.	.	shright†	.	.	.	.	.
.	splurt	.	.	.	.	.	.	.	.
.	.	.	.	sprite*	sprout	.	.	.	.
strut	.	straight*	.	.	strout	.	.	.	.
.	.	.	.	.	.	.	.	.	.
.	squirt	.	.	.	.	.	.	.	.

Final—/ts/ . For inflected forms add /s/ to appropriate words, e.g. nets.
. For uninflected forms, see page 233.

	i	ɪ	ɛ	æ	ɑ/r	ɒ(ɑ	ɔ(oʊ/r	ʊ	u
—	.	id†	.	add*	.	odd*	ord*†	.	.
p	.	.	ped	pad	pard	pod	poured*	.	pooe
b	bead*	bid	*bed*	bad*	bard*	bod	board*	.	booe
t	teed*	tid	ted*	.	tarred	tod*	tawed	.	.
d	deed*	did	dead	Dad	[dad]*†	dod	[daud]†	.	(duc
k	keyed	kid*	[ked]	cad	*card*	cod	cord*	could	cooe
g	.	gid	ged†	gad	guard*	God	gaud*†	good	[gud
f	feed*	fid	fed	fad	fard	.	ford*	.	food
v	.	.	.	.	.	.	.	.	.
θ	.	.	.	.	.	.	thawed	.	.
ð	.	.	.	.	.	.	.	.	.
s	seed*	Cid	said	sad	sard*	sod	*sword*	.	(sue
z	.	.	(Z)*	.	.	.	.	.	.
ʃ	she'd	.	*shed*	shad	shard	shod	shored	should	shoc
ʒ	.	.	.	.	.	.	.	.	.
h	heed*	hid	*head*	had	hard	hod	hoard*	hood	who
tʃ	.	chid	.	.	chard*	.	.	.	chev
dʒ	.	.	.	jad†	jarde*	.	jawed	.	Jude
m	mead*	mid	.	mad	marred	.	maud*	.	moo
n	need*	[nid]	Ned	.	nard*	nod	gnawed	.	(nud
l	lead	lid	lead*	lad	lard	.	lord*	.	(lew
r	read*	rid	*red**	rad†	.	rod	roared	.	rude
w	weed*	whid	wed	.	.	wad*	ward*	wood*	woo
j	yead†	.	.	.	yard*	(yod)†	(yaud)*†	.	you'
pl	plead	.	pled	plaid	.	plod	.	.	.
pr	preed†	.	.	prad	.	prod	.	.	pruc
bl	bleed*	.	bled	blad†	.	.	blaud†	.	blue
br	breed*	.	*bread**	brad	.	brod†	broad	.	broc
tr	.	.	tread	.	.	trod	.	.	.
tw	tweed	.	.	.	.	.	.	.	'twould	.
dr	dreed†	.	dread	drad	.	.	.	.	.
kl	.	.	.	clad	.	clod	Claud*	.	clew
kr	creed	.	.	.	.	.	.	(crud)†	cruc
kw	.	quid	qued†	.	.	quad*†	.	.	.
gl	gleed*	.	[gled]	glad	.	.	.	.	.
gr	greed	grid	.	.	.	.	.	.	.
fl	.	.	fled	.	.	.	flawed*	.	flew
fr	freed	.	Fred	.	.	.	fraud	.	.
θr	.	[thrid]	thread	.	.	.	.	.	.
sp	speed	.	sped	.	sparred*	.	spored	.	.
st	steed	.	stead	.	starred	.	stored	stood	.
sk	skied	skid	.	scad	scarred	.	scored	.	.
sm	.	.	.	.	.	.	(smored)†	.	.
sn	.	.	sned	.	snarred	snod	snored	snood	.
sl	.	slid*	sled	.	.	.	.	.	slue
sw	Swede*	.	swed	.	.	swad	sward	.	.
ʃr	.	.	shred	.	.	.	.	.	shre
spl	.	.	.	.	.	.	.	.	.
spr	spreed†	.	spread	.	.	sprod†	.	.	.
str	.	.	.	.	.	.	strawed†	.	strev
skr	screed	.	.	.	.	.	.	.	screv
skw	.	squid	.	.	.	squad	.	.	.

* homophones—see pages 212–213.
  Total number of words—429

60

ʌ	ɜ/r	eɪ	oʊ	aɪ	aʊ	ɔɪ	i/ə/r	ɛ/ə/r	ju
.	erred	aid*	ode*	eyed*	.	.	eared	aired	you'd
pud	purred	paid*	.	pied	.	.	peered	paired*	.
bud	*bird*	(bade)*	bode*	bide	bowed	buoyed*	beard	bared	.
.	turd	.	toad*	tide*	.	toyed	tiered	.	.
dud	.	dade	.	died*	dowd*	.	.	dared	(dude)†
cud*	curd*	cade*	code	.	cowed	.	.	caird*	cued*
.	gird	gade	goad	guide*	.	.	geared	.	.
fud	(fyrd)*	fade	.	.	foud	.	feared	fared*	fued
.	.	vade	.	vied	vowed	void	veered	.	viewed
thud	third	.	.	.	.	.	.	.	thewed
.	.	they'd	.	.	.	.	.	.	.
sudd	surd	[said]	sewed*	side*	.	.	seared*	.	(sued)
.	.	.	.	.	.	.	.	.	.
.	sherd*	shade	showed	shied	.	.	sheared	shared	.
.	.	.	.	.	.	.	.	.	.
.	herd*	hade	hoed	hide*	.	.	.	haired	hewed
.	.	chode	chide	.	.	.	cheered	chaired*	.
jud	.	jade	.	.	jowed†	joyed	jeered	.	.
mud	.	maid*	mode*	.	mowed	.	mear'd†	.	mewed
.	.	neighed	node	[nide]	.	.	neared	.	(nude)
lud	.	laid*	load*	lied	loud	Lloyd	leered	laird	(lewd)
rudd*	.	raid*	road*	ride	rowed	.	reared*	[raird]†	.
[wud]†	word*	wade*	woad†	wide	.	.	weird	.	.
.	[yird]	.	yode†	.	.	.	.	.	.
.	.	played	.	plied	ploughed.	.	.	.	.
.	.	preyed*	.	pride*	proud	.	.	.	.
blood	blurred	blade	blowed	.	.	.	.	blared	.
.	.	braid*	.	bride	.	.	.	[braird]	.
.	.	trade	[trode]†	tried	.	.	.	.	.
.	.	.	.	dried	.	.	.	.	.
.	.	clayed	.	Clyde*	*cloud*	cloyed	cleared	.	.
(crud)†	.	.	crowed	cried	crowd	.	.	.	.
.	.	quayd†	.	.	.	.	.	.	.
.	.	glade	glowed*	glide	.	.	.	glaired*	.
.	.	grade*	.	gride	.	.	.	.	.
flood	.	flayed	flowed	.	.	Floyd	fleered	flared*	.
.	.	frayed	.	fried	.	Freud	.	.	.
.	.	.	.	.	.	.	.	.	.
spud	spurred	*spade*	spode*	spied	.	.	speared	spared	spewed
stud	stirred	staid*	stowed	stied	.	.	steared	stared	stewed
scud	skirred†	.	.	.	.	.	.	scared	skewed
.	smirred†	.	.	.	.	.	smeared	.	.
.	.	.	snowed	snide	.	.	sneared	snared	.
.	slurred	slade*	slowed	slide	sloughed	sloyd	.	.	.
.	.	suede*	.	.	.	.	[sweard]†	.	.
.	.	.	.	.	shroud	.	.	.	.
.	.	splayed	.	.	.	.	.	.	.
.	.	sprayed	.	.	.	.	.	.	.
.	.	strayed	strode*	stride	stroud	.	.	.	.
.	.	.	.	scried†	.	.	.	.	.
.	[squirred]†	.	.	.	.	.	.	squared	.

Final—/dz/ . For inflected forms add /z/ to appropriate words, e.g. beds
. For uninflected forms, see page 234.

	i	ɪ	ɛ	æ	ɑ/r	ɒ(ɑ	ɔ(oʊ/r	ʊ	u
−	eke	.	.	.	ark*	.	auk*	.	[ou
p	peak*	pick	peck*	pack	park	pock	pork*	[pouke]*	.
b	beak	.	beck*	back	bark*	bok*	balk	*book*	bo
t	teak	tick*	'tec†	tack	[tak]†	.	talk*	took	.
d	.	Dick*	deck	.	dark*	dock*	[dawk]	(douc)	do
k	keek†	kick	keck	.	cark	cock*	cork*	cook	.
g	.	.	geck	.	.	.	gawk	.	.
f	feak	.	feck†	.	.	.	*fork*	.	.
v	.	Vic	.	vac†	.	.	.	.	.
θ	[theek]†	thick	.	[thack]†	.	.	.	.	.
ð	.	.	.	.	.	.	.	.	.
s	seek*	sick*	.	sack*	Sark*	*sock*	.	.	.
z	.	.	.	zack†	.	.	.	.	.
ʃ	chic*	.	.	shack	*shark*	shock*	.	shook	.
ʒ	.	.	.	.	.	.	.	.	.
h	.	hic*	heck	hack	hark	hock*	hawk	hook	.
tʃ	cheek	*chick**	cheque*	.	chack*†	chock	chalk	*chook*	.
dʒ	.	.	.	jack*	jark†	Jock	.	.	juk
m	meek	Mick	.	Mac*	mark*	mock	mauk†	.	.
n	.	nick*	neck*	knack	nark	knock*	.	nook	.
l	leek*	lick	.	lack*	lark	lock	lawk†	look	luk
r	reek*	wrick*	wreck*	wrack*†	.	rock*	.	rook	.
w	weak*	wick	.	whack*	[wark]†	.	walk*	.	.
j	.	.	.	yak	.	.	York	.	[yu
pl	.	.	.	(plack)*	(plaque)*	.	.	.	.
pr	.	prick	.	.	.	.	.	.	.
bl	bleak	.	.	*black*	.	bloc*	.	.	.
br	.	*brick*	.	brack	.	brock*	.	brook*	.
tr	.	trick	trek	track	.	[trock]†	.	.	.
tw	tweak	.	.	.	.	.	.	.	.
dr	.	.	.	.	.	.	.	.	dr
kl	(clique)*	click*	cleck†	clack*	(claque)*	*clock*	.	.	.
kr	(creek)*	crick*	.	crack	.	crock	crawke†	crook	.
kw	.	quick	.	quack	quark†	.	.	quooke†	.
gl	gleek†	.	.	.	.	.	.	.	.
gr	Greek	.	grecque	.	.	.	.	.	.
fl	.	flick	fleck	flak	.	flock*	.	.	flu
fr	freak	.	.	.	frack†	*frock*	.	.	.
θr	.	.	.	.	.	.	.	.	.
sp	speak	spick	speck*	.	spark*	.	.	.	spo
st	steek†	stick*	.	stack	stark	stock	stalk*	stook	.
sk	.	.	.	.	.	.	.	.	.
sm	[smeek]†	.	.	smack	.	smock	.	.	.
sn	sneak	snick	[sneck]†	snack	snark	.	.	snook	sno
sl	sleek	slick	.	slack	.	.	.	.	.
sw	.	.	.	.	swack†	.	.	.	.
ʃr	shriek	.	.	.	.	.	.	.	.
spl	.	.	.	.	.	.	.	.	.
spr	.	.	.	sprack†	.	.	.	.	.
str	streak*	.	.	.	.	.	.	strook†	.
skr	screak	.	.	.	.	.	.	.	.
skw	squeak	.	.	.	.	.	squawk	.	.

* homophones—see pages 213–214.
  Total number of words—304

ʌ	ɜ/r	eɪ	oʊ	aɪ	aʊ	ɔɪ	i/ə/r	ɛ/ə/r	ju
.	irk	ache	oke*	.	.	.	.	.	.
Puck*	perk	paik†	poke	pike	.	.	.	.	puke
buck	[birk]*†	bake	.	bike*†	.	.	.	.	.
tuck	Turk	take	(toque)	tyke	.	.	.	.	tuque
duck	dirk*	.	.	dyke	.	.	.	.	(duke)
.	kirk†	*cake*	coke	.	.	.	.	.	.
.	.	.	.	.	gowk†	.	.	.	.
.	firk	fake*	folk	fike*†	.	.	.	.	.
.	.	.	.	.	.	.	.	.	.
.	.	.	.	.	.	.	.	.	.
suck	[serk]†	sake	soak*	sike†	.	.	.	.	.
.	.	.	.	.	.	.	.	.	.
shuck	shirk	shake*	.	.	.	.	.	.	.
.	.	.	.	.	.	.	.	.	.
huck†	.	hake	holk†	hike*	howk†	hoik	.	.	.
chuck	chirk†	.	choke	.	.	.	.	.	.
.	jerk*	jake†	joke	.	.	.	.	.	.
muck	murk*†	make*	moke†	mike*†	.	.	.	.	.
.	.	.	.	.	.	.	.	.	[neuk]†
luck	lurk	lake*	.	like	.	.	.	.	.
ruck	.	*rake**	[wroke]*†	[ryke]†	.	.	.	.	.
.	work	wake	woke	.	.	.	.	.	.
[yuck]†	yerk†	.	yolk*	yike†	.	[yoik]	.	.	.
pluck	.	.	.	.	.	.	.	.	.
.	.	.	proke	.	.	.	.	.	.
.	.	Blake	bloke†	.	.	.	.	.	.
.	.	brake*	broke	.	.	.	.	.	.
truck	.	traik†	[troke]†	trike†	.	.	.	.	.
.	.	drake	.	.	.	.	.	.	.
cluck	(clerk)	.	cloak	.	.	.	.	.	.
.	.	crake†	croak	.	.	.	.	.	.
.	quirk	quake	.	.	.	.	.	.	.
.	.	glaik†	.	[glike]†	.	.	.	.	.
.	.	flake	.	.	.	.	.	.	.
.	.	.	.	.	.	.	.	.	.
.	.	spake	spoke	spike	.	.	.	.	.
stuck	stirk	steak*	stoke	.	.	.	.	.	.
.	.	.	.	.	.	.	.	.	.
.	smirk	smaik†	smoke	.	.	.	.	.	.
.	.	*snake*	[snoke]†	.	[snowk]†	.	.	.	.
.	.	slake	.	.	.	.	.	.	.
.	.	.	.	shrike	.	.	.	.	.
.	.	.	.	.	.	.	.	.	.
struck	.	strake*†	stroke	strike	.	.	.	.	.
.	.	.	.	scrike	.	.	.	.	.

Final—/kt/ . For inflected forms add /t/ to appropriate words, e.g. walked.
    . For uninflected forms, see page 232.
/ks/ . See pages 118–119.

	i	ɪ	ɛ	æ	ɑ/r	ɒ(ɑ(ɔ	ɔ/r	ʊ	u
–	·	·	*egg*	·	·	·	orgue	·	·
p	[peag]	*pig*	*peg**	·	·	pogge	·	·	·
b	·	big*	beg	*bag*	·	bog	·	·	·
t	Teague†	tig	teg	tag	·	tog	·	·	·
d	·	dig	deg	dag	darg†	*dog*	·	·	·
k	·	·	keg	cag†	·	cog	·	·	·
g	·	gig	·	gag	·	gog	·	·	·
f	feague†	fig	·	fag	·	fog	·	·	·
v	·	·	·	·	·	·	·	·	·
θ	·	thig	·	·	·	·	·	·	·
ð	·	·	·	·	·	·	·	·	·
s	·	·	[seg]†	sag	·	sog	·	·	·
z	·	zig	·	·	·	·	·	·	·
ʃ	·	·	·	shag	·	shog*	·	·	·
ʒ	giguet†	·	·	·	·	·	·	·	·
h	·	·	·	hag*	·	hog*	·	·	·
tʃ	·	·	·	·	·	·	·	·	·
dʒ	·	jig	·	jag*	·	jog	·	·	·
m	·	·	Meg	mag*	·	·	morgue	·	·
n	·	·	·	nag*	·	nog	·	·	·
l	league	[lig]	*leg**	lag	·	*log*	·	·	·
r	·	rig	·	rag*	·	·	·	·	·
w	·	*wig**	·	wag	waag	wog	·	·	·
j	·	·	yegg†	·	·	·	·	·	·
pl	·	·	·	·	·	·	·	·	·
pr	·	prig	·	·	Prague	prog	·	·	·
bl	·	·	·	·	blague	·	·	·	·
br	brigue	brig	·	brag*	·	brog	·	·	·
tr	treague†	trig	·	·	·	·	·	·	·
tw	·	*twig*	·	·	·	·	·	·	·
dr	·	·	dreg	drag	·	·	·	·	·
kl	·	·	cleg	clag†	·	clog	·	·	·
kr	·	·	·	crag	·	·	·	·	·
kw	·	·	·	·	·	quag	·	·	·
gl	·	·	gleg†	·	·	·	·	·	·
gr	·	grig	·	·	·	grog	·	·	·
fl	·	·	fleg†	*flag*	·	flog	·	·	·
fr	·	·	·	·	·	*frog*	·	·	·
θr	·	·	·	·	·	·	·	·	·
sp	·	·	·	·	·	·	·	·	·
st	·	·	·	stag	·	·	·	·	·
sk	·	·	·	·	·	[scog]†	·	·	scoo(
sm	·	·	·	·	·	smog	·	·	·
sn	·	snig	·	snag	·	·	·	·	·
sl	·	·	·	slag	·	slog	·	·	·
sw	·	swig	·	swag	·	·	·	·	·
ʃr	·	·	·	·	·	·	·	·	·
spl	·	·	·	·	·	·	·	·	·
spr	·	sprig	·	sprag	·	·	·	·	·
str	·	strig	·	·	·	·	·	·	·
skr	·	·	·	scrag	·	·	·	·	·
skw	·	·	·	·	·	·	·	·	·

* homophones—see page 214.

Total number of words—138

ʌ	ɜ/r	eɪ	oʊ	aɪ	aʊ	ɔɪ	i/ə/r	ɛ/ə/r	ju
.	erg	ague	.	.	.	.	.	.	.
pug	.	.	.	.	.	.	.	.	.
bug	berg*	.	.	.	.	.	.	.	.
tug	.	.	togue	.	.	.	.	.	.
dug*	.	.	.	.	.	.	.	.	.
.	.	.	cogue†	.	.	.	.	.	.
.	.	.	.	.	.	.	.	.	.
fug	.	.	.	.	.	.	.	.	fugue
vug	.	vague	vogue	.	.	.	.	.	.
thug	.	.	.	.	.	.	.	.	.
.	.	.	.	.	.	.	.	.	.
.	.	.	.	.	.	.	.	.	.
.	.	.	.	.	.	.	.	.	.
.	.	.	.	.	.	.	.	.	.
hug	.	Hague*	.	.	.	.	.	.	.
chug	.	.	.	.	.	.	.	.	.
jug	.	.	.	.	.	.	.	.	.
mug	.	.	.	.	.	.	.	.	.
.	.	.	.	.	.	.	.	.	.
lug	.	.	.	.	.	.	.	.	.
rug	.	.	rogue	.	.	.	.	.	.
.	.	waeg†	.	.	.	.	.	.	.
.	.	.	.	.	.	.	.	.	.
plug	.	plague	.	.	.	.	.	.	.
.	.	(Prague)	.	.	.	.	.	.	.
.	.	.	.	.	.	.	.	.	.
.	.	.	brogue	.	.	.	.	.	.
trug†	.	.	.	.	.	.	.	.	.
.	.	.	.	.	.	.	.	.	.
drug	.	.	drogue	.	.	.	.	.	.
.	.	Craig	.	.	.	.	.	.	.
.	.	.	.	.	.	.	.	.	.
.	.	.	.	.	.	.	.	.	.
.	.	.	.	.	.	.	.	.	.
.	.	.	.	.	.	.	.	.	.
.	.	.	.	.	.	.	.	.	.
.	.	.	.	.	.	.	.	.	.
.	.	staig†	.	.	.	.	.	.	.
skug*†	.	.	.	.	.	.	.	.	.
smug	.	.	.	.	.	.	.	.	.
snug	.	.	.	.	.	.	.	.	.
slug	.	.	.	.	.	.	.	.	.
.	.	.	.	.	.	.	.	.	.
shrug	.	.	.	.	.	.	.	.	.
.	.	.	.	.	.	.	.	.	.
sprug†	.	.	.	.	.	.	.	.	.
.	.	.	.	.	.	.	.	.	.
.	.	.	.	.	.	.	.	.	.
.	.	.	.	.	.	.	.	.	.

Final—/ɡd/ . For inflected forms add /d/ to appropriate words, e.g. tugged.
—/ɡz/ . For inflected forms add /z/ to appropriate words, e.g. tugs.
. For uninflected forms, see page 234.

	i	ɪ	ɛ	æ	ɑ/r	ɒ(ɔ(ɑ	ɔ/r	ʊ	u
–	.	if	*F*	.	.	off	orfe*	.	oof
p	.	.	.	.	.	.	.	.	pou
b	beef	biff	.	(baff)	(baff)	.	.	.	bou
t	.	tiff	teff	.	.	toff†	.	(tuff)	.
d	.	.	deaf	daff†	daff	doff	.	.	.
k	[kief]	[coof]†	[kef]	(calf)	(calf)*	cough*	corf	.	.
g	.	.	.	gaff*	.	goff*†	.	.	goo
f	(fief)*	.	(feoff)	.	.	.	.	.	.
v	.	.	.	.	.	.	.	.	.
θ	thief	.	.	.	.	.	.	.	.
ð	.	.	.	.	.	.	.	.	.
s	.	.	.	.	.	soph†	.	.	.
z	.	Zif	.	.	[zarf]	.	.	.	.
ʃ	sheaf	.	chef	.	.	.	.	.	.
ʒ	.	.	.	.	.	.	.	.	.
h	.	.	.	(half)	(half)*	.	.	(hoof)	hoo
tʃ	chief	.	.	(chaff)	(chaff)	.	[chaufe]†	.	.
dʒ	.	jiff	jeff*	.	.	.	.	.	.
m	.	miff†	.	.	.	.	.	.	.
n	[neif]†	niff†	neff	.	.	.	.	.	.
l	*leaf**	.	lev	(laugh)	(laugh)	.	.	.	loof
r	reef*	riff*	.	raff*	.	.	.	(roof)	roof
w	.	whiff	.	Waaf*	waff†	.	wharf*	.	woo
j	.	.	.	.	yaff*†	.	.	.	.
pl	.	.	.	.	.	.	.	.	.
pr	prief	.	.	.	.	prof†	.	.	pro
bl	.	.	.	.	.	.	.	.	.
br	brief	.	.	.	.	.	.	.	.
tr	.	.	.	.	.	trough	.	.	.
tw	.	.	.	.	.	.	.	.	.
dr	.	.	.	(draff)	(draff)	.	.	.	.
kl	.	cliff*	clef	.	.	cloff	.	.	kloo
kr	.	.	.	.	.	.	.	.	.
kw	.	quiff	.	(quaff)	.	(quaff)	.	.	.
gl	.	glyph*†	.	.	.	.	.	.	.
gr	grief	griff	.	(graph)*	graf*	.	.	groof†	.
fl	.	.	.	(flaff)†	(flaff)†	.	.	.	.
fr	.	.	.	.	.	.	.	.	.
θr	.	.	.	.	.	.	.	.	.
sp	.	spiff	.	.	.	.	.	.	spoo
st	.	stiff	.	(staff)	(staff)	.	.	.	.
sk	.	skiff	.	.	*scarf**	scoff	.	.	.
sm	.	.	.	.	.	.	.	.	.
sn	.	sniff	.	.	.	.	.	.	.
sl	.	.	.	.	.	.	.	.	.
sw	.	.	.	.	.	.	[swarf]	.	.
ʃr	.	.	.	.	.	shroff	.	.	.
spl	.	.	.	.	.	.	.	.	.
spr	.	.	.	.	.	.	.	.	.
str	.	.	.	.	(strafe)	.	.	.	.
skr	.	.	.	.	.	.	.	.	.
skw	.	.	.	.	.	.	.	.	.

* homophones—see page 214.
Total number of words—153

ʌ	ɜ/r	eɪ	oʊ	aɪ	aʊ	ɔɪ	i/ə/r	ɛ/ə/r	ju
.	erf	.	oaf	.	[ouphe]†	.	.	.	.
puff	.	.	.	.	.	.	.	.	.
buff	.	.	.	.	.	.	.	.	.
tough*	turf	.	.	.	.	.	.	.	.
duff	.	.	.	.	.	.	.	.	.
cuff	kerf	.	.	kaif	.	coif	.	.	.
guff	.	.	goaf†	.	gowf†	.	.	.	.
fuff	.	.	.	fife*	.	.	.	.	.
.	.	.	.	.	.	.	.	.	.
.	.	.	.	.	.	.	.	.	.
sough	surf*	safe	.	.	sowf†	.	.	.	.
.	[zurf]	.	.	.	.	.	.	.	.
[shough]	.	.	.	.	.	.	.	.	.
.	.	.	.	.	.	.	.	.	.
huff	.	.	.	.	.	.	.	.	.
chuff*	.	chafe	.	.	.	.	.	.	.
.	.	.	.	.	.	.	.	.	.
muff	.	.	.	.	.	.	.	.	.
.	.	.	.	*knife*	.	.	.	.	.
luff†	.	.	loaf	life	.	.	.	.	.
rough*	.	.	.	rife	.	.	.	.	.
.	.	waif*	.	wife	wowf†	.	.	.	.
.	.	.	.	.	.	.	.	.	.
pluff†	.	.	.	.	.	.	.	.	.
.	.	.	.	.	.	.	.	.	.
bluff	.	.	.	.	.	.	.	.	.
(brough)	.	.	.	.	.	.	.	.	.
.	.	.	.	.	.	.	.	.	.
.	.	.	.	.	.	.	.	.	.
(clough)	.	.	.	.	.	.	.	.	.
.	.	.	.	.	.	.	.	.	.
.	.	.	.	.	.	.	.	.	.
gruff	.	.	.	.	.	.	.	.	.
fluff	.	.	.	.	.	.	.	.	.
.	.	.	.	.	.	.	.	.	.
.	.	.	.	.	.	.	.	.	.
stuff	.	.	.	.	.	.	.	.	.
scuff	scurf	.	.	.	.	.	.	.	.
.	.	.	.	.	.	.	.	.	.
snuff	.	.	.	.	.	.	.	.	.
slough	.	.	.	'slife†	.	.	.	.	.
.	[swerf]†	.	.	.	.	.	.	.	.
.	.	.	.	.	.	.	.	.	.
.	.	.	.	.	.	.	.	.	.
.	.	(strafe)	.	strife	.	.	.	.	.
scruff	.	.	.	.	.	.	.	.	.

Final—/ft/ . See pages 98–99.
—/fs/ . For inflected forms add /s/ to appropriate words, e.g. coughs.

	i	ɪ	ɛ	æ	ɒ/r	ɒ(ɑ	ɔ/r	ʊ	u
—	eve*	.	.	.	.	(of)	.	.	.
p	peeve	.	.	.	.	.	.	.	.
b	.	.	.	.	.	.	.	.	.
t	.	.	.	.	.	.	.	.	.
d	(div)*	div†	.	.	.	.	.	.	.
k	keeve	.	.	.	carve*	.	.	.	.
g	.	give	.	.	.	.	.	.	.
f	.	.	.	.	.	.	.	.	.
v	.	.	.	.	varve	.	.	.	.
θ	thieve*	.	.	.	.	.	.	.	.
ð	.	.	.	.	.	.	.	.	.
s	.	sieve	.	(salve)	(salve)	.	.	.	.
z	.	.	.	.	.	.	.	.	.
ʃ	sheave	shive†	.	.	.	.	.	.	.
ʒ	.	.	.	.	.	.	.	.	.
h	heave	.	.	have*	(halve)	.	.	.	ho
tʃ	cheve†	.	.	.	.	.	.	.	.
dʒ	.	.	.	.	.	.	.	.	.
m	[meve]†	.	mev	.	.	.	.	.	m
n	[nieve]†	.	.	.	.	.	.	.	.
l	leave*	live	.	.	.	.	.	.	.
r	reeve*	.	rev†	.	.	.	.	.	.
w	weave*	.	.	.	.	.	wharve	.	.
j	yeve	.	.	.	.	.	.	.	yo
pl	.	.	.	.	.	.	.	.	.
pr	preeve†	.	.	.	.	.	.	.	pr
bl	.	.	.	.	.	.	.	.	.
br	breve	.	.	.	.	.	.	.	.
tr	.	.	.	.	.	.	.	.	.
tw	.	.	.	.	.	.	.	.	.
dr	.	.	.	.	.	.	.	.	.
kl	cleave*	.	.	.	.	.	.	.	.
kr	.	(cruive)†	.	.	.	.	.	.	(cr
kw	.	.	.	.	.	.	.	.	.
gl	.	.	.	.	.	.	.	.	.
gr	grieve	.	.	.	grave*	.	.	.	gr
fl	.	.	.	.	.	.	.	.	.
fr	.	.	.	.	.	.	.	.	.
θr	[threave]	.	.	.	.	.	.	.	.
sp	.	spiv†	.	.	.	.	.	.	.
st	steeve*	.	.	.	starve	.	.	.	.
sk	.	.	.	.	.	.	.	.	.
sm	.	.	.	.	.	.	.	.	.
sn	.	.	.	.	.	.	.	.	.
sl	sleeve*	.	.	(Slav)	(Slav)	.	.	.	.
sw	.	.	.	.	(suave)	.	.	.	.
ʃr	[shrieve]	.	.	.	.	.	.	.	.
spl	.	.	.	.	.	.	.	.	.
spr	.	.	.	.	.	.	.	.	.
str	.	.	.	.	.	.	.	.	.
skr	screeve*†	.	.	.	.	.	.	.	.
skw	.	.	.	.	.	.	.	.	.

* homophones—see pages 214–215.
  Total number of words—122

ʌ	ɜ/r	eɪ	oʊ	aɪ	aʊ	ɔɪ	i/ə/r	ɛ/ə/r	ju
(of)	.	.	.	I've	.	.	.	.	.
.	.	pave	.	.	.	.	.	.	.
.	.	.	.	.	.	.	.	.	.
dove	.	Dave†	dove	dive*	.	.	.	.	.
.	curve*	cave	cove	kive	.	.	.	.	.
.	.	gave	.	(gyve)	.	.	.	.	.
.	.	.	Fauve	*five*	.	.	.	.	.
.	verve	.	.	vive	.	.	.	.	.
.	.	.	.	.	.	.	.	.	.
.	.	they've	.	.	.	.	.	.	.
.	serve	save	.	[cive]	.	.	.	.	.
.	.	.	.	.	.	.	.	.	.
shove	.	shave	.	.	.	.	.	.	.
.	.	.	.	.	.	.	.	.	.
.	.	.	hove†	hive	.	.	.	.	.
.	.	.	.	[chive]	.	.	.	.	.
.	.	.	Jove	jive*	.	.	.	.	.
.	.	.	mauve	.	.	.	.	.	.
.	nerve	nave*	.	.	.	.	.	.	.
love	.	lave	loave	live	.	.	.	.	.
.	.	rave	rove	rive†	.	.	.	.	.
.	.	wave*	wove	wive	.	.	.	.	.
.	.	.	.	.	.	.	.	.	.
.	.	.	.	.	.	.	.	.	.
.	.	.	.	blive†	.	.	.	.	.
.	.	brave	.	.	.	.	.	.	.
.	.	.	trove	.	.	.	.	.	.
.	.	drave†	drove	drive	.	.	.	.	.
.	.	clave	clove	Clive	.	.	.	.	.
.	.	crave	.	.	.	.	.	.	.
glove	.	glaive†	.	.	.	.	.	.	.
.	.	grave	grove	.	.	.	.	.	.
.	.	.	.	.	.	.	.	.	.
.	.	[thrave]	throve	thrive	.	.	.	.	.
.	sterve†	stave	*stove*	stive†	.	.	.	.	.
.	.	.	.	skive	.	.	.	.	.
.	.	.	.	.	.	.	.	.	.
.	.	slave	.	.	.	.	.	.	.
.	swerve	(suave)	.	.	.	.	.	.	.
.	.	.	shrove	[shrive]	.	.	.	.	.
.	.	.	.	.	.	.	.	.	.
.	.	.	strove	strive	.	.	.	.	.
.	.	.	.	scrive	.	.	.	.	.
.	.	.	.	.	.	.	.	.	.

Final—/vd/. For inflected forms add /d/ to appropriate words, e.g. waved.
/vz/. For inflected forms add /z/ to appropriate words, e.g. waves.
. For uninflected and irregular forms, see page 234.

	i	ɪ	ɛ	æ	ɑ/r	ɒ(ɔ(ɑ	ɔ(oʊ/r	ʊ	u
–	(ethe)†	.	(ethe)†	.	.	.	.	.	.
p	.	pith	.	(path)	(path)	.	.	.	.
b	.	.	(beth)*	(*bath*)	(*bath*)*	.	.	.	booth
t	*teeth*	.	.	.	tath†	.	.	.	*tooth*
d	.	.	death	.	.	.	.	.	.
k	Keith	kith	.	.	.	.	.	.	couth†
g	.	.	.	.	garth	Goth	.	.	.
f	.	.	.	.	.	.	fourth*	.	.
v	.	.	.	.	.	.	.	.	.
θ	.	.	.	.	.	(Thoth)	.	.	.
ð	.	.	.	.	.	.	.	.	.
s	.	sith	saith*†	.	.	.	.	.	sooth
z	.	.	.	.	.	.	.	.	.
ʃ	sheath	.	.	.	.	.	.	.	.
ʒ	.	.	.	.	.	.	.	.	.
h	heath	.	.	hath	hearth	.	.	.	.
tʃ	.	.	.	.	.	.	.	.	.
dʒ	.	.	.	.	.	.	.	.	.
m	meith†	myth	.	math†	.	*moth*	.	.	.
n	neath	.	.	.	.	.	north	.	.
l	.	lith†	.	(lath)	(lath)	.	.	.	.
r	wreath	.	.	(wrath)	(wrath)	(wroth)*	(wrath)	.	ruth*
w	.	(withe)*	.	.	.	.	.	.	.
j	.	.	.	.	.	.	.	.	youth
pl	.	.	.	.	.	.	.	.	.
pr	.	.	.	.	.	.	.	.	.
bl	.	.	.	.	.	.	.	.	.
br	.	.	breath	.	.	broth	.	.	.
tr	.	.	.	.	.	(troth)†	.	.	truth
tw	.	.	.	.	.	.	.	.	.
dr	.	.	.	.	.	.	.	.	.
kl	.	.	.	.	.	cloth	.	.	.
kr	.	.	.	.	.	.	.	crwth	.
kw	queeth	.	.	.	.	.	.	.	.
gl	.	.	.	.	.	.	.	.	.
gr	.	grith†	.	.	.	.	.	.	.
fl	.	.	.	.	.	.	.	.	.
fr	.	frith	.	.	.	froth	.	.	.
θr	.	.	.	.	.	.	.	.	.
sp	.	.	.	.	sparthe	.	.	.	.
st	.	.	.	.	.	.	.	.	[stout]
sk	.	.	.	[scath]†	scarth†	.	.	.	[scout
sm	.	smith*	.	.	.	.	.	.	.
sn	sneath	.	.	snath	.	.	.	.	.
sl	.	.	.	.	.	(sloth)	.	.	sleuth
sw	.	swith	.	.	.	swath	swarth	.	.
ʃr	.	.	.	.	.	.	.	.	.
spl	.	.	.	.	.	.	.	.	.
spr	.	.	.	.	.	.	.	.	.
str	.	.	.	(strath)	(strath)	.	.	.	.
skr	.	.	.	.	.	.	.	.	.
skw	.	.	.	.	.	.	.	.	.

* homophones—see page 215.
  Total number of words—104

ʌ	ɜ/r	eɪ	oʊ	aɪ	aʊ	ɔɪ	i/ə/r	ɛ/ə/r	ju
.	earth	[aith]†	oath	.	.	.	.	.	.
	Perth	.	.						
.	birth*	(beth)	both	.	.	.	.	.	.
.	.					.			
doth	dearth	.	.	.	.	.	.	.	.
	.	.	.						
.	girth		.	.	.	.	.	.	.
.	firth*	faith	.	.	.	.	.	.	.
.	.	.	(Thoth)	.	.	.	.	.	.
.	.		.						
.	.	saithe†	.	.	south*	.	.	.	.
.	.	.	.	.	.	.	.	.	.
.	.	.	.	.	.	.	.	.	.
.	.	haithe†	.	.	.	.	.	.	.
.	.	.	.	.	.	.	.	.	.
.	mirth	.	.	.	*mouth*	.	.	.	.
.	.	.	.	.	.	.	.	.	.
.	.	.	loth†	.	.	.	.	.	lewth†
.	.	wraith	(wroth)*	.	routh†	.	.	.	.
.	worth*	.	.	.	.	.	.	.	.
.	[yearth]†	.	.	.	.	.	.	.	.
.	.	.	.	.	.	.	.	.	.
.	.	.	.	.	.	.	.	.	.
.	.	.	(troth)†	.	.	.	.	.	.
.	.	.	.	.	[drouth]†	.	.	.	.
.	.	.	.	.	.	.	.	.	.
.	.	.	quoth	.	.	.	.	.	.
.	.	graith†	growth	.	.	.	.	.	.
.	.	.	.	.	.	.	.	.	.
.	.	.	.	.	.	.	.	.	.
.	.	staithe	.	[styth]	.	.	.	.	.
.	.	[skaith]†	.	.	[scrowth]†	.	.	.	.
.	.	.	.	.	.	.	.	.	.
.	.	.	(sloth)	.	.	.	.	.	.
.	.	.	.	.	.	.	.	.	.
.	.	.	.	.	.	.	.	.	.
.	.	.	.	.	.	.	.	.	.
.	.	.	.	.	.	.	.	.	.

Final—/θt/ . For inflected forms add /t/ to appropriate words, e.g. bathed.
—/θs/ . For inflected forms add /s/ to appropriate words, e.g. moths.

	i	ɪ	ɛ	æ	ɒ	ɑ	ɔ	ʊ	u
—	.	.	(eth)	.	.	.	.	.	.
p									
b	beath†	.	.	.	.	.	.	.	booth
t	teethe	.	.	.	.	.	.	.	.
d									
k	.	.	.	.	.	.	.	.	.
g									
f	.	.	.	.	.	.	.	.	.
v	.	.	.	.	.	.	.	.	.
θ	.	.	.	.	.	.	.	.	.
ð	.	.	.	.	.	.	.	.	.
s	seethe	.	.	.	.	.	.	.	sooth
z									
ʃ	sheathe	.	.	.	.	.	.	.	.
ʒ	.	.	.	.	.	.	.	.	.
h	.	.	.	.	.	.	.	.	.
tʃ	.	.	.	.	.	.	.	.	.
dʒ	.	.	.	.	.	.	.	.	.
m	[meath]†	.	.	.	.	.	.	.	.
n	.	.	.	.	.	.	.	.	.
l	.	.	.	.	.	.	.	.	.
r	wreathe	.	.	.	.	.	.	.	.
w	.	(with)*	.	.	.	.	.	.	.
j	.	.	.	.	.	.	.	.	.
pl	.	.	.	.	.	.	.	.	.
pr	.	.	.	.	.	.	.	.	.
bl	.	.	.	.	.	.	.	.	.
br	breathe	.	.	.	.	.	.	.	.
tr	.	.	.	.	.	.	.	.	.
tw	.	.	.	.	.	.	.	.	.
dr	.	.	.	.	.	.	.	.	.
kl	.	.	.	.	.	.	.	.	.
kr	.	.	.	.	.	.	.	.	.
kw	.	.	.	.	.	.	.	.	.
gl	.	.	.	.	.	.	.	.	.
gr	.	.	.	.	.	.	.	.	.
fl	.	.	.	.	.	.	.	.	.
fr	.	.	.	.	.	.	.	.	.
θr	.	.	.	.	.	.	.	.	.
sp	.	.	.	.	.	.	.	.	.
st	.	.	.	.	.	.	.	.	.
sk	.	.	.	.	.	.	.	.	.
sm	.	.	.	.	.	.	.	.	smoo
sn	.	.	.	.	.	.	.	.	.
sl	.	.	.	.	.	.	.	.	.
sw	.	.	.	.	.	.	.	.	.
ʃr	.	.	.	.	.	.	.	.	.
spl	.	.	.	.	.	.	.	.	.
spr	[spreathe]†	.	.	.	.	.	.	.	.
str	.	.	.	.	.	.	.	.	.
skr	.	.	.	.	.	.	.	.	.
skw	.	.	.	.	.	.	.	.	.

* homophones—see page 215.
  Total number of words—32

ʌ	ɜ/r	eɪ	oʊ	aɪ	aʊ	ɔɪ	i/ə/r	ɛ/ə/r	ju
		bathe							
				tithe					
				kythe†					
				scythe*					
				hithe					
					mouth				
		lathe	loathe	lithe*					
		rathe†		writhe					
				(withe)					
				blithe					
			clothe						
		spathe							
				[stythe]†					
		scathe							
		snathe							
		swathe							

Final—/ðd/ . For inflected forms add /d/ to appropriate words, e.g. soothed.
—/ðz/ . For inflected forms add /z/ to appropriate words, e.g. soothes.

	i	ɪ	ɛ	æ	ɑ/r	ɒ(ɔ	ɔ(oʊ/r	ʊ	u
–	.	.	S*	*ass*	as*	os	.	.	.
p	peace*	piss	.	(pass)	(pass)*	posst	.	puss	.
b	.	bis	Bess*	bass*	.	boss*	.	.	.
t	.	.	Tess	tass*	tass†	toss	torse	.	.
d	(Dis)	(Dis)*	desse	.	.	doss	dorse	.	douc
k	.	kiss	[kess]†	cass†	carse†	cos*	course*	.	.
g	*geese*	.	guess	gas	.	gosse	gorse	.	*goose*
f	.	.	fesse†	.	farce*	fosse	force	.	.
v	.	.	.	vas	.	.	.	.	.
θ	.	.	.	.	.	.	.	.	.
ð	.	this	.	.	.	.	.	.	.
s	cease	sis	cess*	sass*	.	soss	sauce*	.	.
z	.	.	.	.	.	.	.	.	(Zeus
ʃ	.	.	.	.	chasse	.	.	.	.
ʒ	.	.	.	.	.	.	.	.	.
h	.	hiss	.	.	.	hosst	*horse*	.	.
tʃ	.	.	chess	.	.	.	.	.	.
dʒ	.	.	jess*	.	.	joss	.	.	juice
m	.	miss*	mess	mass*	.	moss	morse*	.	moo
n	niece*	nis*	ness	.	.	.	Norse	.	noos
l	lease*	liss†	less	lass	.	loss	.	.	loose
r	.	Riss	.	wrasse*	ras	Ross*	.	.	.
w	.	whiss*	.	.	.	.	.	.	.
j	.	.	yes	.	.	.	.	.	use
pl	.	.	.	.	.	.	.	.	.
pr	preace	.	press	.	.	.	.	.	Pruc
bl	.	bliss	bless	.	.	.	.	.	.
br	.	.	.	(brass)*	(brass)	.	.	.	Bruc
tr	.	.	tress	(trass)	(trass)	.	.	.	truce
tw	.	.	.	.	.	.	.	.	.
dr	.	.	*dress*	.	.	dross	.	.	.
kl	.	.	.	(class)	(class)	.	.	.	.
kr	crease*	Chris	cress	crass	.	*cross*	.	.	crou
kw	.	[cuisse]	.	.	.	.	.	.	.
gl	.	.	.	(*glass*)	(*glass*)	gloss	.	.	.
gr	grease*	.	.	(*grass*)	(*grass*)	.	.	.	.
fl	fleece	.	.	.	.	floss	.	.	.
fr	.	.	.	.	.	.	.	.	.
θr	.	.	.	.	.	.	.	.	.
sp	.	.	.	.	sparce	.	.	.	.
st	.	.	.	.	.	.	.	.	.
sk	.	.	.	.	.	.	scorset	.	.
sm	.	.	.	.	.	.	.	.	.
sn	.	.	.	.	.	.	.	.	.
sl	.	.	.	.	.	.	.	.	sluic
sw	.	Swiss	.	.	.	.	.	.	.
ʃr	.	.	.	.	.	.	.	.	.
spl	.	.	.	.	.	.	.	.	.
spr	.	.	.	.	.	.	.	.	spru
str	.	.	stress	strass	.	.	.	.	.
skr	.	.	.	.	.	.	.	.	.
skw	.	.	.	.	.	.	.	.	.

* homophones—see page 215.
   Total number of words—212

ʌ	ɜ/r	eɪ	oʊ	aɪ	aʊ	ɔɪ	i/ə/r	ɛ/ə/r	ju
us	Erse*	*ace*	as†	ice	.	.	.	.	.
pus	*purse*	pace*	.	pice	.	.	pierce	.	puce
bus	birse†	base*	.	bice	bouse	.	.	.	.
.	terse*	.	.	tice†	.	.	tierce†	.	.
.	.	dace	dose	*dice*	douse*	.	.	.	(deuce)
cuss	curse	*case*	cose	.	.	.	.	.	.
Gus	.	.	.	.	gauss	.	.	.	.
fuss	.	*face*	.	.	.	.	fierce	.	.
.	verse	(*vase*)	.	vice*	.	voice	.	.	.
.	thyrse	.	.	.	.	.	.	.	.
thus	.	.	.	.	.	.	.	.	.
.	searce	.	.	syce†	souse*	.	.	.	.
.	.	.	.	.	.	.	.	.	(Zeus)
.	.	.	.	.	.	.	.	.	.
.	.	.	.	.	.	.	.	.	.
.	hearse*	.	.	.	*house*	.	.	.	.
.	.	chase	.	.	chouse†	choice	.	.	.
.	.	.	.	.	.	Joyce	.	.	.
muss†	.	mace	.	*mice*	*mouse*	.	.	.	[meuse]
.	*nurse*	.	.	nice*	(nous)	.	.	.	.
.	.	lace	lost†	lice	louse*	.	.	.	(luce)
Rhus	.	race*	.	*rice*	(rouse)	.	.	.	.
.	worse	.	.	.	.	.	.	.	.
plus	.	place*	.	.	.	.	.	.	.
.	.	.	.	price	.	.	.	.	.
.	.	.	.	.	(*blouse*)	.	.	.	.
.	.	brace	.	.	.	.	.	.	.
truss	.	trace	.	trice	.	.	.	.	.
.	.	.	.	twice	.	.	.	.	.
.	.	.	close	.	.	.	.	.	.
crus	.	.	.	.	.	.	.	.	.
.	.	.	.	.	.	.	.	.	.
.	.	.	.	.	.	.	.	.	.
.	.	grace*	gross	grice*	grouse	.	.	.	.
.	.	.	.	.	flouse	.	.	.	.
.	.	.	.	thrice	.	.	.	.	.
.	sperse†	space	.	spice*	spouse	.	.	.	.
.	.	.	.	.	scouse	.	.	scarce	.
.	.	.	.	.	.	.	.	.	.
.	.	.	.	slice	.	.	.	.	.
.	.	.	.	.	.	.	.	.	.
.	.	.	.	splice	.	.	.	.	.
.	.	.	.	.	.	.	.	.	.
.	.	.	.	.	.	.	.	.	.
.	.	.	.	.	.	.	.	.	.
.	.	.	.	.	.	.	.	.	.

Final—/st/ . See pages 100–101.

	i	ɪ	ɛ	æ	ɑ/r	ɒ(ɑ	ɔ(oʊ/r	ʊ	u
–	ease*	is	.	as	(ours)*	.	oars*	.	ooze*
p	*peas**	.	.	.	(parse)	poz	pause*	.	.
b	*bees**	.	.	.	baas*	.	bores*	.	booze
t	tease*	'tis†	.	.	tars*	.	tors*	.	twos
d	D's	.	.	.	.	.	doors*	.	(dues
k	quays*	.	.	.	*cars**	.	cause*	.	coups
g	[Giz]	.	.	.	gars†	.	gauze*	.	[gues]
f	feeze*†	fizz*	fez	.	.	.	fours*	.	.
v	V's	.	.	.	(*vase*)	.	.	.	.
θ	.	.	.	.	.	.	thaws	.	.
ð	these	.	.	.	.	.	.	.	.
s	seize*	.	says	.	.	.	soars*	.	(sues)
z	(Z's)	.	.	.	tsars	.	.	.	zuz*
ʃ	sheas*	.	.	.	shahs	.	shores*	.	shoos
ʒ	.	.	.	.	.	.	.	.	.
h	heeze*†	his*	.	has	.	.	hawse*	.	whose
tʃ	*cheese**	.	.	.	chars*	.	chores*	.	choos
dʒ	gees*	gizz	.	jazz	jars	.	jaws	.	Jews
m	mease*	.	.	.	Mars*	.	mores*	.	moos
n	neeze*	(nys)†	.	.	gnars*	.	gnaws	.	(noos
l	lees*	Liz	Les	.	.	.	lores*	.	lose*
r	rees	.	.	razz†	.	.	roars	.	ruse*
w	wheeze	whizz	.	.	.	was	wars*	.	woos
j	.	.	.	.	.	.	yaws*	.	yews*
pl	please*	.	.	.	.	.	plause	.	.
pr	prees	.	.	.	.	.	prores†	.	.
bl	blees†	.	.	.	.	.	.	.	blues
br	breeze*	.	.	.	.	.	.	.	bruis
tr	*trees*	.	.	.	.	.	.	.	trews
tw	.	.	.	.	.	('twas)	.	.	.
dr	drees†	.	.	.	.	.	draws	.	druse
kl	.	.	.	.	.	.	clause*	.	clews
kr	crees	.	.	.	.	.	craws*	.	cruis
kw	.	quiz	.	.	.	.	.	.	.
gl	(gleys)	.	.	.	.	.	glaurs†	.	glues
gr	(grease)*	.	.	.	.	.	.	.	.
fl	fleas*	.	.	.	.	.	flaws*	.	flues*
fr	freeze*	frizz	.	.	.	.	.	.	.
θr	threes	.	.	.	.	.	.	.	.
sp	.	.	.	.	spars*	.	spores*	.	.
st	.	.	.	.	*stars**	.	stores*	.	stows
sk	skiis	.	.	.	scars	.	scores*	.	.
sm	.	.	.	.	.	.	(smores)†	.	.
sn	sneeze	.	.	.	snars†	.	snores	.	snooz
sl	sleeze	.	.	.	.	.	.	.	(slou
sw	[swees]†	.	.	.	.	.	.	.	.
ʃr	.	.	.	.	.	.	.	.	shrew
spl	.	.	.	.	.	.	.	.	.
spr	sprees*	.	.	.	.	.	.	.	sprue
str	.	.	.	.	.	.	straws	.	strew
skr	screes	.	.	.	.	.	scraws	.	*screw.*
skw	squeeze	.	.	.	.	.	squaws	.	.

* homophones—see pages 215–216.
   Total number of words—383

ʌ	ɜ/r	eɪ	oʊ	aɪ	aʊ	ɔɪ	i/ə/r	ɛ/ə/r	ju
.	errs	A's	owes*	*eyes**	.	.	*ears*	heirs*	use*
.	purrs	pays*	pose	pize*	.	poise*	peers*	pairs*	pews
buzz	burs*	baize*	beaux*	buys	bows*	buoys*	biers*	bares*	.
tuzz†	.	.	tows*	*ties**	touse	toise*	tiers*	tears*	.
does	.	daze*	doze*	dyes*	dowse*	.	dears*	dares	(dues)
coz†	currs*†	[cays]*	cose*	.	*cows*	.	kiers	cares	cues*
.	.	gaze	goes	guise*	gaus	.	gears	.	[gjus]
fuzz	furze*	phase*	foes	.	.	foys	fears*	fares*	fuse*
.	.	(*vase*)*	voes	vise*†	vows	.	veers	vairs*	views
.	.	.	.	thighs	.	.	.	.	thews
.	.	.	those	.	thous†	.	.	theirs	.
.	sirs*	.	sows*	size*	sows*	.	sears*	.	(sues)
.	.	.	.	.	.	.	.	.	.
.	shirrs	chaise	shows	shies	.	.	shears*	shares	.
.	.	.	[zhos]	.	.	.	.	.	.
.	hers	haze*	hose*	.	house*	hoise†	hears	hares*	hues*
.	churrs*	(chays)	chose	(chays)	Chows*†	.	cheers	*chairs**	.
.	.	jays*	joes*†	.	.	joys	jeers	.	.
.	.	maze*	moze*	(mise)†	mows	.	.	mares	Muse*
.	knurrs	naze*	*nose**	.	.	noise*	nears	.	(news)*
luz	.	laze*	lows*	lies	louse*	loys	lehrs*	lairs*	.
.	.	raise*	*rose**	rise	rouse*	.	rears	.	.
.	whirs	weighs*	woes	wise*	.	.	wiers*	wares*	.
.	(years)	.	.	.	[yowes]†	.	(years)	.	.
.	.	plays	.	plies	ploughs	ploys	.	(players)	.
.	.	praise*	prose*	prize*	prows	.	.	(prayers)	.
.	blurs	blaze*	blows	.	(*blouse*)*	.	blears	blares	.
.	.	braze*	brose	.	browse*	.	[breers]*	.	.
.	.	(traits)*	.	tries	(trouse)	.	.	.	.
('twas)	.	.	.	.	.	.	[tweers]	.	.
.	.	dreys*	.	dries*	drowse	.	.	.	.
.	.	clays*	close*	clies†	(cloughs)*	cloys*†	clears	.	.
.	.	craze	croze*	cries	.	croise	.	.	.
.	.	queys†	.	.	.	.	.	.	.
.	.	glaze	gloze*	(gleys)	.	.	.	glairs*	.
.	.	graze*	grows	grise	.	.	.	.	.
.	.	flays	floes*	flies	.	.	fleers	flares*	.
.	.	phrase*	froze	fries	.	froise	.	.	.
.	.	.	throes*	.	.	.	.	.	.
.	spurs*	spays*	.	spies	.	.	*spears**	spares	spews
.	stirs	stays	stows	sties*	.	.	steres*	*stairs**	(stews)
.	skirrs†	.	.	skies	scows	.	skiers	scares	skews*
.	smurs†	smaze	.	.	.	.	smears	.	smews
.	.	.	snows	.	.	.	sneers	snares	.
.	slurs	slays*	sloes*	.	sloughs	.	.	.	.
.	.	sways	.	.	.	.	.	swears	.
.	.	.	[shrows]†.	.	.	.	.	.	.
.	.	splays	.	.	.	.	.	.	.
.	.	sprays	.	.	.	.	.	.	.
.	.	strays	(strows)†	.	.	stroys†	.	.	.
.	.	scrays*	scrows	scries†	.	.	.	.	.
.	[squirrs]†.	.	.	.	.	.	.	squares	.

Final—/zd/ . For inflected forms add /d/ to appropriate words, e.g. paused.

	i	ɪ	ɛ	æ	ɑ/r	ɒ(ɑ(ɔ)	ɔ	ʊ	u
–	·	sh†	·	ash*	·	·	·	·	·
p	·	pish	·	pash	·	posh	·	push	·
b	·	·	·	bash	·	bosh*	·	bush	bou
t	·	·	·	·	tash†	tosh†	·	·	·
d	·	*dish*	·	dash	·	·	·	·	dou
k	·	kish	·	cash*	·	cosh	·	·	·
g	·	·	·	gash	·	gosh†	·	·	·
f	·	*fish*	·	·	fash	·	·	·	·
v	·	·	·	·	·	·	·	·	·
θ	·	·	·	·	·	·	·	·	·
ð	·	·	·	·	·	·	·	·	·
s	·	·	(seiche)	sash	·	·	·	·	·
z	·	·	·	·	·	·	·	·	·
ʃ	·	·	·	·	·	·	·	·	·
ʒ	·	·	·	·	·	·	·	·	·
h	·	hish†	·	hash	harsh	·	·	·	hoos
tʃ	·	·	·	·	·	·	·	·	·
dʒ	·	·	·	·	·	josh†	·	·	·
m	·	·	mesh	mash	marsh	·	·	·	·
n	(niche)	·	nesh†	gnash*	·	·	·	·	·
l	leash	·	·	lash	·	[losh]†	·	·	·
r	·	·	·	rash	rash†	·	·	·	ruc
w	·	wish*	[wesh]	·	·	wash	·	whoosh	·
j	·	·	·	·	·	·	·	·	·
pl	·	·	plesh	plash	·	·	·	·	·
pr	·	·	·	·	·	·	·	·	·
bl	·	·	·	blash	·	·	·	·	·
br	·	·	·	brash	·	·	·	·	·
tr	·	·	·	trash	·	·	·	·	·
tw	·	·	·	·	·	·	·	·	·
dr	·	·	·	·	·	·	·	·	·
kl	·	·	·	clash	·	(cloche)	·	·	·
kr	creesh†	·	(crèche)	crash	·	·	·	·	·
kw	·	[cuish]	·	·	·	quash	·	·	·
gl	·	·	·	·	·	·	·	·	·
gr	·	·	·	·	·	·	·	·	·
fl	·	Flysch	flesh*	flash	·	·	·	·	·
fr	·	fris	fresh	·	·	·	·	·	·
θr	·	·	thresh	thrash	thrash†	·	·	·	·
sp	·	·	·	·	·	sposh	·	·	·
st	·	·	·	·	·	·	·	·	·
sk	·	·	·	·	·	·	·	·	·
sm	·	·	·	smash	·	·	·	·	·
sn	sneesh	·	·	snash	·	·	·	·	·
sl	·	slish†	·	slash	·	slosh	·	·	·
sw	·	swish	·	·	·	swash	·	·	·
ʃr	·	·	·	·	·	·	·	·	·
spl	·	·	·	splash	·	splosh	·	·	·
spr	·	·	·	·	·	·	·	·	(spr
str	·	·	·	·	·	·	·	·	·
skr	·	·	·	·	·	·	·	·	·
skw	·	squish	·	·	·	squash	·	·	·

* homophones—see page 217.
   Total number of words—105

ʌ	ɜ/r	eɪ	oʊ	aɪ	aʊ	ɔɪ	i/ə/r	ɛ/ə/r	ju
.	ersh	.	.	.	.	.	.	.	.
.	.	.	.	.	.	.	.	.	.
tush†	.	.	.	taish	.	.	.	.	.
dush†	.	.	.	.	.	.	.	.	.
[cush]†	.	.	.	.	.	.	kirsch	.	.
gush	.	.	gauche	.	.	.	.	.	.
.	.	.	.	.	.	.	.	.	.
.	.	.	.	.	.	.	.	.	.
.	.	(seiche)	.	.	.	.	.	.	.
.	.	.	.	.	.	.	.	.	.
.	.	.	.	.	.	.	.	.	.
hush	.	.	.	.	.	.	.	.	.
.	.	.	.	.	.	.	.	.	.
mush	.	.	.	.	.	.	.	.	.
lush	.	.	.	.	.	.	.	.	.
rush	.	.	.	.	.	.	.	.	.
.	wersh†	.	.	.	.	.	.	.	.
plush	.	.	.	.	.	.	.	.	.
.	.	.	.	.	.	.	.	.	.
blush	.	.	.	.	.	.	.	.	.
brush	.	.	.	.	.	.	.	.	.
.	.	.	.	.	.	.	.	.	.
.	.	.	.	.	.	.	.	.	.
.	.	.	(cloche)	.	.	.	.	.	.
crush	.	(crèche)	.	.	.	.	.	.	.
.	.	.	.	.	.	.	.	.	.
flush	.	.	.	.	.	.	.	.	.
frush	.	.	.	.	.	.	.	.	.
thrush	.	.	.	.	.	.	.	.	.
.	.	.	.	.	.	.	.	.	.
.	.	.	.	.	.	.	.	.	.
snush†	.	.	.	.	.	.	.	.	.
slush	.	.	.	.	.	.	.	.	.
.	.	.	.	.	.	.	.	.	.
(sprush)	.	.	.	.	.	.	.	.	.
.	.	.	.	.	.	.	.	.	.
.	.	.	.	.	.	.	.	.	.

Final—/ʃt/ . For inflected forms add /t/ to appropriate words, e.g. pushed.

	i	ɪ	ɛ	æ	ɑ/r	ɒ(ɑ(ɔ	ɔ(ou/r	ʊ	u
–	each*	itch*	etch	.	arch	.	.	.	.
p	*peach*	pitch	.	patch	parch	potch	porch	putsch	.
b	beach*	bitch	.	batch*	.	botch	.	.	.
t	teach	.	.	tach	.	.	*torch*	.	.
d	.	ditch*	.	.	.	.	.	.	.
k	keech†	.	ketch	catch	.	.	.	.	(cou
g	.	.	.	.	.	.	.	.	.
f	.	fitch	fetch	.	.	.	.	.	.
v	.	.	vetch	.	.	.	.	.	.
θ	.	.	thetch	thatch	.	.	.	.	.
ð	.	.	.	.	.	.	.	.	.
s	.	[sich]†	.	.	.	.	.	.	.
z	.	.	.	.	.	.	.	.	.
ʃ	.	.	.	.	.	.	.	.	.
ʒ	.	.	.	.	.	.	.	.	.
h	.	hitch	.	hatch	.	hotch†	.	.	hoo
tʃ	.	chich	.	.	.	.	.	.	.
dʒ	.	.	.	.	.	.	.	.	.
m	.	miche	.	*match*	March*	.	.	.	moo
n	.	(niche)*	.	natch†	.	notch	[nautch]	.	.
l	leech*	lich†	letch†	latch	larch	.	.	.	.
r	reach*	rich	wretch*	ratch	.	rotch	.	.	.
w	.	*witch**	.	.	warch	*watch*	.	.	.
j	. .								
pl	pleach	.	.	.	.	.	.	.	.
pr	preach	.	.	.	.	.	.	.	.
bl	bleach	.	.	.	.	blotch	.	.	.
br	breach*	.	.	brach	.	.	.	.	.
tr	.	.	.	.	.	.	.	.	.
tw	.	twitch	.	.	.	.	.	.	.
dr	.	.	.	.	.	.	.	.	.
kl	.	.	.	.	clatch†	.	.	.	.
kr	.	.	.	cratch	.	crotch	.	.	.
kw	queach	quitch*	.	.	.	.	.	.	.
gl	.	.	.	.	.	.	.	.	.
gr	.	.	.	.	.	.	.	.	.
fl	fleech	flitch	fletch	.	.	.	.	.	.
fr	.	.	.	fratch	.	.	.	.	.
θr	.	.	.	.	.	.	.	.	.
sp	speech	.	spetch	.	.	.	.	.	.
st	.	stitch	.	.	starch	.	.	.	.
sk	.	.	sketch	scatch	.	scotch*	scorch	.	.
sm	smeech	.	.	smatch	.	.	.	.	smo
sn	.	snitch	.	snatch	.	.	.	.	.
sl	sleech	.	.	[slatch]†	.	.	.	.	.
sw	.	switch	.	.	.	swatch†	.	.	.
ʃr	.	shrich	.	.	.	.	.	.	.
spl	.	.	.	splatch	.	splotch	.	.	.
spr	.	.	.	.	.	.	.	.	.
str	.	strich	stretch	.	.	.	.	.	.
skr	screech	scritch†	.	scratch*	.	.	.	.	.
skw	.	squitch	.	.	.	.	.	.	.

* homophones—see page 217.
  Total number of words—132

ʌ	ɜ/r	eɪ	oʊ	aɪ	aʊ	ɔɪ	i/ə/r	ɛ/ə/r	ju
.	.	*H**	.	.	ouch	.	.	.	.
.	perch	.	poach	.	pouch	.	.	.	.
.	birch	.	.	.	.	.	.	.	.
touch	.	.	.	.	.	.	.	.	.
Dutch*	.	.	.	.	.	.	.	.	.
cutch*	curch	.	coach	.	couch	.	.	.	.
.	.	.	.	.	.	.	.	.	.
.	.	.	.	.	vouch	.	.	.	.
.	.	.	.	.	.	.	.	.	.
such	search	.	.	.	.	.	.	.	.
.	.	.	.	.	.	.	.	.	.
.	.	.	.	.	.	.	.	.	.
hutch	.	.	.	.	.	.	.	.	.
.	*church*	.	.	.	.	.	.	.	.
.	.	.	.	.	.	.	.	.	.
much*	.	.	.	.	.	.	.	.	.
.	.	nache	.	.	.	.	.	.	.
.	lurch	.	loach	.	louch	.	.	.	.
.	.	.	roach	.	.	.	.	.	.
.	.	.	.	.	.	.	.	.	.
.	.	.	.	.	.	.	.	.	.
.	.	.	.	.	.	.	.	.	.
.	.	.	brooch*	.	.	.	.	.	.
.	.	.	.	.	.	.	.	.	.
.	.	.	.	.	.	.	.	.	.
.	.	.	.	.	.	.	.	.	.
clutch	.	.	.	.	.	.	.	.	.
crutch	.	.	croche	.	crouch	.	.	.	.
.	.	.	.	.	.	.	.	.	.
.	.	.	.	.	.	.	.	.	.
grutch	.	.	.	.	grouch	.	.	.	.
.	.	.	.	.	.	.	.	.	.
.	.	.	.	.	.	.	.	.	.
.	.	.	.	.	.	.	.	.	.
scutch	.	.	.	.	.	.	.	.	.
[smutch] smirch	.	.	.	smouch	.	.	.	.	
.	.	.	.	.	slouch	.	.	.	.
.	.	.	.	.	.	.	.	.	.
.	.	.	.	.	.	.	.	.	.
.	.	.	.	.	.	.	.	.	.
.	.	.	.	.	.	.	.	.	.

Final—/tʃt/ . For inflected forms add /t/ to appropriate words, e.g. arched.

	i	ɪ	ɛ	æ	ɑ/r	ɒ(ɑ	ɔ(oʊ/r	ʊ	u
—	.	.	edge	.	.	.	.	.	.
p	.	.	.	.	.	[podge]	.	.	.
b	.	.	.	badge	barge	bodge	.	.	.
t	.	.	.	.	targe*	.	.	.	.
d	.	.	.	.	.	dodge	.	.	.
k	.	.	kedge	cadge	.	.	.	.	.
g	.	.	.	gadget†	.	.	gorge	.	goug
f	.	.	.	fadge	.	.	forge	.	.
v	.	.	.	.	.	.	.	.	.
θ	.	.	.	.	.	.	.	.	.
ð	.	.	.	.	.	.	.	.	.
s	siege	.	sedge	.	.	.	.	.	.
z	.	.	.	.	.	.	.	.	.
ʃ	.	.	.	.	.	.	.	.	.
ʒ	.	.	.	.	.	.	.	.	.
h	.	.	hedge	hadj	.	Hodge	.	.	.
tʃ	.	.	.	.	charge	.	.	.	.
dʒ	.	.	.	.	.	.	George	.	.
m	.	midge	.	madge	marge*	.	.	.	.
n	.	.	.	.	.	.	.	.	.
l	liege	.	ledge	.	large	lodge	.	.	.
r	.	ridge	Reg	.	raj	.	.	.	roug
w	.	.	wedge	.	.	.	.	.	.
j	.	.	.	.	.	.	.	.	.
pl	.	.	pledge	.	plage	.	.	.	.
pr	.	.	.	.	.	.	.	.	.
bl	.	.	.	.	.	.	.	.	.
br	.	*bridge*	.	.	.	.	.	.	.
tr	.	.	.	.	.	.	.	.	.
tw	.	.	.	.	.	.	.	.	.
dr	.	.	dredge	.	.	.	.	.	.
kl	.	.	.	.	.	.	.	.	.
kr	.	.	.	.	.	.	.	.	.
kw	.	.	.	.	.	.	.	.	.
gl	.	.	gledge†	.	.	.	.	.	.
gr	.	.	.	.	.	.	.	.	.
fl	.	.	fledge	.	.	.	.	.	.
fr	.	frig*†	.	.	.	.	.	.	.
θr	.	.	.	.	.	.	.	.	.
sp	.	.	.	.	sparge	.	.	.	.
st	.	.	.	.	.	stodge	.	.	stoog
sk	.	.	.	.	.	.	.	.	.
sm	.	.	.	.	.	.	.	.	.
sn	.	.	.	.	.	.	.	.	.
sl	.	.	sledge	.	.	.	.	.	.
sw	.	.	.	.	.	.	.	.	.
ʃr	.	.	.	.	.	.	.	.	.
spl	.	.	.	.	.	splodge	.	.	.
spr	.	.	.	.	.	.	.	.	.
str	.	.	.	.	.	.	.	.	.
skr	.	.	.	.	.	.	.	.	scroo
skw	squeedge†	.	.	.	.	.	.	.	.

* homophones—see page 217.
  Total number of words—84

ʌ	ɜ/r	eɪ	oʊ	aɪ	aʊ	ɔɪ	ɪ/ə/r	ɛ/ə/r	ju
.	urge	age	.	.	.	.	.	.	.
[pudge]	purge	page	.	.	.	.	.	.	.
budge	.	.	.	.	.	.	.	.	.
.	.	.	[toge]	.	.	.	.	.	.
.	dirge	.	doge	.	.	.	.	.	.
.	.	*cage*	.	.	.	.	.	.	.
.	gurge†	gauge*	.	.	gouge	.	.	.	.
fudge	.	.	.	.	.	.	.	.	.
.	verge	.	.	.	.	(voyage)	.	.	.
.	.	.	.	.	.	.	.	.	.
.	.	.	.	.	.	.	.	.	.
.	serge*	sage	.	.	.	.	.	.	.
.	.	.	.	.	.	.	.	.	.
.	.	.	.	.	.	.	.	.	.
.	.	.	.	.	.	.	.	.	huge
.	.	.	.	.	.	.	.	.	.
judge	.	.	.	.	.	.	.	.	.
.	merge	mage	.	.	.	.	.	.	.
nudge	.	.	.	.	.	.	.	.	.
.	.	.	.	.	.	.	.	.	.
.	.	rage	.	.	.	.	.	.	.
.	.	wage	.	.	.	.	.	.	.
.	.	.	.	.	.	.	.	.	.
.	.	.	.	.	.	.	.	.	.
.	.	.	.	.	.	.	.	.	.
.	.	.	.	.	.	.	.	.	.
.	.	.	.	.	.	.	.	.	.
trudge	.	.	.	.	.	.	.	.	.
.	.	.	.	.	.	.	.	.	.
drudge	.	.	.	.	.	.	.	.	.
.	.	.	.	.	.	.	.	.	.
.	.	.	.	.	.	.	.	.	.
.	.	.	.	.	.	.	.	.	.
grudge	.	.	.	.	.	.	.	.	.
.	.	.	.	.	.	.	.	.	.
.	.	.	.	.	.	.	.	.	.
.	.	.	.	.	.	.	.	.	.
.	spurge	.	.	.	.	.	.	.	.
.	.	stage	.	.	.	.	.	.	.
.	scourge	.	.	.	.	.	.	.	.
smudge	.	.	.	.	.	.	.	.	.
snudge	.	.	.	.	.	.	.	.	.
sludge	.	.	.	.	.	.	.	.	.
.	.	swage†	.	.	.	.	.	.	.
.	.	.	.	.	.	.	.	.	.
.	splurge	.	.	.	.	.	.	.	.
.	.	.	.	.	.	.	.	.	.
.	.	.	.	.	.	.	.	.	.
.	.	.	.	.	scrouge	.	.	.	.
.	.	.	.	.	.	.	.	.	.

Final—/dʒd/ . For inflected forms add /d/ to appropriate words, e.g. aged.

	i	ɪ	ɛ	æ	ɑ)r	ɒ(ɑ	ɔ/r	ʊ	u
−	emet†	.	*M**	am	*arm**	.	(aam)	.	oom†
p	.	.	.	pam*	*palm*	pom	.	.	.
b	beam	.	.	bam	balm*	(bomb)	.	.	boom
t	team*	Tim†	.	.	.	Tom†	.	.	tomb
d	deem	dim	.	dam*	dam†	Dom	.	.	doom
k	.	Kim	kemb†	cam*	calm*	com*	corm*	.	cooml
g	.	.	.	gam*	gam†	.	gaum	.	.
f	.	.	femet†	fam†	farm	.	form*	.	.
v	.	vim	.	.	.	.	.	.	.
θ	theme	.	.	.	.	.	.	.	.
ð	.	.	them	.	.	.	.	.	.
s	seem*	.	.	sam*†	psalm	(Somme)	.	soum†	soom
z	.	.	.	.	.	.	.	.	zoom
ʃ	.	shim	.	sham	shalm	.	[shawm]	.	.
ʒ	.	.	.	.	.	.	.	.	.
h	[heme]†	hymn*	hem	ham*	harm*	.	hawm*†	.	whom
tʃ	.	.	.	.	charm	.	.	.	.
dʒ	.	Jim*	gem	*jam**	.	.	.	.	jume
m	.	mim†	.	(ma'am)†	malm*	.	.	.	.
n	nim	nim	.	.	naam†	.	norm	.	.
l	leam†	limb*	.	*lamb**	.	.	.	.	loom
r	ream*	rim	.	ram	.	rom*	.	(room)	(room
w	weem†	whim	[wem]	.	.	.	warm	.	womb
j	.	.	.	yam	.	.	.	.	.
pl	.	plim	.	.	.	.	.	.	plume
pr	.	prim	.	*pram*†	praam	prom†	.	.	.
bl	.	.	.	.	.	.	.	.	bloom
br	bream*	brim*	.	.	Brahm	.	.	(Brougham)*	(broom
tr	.	trim	.	*tram*	.	.	.	.	.
tw	.	.	.	.	.	.	.	.	.
dr	dream	.	.	dram*	.	.	.	.	[droom
kl	.	.	clem	clam	.	.	.	.	.
kr	cream	.	creme	cram	.	.	.	.	[crom
kw	quemet†	.	.	.	qualm	.	.	.	.
gl	gleam	glim	.	.	.	.	glaum†	.	gloom
gr	.	grim*	.	gramme*	.	.	.	.	groon
fl	fleam*	.	phlegm	flam*	.	.	.	.	flume
fr	.	.	frem	.	.	(from)	.	.	.
θr	.	.	.	.	.	.	.	.	.
sp	.	.	.	spam	.	.	.	.	spoon
st	steam*	.	stem	.	.	.	storm	.	.
sk	scheme	skim	.	.	.	.	.	.	.
sm	.	.	.	.	smarm	.	.	.	.
sn	.	.	.	.	.	.	.	.	.
sl	.	slim	.	slam	.	.	.	.	sloom
sw	.	swim	.	swam	.	.	swarm	.	.
ʃr	.	shrim†	.	shram†	.	.	.	.	.
spl	.	.	.	.	.	.	.	.	.
spr	.	.	.	.	.	.	.	.	.
str	stream	.	.	.	.	stromb	.	.	.
skr	scream	scrim	.	scram†	.	.	scrawm†	.	.
skw	.	.	.	.	.	.	.	.	.

* homophones—see pages 217–218.
  Total number of words—240

ʌ	ɜ/r	eɪ	oʊ	aɪ	aʊ	ɔɪ	i/ə/r	ɛ/ə/r	ju
.	.	aim	ohm*	I'm	.	.	.	.	.
.	perm†	.	pome	.	.	.	.	.	.
.	berm	.	.	.	.	.	.	.	.
.	term	tame	tome	time*	.	.	.	.	.
.	derm	dame	dome	dime*	(doum)	.	.	.	.
come	.	came*	*comb*	chyme	.	.	.	.	.
gum	.	game	.	.	.	.	.	.	.
fum	firm*	fame	foam	.	.	.	.	.	fume
.	.	.	.	.	.	.	.	.	.
thumb	therm	.	.	.	.	.	.	thairm†	.
.	.	[thaim]†	.	.	.	.	.	.	.
*sum**	.	same*	.	cyme	.	.	.	.	.
.	.	.	.	zyme	.	.	.	.	.
.	.	shame	.	.	.	.	.	.	.
.	.	.	.	.	.	.	.	.	.
hum	herm	hame	home*	.	.	.	.	.	.
chum	chirm	.	.	chime	.	.	.	.	.
.	germ	.	.	.	.	.	.	.	.
mum*	.	maim	mome†	mime	.	.	.	.	.
numb	.	name	gnome*	.	.	.	.	.	neume
lum†	.	lame	loam	lime*	.	.	.	.	.
rum*	.	.	roam*	rhyme*	.	.	.	.	.
.	worm	[wame]†	.	.	.	.	.	.	.
.	.	.	.	.	.	.	.	.	.
*plum**	.	.	.	.	.	.	.	.	.
.	.	.	.	prime	.	.	.	.	.
.	.	blame	.	.	.	.	.	.	.
.	.	brame†	.	.	.	.	.	.	.
.	.	.	.	.	.	.	.	.	.
drum	.	.	drome	.	.	.	.	.	.
.	.	claim*	cloam*	climb*	.	.	.	.	.
crumb	.	crame†	chrome*	crime	.	.	.	.	.
.	.	.	.	.	.	.	.	.	.
glum	.	.	.	.	.	.	.	.	.
grum	.	[grame]	.	grime	.	.	.	.	.
.	.	flame	.	.	.	.	.	.	.
(from)	.	frame	.	.	.	.	.	.	.
thrum	.	.	.	.	.	.	.	.	.
.	sperm	.	.	.	.	.	.	.	spume
stum	.	.	.	stime	.	.	.	.	.
scum	.	.	.	.	.	.	.	.	.
.	.	.	.	.	.	.	.	.	.
slum	.	.	.	slime	.	.	.	.	.
swum	.	.	.	.	.	.	.	.	.
.	.	.	.	.	.	.	.	.	.
.	.	.	.	.	.	.	.	.	.
strum	.	.	stroam	.	.	.	.	.	.
scrum	.	.	.	.	.	.	.	.	.
.	squirm	.	.	.	.	.	.	.	.

Final—/md/ . For inflected forms add /d/ to appropriate words, e.g. aimed.
—/mz/ . For inflected forms add /z/ to appropriate words, e.g. aims.

	i	ɪ	ɛ	æ	ɑ/r	ɒ(ɑ(ɔ	ɔ(oʊ/r	ʊ	u
–	(eine)†	inn*	N*	an*	.	on	awn	.	[oo
p	peen*	*pin*	*pen*	*pan*	[pan]	'pon†	pawn	.	po
b	*bean*	bin*	ben*	ban*	barn	bonne	born*	.	bo
t	teen*	tin	*ten*	tan	tarn	.	torn	.	too
d	dean*	din	den	Dan*	darn	Don*	dawn	.	(du
k	keen*	kin	ken	can*	Khan	con*	*corn*	.	coo
g	gean	gin	gen†	gan	.	gone	[gaun]*†	.	goo
f	phene	fin*	fen	*fan*	.	phon*	fawn*	.	.
v	.	.	.	*van*	.	.	Vaughan	.	.
θ	.	thin	.	tanh	.	.	thorn	.	.
ð	.	.	then	than	.	.	.	.	.
s	seen*	sin	sen	san	.	.	sawn*	.	soo
z	.	.	.	.	.	.	.	.	.
ʃ	sheen	shin*	.	shan†	Shan*	(shone)	shorn	.	sho
ʒ	.	.	.	.	.	.	.	.	.
h	.	hin	*hen*	[han]†	harn	.	*horn*	.	.
tʃ	.	chin	.	.	.	.	.	.	.
dʒ	gene*	gin*	.	Jan	jann	John	.	.	Ju
m	mean*	.	*men*	*man*	(maun)†	.	morn*	.	*mo*
n	.	.	.	Nan	.	non	Norn*	.	noo
l	lean*	linn*	Len	.	.	.	lawn*	.	loo
r	rhine†	rin†	wren*	ran	.	Ron	rawn†	.	ru
w	wean*	win*	when*	wan†	[whan]†	wan	worn*	.	wo
j	yean	yin	yen	.	yarn	yon	yawn	.	.
pl	.	.	.	plan	.	.	.	.	.
pr	preen	.	.	.	.	.	*prawn*	.	pr
bl	.	blin†	.	.	.	.	.	.	.
br	.	.	bren*†	bran	.	.	brawn	.	.
tr	.	.	.	.	.	[tron]	.	.	.
tw	'tween†	twin	.	.	.	.	.	.	.
dr	.	.	.	.	.	.	drawn	.	.
kl	clean	.	.	clan	.	.	.	.	.
kr	.	.	.	cran	.	.	.	.	cr
kw	*queen*	quint	.	.	.	.	.	.	.
gl	glean	.	glen*	.	.	.	.	.	.
gr	*green*	grin	.	Gran	.	.	.	.	.
fl	.	.	.	[flan]	.	.	(flawn)	.	.
fr	.	.	frenne†	.	.	.	[frorn]	.	.
θr	.	.	.	.	.	.	thrawn	.	.
sp	.	spin	.	span	.	.	spawn	.	*spo*
st	stean†	.	Sten	Stan	[starn]†	.	.	.	sto
sk	skene	skin	.	scan	.	(scone)	scorn	.	.
sm	.	.	.	.	.	.	.	.	.
sn	.	.	.	.	.	.	.	.	.
sl	.	.	.	.	.	.	.	.	.
sw	.	.	.	.	.	*swan*	sworn	.	sw
ʃr	.	.	.	.	.	.	.	.	.
spl	spleen	.	.	.	.	.	.	.	.
spr	.	.	.	.	.	.	.	.	.
str	strene†	.	.	.	.	.	.	.	str
skr	screen	.	.	scran	.	.	.	.	.
skw	.	.	.	.	.	.	.	.	.

* homophones—see page 218.

  Total number of words—330

ʌ	ɜ/r	eɪ	oʊ	aɪ	aʊ	ɔɪ	i/ə/r	ɛ/ə/r	ju
un†	urn*	eigne*	own	(eine)†	.	.	Ian	[airn]†	.
pun	pern*	pane*	pone	pine*	pown†	.	Paean*	.	.
bun	burn	bane	*bone**	.	[bowne]	.	.	bairn†	.
ton*	turn*	ta'en†	tone	tine*	town	.	.	.	(tune)
done*	durn*†	deign*	.	dine*	down	.	.	.	(dune)
[con]	kern*	cane*	cone	kine	.	coin*	.	cairn	.
gun	[gerne]*†	gain*	.	gown	.	.	.	.	.
fun	fern*	feign*	*'phone**	fine	.	foin	.	.	.
.	.	vein*	.	vine	.	.	.	.	.
.	.	thane	.	.	.	.	.	.	.
.	.	.	.	thine	.	.	.	.	.
*sun**	cerne*†	sane*	sewn	sign*	[sowne]†	.	.	.	.
.	.	.	zone	.	.	.	.	.	.
shun	.	Shane	shown*	shine*	.	.	.	.	.
.	.	.	.	.	.	.	.	.	.
Hun	[hern]*	hain†	hone	.	.	.	.	.	hewn
.	churn	*chain*	.	chine	.	.	.	.	.
.	.	Jane*	Joan	(Jain)	.	join	.	.	.
[mun]*†	.	mane*	moan*	mine	.	.	.	.	.
*nun**	.	nain†	known*	*nine*	noun	.	.	.	.
.	learn	lane*	loan*	line*	[lown]*†	loin	(lien)	.	(lune)
run	.	*rain**	roan*	Rhine*	.	royne	.	.	.
*one**	.	wane*	[won]†	wine*	.	.	.	.	.
.	yearn*	.	.	.	.	.	.	.	.
.	.	*'plane**	.	.	.	.	.	.	.
.	.	.	prone	.	.	[proin]	.	.	.
.	.	blain	blown	.	.	.	.	.	.
.	.	brain	.	brine	*brown*	.	.	.	.
.	.	*train*	[trone]†	trine	.	.	.	.	.
.	.	twain	.	twine	.	.	.	.	.
.	.	drain	drone	.	drown	.	.	.	.
.	.	.	clone	.	*clown*	.	.	.	.
.	.	*crane*	crone	crine	*crown*	.	.	.	.
.	quern	.	.	.	.	.	.	.	.
.	.	grain*	groan*	.	.	groin*	.	.	.
.	.	.	flown	.	.	.	.	.	.
.	.	.	.	.	frown	.	.	.	.
.	.	.	throne*	.	.	.	.	.	.
spun	spurn*	Spain*	.	spine	.	.	.	.	.
stun	stern	stain*	stone	.	[stown]†	.	.	.	.
.	.	skein	(scone)	.	.	.	.	.	.
.	.	.	.	.	.	.	.	.	.
.	.	slain	sloan†	.	.	.	.	.	.
.	.	swain	.	swine	.	.	.	.	.
.	.	.	.	shrine	.	.	.	.	.
.	.	.	.	spline	.	.	.	.	.
.	.	sprain	.	.	.	.	.	.	.
.	.	strain	.	.	.	.	.	.	.
.	.	.	.	scrine†	.	.	.	.	.
.	.	.	.	.	.	.	.	.	.

Final—/nd/ . See pages 106–107.
    —/ns/ . See pages 120–121.
    —/nz/ . For inflected forms add /z/ to appropriate words, e.g. pens.
      . For uninflected forms see, page 234.

	i	ɪ	ɜ	æ	ɑ	ɒ(ɔ(ɑ	ɔ	ʊ	u
–									
p		ping		pang	pang†	pong			
b		bing		bang*		bong			
t		ting		tang		tong			
d		ding		[dang]		dong			
k		*king*		kang*					
g		ging		gang*		gong			
f				fang					
v				[vang]					
θ		thing				thong			
ð									
s		sing*		sang	sang	song		Sung	
z		zing							
ʃ									
ʒ									
h		hing		hang		hong			
tʃ									
dʒ									
m		ming*	[meng]						
n									
l		ling	leng†	lang†		long			
r		*ring*		rang		wrong*			
w		wing		whang*					
j				yang					
pl						[plong]			
pr				prang		prong			
bl									
br		bring							
tr									
tw				twang					
dr									
kl		cling		clang*					
kr			[kreng]	[krang]					
kw									
gl									
gr									
fl		fling				flong			
fr									
θr				[thrang]		throng			
sp				spang					
st		sting		stang		stong†			
sk									
sm									
sn									
sl		sling		slang					
sw		*swing*		swang					
ʃr									
spl									
spr		spring		sprang		sprong†			
str		*string*				strong			
skr									
skw									

* homophones—see pages 218–219.
 Total number of words—87

88

ʌ	ɜ/r	eɪ	oʊ	aɪ	aʊ	ɔɪ	i/ə/r	ɛ/ə/r	ju
·	·	·	·	·	·	·	· ·	·	·
pung	·	·	·	·	·	·	·	·	·
bung	·	·	·	·	·	·	·	·	·
tongue	·	·	·	·	·	·	·	·	·
dung	·	·	·	·	·	·	·	·	·
·	·	·	·	·	·	·	·	·	·
·	·	·	·	·	·	·	·	·	·
[fung]	·	·	·	·	·	·	·	·	·
·	·	·	·	·	·	·	·	·	·
·	·	·	·	·	·	·	·	·	·
sung	·	·	·	·	·	·	·	·	·
·	·	·	·	·	·	·	·	·	·
·	·	·	·	·	·	·	·	·	·
hung	·	·	·	·	·	·	·	·	·
·	·	·	·	·	·	·	·	·	·
mong†	·	·	·	·	·	·	·	·	·
·	·	·	·	·	·	·	·	·	·
lung	·	·	·	·	·	·	·	·	·
rung*	·	·	·	·	·	·	·	·	·
·	·	·	·	·	·	·	·	·	·
young	·	·	·	·	·	·	·	·	·
·	·	·	·	·	·	·	·	·	·
·	·	·	·	·	·	·	·	·	·
·	·	·	·	·	·	·	·	·	·
·	·	·	·	·	·	·	·	·	·
·	·	·	·	·	·	·	·	·	·
clung	·	·	·	·	·	·	·	·	·
·	·	·	·	·	·	·	·	·	·
·	·	·	·	·	·	·	·	·	·
·	·	·	·	·	·	·	·	·	·
flung	·	·	·	·	·	·	·	·	·
·	·	·	·	·	·	·	·	·	·
·	·	·	·	·	·	·	·	·	·
·	·	·	·	·	·	·	·	·	·
stung	·	·	·	·	·	·	·	·	·
·	·	·	·	·	·	·	·	·	·
·	·	·	·	·	·	·	·	·	·
slung	·	·	·	·	·	·	·	·	·
swung	·	·	·	·	·	·	·	·	·
·	·	·	·	·	·	·	·	·	·
sprung	·	·	·	·	·	·	·	·	·
strung	·	·	·	·	·	·	·	·	·
·	·	·	·	·	·	·	·	·	·
·	·	·	·	·	·	·	·	·	·

Final—/ŋd/ . For inflected forms add /d/ to appropriate words, e.g. hanged.
—/ŋz/ . For inflected forms add /z/ to appropriate words, e.g. hangs.

	i	ɪ	ɛ	æ	ɑ/r	ɒ(ɑ(ɔ	ɔ	ʊ	u
–	eel*	ill	L*	Al	aal	.	all*	.	.
p	peel*	pill	pell†	pal	parle†	Poll*	pall*	pull	pool
b	beal*	bill*	bell*	.	(Baal)*	.	ball*	bull	buh
t	teal*	till*	tell	.	taal	.	tall	.	tool
d	deal*	dill	dell	.	dalle*	doll	.	.	[doo
k	keel	kill*	kell†	.	carl*	col*	call*	.	cool
g	.	gill*	.	gal†	.	.	gall*	.	(gho
f	feel*	fill*	fell	.	farl†	.	fall	full	fool
v	veal*	vill†	.	.	.	vol	.	.	.
θ	.	thill	.	.	.	.	.	.	Thu
ð	.	.	.	.	.	.	.	.	.
s	seal*	sill	sell*	sal*	sal†	sol*	Saul	.	[soo
z	zeal	.	.	.	.	.	.	.	.
ʃ	she'll*	[shill]†	shell	shall	.	.	shawl*	.	shoo
ʒ	.	.	.	.	.	.	.	.	.
h	heel*	hill	hell*	.	harl	.	hall*	.	.
tʃ	[chiel]†	chill	.	chal	.	.	.	.	.
dʒ	geal*	jill*	gel*	.	.	.	.	.	(jou
m	meal	mill*	mell	(Mall)	marl*	Moll	maul*	.	[mo
n	kneel*	nil*	knell*	.	gnarl	Noll	.	.	(new
l	leal	lill	.	.	.	loll	.	.	.
r	real*	rill*	.	.	rale†	.	wrawl†	.	rule
w	wheel*	will	well	.	wharl†	.	wall*	wool	.
j	.	yill	yell	.	jarl	.	yawl	.	you'
pl	.	.	.	.	.	.	.	.	.
pr	.	prill†	.	.	.	.	prawle	.	.
bl	.	.	.	.	.	.	.	.	.
br	.	brill	.	.	.	.	brawl	.	broo
tr	.	trill	.	.	.	.	trawl	.	.
tw	tuille*	twill*	.	.	toile*	.	(twal)†	.	.
dr	.	drill	.	.	.	.	drawl	.	droo
kl	.	.	.	.	.	.	.	.	.
kr	creel	krill	.	.	kraal	.	crawl	.	croo
kw	.	quill	quell	.	.	.	.	.	.
gl	.	.	.	.	.	.	.	.	.
gr	.	grill*	.	.	.	.	.	.	(gru
fl	.	.	.	.	.	.	.	.	.
fr	.	frill	.	.	.	.	.	.	.
θr	.	thrill	.	.	.	.	thrall	.	.
sp	spiel*†	spill	spell	.	.	.	spall*	.	spoo
st	steal*	still	stell	.	.	.	stall	.	stoo
sk	.	skill	.	.	.	.	.	.	scho
sm	.	.	smell	.	.	.	small	.	.
sn	.	.	snell	.	snarl	.	.	.	snoo
sl	.	.	.	.	.	.	.	.	.
sw	[sweal]†	swill	swell	.	.	.	.	.	.
ʃr	.	shrill	.	.	.	.	.	.	.
spl	.	.	.	.	.	.	.	.	.
spr	.	.	.	.	.	.	sprawl	.	.
str	streel†	.	.	.	.	.	.	.	.
skr	.	.	.	.	.	.	scrawl	.	.
skw	squeal	squill	.	.	.	.	squall	.	.

* homophones—see page 219.
  Total number of words—313

ʌ	ɜ/r	eɪ	oʊ	aɪ	aʊ	ɔɪ	i/ə/r	ɛ/ə/r	ju
.	earl*	ale*	.	aisle*	*owl*	oil	.	.	Yule*
.	pearl*	*pail*	pole*	pile	.	.	.	.	pule
.	burl*	bail*	*bowl*	bile	(bowel)	boil	.	.	.
.	tirl	tail*	toll*	tile	(towel)	toil	.	.	(tulle)
dull	dirl†	dale	dole*	dial	dowl†	(Dail)	.	.	(dual)*
cull	curl	kale*	coal*	kyle*	cowl	coil	.	.	.
gull	*girl*	gale*	goal*	guile	gowl*†	.	.	.	.
.	furl	fail*	foal	file*	fowl*	foil	.	.	fuel
.	virl	veil*	vole	vile*	(vowel)	voile	.	.	.
.	thirl†	.	thowl*	.	.	.	.	.	.
.	.	.	.	.	.	.	.	.	.
.	cirl	sail*	soul*	sile	sowl	soil*	.	.	.
.	.	.	.	.	.	.	.	.	.
.	.	shale	shoal*	.	.	.	.	.	.
.	.	.	.	.	.	.	.	.	.
hull	hurl	hail*	hole*	.	howl	.	.	.	.
.	churl	.	.	.	.	.	.	.	.
.	.	jail	jole	.	jowl*	.	.	.	.
mull	merle*	mail*	mole*	mile	.	moil*	.	.	mule*
null	nirl†	*nail*	noll*	Nile	.	noil	.	.	(newel)
lull	.	.	.	lisle	.	(loyal)	.	.	.
.	.	rail*	role*	rile	.	roil*	.	.	.
[wull]	whirl*	*whale*	.	while*	.	.	.	.	.
.	.	Yale	.	.	yowl	.	.	.	.
.	.	.	proll	.	prowl	.	.	.	.
.	.	.	.	.	.	.	.	.	.
.	.	Braille*	.	.	.	broil	.	.	.
trull	.	trail*	troll	(trail)	(trowel)	.	.	.	.
.	twirl	.	.	.	.	.	.	.	.
.	.	drail	droll	.	.	droil	.	.	.
.	.	.	.	.	.	.	.	.	.
.	.	quail	.	.	.	.	.	.	.
.	.	.	.	.	.	.	.	.	.
.	.	grail*	.	.	growl	.	.	.	.
.	.	flail	.	.	.	.	.	.	.
.	.	frail	.	.	.	.	.	.	.
.	.	.	.	.	.	.	.	.	.
.	.	spale	.	spile	.	spoil	.	.	.
stull	.	stale	stole	style*	.	.	.	.	.
skull	skirl†	scale*	skoal	.	scowl	.	.	.	.
.	.	.	.	smile	.	[smoile]	.	.	.
.	.	*snail*	.	.	.	.	.	.	.
.	swirl	swale	.	.	.	.	.	.	.
.	.	.	.	.	.	.	.	.	.
.	.	.	.	.	.	.	.	.	.
.	.	.	stroll	.	.	.	.	.	.
.	.	.	scroll	.	.	scroyle†	.	.	.
.	.	squail	.	.	.	.	.	.	.

Final—/ld/ . See pages 108–109.
— /ls/ . See page 223.
— /lz/ . For inflected forms add /z/ to appropriate words, e.g. owls.
. For uninflected forms, see page 235.

	i	ɪ	ɛ	æ	ɑ	ɒ(ɑ(ɔ)	ɔ	ʊ	u
–	.	.	.	asp	[asp]	.	.	.	.
p	.	.	.	.	.	.	.	.	.
b	.	.	.	.	.	.	.	.	.
t	.	.	.	.	.	.	.	.	.
d	.	.	.	.	.	.	.	.	.
k	.	.	.	.	.	.	.	.	.
g	.	.	.	(gasp)	(gasp)	.	.	.	.
f	.	.	.	.	.	.	.	.	.
v	.	.	.	.	.	.	.	.	.
θ	.	.	.	.	.	.	.	.	.
ð	.	.	.	.	.	.	.	.	.
s	.	.	.	.	.	.	.	.	.
z	.	.	.	.	.	.	.	.	.
ʃ	.	.	.	.	.	.	.	.	.
ʒ	.	.	.	.	.	.	.	.	.
h	.	.	[hesp]†	(hasp)	(hasp)	.	.	.	.
tʃ	.	.	.	.	.	.	.	.	.
dʒ	.	.	.	jasp†	.	.	.	.	.
m	.	.	.	.	.	.	.	.	.
n	.	.	.	.	.	knosp	.	.	.
l	.	lisp	.	.	.	.	.	.	.
r	.	risp†	.	(rasp)	(rasp)	.	.	.	.
w	.	wisp	.	.	.	*wasp*	.	.	.
j	.	.	.	.	.	.	.	.	.
pl	.	.	.	.	.	.	.	.	.
pr	.	.	.	.	.	.	.	.	.
bl	.	.	.	.	.	.	.	.	.
br	.	.	.	.	.	.	.	.	.
tr	.	.	.	.	.	.	.	.	.
tw	.	.	.	.	.	.	.	.	.
dr	.	.	.	.	.	.	.	.	.
kl	.	.	.	(clasp)	(clasp)	.	.	.	.
kr	.	crisp	.	.	.	.	.	.	.
kw	.	.	.	.	.	.	.	.	.
gl	.	.	.	.	.	.	.	.	.
gr	.	.	.	(grasp)	(grasp)	.	.	.	.
fl	.	.	.	.	.	.	.	.	.
fr	.	.	.	.	.	.	.	.	.
θr	.	.	.	.	.	.	.	.	.
sp	.	.	.	.	.	.	.	.	.
st	.	.	.	.	.	.	.	.	.
sk	.	.	.	.	.	.	.	.	.
sm	.	.	.	.	.	.	.	.	.
sn	.	.	.	.	.	.	.	.	.
sl	.	.	.	.	.	.	.	.	.
sw	.	.	.	.	.	.	.	.	.
ʃr	.	.	.	.	.	.	.	.	.
spl	.	.	.	.	.	.	.	.	.
spr	.	.	.	.	.	.	.	.	.
str	.	.	.	.	.	.	.	.	.
skr	.	.	.	.	.	.	.	.	.
skw	.	.	.	.	.	.	.	.	.

Total number of words—21

ʌ	ɜ/r	eɪ	oʊ	aɪ	aʊ	ɔɪ	i/ə/r	ɛ/ə/r	ju
·	·	·	·	·	·	·	·	·	·
·	·	·	·	·	·	·	·	·	·
·	·	·	·	·	·	·	·	·	·
·	·	·	·	·	·	·	·	·	·
cusp	·	·	·	·	·	·	·	·	·
·	·	·	·	·	·	·	·	·	·
·	·	·	·	·	·	·	·	·	·
·	·	·	·	·	·	·	·	·	·
·	·	·	·	·	·	·	·	·	·
·	·	·	·	·	·	·	·	·	·
·	·	·	·	·	·	·	·	·	·
·	·	·	·	·	·	·	·	·	·
·	·	·	·	·	·	·	·	·	·
·	·	·	·	·	·	·	·	·	·
·	·	·	·	·	·	·	·	·	·
·	·	·	·	·	·	·	·	·	·
·	·	·	·	·	·	·	·	·	·
·	·	·	·	·	·	·	·	·	·
·	·	·	·	·	·	·	·	·	·
·	·	·	·	·	·	·	·	·	·
·	·	·	·	·	·	·	·	·	·
·	·	·	·	·	·	·	·	·	·

Final—/spt/ . For inflected forms add /t/ to appropriate words, e.g. gasped.
　　—/sps/ . For inflected forms add /s/ to appropriate words, e.g. gasps.

	i	ɪ	ɛ	æ	ɑ	ɒ(ɑ(ɔ	ɔ	ʊ	u
–	.	imp	.	amp	.	.	.	.	.
p	.	pimp	.	.	.	pomp	.	.	.
b	.	.	.	.	.	.	.	.	.
t	.	tymp	.	tamp	.	.	.	.	.
d	.	.	.	damp	.	.	.	.	.
k	.	.	kempt†	camp	.	compt†	.	.	.
g	.	gimp	.	gamp	.	.	.	.	.
f	.	.	.	.	.	.	.	.	.
v	.	.	.	vamp	.	.	.	.	.
θ	.	.	.	.	.	.	.	.	.
ð	.	.	.	.	.	.	.	.	.
s	.	.	.	samp	.	.	.	.	.
z	.	.	.	.	.	.	.	.	.
ʃ	.	.	.	.	.	.	.	.	.
ʒ	.	.	.	.	.	.	.	.	.
h	.	.	hemp	.	.	.	.	.	.
tʃ	.	.	.	champ	.	.	.	.	.
dʒ	.	jimp	.	.	.	.	.	.	.
m	.	mimpt†	.	.	.	.	.	.	.
n	.	.	.	.	.	.	.	.	.
l	.	limp	.	*lamp*	.	.	.	.	.
r	.	.	.	ramp	.	romp	.	.	.
w	.	.	.	.	.	wamp	.	.	.
j	.	.	.	.	.	.	.	.	.
pl	.	.	.	.	.	.	.	.	.
pr	.	.	.	.	.	.	.	.	.
bl	.	blimp	.	.	.	.	.	.	.
br	.	.	.	.	.	.	.	.	.
tr	.	.	.	tramp	.	trompe	.	.	.
tw	.	.	.	.	.	.	.	.	.
dr	.	.	.	.	.	.	.	.	.
kl	.	.	.	clamp	.	.	.	.	.
kr	.	crimp	.	cramp	.	.	.	.	.
kw	.	.	.	.	.	.	.	.	.
gl	.	.	.	.	.	.	.	.	.
gr	.	.	.	.	.	.	.	.	.
fl	.	flimp	.	.	.	.	.	.	.
fr	.	.	.	.	.	.	.	.	.
θr	.	.	.	.	.	.	.	.	.
sp	.	.	.	.	.	.	.	.	.
st	.	.	.	*stamp*	.	.	.	.	.
sk	.	skimp	.	scamp	.	.	.	.	.
sm	.	.	.	.	.	.	.	.	.
sn	.	.	.	.	.	.	.	.	.
sl	.	.	.	.	.	.	.	.	.
sw	.	.	.	.	.	swamp	.	.	.
ʃr	.	shrimp	.	.	.	.	.	.	.
spl	.	.	.	.	.	.	.	.	.
spr	.	.	.	.	.	.	.	.	.
str	.	.	.	stramp	.	.	.	.	.
skr	.	scrimp	.	.	.	.	.	.	.
skw	.	.	.	.	.	.	.	.	.

Total number of words—58

ʌ	ɜ/r	eɪ	oʊ	aɪ	aʊ	ɔɪ	i/ə/r	ɛ/ə/r	ju
.	.	.	.	.	.	.	.	.	.
pump	.	.	.	.	.	.	.	.	.
bump	.	.	.	.	.	.	.	.	.
tump	.	.	.	.	.	.	.	.	.
dump	.	.	.	.	.	.	.	.	.
.	.	.	.	.	.	.	.	.	.
gump	.	.	.	.	.	.	.	.	.
.	.	.	.	.	.	.	.	.	.
.	.	.	.	.	.	.	.	.	.
thump	.	.	.	.	.	.	.	.	.
.	.	.	.	.	.	.	.	.	.
sump	.	.	.	.	.	.	.	.	.
.	.	.	.	.	.	.	.	.	.
.	.	.	.	.	.	.	.	.	.
.	.	.	.	.	.	.	.	.	.
hump	.	.	.	.	.	.	.	.	.
chump	.	.	.	.	.	.	.	.	.
jump	.	.	.	.	.	.	.	.	.
mump	.	.	.	.	.	.	.	.	.
.	.	.	.	.	.	.	.	.	.
lump	.	.	.	.	.	.	.	.	.
rump	.	.	.	.	.	.	.	.	.
.	.	.	.	.	.	.	.	.	.
.	.	.	.	.	.	.	.	.	.
plump	.	.	.	.	.	.	.	.	.
.	.	.	.	.	.	.	.	.	.
.	.	.	.	.	.	.	.	.	.
.	.	.	.	.	.	.	.	.	.
trump	.	.	.	.	.	.	.	.	.
.	.	.	.	.	.	.	.	.	.
.	.	.	.	.	.	.	.	.	.
clump	.	.	.	.	.	.	.	.	.
crump	.	.	.	.	.	.	.	.	.
.	.	.	.	.	.	.	.	.	.
.	.	.	.	.	.	.	.	.	.
flump	.	.	.	.	.	.	.	.	.
frump	.	.	.	.	.	.	.	.	.
.	.	.	.	.	.	.	.	.	.
.	.	.	.	.	.	.	.	.	.
stump	.	.	.	aɪ	.	ɔɪ	i/ə/r	ɛ/ə/r	ju
.	.	.	.	.	.	.	.	.	.
.	.	.	.	.	.	.	.	.	.
.	.	.	.	.	.	.	.	.	.
slump	.	.	.	.	.	.	.	.	.
.	.	.	.	.	.	.	.	.	.
.	.	.	.	.	.	.	.	.	.
.	.	.	.	.	.	.	.	.	.
.	.	.	.	.	.	.	.	.	.
.	.	.	.	.	.	.	.	.	.

Final—/m(p)t/ . For inflected forms add /t/ to appropriate words, e.g. pumped.
. For uninflected forms, see page 232.
—/mps/ . For inflected forms add /s/ to appropriate words, e.g. pumps.
—/mpnd/ . For inflected forms add /nd/ to appropriate words, e.g. dampened.
—/mpnz/ . For inflected forms add /nz/ to appropriate words, e.g. dampens.

	i	ɪ	ɛ	æ	ɑ	ɒ	ɔ	ʊ	u
–	·	·	·	alp	·	·	·	·	·
p	·	·	·	palp	·	·	·	·	pou
b	·	·	·	·	·	·	·	·	·
t	·	·	·	·	·	·	·	·	·
d	·	·	·	·	·	·	·	·	·
k	·	[kilp]	kelp	calp	·	·	·	·	·
g	·	·	·	·	·	·	·	·	·
f	·	·	·	·	·	·	·	·	·
v	·	·	·	·	·	·	·	·	·
θ	·	·	·	·	·	·	·	·	·
ð	·	·	·	·	·	·	·	·	·
s	·	·	·	salp	·	·	·	·	·
z	·	·	·	·	·	·	·	·	·
ʃ	·	·	·	·	·	·	·	·	·
ʒ	·	·	·	·	·	·	·	·	·
h	·	·	help	·	·	·	·	·	·
tʃ	·	·	·	·	·	·	·	·	·
dʒ	·	·	·	·	·	·	·	·	·
m	·	·	·	·	·	·	·	·	·
n	·	·	·	·	·	·	·	·	·
l	·	·	·	·	·	·	·	·	·
r	·	·	·	·	·	·	·	·	·
w	·	·	whelp	·	·	·	·	·	·
j	·	·	yelp	·	·	·	·	·	·
pl	·	·	·	·	·	·	·	·	·
pr	·	·	·	·	·	·	·	·	·
bl	·	·	·	·	·	·	·	·	·
br	·	·	·	·	·	·	·	·	·
tr	·	·	·	·	·	·	·	·	·
tw	·	·	·	·	·	·	·	·	·
dr	·	·	·	·	·	·	·	·	·
kl	·	·	·	·	·	·	·	·	·
kr	·	·	·	·	·	·	·	·	·
kw	·	·	·	·	·	·	·	·	·
gl	·	·	·	·	·	·	·	·	·
gr	·	·	·	·	·	·	·	·	·
fl	·	·	·	·	·	·	·	·	·
fr	·	·	·	·	·	·	·	·	·
θr	·	·	·	·	·	·	·	·	·
sp	·	·	·	·	·	·	·	·	·
st	·	·	·	·	·	·	·	·	·
sk	·	·	skelp†	scalp	·	·	·	·	·
sm	·	·	·	·	·	·	·	·	·
sn	·	·	·	·	·	·	·	·	·
sl	·	·	·	·	·	·	·	·	·
sw	·	·	·	·	·	·	·	·	·
ʃr	·	·	·	·	·	·	·	·	·
spl	·	·	·	·	·	·	·	·	·
spr	·	·	·	·	·	·	·	·	·
str	·	·	·	·	·	·	·	·	·
skr	·	·	·	·	·	·	·	·	·
skw	·	·	·	·	·	·	·	·	·

Total number of words—16

ʌ	ɜ/r	ɪə	oʊ	aɪ	aʊ	ɔɪ	i/ə/r	ɛ/ə/r	ju
pulp									
gulp									
			holp†						
sculp									

Final—/lpt/ . For inflected forms add /t/ to appropriate words, e.g. helped.
—/lps/ . For inflected forms add /s/ to appropriate words, e.g. helps.

	i	ɪ	ɛ	æ	ɑ/r	ɒ(ɔ(ɑ	ɔ/r	ʊ	u
—	.	.	eft	(aft)	(aft)	oft	.	.	.
p	.	.	.	.	.	.	.	poufed	.
b	.	biffed†	.	(baffed)*	(baft)*	.	.	.	.
t	.	tift*†	.	.	.	toft	.	.	.
d	.	.	deft	(daffed)*	(daft)*	doffed	.	.	.
k	.	.	.	.	.	coughed*	.	.	.
g	.	gift	.	gaffed	.	.	.	.	.
f	.	.	feoffed	.	.	.	.	.	.
v	.	.	.	.	.	.	.	.	.
θ	.	.	theft	.	.	thoft	.	.	.
ð	.	.	.	.	.	.	.	.	.
s	.	sift	.	.	.	soft	.	.	.
z	.	.	.	.	.	.	.	.	.
ʃ	.	shift	.	(shaft)	(shaft)	.	.	.	.
ʒ	.	.	.	.	.	.	.	.	.
h	.	.	heft	(haft)	(haft)	.	.	.	ho
tʃ	.	.	.	(chaffed)*	(chaft)*	.	[chaufed]†	.	.
dʒ	.	.	jeffed	.	.	.	.	.	.
m	.	miffed	.	.	.	.	.	.	.
n	.	.	.	.	.	.	.	.	.
l	.	lift	left*	(laughed)	(laughed)	loft	.	.	.
r	reefed	rift*	reft	(raft)	(raft)	.	.	.	ro
w	.	whiffed	weft	(waft)*	(waffed)*	(waft)*	wharfed†	.	.
j	.	yift†	.	.	yaffed†	.	.	.	.
pl	.	.	.	.	.	.	.	.	.
pr	.	.	.	.	.	.	.	.	pr
bl	.	.	.	.	.	.	.	.	.
br	briefed	.	.	.	.	.	.	.	.
tr	.	.	.	.	.	.	.	.	.
tw	.	.	.	.	.	.	.	.	.
dr	.	drift	.	(draft)*	(draught)*	.	.	.	.
kl	.	[clift]*	cleft*	.	.	.	.	.	.
kr	.	.	.	(craft)	(craft)*	croft	.	.	.
kw	.	quiffed	.	(quaffed)	.	(quaffed)	.	.	.
gl	.	glift†	.	.	.	.	.	.	.
gr	.	.	.	(graphed)*	(graft)*	.	.	.	.
fl	.	.	.	(flaffed)	(flaffed)	.	.	.	.
fr	.	.	.	.	.	.	.	.	.
θr	.	thrift	.	.	.	.	.	.	.
sp	.	.	.	.	.	.	.	.	sp
st	.	.	.	(staffed)	(staffed)	.	.	.	.
sk	.	skiffed†	.	.	scarfed	scoffed†	.	.	.
sm	.	.	.	.	.	.	.	.	.
sn	.	sniffed	sneft	.	.	.	.	.	.
sl	.	.	.	.	.	.	.	.	.
sw	.	swift	.	.	.	.	[swarfed]†	.	.
ʃr	.	shrift	.	.	.	shroffed	.	.	.
spl	.	.	.	.	.	.	.	.	.
spr	.	.	.	.	.	.	.	.	.
str	.	strift†	.	.	(strafed)	.	.	.	.
skr	.	.	.	.	.	.	.	.	.
skw	.	.	.	.	.	.	.	.	.

* homophones—see pages 219–220.
  Total number of words—115

ʌ	ɜ/r	ɪə	oʊ	aɪ	aʊ	ɔɪ	i/ə/r	ɛ/ə/r	ju
puffed									
buffed									
tuft	turfed								
duffed									
cuffed						coifed			
					gowfed†				
fuffed†				fifed					
(soughed)	surfed								
huffed									
		chafed							
muffed									
				knifed					
luffed			loafed						
ruffed*									
yuft									
pluffed†									
bluffed									
fluffed									
stuffed									
scuft*†									
snuffed									
sloughed									
	[swerfed]†								
		(strafed)							

Final—/fts/ . For inflected forms add /s/ to appropriate words, e.g. gifts.

	i	ɪ	ɛ	æ	ɑ	ɒ(ɔ(ɑ	ɔ(oʊ/r	ʊ	u
–	east	is't†	.	.	(asked)	.	.	.	.
p	pieced	pissed	pest	(past)*	(passed)*	.	.	pussed	.
b	beast	.	best	(bast)	(bast)	bossed	.	.	bo‹
t	.	.	test	.	.	tossed	.	.	.
d	.	.	.	.	.	dossed	.	.	(de‹
k	.	kissed*	[kest]	(cast)*	(caste)*	cost*	coursed	.	.
g	geest	.	guest*	gassed*	(ghast)	.	.	.	.
f	feast	fist	fest	(fast)	(fast)	fossed	forced	.	.
v	.	.	vest	(vast)	(vast)	.	.	.	.
θ	.	.	.	.	.	.	.	.	.
ð	.	.	.	.	.	.	.	.	.
s	ceased	cyst*	cest*	.	.	sossed	sauced	.	.
z	.	xyst†	zest	.	.	.	.	.	.
ʃ	.	schist	.	.	.	.	.	.	.
ʒ	.	.	.	.	.	.	.	.	.
h	.	hist*†	hest	hast	.	.	horst*	.	.
tʃ	.	.	chest	.	.	.	.	.	.
dʒ	.	gist	jest*	.	.	.	.	.	(jo‹
m	.	mist*	messed	massed*	(mast)	mossed	.	[moust]†	.
n	neist	.	*nest*	.	.	.	.	.	no‹
l	least*	list*	lest	(last)	(last)	lost	.	.	lo‹
r	reast*	wrist	rest*	wrast†.	(rast)†	.	.	.	ro‹
w	.	whist*	west	.	.	wast	.	.	.
j	yeast	.	[yest]	.	.	.	.	.	us‹
pl	.	.	.	(plast)	(plast)	.	.	.	.
pr	priest*	.	pressed*	.	.	.	.	.	.
bl	.	blist†	blest*	(blast)	(blast)	.	.	.	.
br	.	.	breast*	brast	.	.	.	.	.
tr	.	tryst*†	tressed	.	.	.	.	.	.
tw	.	twist	.	.	.	.	.	.	.
dr	.	.	dressed	.	.	.	.	.	.
kl	.	.	.	(classed)	(classed)	.	.	.	.
kr	creased	.	crest	.	.	crossed	.	.	.
kw	[queest]	[quist]	quest	.	.	.	.	.	.
gl	.	.	.	(glassed)	(glassed)	glossed	.	.	.
gr	(greased)*	grist	.	(grassed)	(grassed)	.	.	.	.
fl	fleeced	.	.	.	.	.	.	.	.
fr	.	frist	.	.	.	frost	.	.	.
θr	.	[thrist]†	.	.	.	.	.	.	.
sp	.	.	.	.	.	.	.	.	.
st	.	.	.	.	.	.	.	.	.
sk	.	.	.	.	.	.	.	.	.
sm	.	.	.	.	.	.	.	.	.
sn	.	.	.	.	.	.	.	.	.
sl	.	.	.	.	.	.	.	.	slu‹
sw	.	.	.	.	.	.	.	.	.
ʃr	.	.	.	.	.	.	.	.	.
spl	.	.	.	.	.	.	.	.	.
spr	.	.	.	.	.	.	.	.	sp‹
str	.	.	stressed	.	.	.	.	.	.
skr	.	.	.	.	.	.	.	.	.
skw	.	.	.	.	.	.	.	.	.

* homophones—see page 220.
  Total number of words—204

ʌ	ɜ/r	eɪ	oʊ	aɪ	aʊ	ɔɪ	i/ə/r	ɛ/ə/r	ju
.	erst	.	oast	iced	oust	.	.	.	used
.	pursed	paste*	post	.	.	.	pierced	.	.
bust*	burst	baste*	boast	.	bowsed	.	.	.	.
.	.	taste	toast	ticed†	.	.	.	.	.
dust*	durst†	.	dosed	diced	dowsed*	.	.	.	(deuced)
cussed	cursed	cased	coast	.	.	.	.	.	.
gust	.	.	ghost	geist	.	.	.	.	.
fust*	first	faced	.	.	Faust	foist	.	.	.
.	verst*	.	.	viced†	.	voiced	.	.	.
.	thirst	.	.	.	.	.	.	.	.
.	.	.	.	.	.	.	.	.	.
.	searced	[saist]†	.	.	soused	.	.	.	.
.	.	.	.	.	.	.	.	.	.
.	.	.	.	.	.	.	.	.	.
.	.	.	.	.	.	.	.	.	.
.	hurst*	haste	host*	.	.	hoist	.	.	.
.	.	chaste*	.	.	choused	.	.	.	.
just*	.	.	.	.	(joust)	joist	.	.	.
must*	.	[mayst]†	most	.	.	moist	.	.	.
.	nursed	.	.	.	.	.	.	.	.
lust	.	laced	.	.	(lowsed)†	.	.	.	.
rust	.	raced*	roast	.	roust	.	.	.	.
.	worst	waist*	.	.	.	.	.	.	.
.	.	placed	.	.	.	.	.	.	.
.	.	.	.	priced	.	.	.	.	.
.	.	braced	.	.	.	.	.	.	.
trust*	.	traced	.	.	.	.	.	.	.
.	.	.	.	.	.	.	.	.	.
.	.	.	.	.	.	.	.	.	.
crust	.	.	.	Christ	.	.	.	.	.
.	.	.	.	.	.	[quoist]	.	.	.
.	.	.	.	.	.	.	.	.	.
.	.	graced	grossed	.	groused	.	.	.	.
.	.	.	.	.	.	.	.	.	.
frust	.	.	.	.	frowst	.	.	.	.
thrust	.	.	.	.	.	.	.	.	.
.	spersed†	spaced	.	spiced	.	.	.	.	.
.	.	.	.	.	.	.	.	.	.
.	.	.	.	.	.	.	.	.	.
.	.	snaste	.	.	.	.	.	.	.
.	.	.	.	sliced	.	.	.	.	.
.	.	.	.	.	.	.	.	.	.
.	.	.	.	spliced	.	.	.	.	.
.	.	.	.	.	.	.	.	.	.
.	.	.	.	.	.	.	.	.	.
.	.	.	.	.	.	.	.	.	.
.	.	.	.	.	.	.	.	.	.

Final—/sts/ . For inflected forms add /s/ to appropriate words, e.g. tests.

	i	ɪ	ɛ	æ	ɑ	ɒ(ɑɔ)	ɔ(ɑɒ)	ʊ	u
—	·	·	·	ant*	(aunt)*	·	·	·	oo
p	·	·	pent	pant	·	·	·	·	·
b	·	·	bent	bant	·	·	·	(bund)	·
t	·	tint	*tent*	·	·	·	taunt	·	·
d	·	dint	dent	·	·	·	daunt	·	·
k	·	·	Kent*	cant*	(can't)	·	·	·	·
g	·	·	Ghent	·	[gant]*†	·	gaunt	·	·
f	·	·	fent	·	·	font	·	·	·
v	·	vint	vent	·	·	·	vaunt	·	·
θ	·	·	·	·	·	·	·	·	·
ð	·	·	·	·	·	·	·	·	·
s	·	·	scent*	·	·	·	[saunt]†	·	·
z	·	·	·	·	·	·	·	·	·
ʃ	·	·	shent†	(shan't)	(shan't)	·	·	·	·
ʒ	·	·	·	·	·	·	·	·	·
h	·	hint	hent	(ha'n't)†	(ha'n't)†	·	haunt	·	·
tʃ	·	·	·	(chant)	(chant)	·	·	·	·
dʒ	·	·	gent	·	·	·	jaunt	·	·
m	·	mint	meant*	·	·	·	·	·	·
n	·	·	·	·	[naunt]†	·	·	·	·
l	·	lint	lent*	lant	·	·	·	·	·
r	·	·	rent	rant	·	·	·	·	·
w	·	win't†	went	·	·	want*	·	·	·
j	·	·	·	·	·	·	·	·	·
pl	·	·	·	(plant)	(plant)	·	·	·	·
pr	·	print	·	·	·	·	·	·	·
bl	·	·	blent†	·	·	·	·	·	·
br	·	·	brent†	brant	·	·	·	·	·
tr	·	·	Trent	trant†	·	·	·	·	·
tw	·	·	·	·	·	·	·	·	·
dr	·	·	drent†	(drant)	(drant)	dronte	draunt	·	·
kl	·	·	·	·	·	·	·	·	·
kr	·	·	·	·	·	·	·	·	·
kw	·	quint	·	·	(quant)	(quant)	·	·	·
gl	·	glint	glent†	·	·	·	·	·	·
gr	·	·	·	(grant)*	(grant)*	·	·	·	·
fl	·	flint	·	·	·	·	flaunt	·	·
fr	·	·	·	·	·	·	·	·	·
θr	·	·	·	·	·	·	·	·	·
sp	·	·	spent	·	·	·	·	·	·
st	·	stint	stent	·	·	·	·	·	·
sk	·	·	·	scant	·	·	·	·	·
sm	·	·	·	·	·	·	·	·	·
sn̩	·	·	·	·	·	·	·	·	·
sl	·	·	·	(slant)	(slant)	·	·	·	·
sw	·	suint	·	·	·	·	·	·	·
ʃr	·	·	·	·	·	·	·	·	·
spl	·	splint	[splent]	·	·	·	·	·	·
spr	·	sprint	sprent	·	·	·	·	·	·
str	·	·	·	·	·	·	·	·	·
skr	·	·	·	·	·	·	·	·	·
skw	·	squint	·	·	·	·	·	·	·

* homophones—see page 220.
   Total number of words—126

ʌ	ɜ/r	eɪ	oʊ	aɪ	aʊ	ɔɪ	i/ə/r	ɛ/ə/r	ju
.	(earned)	ain't†	.	.	.	oint†	.	.	.
punt	.	paint	.	pint	.	point	.	.	.
bunt	burnt	.	.	.	.	.	.	.	.
.	.	taint	.	.	.	.	.	.	.
dunt	.	.	don't	.	.	.	.	.	.
.	.	.	.	.	count*	.	.	.	.
.	.	.	.	.	.	.	.	.	.
.	.	faint*	.	.	fount	.	.	.	.
.	.	.	.	.	.	.	.	.	.
.	.	.	.	.	.	.	.	.	.
.	.	.	.	.	.	.	.	.	.
.	.	saint	.	.	.	.	.	.	.
.	.	.	.	.	.	.	.	.	.
shunt	.	.	.	.	.	.	.	.	.
.	.	.	.	.	.	.	.	.	.
hunt	.	.	.	.	.	.	.	.	.
.	.	.	.	.	.	joint	.	.	.
.	.	meyn't†	.	.	mount	.	.	.	.
.	.	.	.	.	.	noint	.	.	.
lunt	learnt	.	.	.	.	.	.	.	.
runt	.	.	.	.	.	.	.	.	.
(wont)†	weren't	.	(wont)*	.	.	.	.	.	.
.	.	.	.	.	.	.	.	.	.
.	.	plaint	.	.	.	.	.	.	.
prunt	.	.	.	.	.	.	.	.	.
blunt	.	.	.	.	.	.	.	.	.
brunt	.	.	.	.	.	.	.	.	.
.	.	.	.	.	.	.	.	.	.
.	.	.	.	.	.	.	.	.	.
.	.	.	.	.	.	.	.	.	.
.	.	.	.	.	.	.	creant	.	.
.	.	quaint*	.	.	.	.	.	.	.
.	.	.	.	.	.	.	.	.	.
grunt*	.	.	.	.	.	.	.	.	.
.	.	.	.	.	.	.	.	.	.
front	.	.	.	.	.	.	.	.	.
.	.	.	.	.	.	.	.	.	.
.	.	.	.	.	.	.	.	.	.
stunt	.	.	.	.	.	.	.	.	.
.	.	.	.	.	.	.	.	.	.
.	.	.	.	.	.	.	.	.	.
.	.	.	.	.	.	.	.	.	.
.	.	.	.	.	.	.	.	.	.
.	.	.	.	.	.	.	.	.	.
sprunt	.	spraint	.	.	.	.	.	.	.
strunt	.	straint†	.	.	.	.	.	.	.
scrunt	.	.	.	.	.	.	.	.	.
.	.	.	.	.	.	.	.	.	.

Final—/nts/ . For inflected forms add /s/ to appropriate words, e.g. ants.

	i	ɪ	ɛ	æ	ɑ	ɒ	ɔ	ʊ	u
–	.	.	elt	alt	.	.	.	.	.
p	.	.	pelt	.	.	.	.	.	.
b	.	built	*belt*	.	.	(bolt)	Balt	.	.
t	.	tilt	telt	.	.	.	.	.	.
d	.	.	dealt	.	.	(dolt)	dault	.	.
k	.	kilt	kelt*	.	.	(colt)	.	.	.
g	.	guilt*	gelt	.	.	.	gault*	.	.
f	.	.	felt*	.	.	.	fault	.	.
v	.	.	(veld)	.	.	(volt)	vault	.	.
θ	.	.	.	.	.	.	.	.	.
ð	.	.	.	.	.	.	.	.	.
s	.	silt	celt*	.	.	(salt)	(salt)	.	.
z	.	.	.	.	.	.	.	.	.
ʃ	.	.	.	shalt	.	.	.	.	.
ʒ	.	.	.	.	.	.	.	.	.
h	.	hilt	.	.	.	(halt)	(halt)	.	.
tʃ	.	.	.	.	.	.	.	.	.
dʒ	.	jilt	.	.	.	.	.	.	.
m	.	milt	melt	.	.	(malt)	(malt)	.	.
n	.	.	knelt	.	.	.	.	.	.
l	.	lilt	.	.	.	.	.	.	.
r	.	.	.	.	.	.	.	.	.
w	.	wilt	welt	.	.	.	.	.	.
j	.	.	.	.	.	.	.	.	.
pl	.	.	.	.	.	.	.	.	.
pr	.	.	.	.	.	.	.	.	.
bl	.	.	.	.	.	.	.	.	.
br	.	.	.	.	.	.	.	.	.
tr	.	.	.	.	.	.	.	.	.
tw	.	[twilt]†	.	.	.	.	.	.	.
dr	.	.	.	.	.	.	.	.	.
kl	.	.	.	.	.	.	.	.	.
kr	.	.	.	.	.	.	.	.	.
kw	.	quilt	.	.	.	.	.	.	.
gl	.	.	.	.	.	.	.	.	.
gr	.	.	.	.	.	.	.	.	.
fl	.	.	.	.	.	.	.	.	.
fr	.	.	.	.	.	.	.	.	.
θr	.	.	.	.	.	.	.	.	.
sp	.	spilt	spelt	.	.	(spalt)	(spalt)	.	.
st	.	stilt	stealt†	.	.	.	.	.	.
sk	.	.	.	.	.	.	.	.	.
sm	.	.	smelt	.	.	(smalt)	(smalt)	.	.
sn	.	.	.	.	.	.	.	.	.
sl	.	.	.	.	.	.	.	.	.
sw	.	.	swelt†	.	.	.	.	.	.
ʃr	.	.	.	.	.	.	.	.	.
spl	.	.	.	.	.	.	.	.	.
spr	.	.	.	.	.	.	.	.	.
str	.	.	.	.	.	.	.	.	.
skr	.	.	.	.	.	.	.	.	.
skw	.	.	.	.	.	.	.	.	.

* homophones—see page 220.
   Total number of words—65

104

ʌ	ɜ/r	eɪ	oʊ	aɪ	aʊ	ɔɪ	i/ə/r	ɛ/ə/r	ju
			poult*						
			(bolt)*						
			tolt						
			(dolt)			doilt			
cult			(colt)*						
			(volt)						
			holt*						
			jolt						
			moult*						
						spoilt			
			smolt						

Final—/lts/ . For inflected forms add /s/ to appropriate words, e.g. belts.

	i	ɪ	ɛ	æ	ɑ/r	ɒ(ɑ	ɔ/r	ʊ	u
−	.	[Ind]	end	and	.	.	awned	.	.
p	piend*	pinned*	pend*	panned*	.	pond	pawned	.	.
b	.	.	bend	band*	.	bond*	.	.	.
t	teind*	tinned*	tend	tanned	.	.	.	.	(tune⊕
d	.	dinned	.	.	darned	donned	dawned	.	.
k	.	.	kenned†	canned	.	[conned]*	.	.	.
g	.	.	.	.	.	.	.	.	.
f	fiend	finned	fend	fanned	fand†	fond*	fawned	.	.
v	.	.	vend	.	.	.	.	.	.
θ	.	thinned	.	.	.	.	.	.	.
ð	.	.	.	.	.	.	.	.	.
s	.	sinned	send	sand	.	.	sorned†	.	.
z	.	.	zend	.	.	.	.	.	.
ʃ	.	shinned	shend	[shand]	.	.	.	.	.
ʒ	.	.	.	.	.	.	.	.	.
h	.	.	hend	*hand*	.	[hond]	horned	.	.
tʃ	.	.	.	.	.	.	.	.	.
dʒ	.	.	.	.	.	.	.	.	.
m	meaned†	.	mend	manned	(mauned)†	.	maund*	.	moon⊕
n	.	.	.	.	.	.	.	.	.
l	leaned	lind*	lend	land	.	.	laund†	.	.
r	.	.	rend	rand	.	ronde	.	.	.
w	weaned*	wind	wend*	.	.	wand*	warned	.	woun⊕
j	yeaned†	.	yenned†	.	yarned	yond†	yawned	.	.
pl	.	.	.	planned	.	.	.	.	.
pr	preened	.	.	.	.	.	prawned	.	prune⊕
bl	.	blinned†	blend*	bland	.	blonde*	.	.	.
br	.	.	.	brand	.	brond†	brawned	.	.
tr	.	.	trend	.	.	.	.	.	.
tw	.	twinned	.	.	.	.	.	.	.
dr	.	.	.	.	.	.	.	.	.
kl	cleaned	.	.	.	.	.	.	.	.
kr	.	.	.	.	.	.	.	.	croon⊕
kw	queened	.	.	.	.	.	.	.	.
gl	gleaned	.	.	gland	.	.	.	.	.
gr	.	grinned	.	grand	.	.	.	.	.
fl	.	.	.	.	.	.	.	.	.
fr	.	.	friend	.	.	frond	.	.	.
θr	.	.	.	.	.	.	.	.	.
sp	.	spinned	spend	spanned	.	.	spawned	.	spoon⊕
st	.	.	stend†	stand	.	[stond]†	.	.	(stow⊕
sk	.	skinned	.	scanned	.	.	scorned	.	.
sm	.	.	.	.	.	.	.	.	.
sn	.	.	.	.	.	.	.	.	.
sl	.	.	.	.	.	.	.	.	.
sw	.	.	.	.	.	.	.	.	swoon⊕
ʃr	.	.	.	.	.	.	.	.	.
spl	.	.	.	.	.	.	.	.	.
spr	.	.	.	.	.	.	.	.	.
str	.	.	.	strand	.	[strond]†	.	.	.
skr	screened	.	.	.	.	.	.	.	.
skw	.	.	.	.	.	.	.	.	.

* homophones—see page 221.
  Total number of words—212

ʌ	ɜ/r	eɪ	oʊ	aɪ	aʊ	ɔɪ	i/ə/r	ɛ/ə/r	ju
.	earned*	.	owned	[Ind]	.	.	.	.	.
punned	.	pained*	.	pined	pound	.	.	.	.
bund	burned	.	boned	bind	bound	.	.	.	.
tund*	turned	.	toned	tined*	.	.	.	.	(tuned)
dunned	.	deigned	.	dined	downed	.	.	.	.
(cunned)	kerned	caned	coned	kind	.	coined	.	.	.
gunned	[gerned]†	gained	.	.	gowned	.	.	.	.
fund	.	feigned	'phoned	find*	found	.	.	.	.
.	.	veined	.	.	.	.	.	.	.
.	.	.	.	.	.	.	.	.	.
sunned	scerned†	sained†	.	signed*	sound*	.	.	.	.
.	.	.	zoned	.	.	.	.	.	.
shunned	.	.	.	shined	.	.	.	.	.
.	.	hained†	honed	hind	hound	.	.	.	.
.	churned	chained	.	chynd*†	.	.	.	.	.
.	.	.	.	.	.	joined	.	.	.
(mauned)†	.	maned*	moaned	mind*	mound	.	.	.	.
.	learned	.	loaned	lined	(lound)†	.	.	.	.
[rund]	.	reigned*	.	rind*	round	royned†	.	.	.
.	.	waned	.	wind*	wound	.	.	.	.
.	yearned	.	.	.	.	.	.	.	.
.	.	planed	.	.	.	.	.	.	.
.	.	.	.	blind	.	.	.	.	.
.	.	brained	.	.	browned	.	.	.	.
.	.	trained	.	trined†	.	.	.	.	.
.	.	.	.	twined	.	.	.	.	.
.	.	drained	droned	.	drowned	.	.	.	.
.	.	.	.	.	clowned	.	.	.	.
.	.	craned	.	crined†	crowned	.	.	.	.
.	.	.	.	.	.	.	.	.	.
.	.	grained	groaned	grind	ground	groined†	.	.	.
.	.	.	.	.	frowned	.	.	.	.
.	.	.	throned	.	.	.	.	.	.
.	spurned	spaned†	.	spined	.	.	.	.	.
stunned	.	stained	stoned	.	(stound)*†	.	.	.	.
.	.	.	.	.	.	.	.	.	.
.	.	.	.	.	.	.	.	.	.
.	.	.	.	.	[swound]†	.	.	.	.
.	.	.	.	shrined	.	.	.	.	.
.	.	.	.	.	.	.	.	.	.
.	.	sprained	.	.	.	.	.	.	.
.	.	strained	.	.	.	.	.	.	.
.	.	.	.	.	.	.	.	.	.
.	.	.	.	.	.	.	.	.	.

Final—/ndz/ . For inflected forms add /z/ to appropriate words, e.g. ends.

	i	ɪ	ɛ	æ	ɑ/r	ɒ(ɑ(ɔ)	ɔ	ʊ	u
—	eild	.	eld	.	.	.	auld†	.	.
p	pealed*	.	.	palled	parled†	polled	palled	pulled	poole
b	bield*†	build*	.	.	.	.	bald*	.	.
t	.	tilled	teld	.	.	.	[tauld]†	.	toole
d	.	.	.	.	.	dolled	.	.	(duel
k	keeled	killed	keld†	.	.	colled†	called*	.	coole
g	.	guild*	geld·	.	.	.	galled	.	goold
f	field*	filled	felled	.	.	.	.	.	foole
v	.	.	.	.	.	.	.	.	.
θ	.	.	.	.	.	.	.	.	.
ð	.	.	.	.	.	.	.	.	.
s	ceiled*	.	celled*	.	.	sold†	.	.	[soole
z	.	.	.	.	.	.	.	.	.
ʃ	shield*	[shilled]†	shelled	.	.	.	.	.	shoole
ʒ	.	.	.	.	.	.	.	.	.
h	healed*	[hild]†	held	.	harled†	.	hauled*	.	.
tʃ	chield	chilled	.	.	.	.	.	.	.
dʒ	gealed*	.	jelled*	.	.	.	.	.	(jewe
m	.	milled	meld*	.	marled	.	mauled*	.	.
n	kneeled*	nilled†	knelled	.	gnarled	.	.	.	.
l	.	lilled†	.	.	.	lolled	.	.	.
r	reeled	rilled	.	.	.	.	wrawled	.	ruled
w	wield*	willed	weld*	[wald]†	.	.	walled*	.	woold
j	yield	.	yeld*†	.	[yald]†	.	yawled*	.	.
pl	.	.	.	.	.	.	.	.	.
pr	.	.	.	.	.	.	.	.	.
bl	.	.	.	.	.	.	.	.	.
br	.	.	.	.	.	.	brawled	.	.
tr	.	trilled	.	.	.	.	trawled	.	.
tw	[tweeled]†	twilled	.	.	.	.	.	.	.
dr	.	drilled	.	.	.	.	drawled	.	droole
kl	.	.	.	.	.	.	.	.	.
kr	.	.	.	.	.	.	crawled	.	.
kw	.	quilled	quelled	.	.	.	.	.	.
gl	.	.	.	.	.	.	.	.	.
gr	.	grilled	.	.	.	.	.	.	.
fl	.	.	.	.	.	.	.	.	.
fr	.	frilled	.	.	.	.	.	.	.
θr	.	thrilled	.	.	.	.	thralled	.	.
sp	speeled*†	spilled	spelled*	.	.	.	spauld*†	.	spoole
st	steeled*	stilled	stelled	.	.	.	stalled	.	.
sk	.	skilled	.	.	.	.	scald*	.	schoo.
sm	.	.	smelled	.	.	.	.	.	.
sn	.	.	.	.	snarled	.	.	.	snoole
sl	.	.	.	.	.	.	.	.	.
sw	[swealed]	swilled	swelled	.	.	.	.	.	.
ʃr	.	shrilled	.	.	.	.	.	.	.
spl	.	.	.	.	.	.	.	.	.
spr	.	.	.	.	.	.	sprawled	.	.
str	streeled†	.	.	.	.	.	.	.	.
skr	.	.	.	.	.	.	scrawled	.	.
skw	squealed	.	.	.	.	.	.	.	.

* homophones—see page 221.
  Total number of words—218

ʌ	ɜ/r	eɪ	oʊ	aɪ	aʊ	ɔɪ	i/ə/r	ɛ/ə/r	ju
.	.	ailed	old	.	.	oiled	.	.	.
.	purled*	paled	polled*	piled	.	.	.	.	puled
.	birled*†	baled*	bold*	.	.	boiled	.	.	.
.	tirled†	tailed	told*	tiled	.	toiled	.	.	.
dulled	.	.	doled	dialed	.	doiled†	.	.	(duelled)
culled	curled	.	cold*	.	cowled	coiled	.	.	.
gulled	gurled†	.	gold	guiled	.	.	.	.	.
.	furled	failed	fold*	filed	fouled	foiled	.	.	fuelled
.	.	veiled*	.	[vild]†	.	.	.	.	.
.	thirled†	.	tholed†	.	.	.	.	.	.
.	.	sailed	sold*	siled†	[sowled]†	soiled	.	.	.
.	.	.	.	.	.	.	.	.	.
.	.	.	.	.	.	.	.	.	.
.	hurled	hailed*	hold*	.	howled	.	.	.	.
.	.	.	.	child	.	.	.	.	.
.	.	jailed	[joled]	.	jowled	.	.	.	.
mulled	murled†	mailed	mould	mild	.	moiled	.	.	mewled
nulled	nirled†	nailed	knolled*	.	.	.	.	.	.
lulled	.	.	.	.	.	.	.	.	.
.	.	railed	rolled	riled	.	roiled	.	.	.
[wulled]†	world*	wailed*	wold	wild*	.	.	.	.	.
.	.	.	[yold]†	.	yowled	.	.	.	.
.	.	.	[prolled]	.	prowled	.	.	.	.
.	.	.	.	.	.	broiled	.	.	.
.	.	trailed	trolled	.	.	.	.	.	.
.	twirled	.	.	.	.	.	.	.	.
.	.	drailed	drolled	.	.	droiled	.	.	.
.	.	.	.	.	.	.	.	.	.
.	.	quailed	.	.	.	.	.	.	.
.	.	.	.	.	growled	.	.	.	.
.	.	flailed	.	.	.	.	.	.	.
.	.	.	.	.	.	.	.	.	.
.	.	.	.	spiled	.	spoiled	.	.	.
.	.	.	stoled	styled	.	.	.	.	.
sculled	skirled†	scaled*	scold	.	scowled	.	.	.	.
.	.	.	.	smiled	.	.	.	.	.
.	swirled	swaled	.	.	.	.	.	.	.
.	.	.	.	.	.	.	.	.	.
.	.	.	.	.	.	.	.	.	.
.	.	.	strolled	.	.	.	.	.	.
.	.	.	scrolled	.	.	.	.	.	.
.	.	squailed	.	.	.	.	.	.	.

Final—/ldz/ . For inflected forms add /z/ to appropriate words, e.g. builds.

	i	ɪ	ε	æ	ɑ	ɒ(ɑ(ɔ)	ɔ/r	ʊ	u
–	·	·	·	(ask)	(ask)	·	·	·	·
p	·	·	·	(Pasch)	(Pasch)	·	·	·	·
b	·	bisque*	·	(Basque)*	(bask)*	bosk	·	·	·
t	·	·	·	(task)	(task)	·	torsk	·	·
d	·	disc	desk	·	·	·	·	·	·
k	·	·	·	(casque)*	(cask)*	·	·	·	·
g	·	·	·	·	·	·	·	·	·
f	·	fisk*†	·	·	·	·	·	·	·
v	·	·	·	·	·	·	·	·	·
θ	·	·	·	·	·	·	·	·	·
ð	·	·	·	·	·	·	·	·	·
s	·	·	·	·	·	·	·	·	·
z	·	·	·	·	·	·	·	·	·
ʃ	·	·	·	·	·	·	·	·	·
ʒ	·	·	·	·	·	·	·	·	·
h	·	·	·	hask†	·	·	·	·	·
tʃ	·	·	·	·	·	·	·	·	·
dʒ	·	·	·	·	·	·	·	·	·
m	·	·	·	(masque)*	(mask)*	mosque	·	·	·
n	·	·	·	·	·	·	Norsk	·	·
l	·	·	·	·	·	·	·	·	·
r	·	risk	·	·	·	·	·	·	·
w	·	whisk	·	·	·	·	·	·	·
j	·	·	[yesk]†	·	·	·	·	·	·
pl	·	·	·	·	·	·	·	·	·
pr	·	·	·	·	·	·	·	·	·
bl	·	·	·	·	·	·	·	·	·
br	·	brisk	·	·	·	·	·	(brusque)	(brus...
tr	·	·	·	·	·	·	·	·	·
tw	·	·	·	·	·	·	·	·	·
dr	·	·	·	·	·	·	·	·	·
kl	·	·	·	·	·	·	·	·	·
kr	·	·	·	·	·	·	·	·	·
kw	·	·	·	·	·	·	·	·	·
gl	·	glisk†	·	·	·	·	·	·	·
gr	·	·	·	·	·	·	·	·	·
fl	·	flisk†	·	(flask)	(flask)	·	·	·	·
fr	·	frisk	·	·	·	·	·	·	·
θr	·	·	·	·	·	·	·	·	·
sp	·	·	·	·	·	·	·	·	·
st	·	·	·	·	·	·	·	·	·
sk	·	·	·	·	·	·	·	·	·
sm	·	·	·	·	·	·	·	·	·
sn	·	·	·	·	·	·	·	·	·
sl	·	·	·	·	·	·	·	·	·
sw	·	·	·	·	·	·	·	·	·
ʃr	·	·	·	·	·	·	·	·	·
spl	·	·	·	·	·	·	·	·	·
spr	·	·	·	·	·	·	·	·	·
str	·	·	·	·	·	·	·	·	·
skr	·	·	·	·	·	·	·	·	·
skw	·	·	·	·	·	·	·	·	·

* homophones—see page 221.
  Total number of words—41

110

ʌ	ɜ/r	eɪ	oʊ	aɪ	aʊ	ɔɪ	i/ə/r	ɛ/ə/r	ju
.	.	.	.	.	.	.	.	.	.
.	.	.	.	.	.	.	.	.	.
busk	.	.	.	.	.	.	.	.	.
tusk	.	.	.	.	.	.	.	.	.
dusk	.	.	.	.	.	.	.	.	.
cusk	.	.	.	.	.	.	.	.	.
.	.	.	.	.	.	.	.	.	.
.	.	.	.	.	.	.	.	.	.
.	.	.	.	.	.	.	.	.	.
.	.	.	.	.	.	.	.	.	.
.	.	.	.	.	.	.	.	.	.
.	.	.	.	.	.	.	.	.	.
.	.	.	.	.	.	.	.	.	.
husk	.	.	.	.	.	.	.	.	.
.	.	.	.	.	.	.	.	.	.
musk	.	.	.	.	.	.	.	.	.
.	.	.	.	.	.	.	.	.	.
lusk†	.	.	.	.	.	.	.	.	.
rusk	.	.	.	.	.	.	.	.	.
.	.	.	.	.	.	.	.	.	.
.	.	.	.	.	.	.	.	.	.
.	.	.	.	.	.	.	.	.	.
(brusque)	.	.	.	.	.	.	.	.	.
.	.	.	.	.	.	.	.	.	.
.	.	.	.	.	.	.	.	.	.
.	.	.	.	.	.	.	.	.	.
.	.	.	.	.	.	.	.	.	.
.	.	.	.	.	.	.	.	.	.
.	.	.	.	.	.	.	.	.	.
.	.	.	.	.	.	.	.	.	.
.	.	.	.	.	.	.	.	.	.
.	.	.	.	.	.	.	.	.	.
.	.	.	.	.	.	.	.	.	.
.	.	.	.	.	.	.	.	.	.
.	.	.	.	.	.	.	.	.	.
.	.	.	.	.	.	.	.	.	.
.	.	.	.	.	.	.	.	.	.
.	.	.	.	.	.	.	.	.	.
.	.	.	.	.	.	.	.	.	.
.	.	.	.	.	.	.	.	.	.
.	.	.	.	.	.	.	.	.	.
.	.	.	.	.	.	.	.	.	.

Final—/skt/ . For inflected forms add /t/ to appropriate words, e.g. asked.
—/sks/ . For inflected forms add /s/ to appropriate words, e.g. asks.

111

	i	ɪ	ɛ	æ	ɑ	ɒ(ɑ(ɔ	ɔ	ʊ	u
—	.	*ink*	.	ankh	.	.	.	.	.
p	.	*pink*	[penk]	.	.	.	.	.	.
b	.	bink	.	bank*	.	.	.	.	.
t	.	tink	.	*tank*	.	.	.	.	.
d	.	dink	.	dank	.	.	.	.	.
k	.	kink	.	.	.	conch*	.	.	.
g	.	gink	.	.	.	.	.	.	.
f	.	.	.	fank	.	.	.	.	.
v	.	.	.	.	.	.	.	.	.
θ	.	think	.	thank	.	.	.	.	.
ð	.	.	.	.	.	.	.	.	.
s	.	*sink**	.	sank	.	.	.	.	.
z	.	zinc	.	.	.	.	.	.	.
ʃ	.	.	.	shank	.	.	.	.	.
ʒ	.	.	.	.	.	.	.	.	.
h	.	.	.	hank	.	honk	.	.	.
tʃ	.	chink*	.	chank	.	.	.	.	.
dʒ	.	jink	.	.	.	.	.	.	.
m	.	mink	.	.	.	.	.	.	.
n	.	.	.	.	.	.	.	.	.
l	.	link	.	lank	.	.	.	.	.
r	.	rink	.	rank*	.	.	.	.	.
w	.	wink	.	.	.	.	.	.	.
j	.	.	.	yank*	.	.	.	.	.
pl	.	.	.	plank	.	.	.	.	.
pr	.	prink	.	prank*	.	.	.	.	.
bl	.	blink	blenk	blank	.	.	.	.	.
br	.	brink	.	brank	.	.	.	.	.
tr	.	.	.	.	.	.	.	.	.
tw	.	twink	.	twank†	.	.	.	.	.
dr	.	drink	.	drank	.	.	.	.	.
kl	.	clink	.	clank	.	.	.	.	.
kr	.	.	.	crank	.	.	.	.	.
kw	.	.	.	.	.	.	.	.	.
gl	.	.	.	.	.	.	.	.	.
gr	.	.	.	.	.	.	.	.	.
fl	.	.	.	flank	.	.	.	.	.
fr	.	.	.	frank*	.	.	.	.	.
θr	.	.	.	.	.	.	.	.	.
sp	.	spink	.	spank	.	.	.	.	.
st	.	stink	.	stank	.	.	.	.	.
sk	.	skink	.	.	.	.	.	.	.
sm	.	.	.	.	.	.	.	.	.
sn	.	.	.	.	.	.	.	.	.
sl	.	slink	.	slank	.	.	.	.	.
sw	.	swink	.	swank	.	.	.	.	.
ʃr	.	shrink	.	shrank	.	.	.	.	.
spl	.	.	.	.	.	.	.	.	.
spr	.	.	.	.	.	.	.	.	.
str	.	.	.	.	.	.	.	.	.
skr	.	.	.	.	.	.	.	.	.
skw	.	.	.	.	.	.	.	.	.

* homophones—see pages 221–222.
   Total number of words—79

ʌ	ɜ/r	eɪ	oʊ	aɪ	aʊ	ɔɪ	i/ə/r	ɛ/ə/r	ju
.	.	.	.	.	.	.	.	.	.
punk	.	.	.	.	.	.	.	.	.
bunk	.	.	.	.	.	.	.	.	.
.	.	.	.	.	.	.	.	.	.
dunk	.	.	.	.	.	.	.	.	.
.	.	.	.	.	.	.	.	.	.
.	.	.	.	.	.	.	.	.	.
funk	.	.	.	.	.	.	.	.	.
.	.	.	.	.	.	.	.	.	.
.	.	.	.	.	.	.	.	.	.
sunk	.	.	.	.	.	.	.	.	.
.	.	.	.	.	.	.	.	.	.
.	.	.	.	.	.	.	.	.	.
.	.	.	.	.	.	.	.	.	.
hunk	.	.	.	.	.	.	.	.	.
chunk	.	.	.	.	.	.	.	.	.
junk	.	.	.	.	.	.	.	.	.
monk	.	.	.	.	.	.	.	.	.
.	.	.	.	.	.	.	.	.	.
.	.	.	.	.	.	.	.	.	.
.	.	.	.	.	.	.	.	.	.
.	.	.	.	.	.	.	.	.	.
plunk	.	.	.	.	.	.	.	.	.
.	.	.	.	.	.	.	.	.	.
blunk	.	.	.	.	.	.	.	.	.
.	.	.	.	.	.	.	.	.	.
trunk	.	.	.	.	.	.	.	.	.
.	.	.	.	.	.	.	.	.	.
drunk	.	.	.	.	.	.	.	.	.
.	.	.	.	.	.	.	.	.	.
.	.	.	.	.	.	.	.	.	.
.	.	.	.	.	.	.	.	.	.
.	.	.	.	.	.	.	.	.	.
flunk	.	.	.	.	.	.	.	.	.
.	.	.	.	.	.	.	.	.	.
.	.	.	.	.	.	.	.	.	.
spunk	.	.	.	.	.	.	.	.	.
stunk	.	.	.	.	.	.	.	.	.
skunk	.	.	.	.	.	.	.	.	.
.	.	.	.	.	.	.	.	.	.
.	.	.	.	.	.	.	.	.	.
slunk	.	.	.	.	.	.	.	.	.
.	.	.	.	.	.	.	.	.	.
shrunk	.	.	.	.	.	.	.	.	.
.	.	.	.	.	.	.	.	.	.
.	.	.	.	.	.	.	.	.	.
.	.	.	.	.	.	.	.	.	.
.	.	.	.	.	.	.	.	.	.
.	.	.	.	.	.	.	.	.	.

Final—/ŋkt/ . For inflected forms add /t/ to appropriate words, e.g. blinked.
—/ŋks/ . For inflected forms add /s/ to appropriate words, e.g. blinks.
. For uninflected forms, see page 233.

	i	ɪ	ɛ	æ	ɑ	ɒ	ɔ	ʊ	u
–	·	ilk	elk	·	·	·	·	·	·
p	·	·	·	·	·	·	·	·	·
b	·	bilk	·	·	·	·	(balk)	·	·
t	·	·	·	talc	·	·	·	·	·
d	·	·	·	·	·	·	·	·	·
k	·	·	kelk	[calque]	·	·	·	·	·
g	·	·	·	·	·	·	·	·	·
f	·	·	·	·	·	·	·	Fulk	·
v	·	·	·	·	·	·	·	·	·
θ	·	·	·	·	·	·	·	·	·
ð	·	thilk†	·	·	·	·	·	·	·
s	·	silk	·	·	·	·	·	·	·
z	·	·	·	·	·	·	·	·	·
ʃ	·	·	·	·	·	·	·	·	·
ʒ	·	·	·	·	·	·	·	·	·
h	·	·	·	·	·	·	·	·	·
tʃ	·	·	·	·	·	·	·	·	·
dʒ	·	·	·	·	·	·	·	·	·
m	·	milk	·	·	·	·	·	·	·
n	·	·	·	·	·	·	·	·	·
l	·	·	·	·	·	·	·	·	·
r	·	·	·	·	·	·	·	·	·
w	·	[whilk]*†	whelk*	·	·	·	·	·	·
j	·	·	[yelk]	·	·	·	·	·	·
pl	·	·	·	·	·	·	·	·	·
pr	·	·	·	·	·	·	·	·	·
bl	·	·	·	·	·	·	·	·	·
br	·	·	·	·	·	·	·	·	·
tr	·	·	·	·	·	·	·	·	·
tw	·	·	·	·	·	·	·	·	·
dr	·	·	·	·	·	·	·	·	·
kl	·	·	·	·	·	·	·	·	·
kr	·	·	·	·	·	·	·	·	·
kw	·	·	·	·	·	·	·	·	·
gl	·	·	·	·	·	·	·	·	·
gr	·	·	·	·	·	·	·	·	·
fl	·	·	·	·	·	·	·	·	·
fr	·	·	·	·	·	·	·	·	·
θr	·	·	·	·	·	·	·	·	·
sp	·	·	·	·	·	·	·	·	·
st	·	·	·	·	·	·	·	·	·
sk	·	·	·	·	·	·	·	·	·
sm	·	·	·	·	·	·	·	·	·
sn	·	·	·	·	·	·	·	·	·
sl	·	·	·	·	·	·	·	·	·
sw	·	·	·	·	·	·	·	·	·
ʃr	·	·	·	·	·	·	·	·	·
spl	·	·	·	·	·	·	·	·	·
spr	·	·	·	·	·	·	·	·	·
str	·	·	·	·	·	·	·	·	·
skr	·	·	·	·	·	·	·	·	·
skw	·	·	·	·	·	·	·	·	·

* homophones—see page 222.
  Total number of words—19

ʌ	ɜ/r	ɪə	oʊ	aɪ	aʊ	ɔɪ	i/ə/r	ɛ/ə/r	ju
·	·	·	·	·	·	·	·	·	·
·	·	·	polk	·	·	·	·	·	·
bulk	·	·	·	·	·	·	·	·	·
·	·	·	·	·	·	·	·	·	·
·	·	·	·	·	·	·	·	·	·
·	·	·	·	·	·	·	·	·	·
·	·	·	·	·	·	·	·	·	·
·	·	·	·	·	·	·	·	·	·
·	·	·	·	·	·	·	·	·	·
sulk	·	·	·	·	·	·	·	·	·
·	·	·	·	·	·	·	·	·	·
·	·	·	·	·	·	·	·	·	·
·	·	·	·	·	·	·	·	·	·
hulk	·	·	·	·	·	·	·	·	·
·	·	·	·	·	·	·	·	·	·
·	·	·	·	·	·	·	·	·	·
·	·	·	·	·	·	·	·	·	·
·	·	·	·	·	·	·	·	·	·
·	·	·	·	·	·	·	·	·	·
·	·	·	·	·	·	·	·	·	·
·	·	·	·	·	·	·	·	·	·
·	·	·	·	·	·	·	·	·	·
·	·	·	·	·	·	·	·	·	·
·	·	·	·	·	·	·	·	·	·
·	·	·	·	·	·	·	·	·	·
·	·	·	·	·	·	·	·	·	·
·	·	·	·	·	·	·	·	·	·
·	·	·	·	·	·	·	·	·	·
·	·	·	·	·	·	·	·	·	·
·	·	·	·	·	·	·	·	·	·
·	·	·	·	·	·	·	·	·	·
·	·	·	·	·	·	·	·	·	·
·	·	·	·	·	·	·	·	·	·
·	·	·	·	·	·	·	·	·	·
·	·	·	·	·	·	·	·	·	·
·	·	·	·	·	·	·	·	·	·
·	·	·	·	·	·	·	·	·	·
skulk	·	·	·	·	·	·	·	·	·
·	·	·	·	·	·	·	·	·	·
·	·	·	·	·	·	·	·	·	·
·	·	·	·	·	·	·	·	·	·
·	·	·	·	·	·	·	·	·	·
·	·	·	·	·	·	·	·	·	·
·	·	·	·	·	·	·	·	·	·
·	·	·	·	·	·	·	·	·	·

Final—/lkt/ . For inflected forms add /t/ to appropriate words, e.g. milked.
—/lks/ . For inflected forms add /s/ to appropriate words, e.g. milks.

	i	ɪ	ɛ	æ	ɑ	ɒ(ɑ(ɔ	ɔ	ʊ	u
–	·	·	elf	Alf	·	·	·	·	·
p	·	·	pelf	·	·	·	·	·	·
b	·	·	·	·	·	·	·	·	·
t	·	·	·	·	·	·	·	·	·
d	·	·	delf*	·	·	·	·	·	·
k	·	·	·	·	·	·	·	·	·
g	·	·	·	·	·	(golf)	·	·	·
f	·	·	·	·	·	·	·	·	·
v	·	·	·	·	·	·	·	·	·
θ	·	·	·	·	·	·	·	·	·
ð	·	·	·	·	·	·	·	·	·
s	·	sylph	self	·	·	·	·	·	·
z	·	·	·	·	·	·	·	·	·
ʃ	·	·	shelf	·	·	·	·	·	·
ʒ	·	·	·	·	·	·	·	·	·
h	·	·	·	·	·	·	·	·	·
tʃ	·	·	·	·	·	·	·	·	·
dʒ	·	·	·	·	·	·	·	·	·
m	·	·	·	·	·	·	·	·	·
n	·	·	·	·	·	·	·	·	·
l	·	·	·	·	·	·	·	·	·
r	·	·	·	Ralph	·	(Rolfe)	·	·	·
w	·	Wilf	·	·	·	·	·	·	*wolf**
j	·	·	·	·	·	·	·	·	·
pl	·	·	·	·	·	·	·	·	·
pr	·	·	·	·	·	·	·	·	·
bl	·	·	·	·	·	·	·	·	·
br	·	·	·	·	·	·	·	·	·
tr	·	·	·	·	·	·	·	·	·
tw	·	·	·	·	·	·	·	·	·
dr	·	·	·	·	·	·	·	·	·
kl	·	·	·	·	·	·	·	·	·
kr	·	·	·	·	·	·	·	·	·
kw	·	·	·	·	·	·	·	·	·
gl	·	·	·	·	·	·	·	·	·
gr	·	·	·	·	·	·	·	·	·
fl	·	·	·	·	·	·	·	·	·
fr	·	·	·	·	·	·	·	·	·
θr	·	·	·	·	·	·	·	·	·
sp	·	·	·	·	·	·	·	·	·
st	·	·	·	·	·	·	·	·	·
sk	·	·	·	·	·	·	·	·	·
sm	·	·	·	·	·	·	·	·	·
sn	·	·	·	·	·	·	·	·	·
sl	·	·	·	·	·	·	·	·	·
sw	·	·	·	·	·	·	·	·	·
ʃr	·	·	·	·	·	·	·	·	·
spl	·	·	·	·	·	·	·	·	·
spr	·	·	·	·	·	·	·	·	·
str	·	·	·	·	·	·	·	·	·
skr	·	·	·	·	·	·	·	·	·
skw	·	·	·	·	·	·	·	·	·

* homophones—see page 222.
Total number of words—14

ʌ	ɜ/r	eɪ	oʊ	aɪ	aʊ	ɔɪ	i/ə/r	ɛ/ə/r	ju
·	·	·	·	·	·	·	·	·	·
·	·	·	·	·	·	·	·	·	·
·	·	·	·	·	·	·	·	·	·
·	·	·	·	·	·	·	·	·	·
gulf	·	·	·	·	·	·	·	·	·
·	·	·	·	·	·	·	·	·	·
·	·	·	·	·	·	·	·	·	·
·	·	·	·	·	·	·	·	·	·
·	·	·	·	·	·	·	·	·	·
·	·	·	·	·	·	·	·	·	·
·	·	·	·	·	·	·	·	·	·
·	·	·	·	·	·	·	·	·	·
·	·	·	·	·	·	·	·	·	·
·	·	·	·	·	·	·	·	·	·
·	·	·	(Rolfe)	·	·	·	·	·	·
·	·	·	·	·	·	·	·	·	·

Final—/lft/ . For inflected forms add /t/ to appropriate words, e.g. golfed.
—/lfs/ . For inflected forms add /s/ to appropriate words, e.g. golfs.

	i	ɪ	ɛ	æ	ɑ/r	ɒ(ɑ	ɔ/r	ʊ	u
–	ekes	.	*X*	*axe*	arcs*	*ox*	orcs*	.	.
p	peeks*	pyx*	pecs*	pax*	parks	pox*	pawks†	pooks*†	.
b	beaks	.	becks*	backs	barques*	*box*	baulks	*books*	.
t	teaks	tics*	'tecs†	tax*	.	.	torques*	.	.
d	.	.	decks	.	dhaks	docks	[dawks]	(doucs)	dooks
k	keeks†	kicks	kex*	.	carks†	cox*	calks*	cooks	.
g	.	.	gecks	.	.	.	gawks	.	.
f	feaks	fix	.	.	.	*fox*	forks*	.	.
v	.	.	vex	.	.	vox	.	.	.
θ	.	.	.	[thacks]†	.	.	.	.	.
ð	.	.	.	.	.	.	.	.	.
s	(Sikhs)*	*six*	sex	sax*	[sarks]†	*socks*	.	.	.
z	.	.	.	[zax]†	.	.	.	.	zooks
ʃ	(sheiks)	.	.	shacks	*sharks*	(shoughs)*	.	.	.
ʒ	.	.	.	.	.	.	.	.	.
h	.	hicks	hecks†	hacks	harks	hox*†	hawks	hooks	.
tʃ	cheeks	*chicks*	checks*	.	charks*	chocks	chalks	*chooks*	.
dʒ	.	.	.	jaks*	.	.	.	.	jouks*
m	.	mix	.	max*†	marques*†	mocks	mawks	.	.
n	.	nix*	neks*	knacks	narks	nocks*	.	nooks	.
l	leaks*	licks	Lex	lax*	larks	lox*	lawks†	looks	(luxe)
r	wreaks*†	ricks*	rex*	racks*	.	rocs*	.	rooks	[rukhs
w	weeks	wicks	[wex]†	wax*	[warks]†	[wox]†	walks*	.	.
j	.	.	[yex]†	yaks	jarks†	.	.	.	[yukes
pl	.	.	.	(plaques)*	(placks)*	.	.	.	.
pr	.	pricks	prex†	.	.	.	.	.	.
bl	bleaks	.	.	blacks	.	*blocks*	.	.	.
br	breeks†	*bricks*	.	bracks	.	brocks*	.	brooks	.
tr	.	tricks	treks	tracks	.	[trocks]†	.	.	.
tw	tweeks	.	.	.	.	.	.	.	.
dr	.	.	.	.	.	.	.	.	.
kl	cleeks*†	clicks*	clecks†	clacks	(clerks)*	*clocks*	.	.	.
kr	creaks*	cricks*	.	Crax*	.	crocks	.	crooks	.
kw	.	.	.	quacks	quarks†	.	.	.	.
gl	gleeks†	.	.	.	.	.	Glaux	.	.
gr	Greeks	.	grecques	.	.	.	.	.	.
fl	.	flix*	flex*	flax	.	Phlox*	.	.	flukes
fr	freaks	.	.	.	.	*frocks*	.	.	.
θr	.	.	.	.	.	.	.	.	.
sp	speaks	spicks	specs*†	.	sparks*	.	.	.	spook
st	steeks†	Styx*	.	stacks	starks	stocks	storks*	stooks	.
sk	.	.	.	.	.	.	.	.	.
sm	.	.	.	smacks	.	smocks	.	.	.
sn	sneaks	snicks	snecks†	snacks	snarks	.	.	snooks	[snoek
sl	sleeks	slicks	.	slacks	.	.	.	.	.
sw	.	.	.	.	.	.	.	.	.
ʃr	shrieks	.	.	.	.	.	.	.	.
spl	.	.	.	.	.	.	.	.	.
spr	.	.	.	.	.	.	.	.	.
str	streeks*†	.	.	.	.	.	.	.	.
skr	screaks	.	.	.	.	.	.	.	.
skw	squeaks	.	.	.	.	.	squawks	.	.

* homophones—see page 222.
  Total number of words—292

ʌ	ɜ/r	eɪ	oʊ	aɪ	aʊ	ɔɪ	i/ə/r	ɛ/ə/r	ju
.	irks	aches	oaks*	.	.	.	.	.	.
pucks	perks	paiks	pokes	pikes	.	.	.	.	pukes
bucks	burkes*	bakes	.	bykes*†	.	.	.	.	.
tucks*	Turks	takes	toques	tykes	.	.	.	.	tuques
dux*	[dirkes]*†.	.	.	dykes	.	.	.	.	(dukes)
.	kirks†	*cakes*	coax*	.	.	.	.	.	.
.	.	.	.	.	gowks†	.	.	.	.
.	firks	faikes*	folks	fykes*†	.	.	.	.	.
.	.	.	.	.	.	.	.	.	.
.	.	.	.	.	.	.	.	.	.
sucks	[serks]*†	sakes	soaks*	sikes†	.	.	.	.	.
shucks	shirks	shakes*	.	.	.	.	.	.	.
hucks	.	hakes	hoax*	haiks*	howks†	hoicks*†	.	.	.
chucks	chirks	.	chokes	.	.	.	.	.	.
.	jerques*	jakes†	jokes	.	.	.	.	.	.
mux*†	merks	makes*	mokes†	mikes	.	.	.	.	.
.	.	.	.	.	.	.	.	.	[neuks]†
lux*	lurks	lakes*	.	likes	.	.	.	.	.
rucks	.	raiks*	rokes	.	.	.	.	.	.
.	works	wakes	.	.	.	.	.	.	.
[yucks]†	yerks†	.	yokes*	.	.	yoiks†	.	.	.
plucks	.	.	.	.	.	.	.	.	.
.	.	.	prokes†	.	.	.	.	.	.
.	.	.	blockes†	.	.	.	.	.	.
.	.	breaks*	.	.	.	.	.	.	.
trucks	.	traiks†	[trokes]†	trikes	.	.	.	.	.
.	.	drakes	.	.	.	.	.	.	.
clucks	(clerks)	.	cloaks	.	.	.	.	.	.
crux	.	crakes†	croaks	.	.	.	.	.	.
.	quirks	quakes	.	.	.	.	.	.	.
.	.	glaiks†	.	[glikes]†	.	.	.	.	.
flux	.	flakes	.	.	.	.	.	.	.
.	.	.	.	.	.	.	.	.	.
.	.	.	spokes	spikes	.	.	.	.	.
.	stirks	stakes*	stokes	.	.	.	.	.	.
.	smirks	smaiks†	smokes	.	.	.	.	.	.
.	.	*snakes*	[snokes]	.	[snowks]†	.	.	.	.
.	.	slakes	.	.	.	.	.	.	.
.	.	.	.	shrikes	.	.	.	.	.
.	.	straiks†	strokes	strikes	.	.	.	.	.
.	.	.	.	scrikes†	.	.	.	.	.

Final—/kst/ . For inflected forms add /t/ to appropriate words, e.g. fixed.

119

	i	ɪ	ɛ	æ	ɑ	ɒ(ɑ	ɔ(ɑ(ɒ	ʊ	u
–	·	·	·		·		·		·
p	·	·	pence	·	[panse]†	·	[paunce]†	·	·
b	·	·	·	·	·	·	·	·	·
t	·	·	tense	·	·	·	·	·	·
d	·	·	dense	(dance)	(dance)	·	·	·	·
k	·	·	·	·	kans	·	·	·	·
g	·	·	·	·	·	·	·	·	·
f	·	·	*fence*	·	·	·	·	·	·
v	·	·	·	·	·	·	[vaunce]†	·	·
θ	·	·	·	·	·	·	·	·	·
ð	·	·	thence	·	·	·	·	·	·
s	·	since	sense*	·	·	sonse	·	·	·
z	·	·	·	·	·	·	·	·	·
ʃ	·	·	·	·	·	·	·	·	·
ʒ	·	·	·	·	·	·	·	·	·
h	·	·	hence	Hanse*	hance†	·	·	·	·
tʃ	·	·	·	(chance)	(chance)	·	chaunce	·	·
dʒ	·	·	·	·	[jaunce]	·	[jaunce]	·	·
m	·	mince	mense	manse	·	·	·	·	·
n	·	·	·	·	·	nonce	·	·	·
l	·	·	·	(lance)	(lance)*	·	(launce)	·	·
r	·	rinse	·	(rance)	(rance)	·	·	·	·
w	·	wince	whence	·	·	·	·	·	·
j	·	yince†	·	·	·	·	·	·	·
pl	·	·	·	·	·	·	·	·	·
pr	·	prince	·	(prance)	(prance)	·	·	·	·
bl	·	·	·	·	·	·	·	·	·
br	·	·	·	·	·	·	·	·	·
tr	·	·	·	(trance)	(trance)	·	·	·	·
tw	·	·	·	·	·	·	·	·	·
dr	·	·	·	·	·	·	·	·	·
kl	·	·	·	·	·	·	·	·	·
kr	·	·	·	·	·	·	·	·	·
kw	·	quince	·	·	·	·	·	·	·
gl	·	·	·	(glance)	(glance)	·	·	·	·
gr	·	·	·	·	·	·	·	·	·
fl	·	·	[flense]	·	·	·	·	·	·
fr	·	·	·	(France)	(France)	·	·	·	·
θr	·	·	·	·	·	·	·	·	·
sp	·	·	spence	·	·	·	·	·	·
st	·	·	·	(stance)	(stance)	·	·	·	·
sk	·	·	·	·	·	sconce	·	·	·
sm	·	·	·	·	·	·	·	·	·
sn	·	·	·	·	·	·	·	·	·
sl	·	·	·	·	·	·	·	·	·
sw	·	·	·	·	·	·	·	·	·
ʃr	·	·	·	·	·	·	·	·	·
spl	·	·	·	·	·	·	·	·	·
spr	·	·	·	·	·	·	·	·	·
str	·	·	·	·	·	·	·	·	·
skr	·	·	·	·	·	·	·	·	·
skw	·	·	·	·	·	·	·	·	·

* homophones—see page 222.
  Total number of words—62

ʌ	ɜ/r	eɪ	oʊ	aɪ	aʊ	ɔɪ	i/ə/r	ɛ/ə/r	ju
[unce]†	.	.	.	.	ounce	.	.	.	.
punce	.	.	.	.	pounce	.	.	.	.
.	.	.	.	.	bounce	.	.	.	.
.	.	.	.	.	.	.	.	.	.
dunce	.	.	.	.	.	.	.	.	.
.	.	.	.	.	.	.	.	.	.
.	.	.	.	.	.	.	.	.	.
.	.	.	.	.	.	.	.	.	.
.	.	.	.	.	.	.	.	.	.
.	.	.	.	.	.	.	.	.	.
.	.	.	.	.	.	.	.	.	.
.	.	.	.	.	.	.	.	.	.
.	.	.	.	.	.	.	.	.	.
.	.	.	.	.	.	.	.	.	.
.	.	.	.	.	jounce	.	.	.	.
.	.	.	.	.	.	.	.	.	.
.	.	.	.	.	.	.	.	.	.
.	.	.	.	.	rounce	.	.	.	.
once	.	.	.	.	.	.	.	.	.
.	.	.	.	.	.	.	.	.	.
.	.	.	.	.	.	.	.	.	.
.	.	.	.	.	.	.	.	.	.
.	.	.	.	.	.	.	.	.	.
.	.	.	.	.	.	.	.	.	.
.	.	.	.	.	.	.	.	.	.
.	.	.	.	.	.	.	creance	.	.
.	.	.	.	.	.	.	.	.	.
.	.	.	.	.	.	.	.	.	.
.	.	.	.	.	.	.	.	.	.
.	.	.	.	.	flounce	.	.	.	.
.	.	.	.	.	frounce	.	.	.	.
.	.	.	.	.	.	.	.	.	.
.	.	.	.	.	.	.	.	.	.
.	.	.	.	.	.	.	.	.	.
.	.	.	.	.	.	.	.	.	.
.	.	.	.	.	.	.	.	.	.
.	.	.	.	.	.	.	.	.	.
.	.	.	.	.	.	.	.	.	.
.	.	.	.	.	.	.	.	.	.
.	.	.	.	.	.	.	.	.	.

Final—/nst/ . For inflected forms add /t/ to appropriate words, e.g. danced.

	i	ɪ	ɛ	æ	ɑ	ɒ	ɔ(ɑ(ɒ)	ʊ	u
—	.	inch	.	.	.	.		.	.
p	.	pinch	.	.	.	.	paunch	.	.
b	.	.	bench	.	.	.		.	.
t	.	.	tench	.	.	.		.	.
d	.	.	.	.	.	.		.	.
k	.	.	.	.	.	.		.	.
g	.	.	.	.	[ganch]	.	[gaunch]	.	.
f	.	finch	.	.	.	.		.	.
v	.	.	.	.	.	.		.	.
θ	.	.	.	.	.	.		.	.
ð	.	.	.	.	.	.		.	.
s	.	cinch	.	.	.	.		.	.
z	.	.	.	.	.	.		.	.
ʃ	.	.	.	.	.	.		.	.
ʒ	.	.	.	.	.	.		.	.
h	.	.	.	(hanch)	(hanch)	.	haunch	.	.
tʃ	.	chinch	.	.	.	.		.	.
dʒ	.	.	.	.	.	.		.	.
m	.	.	.	(manche)	(manche)	.		.	.
n	.	.	.	.	.	.		.	.
l	.	lynch*	.	[lanch]†	.	.	launch	.	.
r	.	.	wrench	(ranch)	(ranch)	.	raunch	.	.
w	.	winch	wench	.	.	.		.	.
j	.	.	.	.	.	.		.	.
pl	.	.	.	.	planch†	.		.	.
pr	.	.	.	.	.	.		.	.
bl	.	.	blench	(Blanche)*	(blanch)*	.		.	.
br	.	.	.	(branch)	(branch)	.		.	.
tr	.	.	trench	.	.	.		.	.
tw	.	.	.	.	.	.		.	.
dr	.	.	drench	.	.	.		.	.
kl	.	clinch	clench	.	.	.		.	.
kr	.	.	.	.	[cranch]	.	[craunch]	.	.
kw	.	quinche†	quench	.	.	.		.	.
gl	.	.	.	.	.	.		.	.
gr	.	.	.	.	.	.		.	.
fl	.	flinch	flench	(flanch)	(flanch)	.		.	.
fr	.	.	French	.	.	.		.	.
θr	.	.	.	.	.	.		.	.
sp	.	.	.	.	.	.		.	.
st	.	.	stench	.	[stanch]	.	[staunch]	.	.
sk	.	.	.	.	.	.		.	.
sm	.	.	.	.	.	.		.	.
sn	.	.	.	.	.	.		.	.
sl	.	.	.	.	.	.		.	.
sw	.	.	.	.	.	.		.	.
ʃr	.	.	.	.	.	.		.	.
spl	.	.	.	.	.	.		.	.
spr	.	.	.	.	.	.		.	.
str	.	.	.	.	.	.		.	.
skr	.	.	.	scranch	.	.		.	.
skw	.	squinch	.	.	.	.		.	.

* homophones—see page 223.
  Total number of words—60

ʌ	ɜ/r	eɪ	oʊ	aɪ	aʊ	ɔɪ	i/ə/r	ɛ/ə/r	ju
punch*									
bunch									
duncht†									
hunch		[hainch]							
munch									
lunch									
runch									
brunch									
clunch									
[crunch]									
scrunch									

Final—/n(t)ʃt/ . For inflected forms add /t/ to appropriate words, e.g. punched.

	i	ɪ	ɛ	æ	ɑ	ɒ	ɔ	ʊ	u
—	.	.	.	.	.	.	.	.	.
p	peenge†	.	.	.	.	.	.	.	.
b	.	binge	benj	.	.	.	.	.	.
t	.	tinge	.	.	.	.	.	.	.
d	.	dinge†	.	.	.	.	.	.	.
k	.	.	.	.	.	.	.	.	.
g	.	.	.	.	.	.	.	.	.
f	.	.	.	.	.	.	.	.	.
v	.	.	venge†	.	.	.	.	.	.
θ	.	.	.	.	.	.	.	.	.
ð	.	.	.	.	.	.	.	.	.
s	.	singe	.	.	.	.	.	.	.
z	.	.	.	.	.	.	.	.	.
ʃ	.	.	.	.	.	.	.	.	.
ʒ	.	.	.	.	.	.	.	.	.
h	.	hinge	.	.	.	.	.	.	.
tʃ	.	.	.	.	.	.	.	.	.
dʒ	.	.	.	.	.	.	.	.	.
m	.	.	[menge]†	.	.	.	.	.	.
n	.	.	.	.	.	.	.	.	.
l	.	.	.	.	.	.	.	.	.
r	.	.	.	.	.	.	[raunge]†	.	.
w	.	whinge	.	.	.	.	.	.	.
j	.	.	.	.	.	.	.	.	.
pl	.	.	.	.	.	.	.	.	.
pr	.	.	.	.	.	.	.	.	.
bl	.	.	.	.	.	.	.	.	.
br	.	.	.	.	.	.	.	.	.
tr	.	.	.	.	.	.	.	.	.
tw	.	twinge	.	.	.	.	.	.	.
dr	.	.	.	.	.	.	.	.	.
kl	.	.	.	.	.	.	.	.	.
kr	.	cringe	.	.	.	.	.	.	.
kw	.	.	.	.	.	.	.	.	.
gl	.	.	.	.	.	.	.	.	.
gr	.	.	.	.	.	.	.	.	.
fl	.	.	.	flange	.	.	.	.	.
fr	.	fringe	.	.	.	.	.	.	.
θr	.	.	.	.	.	.	.	.	.
sp	.	.	.	.	.	.	.	.	.
st	.	.	.	.	.	.	.	.	.
sk	.	.	.	.	.	.	.	.	.
sm	.	.	.	.	.	.	.	.	.
sn	.	.	.	.	.	.	.	.	.
sl	.	.	.	.	.	.	.	.	.
sw	.	swinge	.	.	.	.	.	.	.
ʃr	.	.	.	.	.	.	.	.	.
spl	.	.	.	.	.	.	.	.	.
spr	.	springe	.	.	.	.	.	.	.
str	.	.	.	.	.	.	[straunge]†	.	.
skr	.	.	.	.	.	.	.	.	.
skw	.	.	.	.	.	.	.	.	.

* homophones—see page 223.
  Total number of words—28

ʌ	ɜ/r	eɪ	oʊ	aɪ	aʊ	ɔɪ	i/ə/r	ɛ/ə/r	ju
.	.	.	.	.	.	.	.	.	.
.	.	.	.	.	.	.	.	.	.
.	.	.	.	.	.	.	.	.	.
.	.	.	.	.	.	.	.	.	.
.	.	.	.	.	.	.	.	.	.
.	.	.	.	.	.	.	.	.	.
.	.	.	.	.	.	.	.	.	.
.	.	.	.	.	.	.	.	.	.
.	.	.	.	.	.	.	.	.	.
.	.	.	.	.	.	.	.	.	.
.	.	.	.	.	.	.	.	.	.
.	.	.	.	.	.	.	.	.	.
.	.	change	.	.	.	.	.	.	.
.	.	.	.	.	.	.	.	.	.
.	.	mange	.	.	.	.	.	.	.
.	.	.	.	.	.	.	.	.	.
lunge*	.	.	.	.	lounge	.	.	.	.
.	.	range	.	.	.	.	.	.	.
.	.	.	.	.	.	.	.	.	.
plunge	.	.	.	.	.	.	.	.	.
.	.	.	.	.	.	.	.	.	.
.	.	.	.	.	.	.	.	.	.
.	.	.	.	.	.	.	.	.	.
.	.	.	.	.	.	.	.	.	.
.	.	.	.	.	.	.	.	.	.
.	.	.	.	.	.	.	.	.	.
.	.	.	.	.	.	.	.	.	.
.	.	.	.	.	.	.	.	.	.
.	.	grange	.	.	.	.	.	.	.
.	.	.	.	.	.	.	.	.	.
sponge	.	.	.	.	.	.	.	.	.
.	.	.	.	.	.	.	.	.	.
.	.	.	.	.	.	.	.	.	.
.	.	.	.	.	.	.	.	.	.
.	.	.	.	.	.	.	.	.	.
.	.	.	.	.	.	.	.	.	.
.	.	strange	.	.	.	.	.	.	.
.	.	.	.	.	scrounge	.	.	.	.
.	.	.	.	.	.	.	.	.	.

Final—/n(d)ʒd/ . For inflected forms add /d/ to appropriate words, e.g. changed.

	i	ɪ	ɛ	æ	ɑ	ɒ(ɑ	ɔ	ʊ	u
–	·	·	·	atom	·	·	autumn	·	·
p	·	·	·	·	·	·	·	·	·
b	·	·	·	·	·	bottom	·	·	·
t	·	·	·	·	·	·	·	·	·
d	·	·	·	·	(datum)	·	·	·	·
k	·	·	·	·	·	·	·	·	·
g	·	·	·	·	·	·	·	·	·
f	·	·	·	·	·	·	·	·	·
v	·	·	·	·	·	·	·	·	·
θ	·	·	·	·	·	·	·	·	·
ð	·	·	·	·	·	·	·	·	·
s	·	·	·	·	·	·	·	·	·
z	·	·	·	·	·	·	·	·	·
ʃ	·	shittim	·	·	·	·	·	·	·
ʒ	·	·	·	·	·	·	·	·	·
h	·	·	·	·	·	·	·	·	·
tʃ	·	·	·	·	·	·	·	·	·
dʒ	·	·	·	·	·	·	·	·	·
m	·	·	·	·	·	·	·	·	·
n	gnetum	·	·	·	·	·	·	·	·
l	·	·	·	·	·	·	·	·	·
r	·	·	·	·	·	·	·	·	·
w	·	·	·	·	·	·	·	·	·
j	·	·	·	·	·	·	·	·	·
pl	·	·	·	·	·	·	·	·	·
pr	·	·	·	·	·	·	·	·	·
bl	·	·	·	·	·	·	·	·	·
br	·	·	·	·	·	·	·	·	·
tr	·	·	·	·	·	·	·	·	·
tw	·	·	·	·	·	·	·	·	·
dr	·	·	·	·	·	·	·	·	·
kl	·	·	·	·	·	·	·	·	·
kr	·	·	·	·	·	·	·	·	·
kw	·	·	·	·	·	·	·	·	·
gl	·	·	·	·	·	·	·	·	·
gr	·	·	·	·	·	·	·	·	·
fl	·	·	·	·	·	·	·	·	·
fr	·	·	·	·	·	·	·	·	·
θr	·	·	·	·	·	·	·	·	·
sp	·	·	·	·	·	·	·	·	·
st	·	·	·	·	·	·	·	·	·
sk	·	·	·	·	·	·	·	·	·
sm	·	·	·	·	·	·	·	·	·
sn	·	·	·	·	·	·	·	·	·
sl	·	·	·	·	·	·	·	·	·
sw	·	·	·	·	·	·	·	·	·
ʃr	·	·	·	·	·	·	·	·	·
spl	·	·	·	·	·	·	·	·	·
spr	·	·	·	·	·	·	·	·	·
str	·	·	Streatham.	·	(stratum)	·	·	·	·
skr	·	·	·	·	·	·	·	·	·
skw	·	·	·	·	·	·	·	·	·

Total number of words—16

ʌ	ɜ/r	eɪ	oʊ	aɪ	aʊ	ɔɪ	i/ə/r	ɛ/ə/r	ju
.	.	.	.	item	.	.	.	.	.
.	.	.	.	.	.	.	.	.	.
.	.	.	totem	.	.	.	.	.	.
.	.	datum	.	.	.	.	.	.	.
.	.	.	.	.	.	.	.	.	.
.	.	.	.	.	.	.	.	.	.
.	.	.	.	.	.	.	.	.	.
.	.	.	.	.	.	.	.	.	.
.	.	.	.	.	.	.	.	.	.
.	.	.	.	.	.	.	.	.	.
.	.	.	.	.	.	.	.	.	.
.	.	.	.	.	.	.	.	.	.
.	.	.	.	.	.	.	.	.	.
.	.	.	.	.	.	.	.	.	.
.	.	.	.	.	.	.	.	.	.
.	.	.	notum	.	.	.	.	.	.
.	.	.	.	.	.	.	.	.	.
.	.	.	.	.	.	.	.	.	.
.	.	.	.	.	.	.	.	.	.
.	.	.	.	.	.	.	.	.	.
.	.	.	.	.	.	.	.	.	.
.	.	.	.	.	.	.	.	.	.
.	.	.	.	.	.	.	.	.	.
.	.	.	.	.	.	.	.	.	.
.	.	.	.	.	.	.	.	.	.
.	.	.	.	.	.	.	.	.	.
.	.	.	.	.	.	.	.	.	.
.	.	.	.	.	.	.	.	.	.
.	.	.	.	.	.	.	.	.	.
.	.	.	.	.	.	.	.	.	.
.	.	.	.	.	.	.	.	.	.
.	.	.	.	.	.	.	.	.	sputum
.	.	.	.	.	.	.	.	.	.
.	.	.	.	.	.	.	.	.	scutum†
.	.	.	.	.	.	.	.	.	.
.	.	.	.	.	.	.	.	.	.
.	.	.	.	.	.	.	.	.	.
.	.	.	.	.	.	.	.	.	.
.	.	(stratum).	.	.	.	.	.	.	.
.	.	.	scrotum	.	.	.	.	.	.
.	.	.	.	.	.	.	.	.	.

Final—/tmd/ . For inflected forms add /d/ to appropriate words, e.g. bottomed.
—/tmz/ . For inflected forms add /z/ to appropriate words, e.g. bottoms.

	i	ɪ	ɛ	æ	ɑ	ɒ(ɑ	ɔ	ʊ	u
–	·	·	·	alum	·	·	·	·	·
p	·	·	·	·	·	·	·	·	·
b	·	·	·	Balham	·	·	·	·	·
t	·	·	·	·	·	·	·	·	·
d	·	·	·	·	·	·	·	·	·
k	·	·	·	·	·	column	·	·	·
g	·	·	·	·	·	·	·	·	·
f	·	·	phellem†	·	·	·	·	Fulham	·
v	velum	·	vellum	vallum	·	·	·	·	·
θ	·	·	·	·	·	·	·	·	·
ð	·	·	·	·	·	·	·	·	·
s	·	·	·	·	·	solemn	·	·	·
z	·	·	·	·	·	·	·	·	·
ʃ	·	·	·	·	·	·	·	·	·
ʒ	·	·	·	·	·	·	·	·	·
h	·	·	·	·	·	·	·	·	·
tʃ	·	chillum	·	·	·	·	·	·	·
dʒ	·	·	·	·	·	·	·	·	·
m	·	·	·	·	·	·	·	·	·
n	·	·	·	·	·	·	·	·	·
l	·	·	·	·	·	·	·	·	·
r	·	·	·	·	·	·	·	·	·
w	·	·	·	·	·	·	·	·	·
j	·	·	·	·	·	·	·	·	·
pl	·	·	·	·	·	·	·	·	·
pr	·	·	·	·	·	·	·	·	·
bl	·	·	·	·	·	·	·	·	·
br	·	·	·	·	·	·	·	·	·
tr	·	·	·	·	·	·	·	·	·
tw	·	·	·	·	·	·	·	·	·
dr	·	·	·	·	·	·	·	·	·
kl	·	·	·	·	·	·	·	·	·
kr	·	·	·	·	·	·	·	·	·
kw	·	·	·	·	·	·	·	·	·
gl	·	·	·	·	·	·	·	·	·
gr	·	·	·	·	·	·	·	·	·
fl	·	·	·	·	·	·	·	·	·
fr	·	·	·	·	·	·	·	·	·
θr	·	·	·	·	·	·	·	·	·
sp	·	·	·	·	·	·	·	·	·
st	·	·	·	·	·	·	·	·	·
sk	·	·	skellum†	·	·	·	·	·	·
sm	·	·	·	·	·	·	·	·	·
sn	·	·	·	·	·	·	·	·	·
sl	·	·	·	·	slalom	·	·	·	·
sw	·	·	·	·	·	·	·	·	·
ʃr	·	·	·	·	·	·	·	·	·
spl	·	·	·	·	·	·	·	·	·
spr	·	·	·	·	·	·	·	·	·
str	·	·	·	·	·	·	·	·	·
skr	·	·	·	·	·	·	·	·	·
skw	·	·	·	·	·	·	·	·	·

Total number of words—17

128

ʌ	ɜ/r	eɪ	oʊ	aɪ	aʊ	ɔɪ	i/ə/r	ɛ/ə/r	ju
.	.	.	.	pilum	.	.	.	.	.
.	.	.	.	.	.	.	.	.	.
.	.	.	.	.	.	.	.	.	.
.	.	.	.	.	.	.	.	.	.
.	.	.	.	phylum	.	.	.	.	.
.	.	.	.	.	.	.	.	.	.
.	.	.	.	.	.	.	.	.	.
.	.	.	.	xylem	.	.	.	.	.
.	.	.	.	hilum	.	.	.	.	.
.	.	.	.	.	.	.	.	.	.
.	.	.	.	.	.	.	.	.	.
.	.	.	.	whilom	.	.	.	.	.

Final—/lmd/ . For inflected forms add /d/ to appropriate words, e.g. columned.
—/lmz/ . For inflected forms add /z/ to appropriate words, e.g. columns.

	i	ɪ	ɛ	æ	ɑ	ɒ	ɔ(oʊ	ʊ	ʊə
–	.	.	.	.	.	.	.	.	.
p	.	.	.	.	.	.	.	.	.
b	.	.	.	.	.	.	.	.	.
t	.	.	.	.	.	.	.	.	.
d	.	.	.	.	.	.	.	.	.
k	.	.	.	carom†	.	.	.	.	.
g	.	.	.	.	.	.	.	.	.
f	.	.	.	.	.	.	forum	.	.
v	.	.	.	.	.	.	.	.	.
θ	.	.	.	.	.	.	.	.	.
ð	.	.	.	.	.	.	.	.	.
s	.	.	.	.	.	.	.	.	.
z	.	.	.	.	.	.	.	.	.
ʃ	.	.	.	.	.	.	.	.	.
ʒ	.	.	.	.	.	.	.	.	.
h	.	.	.	.	.	.	.	.	.
tʃ	.	.	.	.	.	.	.	.	.
dʒ	.	.	.	.	.	.	jorum	.	.
m	.	.	.	[marrum] .	.	.	.	.	.
n	.	.	.	.	.	.	.	.	.
l	.	.	.	larum	.	.	.	.	.
r	.	.	.	.	.	.	.	.	.
w	.	.	.	.	.	.	.	(Urim)	(Uri
j	.	.	.	.	.	.	.	.	.
pl	.	.	.	.	.	.	.	.	.
pr	.	.	.	.	.	.	.	.	.
bl	.	.	.	.	.	.	.	.	.
br	.	.	.	.	.	.	.	.	.
tr	.	.	.	.	.	.	.	.	.
tw	.	.	.	.	.	.	.	.	.
dr	.	.	.	.	.	.	.	.	.
kl	.	.	.	.	.	.	.	.	.
kr	.	.	.	.	.	.	.	.	.
kw	.	.	.	.	.	.	quorum	.	.
gl	.	.	.	.	.	.	.	.	.
gr	.	.	.	.	.	.	.	.	.
fl	.	.	.	.	.	.	.	.	.
fr	.	.	.	.	.	.	.	.	.
θr	.	.	.	.	.	.	.	.	.
sp	.	.	.	.	.	.	.	.	.
st	.	.	.	.	.	.	.	.	.
sk	.	.	.	.	.	.	.	.	.
sm	.	.	.	.	.	.	.	.	.
sn	.	.	.	.	.	.	.	.	.
sl	.	.	.	.	.	.	.	.	.
sw	.	.	.	.	.	.	.	.	.
ʃr	.	.	.	.	.	.	.	.	.
spl	.	.	.	.	.	.	.	.	.
spr	.	.	.	.	.	.	.	.	.
str	.	.	.	.	.	.	.	.	.
skr	.	.	.	.	.	.	.	.	.
skw	.	.	.	.	.	.	.	.	.

Total number of words—15

ʌ	ɜ/r	eɪ	oʊ	aɪ	aʊ	ɔɪ	i/ə/r	ɛ/ə/r	jʊə
.	.	.	.	.	.	.	.	Arum	(Urim)
.	.	.	.	.	.	.	.	.	purim
.	.	.	.	.	.	.	.	.	.
Durham	.	.	.	.	.	.	.	.	.
.	.	.	.	.	.	.	.	.	.
.	.	.	.	.	.	.	.	.	.
.	.	.	.	.	.	.	.	.	.
.	.	.	.	.	.	.	.	.	.
.	.	.	.	.	.	.	serum	.	.
.	.	.	.	.	.	.	.	.	.
.	.	.	.	.	.	.	.	.	.
.	.	.	.	.	.	.	.	harem	.
.	.	.	.	.	.	.	.	.	.
[murram]	.	.	.	.	.	.	.	.	.

Final—/rmz/ . For inflected forms add /z/ to appropriate words, e.g. forums.

	i	ɪ	ɛ	æ	a/r	ɒ(a	ɔ/r	ʊ	u
−	·	·	·	·	·	·	orpin	·	·
p	·	pippin†	·	·	parpen	·	·	·	·
b	·	·	·	·	·	·	·	·	·
t	·	·	·	·	tarpon*	·	·	·	·
d	deepen	·	·	·	·	·	·	·	·
k	·	·	·	·	·	coppin	·	·	coupᴅ
g	·	·	·	·	·	·	·	·	·
f	·	·	·	·	·	·	·	·	·
v	·	·	·	·	·	·	·	·	·
θ	·	·	·	·	·	·	·	·	·
ð	·	·	·	·	·	·	·	·	·
s	·	·	·	sappan	·	·	·	·	·
z	·	·	·	·	·	·	·	·	·
ʃ	·	shippen†	·	·	sharpen	·	·	·	·
ʒ	·	·	·	·	·	·	·	·	·
h	·	·	·	happen	·	·	·	·	·
tʃ	cheapen	·	·	·	·	chopin	·	·	·
dʒ	·	·	·	·	·	·	·	·	jupoⁿ
m	·	·	·	·	·	·	·	·	·
n	·	Nippon	·	·	·	·	·	·	·
l	·	lippen†	·	lappen†	·	·	·	·	(lupiⁿ
r	·	Rippon*†	·	·	·	·	·	·	·
w	·	·	weapon	·	·	·	·	·	·
j	·	·	·	·	·	·	[yaupon]	·	[yupᴅ
pl	·	·	·	·	·	·	·	·	·
pr	·	·	·	·	·	·	·	·	·
pl	·	·	·	·	·	·	·	·	·
br	·	·	·	·	·	·	·	·	·
tr	·	·	·	·	·	·	·	·	·
tw	·	·	·	·	·	·	·	·	·
dr	·	·	·	·	·	·	·	·	·
kl	·	·	·	·	·	·	·	·	·
kr	·	·	·	·	·	·	·	·	crouᴘ
kw	·	·	·	·	·	·	·	·	·
gl	·	·	·	·	·	·	·	·	·
gr	·	·	·	·	·	·	·	·	·
fl	·	·	·	·	·	·	·	·	·
fr	·	·	·	·	·	·	·	·	·
θr	·	·	·	·	·	·	·	·	·
sp	·	·	·	·	·	·	·	·	·
st	steepen	·	·	·	·	·	·	·	·
sk	·	·	·	·	·	·	·	·	·
sm	·	·	·	·	·	·	·	·	·
sn	·	·	·	·	·	·	·	·	·
sl	·	·	·	·	·	·	·	·	·
sw	·	·	·	·	·	·	·	·	·
ʃr	·	·	·	·	·	·	·	·	·
spl	·	·	·	·	·	·	·	·	·
spr	·	·	·	·	·	·	·	·	·
str	·	·	·	·	·	·	·	·	·
skr	·	·	·	·	·	·	·	·	·
skw	·	·	·	·	·	·	·	·	·

* homophones—see page 223.
  Total number of words—32

ʌ	ɜ/r	eɪ	oʊ	aɪ	aʊ	ɔɪ	i/ə/r	ɛ/ə/r	ju
·	·	·	open	·	·	·	·	·	·
·	·	·	·	·	·	·	·	·	·
·	·	·	·	·	·	·	·	·	·
·	·	capon	·	·	·	·	·	·	·
·	·	·	·	·	gowpen† ·	·	·	·	·
·	·	·	·	·	·	·	·	·	·
·	·	·	·	·	·	·	·	·	·
·	·	·	·	·	·	·	·	·	·
·	·	·	·	·	·	·	·	·	·
·	·	shapen	·	·	·	·	·	·	·
·	·	·	·	·	·	·	·	·	·
·	·	·	·	·	·	·	·	·	·
·	·	·	·	·	·	·	·	·	·
·	·	·	·	·	·	·	·	·	·
[luppen]† ·	·	·	·	·	loupen† ·	·	·	·	(lupin)
·	·	·	·	ripen	·	·	·	·	·
·	·	·	·	·	·	·	·	·	·
·	·	·	·	·	·	·	·	·	·
·	·	·	·	·	·	·	·	·	·
·	·	·	·	·	·	·	·	·	·
·	·	·	·	·	·	·	·	·	·
·	·	·	·	·	·	·	·	·	·
·	·	·	·	·	·	·	·	·	·
·	·	·	·	·	·	·	·	·	·
·	·	·	·	·	·	·	·	·	·
·	·	·	·	·	·	·	·	·	·
·	·	·	·	·	·	·	·	·	·
·	ɜ/r	·	·	·	·	·	i/ə/r	·	·
·	·	·	·	·	·	·	·	·	·
·	·	·	·	·	·	·	·	·	·
·	·	·	·	·	·	·	·	·	·
·	·	·	·	·	·	·	·	·	·
·	·	·	·	·	·	·	·	·	·
·	·	·	·	·	·	·	·	·	·
·	·	·	·	·	·	·	·	·	·
·	·	·	·	·	·	·	·	·	·

Final—/pn̩d/ . For inflected forms add /d/ to appropriate words, e.g. happened.
—/pn̩z/ . For inflected forms add /z/ to appropriate words, e.g. happens.

	i	ɪ	ɛ	æ	ɑ/r	ɒ(ɑ	ɔ	ʊ/r	u
—	.	.	ebon	.	.	.	auburn	.	.
p	.	.	.	.	.	.	.	.	.
b	.	.	.	.	.	bobbin	.	(Bourbon)*	.
t	.	.	.	.	.	.	.	.	.
d	.	.	.	.	.	dobbin	.	.	.
k	.	.	.	cabin	carbon	.	.	.	.
g	.	gibbon*	.	.	.	.	.	.	.
f	.	.	.	.	.	.	.	.	.
v	.	.	.	.	.	.	.	.	.
θ	Theban	.	.	.	.	.	.	.	.
ð	.	.	.	.	.	.	.	.	.
s	.	.	.	.	.	.	.	.	.
z	.	.	.	.	.	.	.	.	.
ʃ	.	.	.	.	.	.	.	.	.
ʒ	.	.	.	.	.	.	.	.	.
h	.	.	[heben]†	.	.	.	.	.	.
tʃ	.	.	.	.	.	.	.	.	.
dʒ	.	.	.	.	.	.	.	.	.
m	.	.	.	.	.	.	.	.	.
n	.	.	.	.	.	.	.	.	.
l	.	.	.	.	.	.	.	.	.
r	.	ribbon	.	.	.	robin*	.	.	ru
w	.	.	.	.	.	.	.	.	.
j	.	.	.	.	.	.	.	.	.
pl	.	.	.	.	.	.	.	.	.
pr	.	.	.	.	.	.	.	.	.
bl	.	.	.	.	.	.	.	.	.
br	.	.	.	.	.	.	.	.	.
tr	.	.	.	.	.	.	.	.	.
tw	.	.	.	.	.	.	.	.	.
dr	.	.	.	.	.	.	.	.	.
kl	.	.	.	.	.	.	.	.	.
kr	.	.	.	.	.	.	.	.	.
kw	.	.	.	.	.	.	.	.	.
gl	.	.	.	.	.	.	.	.	.
gr	.	.	.	.	.	.	.	.	.
fl	.	.	.	.	.	.	.	.	.
fr	.	.	.	.	.	.	.	.	.
θr	.	.	.	.	.	.	.	.	.
sp	.	.	.	.	.	.	.	.	.
st	.	.	.	.	.	.	.	.	.
sk	.	.	.	.	.	.	.	.	.
sm	.	.	.	.	.	.	.	.	.
sn	.	.	.	.	.	.	.	.	.
sl	.	.	.	.	.	.	.	.	.
sw	.	.	.	.	.	.	.	.	.
ʃr	.	.	.	.	.	.	.	.	.
spl	.	.	.	.	.	.	.	.	.
spr	.	.	.	.	.	.	.	.	.
str	.	.	.	.	.	.	.	.	.
skr	.	.	.	.	.	.	.	.	.
skw	.	.	.	.	.	.	.	.	.

* homophones—see page 223.
  Total number of words—21

ʌ	ɜ/r	eɪ	oʊ	aɪ	aʊ	ɔɪ	i/ə/r	ε/ə/r	ju
.	urban	.	.	.	.	.	.	.	.
.	.	.	.	.	.	.	.	.	.
.	(bourbon).	.	.	.	.	.	.	.	.
.	turban	.	.	Tyburn	.	.	.	.	.
.	Durban	.	.	.	.	.	.	.	.
.	.	.	Koban	.	.	.	.	.	Cuban
.	.	.	.	.	.	.	.	.	.
.	.	.	.	.	.	.	.	.	.
.	.	.	.	.	.	.	.	.	.
.	.	.	.	.	.	.	.	.	.
.	.	.	.	.	.	.	.	.	.
.	.	.	.	.	.	.	.	.	.
.	.	.	.	.	.	.	.	.	.
.	.	.	.	.	.	.	.	.	.
.	.	.	.	.	.	.	.	.	.
.	.	.	.	.	.	.	.	.	.
.	.	.	.	.	.	.	.	.	.
.	.	.	.	.	.	.	.	.	.
.	.	.	.	.	.	.	.	.	.
.	.	.	.	.	.	.	.	.	.
.	.	.	.	.	.	.	.	.	.
.	.	.	.	.	.	.	.	.	.
.	.	.	.	.	.	.	.	.	.
.	.	.	.	.	.	.	.	.	.
.	.	.	.	.	.	.	.	.	.
.	.	.	.	.	.	.	.	.	.
.	.	.	.	.	.	.	.	.	.
.	.	.	.	.	.	.	.	.	.
.	.	.	.	.	.	.	.	.	.
.	.	.	.	.	.	.	.	.	.
.	.	.	.	.	.	.	.	.	.
stubborn	.	.	.	.	.	.	.	.	.
.	.	.	.	.	.	.	.	.	.
.	.	.	.	.	.	.	.	.	.
.	.	.	.	.	.	.	.	.	.
.	.	.	.	.	.	.	.	.	.
.	.	.	.	.	.	.	.	.	.
.	.	.	.	.	.	.	.	.	.
.	.	.	.	.	.	.	.	.	.
.	.	.	.	.	.	.	.	.	.

Final—/bnz/ . For inflected forms add /z/ to appropriate words, e.g. cabins.

	i	ɪ	ɛ	æ	ɑ/r	ɒ(ɑ	ɔ/r	ʊ	u
−	eaten*	.	.	.	.	.	.	.	.
p	.	[pitten]†	.	pattern*	partan†	.	.	.	.
b	beaten	bitten*	.	baton*	.	.	(Boughton).	.	.
t	.	.	.	.	tartan	.	tauten	.	.
d	.	.	.	.	.	.	.	.	.
k	.	kitten	.	.	carton	cotton	.	.	.
g	.	gittern	.	.	.	gotten	Gorton	.	.
f	.	.	.	fatten	.	.	.	.	.
v	.	.	.	.	.	.	.	.	.
θ	.	.	.	.	.	.	thoughten†.	.	.
ð	.	.	.	.	.	.	.	.	.
s	seton	[cittern]	.	satin*	.	.	.	.	.
z	.	.	.	.	.	.	.	.	.
ʃ	.	.	.	.	.	shotten†	shorten	.	.
ʒ	.	.	.	.	.	.	.	.	.
h	.	.	.	.	hearten*	.	Horton	.	.
tʃ	.	.	.	.	.	.	.	.	.
dʒ	.	.	jetton	.	.	.	.	.	.
m	.	*mitten*	.	matin	martin*	.	.	.	mouta
n	.	.	.	.	.	.	.	.	(New
l	.	(luiten)*†	[lettern]†	Latin*	.	.	Laughton .	.	Luto
r	.	written	.	ratton*†	.	rotten	.	.	.
w	wheaten*	witan	wetten	.	.	whaten†	.	.	.
j	.	.	.	.	.	.	.	.	.
pl	.	.	.	platen*	.	.	.	.	.
pr	.	.	.	.	.	.	.	.	.
bl	.	.	.	.	.	.	.	.	.
br	.	Briton*	Breton	.	.	.	Broughton.	.	.
tr	.	.	.	.	.	.	.	.	.
tw	.	.	.	.	.	.	.	.	.
dr	.	.	.	.	.	.	.	.	.
kl	.	.	.	.	.	.	.	.	.
kr	Cretan*	.	(cretin)*	.	.	.	.	.	.
kw	.	.	.	.	.	.	quartan*	.	.
gl	.	.	.	.	.	.	.	.	glute
gr	.	.	.	.	.	.	.	.	.
fl	.	flittern†	.	flatten	.	.	.	.	.
fr	.	.	.	.	.	.	.	.	.
θr	.	.	threaten	.	.	.	.	.	.
sp	.	spitten†	.	.	Spartan	.	.	.	.
st	.	.	.	.	.	.	.	.	.
sk	.	.	.	.	.	.	.	.	.
sm	.	smitten	.	.	smarten	.	.	.	.
sn	.	.	.	.	.	.	.	.	.
sl	.	.	.	slattern	.	.	.	.	.
sw	sweeten	.	.	.	.	.	.	.	.
ʃr	.	.	.	.	.	.	.	.	.
spl	.	.	.	.	.	.	.	.	.
spr	.	.	.	.	.	.	.	.	.
str	.	.	.	Stratton	.	.	.	.	.
skr	.	.	.	.	.	.	.	.	.
skw	.	.	.	.	.	.	.	.	.

* homophones—see page 223.
  Total number of words—101

ʌ	ɜ/r	eɪ	oʊ	aɪ	aʊ	ɔɪ	i/ə/r	ɛ/ə/r	ju
.	.	.	oaten	.	.	.	.	.	.
[putten]†.	.	.		.	.	.	.	.	.
button	Burton*	.	.	.	(Boughton).	.	.	.	.
.	.	.	.	Titan*	.	.	.	.	Teuton
.	.	.	.	.	.	.	.	.	.
.	*curtain*	.	.	chitin*	.	.	.	.	.
.	.	.	.	.	.	.	.	.	.
.	.	(phaeton)	photon	.	.	.	.	.	.
.	.	.	.	.	.	.	.	.	.
.	.	.	.	.	.	.	.	.	.
Sutton	certain	Satan	.	.	.	.	.	.	.
.	.	.	.	.	.	.	.	.	.
.	.	.	.	.	.	.	.	.	.
Hutton	.	.	[hoten]	heighten	.	.	.	.	.
.	.	.	.	.	.	.	.	.	.
.	.	.	.	.	.	.	.	.	.
mutton	Merton	.	.	.	.	.	.	.	mutine†
.	.	.	.	niton	.	.	.	.	(Newton)
.	.	Leyton	.	lighten	.	.	.	.	.
.	.	.	.	rhyton*	.	.	.	.	.
.	.	.	Wotan	whiten	.	.	.	.	.
.	.	.	[jotun]	.	.	.	.	.	.
.	.	.	.	.	.	.	.	.	.
.	.	.	proton	.	.	.	.	.	.
.	.	.	.	.	.	.	.	.	.
.	.	.	.	brighten*.	.	.	.	.	.
.	.	.	.	Triton	.	.	.	.	.
.	.	.	.	.	.	.	.	.	.
.	.	Drayton	.	.	.	.	.	.	.
.	.	Clayton	.	.	.	.	.	.	.
.	.	.	croton	Crichton	.	.	.	.	.
.	.	.	.	.	.	.	.	.	.
glutton	.	.	.	.	.	.	.	.	.
[grutten]†.	.	.	.	.	.	.	.	.	.
.	.	.	.	.	.	.	.	.	.
.	.	.	.	frighten	.	.	.	.	.
.	.	.	.	.	.	.	.	.	.
.	.	.	.	.	stouten	.	.	.	.
.	.	.	.	.	.	.	.	.	.
.	.	.	.	.	.	.	.	.	.
.	.	.	.	.	.	.	.	.	.
.	.	.	.	.	.	.	.	.	.
.	.	straighten*.	.	.	.	.	.	.	.
.	.	.	.	.	.	.	.	.	.
.	.	.	.	.	.	.	.	.	.

Final—/tn̩d/ . For inflected forms add /d/ to appropriate words, e.g. buttoned.
—/tn̩z/ . For inflected forms add /z/ to appropriate words, e.g. buttons.

	i	ɪ	ɛ	æ	ɑ/r	ɒ(ɑ	ɔ/r	ʊ/r	u
–	Eden				Arden				
p				Paddon	pardon			(pudden)	
b		bidden			(Baden)		(bourdon)	(bourdon)	
t									
d			deaden						
k							cordon		
g					*garden*		Gordon		
f					farden*				
v									
θ									
ð									
s				sadden		sodden			
z									
ʃ									
ʒ									
h		hidden			harden*	hodden	Hordern		ho
tʃ		chidden							
dʒ							Jordan		
m		midden		madden*		modern			
n									
l			leaden*		lardon				
r	reeden	ridden	redden						
w							warden	wooden	
j									
pl									
pr									
bl									
br							broaden		
tr						trodden			
tw									
dr									
kl									
kr									
kw									
gl				gladden*					
gr				graddan					
fl									
fr									
θr			threaden†						
sp									
st									
sk									
sm									
sn			Sneddon						
sl		slidden†							
sw	Sweden								
ʃr									
spl									
spr			spredden						
str		stridden							
skr									
skw									

* homophones—see page 223.
  Total number of words—69

ʌ	ɜ/r	eɪ	oʊ	aɪ	aʊ	ɔɪ	i/ə/r	ɛ/ə/r	ju
.	.	Aden	Odin	.	.	.	.	.	.
(pudden).	.	.	.	.	.	.	.	.	.
.	burden	(Baden)	.	.	Bowden	.	.	.	.
.	.	.	.	.	.	.	.	.	.
.	.	.	.	.	.	.	.	.	.
.	guerdon	.	.	guidon	.	.	.	.	.
.	.	.	.	.	.	.	.	.	.
.	.	.	.	.	.	.	.	.	.
.	.	.	.	.	.	.	.	.	.
sudden	.	.	.	.	.	.	.	.	.
.	.	.	.	.	.	.	.	.	.
.	.	.	.	.	.	.	.	.	.
hudden†*	herden	Hayden	.	Haydn	.	hoyden	.	.	.
.	.	.	.	.	.	.	.	.	.
.	.	maiden	.	.	.	.	.	.	.
.	lurdan	laden	loaden	Leiden	louden	.	.	.	.
.	.	radon	Roden	.	.	.	.	.	.
.	.	.	Woden	widen	.	.	.	.	.
.	.	.	.	.	.	.	.	.	.
.	.	.	.	.	.	.	.	.	.
.	.	.	.	.	.	.	.	.	.
.	.	.	.	.	.	.	.	.	.
.	.	.	.	Dryden	.	.	.	.	.
.	.	.	.	.	.	.	.	.	.
.	.	.	.	.	.	.	.	.	.
.	.	(gradin)	.	.	.	.	.	.	.
.	.	.	.	.	.	.	.	.	.
.	.	.	.	.	.	.	.	.	.
.	.	.	.	.	.	.	.	.	.
.	.	.	.	.	.	.	.	.	.
.	.	.	.	.	.	.	.	.	.
.	.	.	.	.	.	.	.	.	.
.	.	.	.	.	.	.	.	.	.
.	.	.	.	.	.	.	.	.	.
.	.	.	.	.	.	.	.	.	.
.	.	.	.	.	.	.	.	.	.

Final— /dnd . For inflected forms add /d/ to appropriate words, e.g. pardoned.
—/dnz/ . For inflected forms add /z/ to appropriate words, e.g. pardons.

	i	ɪ	ɛ	æ	ɑ/r	ɒ(ɑ	ɔ/r	ʊ	u
—	.	.		.	archon	.	.	.	.
p	.	.	pekan	.	[parkin]†	.			
b	beacon	.	beckon	.	barken*	.			
t	.	ticken	.	.	(takin)			.	(touc...
d	deacon	.	.	.	darken	docken†	.	.	
k	.	.	.	.	.	.	.	.	.
g	.	.	.	.	.	.	.	.	.
f	.	.	.	.	.	.	(falcon)	.	.
v	.	.	.	.	.	.	.	.	.
θ	.	thicken*	.	.	.	.	.	.	.
ð	.	.	.	.	.	.	.	.	.
s	.	sicken*	.	.	.	.	.	.	.
z	.	.	.	.	.	.	.	.	.
ʃ	.	.	.	.	.	.	.	.	.
ʒ	.	.	.	.	.	.	.	.	.
h	.	.	.	.	harken	.	.	.	.
tʃ	.	*chicken*	.	.	.	.	.	.	.
dʒ	.	.	.	.	.	.	.	.	.
m	meeken	.	.	.	.	.	morkin*	.	.
n	.	.	.	.	.	.	.	.	.
l	.	.	.	.	.	.	.	.	.
r	.	.	reckon*	.	.	.	.	.	.
w	weaken	[wicken]	.	.	.	.	.	.	.
j	.	.	.	.	.	.	.	.	.
pl	.	.	.	.	.	.	.	.	.
pr	.	.	.	.	.	.	.	.	.
bl	.	.	.	blacken	.	.	.	.	.
br	.	bricken	.	bracken	.	.	.	.	.
tr	.	.	.	.	.	.	.	.	.
tw	.	.	.	.	.	.	.	.	.
dr	.	.	.	.	.	.	.	.	.
kl	.	.	.	.	.	.	.	.	.
kr	.	.	.	.	kraken	.	.	.	.
kw	.	quicken	.	.	.	.	.	.	.
gl	.	.	.	.	.	.	.	.	.
gr	.	.	.	.	.	.	.	.	.
fl	.	.	.	.	.	.	.	.	.
fr	.	.	.	.	.	.	.	.	.
θr	.	.	.	.	.	.	.	.	.
sp	.	.	.	.	.	.	.	.	.
st	.	.	.	.	starken	.	.	.	.
sk	.	.	.	.	.	.	.	.	.
sm	.	.	.	.	.	.	.	.	.
sn	.	.	.	.	.	.	.	.	.
sl	sleeken	slicken	.	slacken	.	[slocken]†	.	.	.
sw	.	.	.	.	.	.	.	.	.
ʃr	.	.	.	.	.	.	.	.	.
spl	.	.	.	.	.	.	.	.	.
spr	.	.	.	.	.	.	.	.	.
str	.	stricken	.	.	.	.	.	.	stroo...
skr	.	.	.	.	.	.	.	.	.
skw	.	.	.	.	.	.	.	.	.

* homophones—see page 223.
  Total number of words—63

ʌ	ɜ/r	eɪ	oʊ	aɪ	aʊ	ɔɪ	i/ə/r	ɛ/ə/r	ju
.		Aikin	oaken	icon	.	.	.	.	.
.	[perkin]*†	.	.	.	.	.	.	.	.
.	birken†	bacon	.	.	.	.	.	.	.
.	.	taken	token	.	.	.	.	.	.
.	.	.	.	.	.	.	.	.	.
.	(kirkin')	.	.	.	.	.	.	.	.
.	gherkin	.	.	.	.	.	.	.	.
.	firkin	.	.	.	.	.	.	.	.
.	.	.	.	.	.	.	.	.	.
.	.	.	.	.	.	.	.	.	.
.	.	.	.	.	.	.	.	.	.
sucken†	.	.	soaken*	(Sican)	.	.	.	.	.
.	zircon	.	.	.	.	.	.	.	.
.	.	shaken	.	.	.	.	.	.	.
.	.	.	.	.	.	.	.	.	.
.	.	.	.	.	.	.	.	.	.
.	.	.	.	.	.	.	.	.	.
.	jerkin	.	.	.	.	.	.	.	.
.	murken†	.	.	.	.	.	.	.	.
.	.	.	.	.	.	.	.	.	.
lucken†	.	lakin†	.	liken*	.	.	.	.	.
.	.	.	wroken†	.	.	.	.	.	.
.	.	waken	woken	.	.	.	.	.	.
.	.	.	.	.	.	.	.	.	.
.	.	.	.	.	.	.	.	.	.
.	.	.	broken	.	.	.	.	.	.
.	.	.	.	.	.	.	.	.	.
.	.	.	.	.	.	.	.	.	.
.	.	.	.	.	.	.	.	.	.
.	.	.	.	.	.	.	.	.	.
.	querken	.	.	.	.	.	.	.	.
.	.	.	.	.	.	.	.	.	.
.	.	.	.	.	.	.	.	.	.
.	.	.	.	.	.	.	.	.	.
.	.	.	.	.	.	.	.	.	.
.	.	.	spoken	.	.	.	.	.	.
.	.	.	.	.	.	.	.	.	.
.	.	.	.	.	.	.	.	.	.
.	.	.	[sloken]†	.	.	.	.	.	.
.	.	.	.	.	.	.	.	.	.
.	.	.	.	.	.	.	.	.	.
strucken†	.	.	.	.	.	.	.	.	.
.	.	.	.	.	.	.	.	.	.
.	.	.	.	.	.	.	.	.	.

Final—/knd/ . For inflected forms add /d/ to appropriate words, e.g. thickened.
—/knz/ . For inflected forms add /z/ to appropriate words, e.g. thickens.

	i	ɪ	ɛ	æ	ɑ/r	ɒ(ɑ	ɔ/r	ʊ	u
–					(argon)*		organ		
p		piggin							
b		biggin			bargain				
t									
d	Deegan								Dug
k									
g							Gorgon		
f									
v									
θ									
ð									
s									
z									
ʃ									
ʒ									
h						hoggin			
tʃ									
dʒ					jargon				
m			Megan			moggan†	Morgan*		
n						noggin*			
l		[liggen]†		[lagan]	laggen†				
r	Regan								
w		Wigan*		waggon*					
j									
pl									
pr									
bl									
br									
tr									
tw		twiggen†							
dr				*dragon**					
kl									
kr									
kw									
gl									
gr									
fl				flagon					
fr									
θr									
sp									
st									
sk						Scoggin			
sm									
sn									
sl									
sw									
ʃr									
spl									
spr									
str									
skr									
skw									

* homophones—see page 224.
  Total number of words—37

ʌ	ɜ/r	eɪ	oʊ	aɪ	aʊ	ɔɪ	i/ə/r	ɛ/ə/r	ju
		pagan							
	durgan	Dagon							
		Fagin							
				zygon					
		Hogan*							
		logan*	[ligan]						
		Reagan							
			brogan*†						
			trogan	trigon*					
			slogan						

Final—/gnd/ . For inflected forms add /d/ to appropriate words, e.g. bargained.
—/gnz/ . For inflected forms add /z/ to appropriate words, e.g. bargains.

	i	ɪ	ε	æ	ɑ	ɒ(ɔ	ɔ/r	ʊ	u
p	·	·	·	·	·	(often)	orphan*	·	·
b	·	biffin	·	·	·	boffin†	·	·	·
t	·	tiffin†	·	·	·	·	·	·	·
d	·	·	deafen	·	·	·	·	dauphin	·
k	·	·	·	·	·	coffin	·	·	·
g	·	·	·	·	·	·	·	·	·
f	·	·	·	·	·	·	·	·	·
v	·	·	·	·	·	·	·	·	·
θ	·	·	·	·	·	·	·	·	·
ð	·	·	·	·	·	·	·	·	·
s	·	·	sephen	·	·	soften	·	·	·
z	·	·	·	·	·	·	·	·	·
ʃ	·	·	·	·	·	·	·	·	·
ʒ	·	·	·	·	·	·	·	·	·
h	·	·	·	·	·	·	·	·	·
tʃ	·	·	·	·	·	·	·	·	·
dʒ	·	·	·	·	·	·	·	·	·
m	·	·	·	·	·	·	·	·	·
n	·	·	·	·	·	·	·	·	·
l	·	·	·	·	·	·	·	·	·
r	·	·	·	·	·	·	·	·	·
w	·	·	·	·	·	·	·	·	·
j	·	·	·	·	·	·	·	·	·
pl	·	·	·	·	·	·	·	·	·
pr	·	·	·	·	·	·	·	·	·
bl	·	·	·	·	·	·	·	·	·
br	·	·	·	·	·	·	·	·	·
tr	·	·	·	·	·	·	·	·	·
tw	·	·	·	·	·	·	·	·	·
dr	·	·	·	·	·	·	·	·	·
kl	·	·	·	·	·	·	·	·	·
kr	·	·	·	·	·	·	·	·	·
kw	·	·	·	·	·	·	·	·	·
gl	·	·	·	·	·	·	·	·	·
gr	·	griffin*	gräfin	·	·	·	·	·	·
fl	·	·	·	·	·	·	·	·	·
fr	·	·	·	·	·	·	·	·	·
θr	·	·	·	·	·	·	·	·	·
sp	·	·	·	·	·	·	·	·	·
st	·	stiffen	·	·	·	·	·	·	·
sk	·	·	·	·	·	·	·	·	·
sm	·	·	·	·	·	·	·	·	·
sn	·	·	·	·	·	·	·	·	·
sl	·	·	·	·	·	·	·	·	·
sw	·	·	·	·	·	·	·	·	·
ʃr	·	·	·	·	·	·	·	·	·
spl	·	·	·	·	·	·	·	·	·
spr	·	·	·	·	·	·	·	·	·
str	·	·	Strephon	·	·	·	·	·	·
skr	·	·	·	·	·	·	·	·	·
skw	·	·	·	·	·	·	·	·	·

* homophones—see page 224.
  Total number of words—23

Λ	ɜ/r	eɪ	oʊ	aɪ	aʊ	ɔɪ	i/ə/r	ɛ/ə/r	ju
puffin									
toughen	turfen			Typhon					
cuffin									
				siphon					
				hyphen					
muffin									
roughen*.									

Final—/fnd/ . For inflected forms add /d/ to appropriate words, e.g. softened.
—/fnz/ . For inflected forms add /z/ to appropriate words, e.g. softens.

	i	ɪ	ɛ	æ	ɑ/r	ɒ	ɔ/r	ʊ	u
—	even	·	·	·	·	·	·	·	·
p	·	·	·	·	·	·	·	·	·
b	·	·	Bevin	bavin	·	·	·	·	·
t	·	·	·	tavern	·	·	·	·	·
d	·	·	Devon	·	·	·	·	·	·
k	·	·	Kevin	cavern	carven	·	·	·	·
g	·	given	·	Gavin	·	·	·	·	·
f	·	·	·	·	·	·	·	·	·
v	·	·	·	·	·	·	·	·	·
θ	·	·	·	·	·	·	·	·	·
ð	·	·	·	·	·	·	·	·	·
s	·	·	*seven*	savin	·	·	·	·	·
z	·	·	·	·	·	·	·	·	·
ʃ	·	·	·	·	·	·	·	·	·
ʒ	·	·	·	·	·	·	·	·	·
h	·	·	heaven	·	·	·	·	·	·
tʃ	·	·	cheven	·	·	·	·	·	·
dʒ	·	·	·	·	·	·	·	·	·
m	·	·	·	·	·	·	·	·	·
n	·	·	·	·	·	·	·	·	·
l	·	·	leaven*	·	·	·	·	·	·
r	·	riven	·	ravin	·	·	·	·	·
w	·	·	·	·	·	·	·	·	·
j	·	·	·	·	·	·	·	·	·
pl	·	·	·	·	·	·	·	·	·
pr	·	·	·	·	·	·	·	·	prov
bl	·	·	·	·	·	·	·	·	·
br	·	·	·	·	·	·	·	·	·
tr	·	·	·	·	·	·	·	·	·
tw	·	·	·	·	·	·	·	·	·
dr	·	driven	·	·	·	·	·	·	·
kl	·	·	·	·	·	·	·	·	·
kr	·	·	·	·	·	·	·	·	·
kw	·	·	·	·	·	·	·	·	·
gl	·	·	·	·	·	·	·	·	·
gr	·	·	·	·	·	·	·	·	·
fl	·	·	·	·	·	·	·	·	·
fr	·	·	·	·	·	·	·	·	·
θr	·	·	·	·	·	·	·	·	·
sp	·	·	·	spavin	·	·	·	·	·
st	Steven*	·	·	·	·	·	[storven]†	·	·
sk	·	·	·	·	·	·	·	·	·
sm	·	·	·	·	·	·	·	·	·
sn	·	·	·	·	·	·	·	·	·
sl	·	·	·	·	·	·	·	·	·
sw	·	·	sweven	·	·	·	·	·	·
ʃr	·	shriven	·	·	·	·	·	·	·
spl	·	·	·	·	·	·	·	·	·
spr	·	·	·	·	·	·	·	·	·
str	·	striven	·	·	·	·	·	·	·
skr	·	scriven	·	·	·	·	·	·	·
skw	·	·	·	·	·	·	·	·	·

* homophones—see page 224.
  Total number of words—45

146

ʌ	ɜ/r	eɪ	oʊ	aɪ	aʊ	ɔɪ	i/ə/r	ɛ/ə/r	ju
oven	.	.	.	Ivan	.	.	.	.	.
.	.	.	.	.	.	.	.	.	.
.	.	.	.	.	.	.	.	.	.
.	.	.	.	.	.	.	.	.	.
.	.	.	.	.	.	.	.	.	.
[coven]	.	.	[covin]	.	.	.	.	.	.
govern	.	.	.	.	.	.	.	.	.
.	.	.	.	.	.	.	.	.	.
.	[verven]†.	.	.	.	.	.	.	.	.
.	.	.	.	.	.	.	.	.	.
.	.	.	.	.	.	.	.	.	.
.	.	.	.	.	.	.	.	.	.
.	.	shaven	.	.	.	.	.	.	.
.	.	.	.	.	.	.	.	.	.
.	.	haven	hoven†	.	.	.	.	.	.
.	.	.	.	.	.	.	.	.	.
.	jervin	.	.	.	.	.	.	.	.
.	.	.	.	.	.	.	.	.	.
.	.	.	.	liven	.	.	.	.	.
.	.	raven	.	.	.	.	.	.	.
.	.	.	woven	wivern†	.	.	.	.	.
.	.	.	.	.	.	.	.	.	.
.	.	.	.	.	.	.	.	.	.
.	.	.	.	.	.	.	.	.	.
.	.	.	.	.	.	.	.	.	.
.	.	.	.	.	.	.	.	.	.
.	.	.	.	.	.	.	.	.	.
.	.	.	cloven	.	.	.	.	.	.
.	.	craven	.	.	.	.	.	.	.
.	.	.	.	.	.	.	.	.	.
.	.	graven	.	.	.	.	.	.	.
.	.	flavin	.	.	.	.	.	.	.
.	.	.	.	.	.	.	.	.	.
.	.	.	.	.	.	.	.	.	.
.	.	.	.	.	.	.	.	.	.
sloven	.	.	.	.	.	.	.	.	.
.	.	.	.	.	.	.	.	.	.
.	.	.	.	.	.	.	.	.	.
.	.	.	.	.	.	.	.	.	.
.	.	.	.	.	.	.	.	.	.
.	.	.	.	.	.	.	.	.	.

Final—/vnd/ . For inflected forms add /d/ to appropriate words, e.g. livened.
—/vnz/ . For inflected forms add /z/ to appropriate words, e.g. livens.

	i	ɪ	ɛ	æ	ɑ/r	ɒ(ɑ	ɔ(oʊ/r	ʊ	
—	·	·	·	·	arson	·	·	·	·
p	·	·	·	·	parson	·	·	·	·
b	·	bisson	·	·	·	·	·	·	·
t	·	·	·	·	·	[tossen]†	·	·	·
d	Deason	·	·	·	·	·	Dawson	·	·
k	·	·	·	·	·	·	·	·	·
g	·	·	·	·	Garson	[gossan]	·	·	·
f	·	·	·	(fasten)	(fasten)*	·	·	·	·
v	·	viscin	·	·	·	·	·	·	·
θ	·	·	·	·	·	·	·	·	·
ð	·	·	·	·	·	·	·	·	·
s	·	·	·	sasin	sarsen	·	·	·	·
z	·	·	·	·	·	·	·	·	·
ʃ	·	·	·	·	·	·	·	·	·
ʒ	·	·	·	·	·	·	·	·	·
h	·	·	·	·	·	·	whoreson	·	·
tʃ	·	·	·	·	·	·	·	·	·
dʒ	·	·	·	·	·	·	·	·	·
m	·	·	(meson)*	·	·	·	·	·	·
n	·	Nissen	·	·	·	·	·	·	·
l	·	listen	lesson*	·	·	·	Lawson	·	loos
r	·	·	·	·	·	·	·	·	·
w	·	·	·	·	·	·	·	·	·
j	·	·	·	·	·	·	·	·	·
pl	·	·	·	·	·	·	·	·	·
pr	·	·	·	·	·	·	·	·	·
bl	·	·	·	·	·	·	·	·	·
br	·	·	·	·	·	·	·	·	·
tr	·	·	·	·	·	·	·	·	·
tw	·	·	·	·	·	·	·	·	·
dr	·	·	·	·	·	·	·	·	·
kl	·	·	·	·	·	·	·	·	·
kr	·	·	·	·	·	·	·	·	·
kw	·	·	·	·	·	·	·	·	·
gl	Gleeson	glisten*	·	(glassen)†	(glassen)†	·	·	·	·
gr	·	·	·	·	·	·	·	·	·
fl	·	·	·	·	·	·	·	·	·
fr	·	·	·	·	·	·	·	·	·
θr	·	·	·	·	·	·	·	·	·
sp	·	·	·	·	·	·	·	·	·
st	·	·	·	·	·	·	·	·	·
sk	·	·	·	·	·	·	·	·	·
sm	·	·	·	·	·	·	·	·	·
sn	·	·	·	·	·	·	·	·	·
sl	·	·	·	·	·	·	·	·	·
sw	·	·	·	·	·	·	·	·	·
ʃr	·	·	·	·	·	·	·	·	·
spl	·	·	·	·	·	·	·	·	·
spr	·	·	·	·	·	·	·	·	·
str	·	·	·	·	·	·	·	·	·
skr	·	·	·	·	·	·	·	·	·
skw	·	·	·	·	squarson	·	·	·	·

* homophones—see page 224.
  Total number of words—50

Λ	ɜ/r	eɪ	oʊ	aɪ	aʊ	ɔɪ	i/ə/r	ɛ/ə/r	ju
.	urson	.	.	.	[owsen]†	.	.	.	.
.	person*	.	.	.	.	.	Pearson	.	.
.	.	basin	bosun	bison	.	.	.	.	.
.	.	.	.	Tyson	.	.	.	.	.
.	.	.	.	.	.	.	.	.	.
.	.	caisson	.	.	.	.	.	.	.
.	.	.	.	.	.	.	.	.	.
.	versin†	.	.	vison	.	.	.	.	.
.	.	.	.	.	.	.	.	.	.
.	.	sasine	.	.	.	.	.	.	.
.	.	.	.	.	.	.	.	.	.
.	.	.	.	.	.	.	.	.	.
.	.	hasten	.	hyson	.	.	.	.	.
.	.	chasten	.	.	.	.	.	.	.
.	.	Jason	.	.	.	.	.	.	.
.	.	mason*	.	.	.	moisten	.	.	.
.	.	.	.	(Nisan)	.	.	.	.	.
.	.	.	.	lysin	.	.	.	.	(leucine)
.	worsen	.	.	.	.	.	.	.	.
.	.	.	.	.	.	.	.	.	.
.	.	.	.	.	.	.	.	.	.
.	.	.	.	.	.	.	.	.	.
.	.	.	.	.	.	.	.	.	.
.	.	.	.	.	.	.	.	.	.
.	.	.	.	.	.	.	.	.	.
.	.	.	.	.	.	.	.	.	.
.	.	.	.	.	.	.	.	.	.
.	.	.	.	.	.	.	.	.	.
.	.	.	.	[glycine]	.	.	.	.	.
.	.	Grayson	.	(grison)	.	.	.	.	.
.	.	.	.	.	.	.	.	.	.
.	.	.	.	.	.	.	.	.	.
.	.	.	.	.	.	.	.	.	.
.	.	.	.	.	.	.	.	.	.
.	.	.	.	.	.	.	.	.	.
.	.	.	.	.	.	.	.	.	.
.	.	.	.	.	.	.	.	.	.
.	.	.	.	.	.	.	.	.	.
.	.	.	.	.	.	.	.	.	.

Final—/snd/ . For inflected forms add /d/ to appropriate words, e.g. fastened.
—/snz/ . For inflected forms add /z/ to appropriate words, e.g. fastens.

	i	ɪ	ɛ	æ	ɑ	ɒ(ɑ	ɔ	ʊ	u
—									
p	[peason]†	.	.	.	.	.	.	.	.
b	.	.	.	basan	.	.	.	.	.
t	.	(ptisan)	.	.	.	.	.	.	.
d	.	(dizen)†	.	.	.	.	.	.	.
k	.	.	.	.	.	.	[causen]†	.	.
g	geason†	gizzen†	.	.	.	[gozzan]	.	.	.
f	.	[fizzen]	.	.	.	.	.	.	.
v	.	.	.	.	.	.	.	.	.
θ	.	.	.	.	.	.	.	.	.
ð	.	.	.	.	.	.	.	.	.
s	season*	.	.	.	.	.	.	.	Sus
z	.	.	.	.	.	.	.	.	.
ʃ	.	.	.	.	.	.	.	.	.
ʒ	.	.	.	.	.	.	.	.	.
h	.	.	.	.	.	.	.	.	.
tʃ	.	.	.	.	.	.	.	.	.
dʒ	.	.	.	.	.	.	.	.	.
m	(meson)	mizzen	.	.	.	.	.	.	.
n	.	.	.	.	.	.	.	.	.
l	.	.	.	.	.	lozen	.	.	.
r	reason	risen	resin	.	.	rosin	.	.	.
w	[weazen]	wizen	.	.	.	.	.	.	.
j	.	.	.	.	.	.	.	.	.
pl	.	.	.	.	.	.	.	.	.
pr	.	prison	.	.	.	.	.	.	.
bl	.	.	.	.	.	.	.	.	.
br	.	.	.	.	.	.	.	.	.
tr	treason	.	.	.	.	.	.	.	.
tw	.	.	.	.	.	.	.	.	.
dr	.	.	.	.	.	.	.	.	.
kl	.	.	.	.	.	.	.	.	.
kr	.	.	.	.	.	.	.	.	.
kw	.	.	.	.	.	.	.	.	.
gl	.	.	.	.	.	.	.	.	.
gr	.	(grison)	.	.	.	.	.	.	.
fl	.	.	.	.	.	.	.	.	.
fr	.	.	.	.	.	.	.	.	.
θr	.	.	.	.	.	.	.	.	.
sp	.	.	.	.	.	.	.	.	.
st	.	.	.	.	.	.	.	.	.
sk	.	.	.	.	.	.	.	.	.
sm	.	.	.	.	.	.	.	.	.
sn	.	.	.	.	.	.	.	.	.
sl	.	.	.	.	.	.	.	.	.
sw	.	.	.	.	.	.	.	.	.
ʃr	.	.	.	.	.	.	.	.	.
spl	.	.	.	.	.	.	.	.	.
spr	.	.	.	.	.	.	.	.	.
str	.	.	.	.	.	.	.	.	.
skr	.	.	.	.	.	.	.	.	.
skw	.	.	.	.	.	.	.	.	.

* homophones—see page 224.
  Total number of words—41

ʌ	ɜ/r	eɪ	oʊ	aɪ	aʊ	ɔɪ	i/ə/r	ɛ/ə/r	ju
						poison			
				(bison)					
dozen				(dizen)†					
cousin*									
						foison			
									(Susan)
			hosen†						
			chosen						
		raisin	rosen*						
		blazon							
		brazen							
						(cloison)			
		glazen							
				greisen*					
			frozen						
		scazon							

Final—/znd/ . For inflected forms add /d/ to appropriate words, e.g. poisoned.
—/znz/ . For inflected forms add /z/ to appropriate words, e.g. poisons.

	i	ɪ	ɛ	æ	ɑ/r	ɒ(ɑ	ɔ(oʊ/r	ʊ	u
–	·	·	·	ashen	·	·	·	·	·
p	·	·	·	passion	·	·	portion	·	·
b	·	·	·	·	·	·	·	·	·
t	·	Titian	·	·	·	·	tortion	·	·
d	·	·	·	·	·	·	·	·	·
k	·	·	·	·	·	·	caution	cushion	·
g	·	·	·	·	·	·	·	·	·
f	·	fission	·	fashion	·	·	·	·	·
v	·	·	·	·	·	·	·	·	·
θ	·	·	·	·	·	·	·	·	·
ð	·	·	·	·	·	·	·	·	·
s	·	(scission)	session*	·	·	·	·	·	·
z	·	·	·	·	·	·	·	·	·
ʃ	·	·	·	·	·	·	·	·	·
ʒ	·	·	·	·	·	·	·	·	·
h	·	·	(hessian)	·	·	·	·	·	·
tʃ	·	·	·	·	·	·	·	·	·
dʒ	·	·	·	·	·	·	·	·	·
m	·	mission	·	·	Martian	·	·	·	·
n	·	·	·	·	·	·	·	·	·
l	·	·	·	·	·	·	·	·	·
r	·	·	·	ration	·	·	·	·	·
w	·	·	·	·	·	[washen]† ·	·	·	·
j	·	·	·	·	·	·	·	·	·
pl	·	·	·	·	·	·	·	·	·
pr	·	·	·	·	·	·	·	·	·
bl	·	·	·	·	·	·	·	·	·
br	·	·	·	·	·	·	·	·	·
tr	·	·	·	·	·	·	·	·	·
tw	·	·	·	·	·	·	·	·	·
dr	·	·	·	·	·	·	·	·	·
kl	·	·	·	·	·	·	·	·	·
kr	·	·	·	·	·	·	·	·	cru⦇
kw	·	·	·	·	·	·	·	·	·
gl	·	·	·	·	·	·	·	·	·
gr	Grecian	·	·	·	·	·	·	·	·
fl	·	·	·	·	·	·	·	·	·
fr	·	·	·	·	·	·	·	·	·
θr	·	·	·	·	·	·	·	·	·
sp	·	·	·	·	·	·	·	·	·
st	·	·	·	·	·	·	·	·	·
sk	·	·	·	·	·	·	·	·	·
sm	·	·	·	·	·	·	·	·	·
sn	sneeshan† ·	·	·	·	·	· ·	·	·	·
sl	·	·	·	·	·	·	·	·	·
sw	·	·	·	·	·	·	·	·	·
ʃr	·	·	·	·	·	·	·	·	·
spl	·	·	·	·	·	·	·	·	·
spr	·	·	·	·	·	·	·	·	·
str	·	·	·	·	·	·	·	·	·
skr	·	·	·	·	·	·	·	·	·
skw	·	·	·	·	·	·	·	·	·

* homophones—see page 224.
  Total number of words—35

ʌ	ɜ/r	eɪ	oʊ	aɪ	aʊ	ɔɪ	i/ə/r	ɛ/ə/r	ju
.	.	(Asian)	ocean	.	.	.	.	.	.
.	(Persian)	.	potion	.	.	.	.	.	.
.	.	.	.	.	.	.	.	.	.
.	.	.	.	.	.	.	.	.	.
.	.	.	Goshen	.	.	.	.	.	.
.	.	.	.	.	.	.	.	.	.
.	(version)	.	.	.	.	.	.	.	.
.	.	.	.	.	.	.	.	.	.
.	.	.	.	.	.	.	.	.	.
.	.	.	.	.	.	.	.	.	.
.	.	.	.	.	.	.	.	.	.
.	.	.	.	.	.	.	.	.	.
.	.	.	.	.	.	.	.	.	.
.	.	.	.	.	.	.	.	.	.
.	.	.	.	.	.	.	.	.	.
.	mersion	.	motion	.	.	.	.	.	.
.	.	nation	notion	.	.	.	.	.	.
.	.	.	lotion	.	.	.	.	.	.
Russian	.	.	.	.	.	.	.	.	.
.	.	.	.	.	.	.	.	.	.
.	.	.	.	.	.	.	.	.	.
Prussian	.	.	.	.	.	.	.	.	.
.	.	.	.	.	.	.	.	.	.
.	.	.	.	.	.	.	.	.	.
.	.	.	.	.	.	.	.	.	.
.	.	.	.	.	.	.	.	.	.
.	.	.	.	.	.	.	.	.	.
.	.	.	.	.	.	.	.	.	.
.	.	.	.	.	.	.	.	.	.
.	.	.	.	.	.	.	.	.	.
.	.	.	groschen	.	.	.	.	.	.
.	.	.	.	.	.	.	.	.	.
.	.	.	.	.	.	.	.	.	.
.	.	.	.	.	.	.	.	.	.
.	.	station	.	.	.	.	.	.	.
.	.	.	Scotian†	.	.	.	.	.	.
.	.	.	.	.	.	.	.	.	.
.	.	.	.	.	.	.	.	.	.
.	.	.	.	.	.	.	.	.	.
.	.	.	.	.	.	.	.	.	.
.	.	.	.	.	.	.	.	.	.
.	.	.	.	.	.	.	.	.	.
.	.	.	.	.	.	.	.	.	.
.	.	.	.	.	.	.	.	.	.

Final—/ʃnd/ . For inflected forms add /d/ to appropriate words, e.g. fashioned.
   —/ʃnz/ . For inflected forms add /z/ to appropriate words, e.g. fashions.

153

	i	ɪ	ɛ	æ	ɑ/r	ɒ	ɔ	ʊ	u
–	·	·	·	·	·	·	·	·	·
p	·	pigeon*	·	·	·	·	·	·	·
b	[bejan]†	·	·	·	·	·	·	·	·
t	·	·	·	·	·	·	·	·	·
d	·	·	·	·	·	·	·	·	·
k	·	·	·	·	·	·	·	·	·
g	·	·	·	·	·	·	·	·	·
f	·	·	·	·	·	·	·	·	·
v	·	·	·	·	·	·	·	·	·
θ	·	·	·	·	·	·	·	·	·
ð	·	·	·	·	·	·	·	·	·
s	·	·	·	·	·	(sojourn)	·	·	·
z	·	·	·	·	·	·	·	·	·
ʃ	·	·	·	·	·	·	·	·	·
ʒ	·	·	·	·	·	·	·	·	·
h	·	·	·	·	·	·	·	·	·
tʃ	·	·	·	·	·	·	·	·	·
dʒ	·	·	·	·	·	·	·	·	·
m	·	·	·	·	margin	·	·	·	·
n	·	·	·	·	·	·	·	·	·
l	legion*	·	·	·	·	·	·	·	·
r	region	·	·	·	·	·	·	·	·
w	·	widgeon	·	·	·	·	·	·	·
j	·	·	·	·	·	·	·	·	·
pl	·	·	·	·	·	·	·	·	·
pr	·	·	·	·	·	·	·	·	·
bl	·	·	·	·	·	·	·	·	·
br	·	·	·	·	·	·	·	·	·
tr	·	·	·	·	·	·	·	·	·
tw	·	·	·	·	·	·	·	·	·
dr	·	·	·	·	·	·	·	·	·
kl	·	·	·	·	·	·	·	·	·
kr	·	·	·	·	·	·	·	·	·
kw	·	·	·	·	·	·	·	·	·
gl	·	·	·	·	·	·	·	·	·
gr	·	·	·	·	·	·	·	·	·
fl	·	·	·	·	·	·	·	·	·
fr	·	·	·	·	·	·	·	·	·
θr	·	·	·	·	·	·	·	·	·
sp	·	·	·	·	·	·	·	·	·
st	·	·	·	æ	·	·	·	·	·
sk	·	·	·	·	·	·	·	·	·
sm	·	·	·	·	·	·	·	·	·
sn	·	·	·	·	·	·	·	·	·
sl	·	·	·	·	·	·	·	·	·
sw	·	·	·	·	·	·	·	·	·
ʃr	·	·	·	·	·	·	·	·	·
spl	·	·	·	·	·	·	·	·	·
spr	·	·	·	·	·	·	·	·	·
str	·	·	·	·	·	·	·	·	·
skr	·	·	·	·	·	·	·	·	·
skw	·	·	·	·	·	·	·	·	·

* homophones—see page 224.
  Total number of words—22

Λ	ɜ/r	eɪ	oʊ	aɪ	aʊ	ɔɪ	i/ə/r	ɜ/ə/r	ju
	bourgeon [bajan]†								
dudgeon									
gudgeon	gurjun								
	virgin								
	surgeon		(sojourn)						
	murgeon†								
			yojan						
bludgeon									
trudgen		Trajan	Trojan						
	sturgeon								

Final—/dʒnd/ . For inflected forms add /d/ to appropriate words, e.g. sojourned.
 —/dʒnz/ . For inflected forms add /z/ to appropriate words, e.g. regions.

	i	ɪ	ɛ	æ	ɑ/r	ɒ(ɑ	ɔ(oʊ/r	ʊ	u
–	.	.	.	Ammon	.	.	.	.	.
p	.	.	.	.	.	.	.	.	.
b	.	.	.	.	barmen	.	.	.	.
t	.	.	.	tamin	.	.	.	.	.
d	demon*	.	(daimen)	daman	.	.	doormen	.	.
k	.	.	.	caman	Carmen*	common	.	.	.
g	.	.	.	gammon*	.	.	.	.	.
f	.	.	.	famine	.	.	foremen	.	.
v	.	.	.	.	.	.	.	.	.
θ	.	.	.	.	.	.	.	.	.
ð	.	.	.	.	.	.	.	.	.
s	semen	'simmon	.	salmon	.	.	.	.	.
z	.	.	.	.	.	.	.	.	.
ʃ	.	.	.	shaman	.	.	.	.	Schu
ʒ	.	.	.	.	.	.	.	.	.
h	.	.	.	.	harman	.	.	.	.
tʃ	.	.	.	.	.	.	.	.	.
dʒ	.	.	gemman†	.	.	.	.	.	.
m	.	.	.	mammon	.	.	Mormon	.	.
n	.	.	.	.	.	.	Norman*	.	.
l	(leman)	.	*lemon**	.	.	.	lawmen	.	lum
r	.	.	.	.	.	.	.	.	rum
w	.	women	.	.	.	.	.	woman	.
j	.	.	Yemen	.	yamen	.	.	.	.
pl	.	.	.	.	.	.	.	.	.
pr	.	.	.	.	.	.	.	.	.
bl	.	.	.	.	.	.	.	.	.
br	(Bremen)	.	.	.	Brahmen*	.	.	.	.
tr	.	.	.	.	.	.	.	.	Tru
tw	.	.	.	.	.	.	.	.	.
dr	.	.	.	.	.	[dromon]	.	.	.
kl	.	.	.	.	.	.	.	.	.
kr	.	.	.	.	.	.	.	.	crur
kw	.	.	.	.	.	.	.	.	.
gl	.	.	.	.	.	.	.	.	.
gr	.	.	.	.	.	.	.	.	.
fl	.	.	.	.	.	.	floormen	.	.
fr	.	.	.	.	.	.	.	.	.
θr	.	.	.	.	.	.	.	.	.
sp	.	.	.	.	.	.	.	.	.
st	.	.	.	.	.	.	.	.	.
sk	.	.	.	.	.	.	.	.	.
sm	.	.	.	.	.	.	.	.	.
sn	.	.	.	.	.	.	.	.	.
sl	.	.	.	.	.	.	.	.	.
sw	.	.	.	.	.	.	.	.	.
ʃr	.	.	.	.	.	.	.	.	.
spl	.	.	.	.	.	.	.	.	.
spr	.	.	.	.	.	.	.	.	.
str	.	.	.	.	.	.	.	.	.
skr	.	.	.	.	.	.	.	.	.
skw	.	.	.	.	.	.	.	.	.

* homophones—see pages 224–225.

Total number of words—75

ʌ	ɜ/r	eɪ	oʊ	aɪ	aʊ	ɔɪ	i/ə/r	ɛ/ə/r	ju
.	ermine	.	omen	.	.	.	.	airmen	.
.	.	.	.	.	.	.	.	.	.
.	.	.	.	Timon*	.	toymen	.	.	.
.	.	Damon*	.	(daimon)	.	.	.	.	.
cumin	.	.	.	cayman	cowmen	.	.	.	.
.	firman	.	.	.	.	.	.	.	.
.	vermin	.	.	.	.	.	.	.	.
.	.	.	.	.	.	.	.	.	.
.	.	.	.	.	.	.	.	.	.
summon	sermon	.	.	Simon	.	.	.	.	.
.	.	.	.	.	.	.	.	.	.
.	Sherman	.	showmen	.	.	.	.	.	.
.	Herman	Haman	.	hymen*	.	.	.	.	human
.	.	.	.	.	.	.	.	chairmen	.
.	German*	.	.	.	.	.	.	.	.
.	merman	.	.	.	.	.	.	.	.
.	.	.	nomen*	.	.	.	.	.	.
.	.	laymen	.	limen	.	.	.	.	.
.	.	.	Roman	.	.	.	.	.	.
.	.	.	.	.	.	.	.	.	.
.	.	.	yeoman	.	.	.	.	.	.
.	.	.	.	.	ploughmen	.	.	.	.
.	.	.	.	primine	.	.	.	.	.
.	.	(Bremen)	(bromine)	.	.	.	.	.	.
.	.	.	.	.	.	.	.	.	.
.	.	.	.	.	.	.	.	.	.
.	.	.	.	.	.	.	.	.	.
.	.	.	.	.	.	.	.	.	.
.	.	.	.	.	.	.	.	.	.
.	.	.	.	.	.	.	.	.	.
.	.	.	.	.	.	.	.	.	.
.	.	flamen	.	.	.	.	.	.	.
.	.	.	.	.	.	.	.	.	.
.	.	.	.	.	.	.	.	.	.
.	.	.	.	.	.	.	spearmen	.	.
.	.	stamen	.	.	.	.	.	.	ju
.	.	.	.	.	.	.	.	.	.
.	.	.	snowmen	.	.	.	.	.	.
.	.	.	.	.	.	.	.	.	.
.	.	.	.	.	.	.	.	.	.
.	.	.	.	.	.	.	.	.	.
.	.	.	.	.	.	.	.	.	.
.	.	.	.	.	.	.	.	.	.

Final—/mnd/ . For inflected forms add /d/ to appropriate words, e.g. summoned.
—/mnz/ . For inflected forms add /z/ to appropriate words, e.g. summons.

	i	ɪ	ɛ	æ	ɑ/r	ɒ(ɑ	ɔ/r	ʊ	u
–	.	.	Ellen	Allan	.	.	orlon	.	.
p	.	.	.	.	.	pollen*	.	.	.
b	.	billon	.	ballan	.	.	.	.	.
t	.	.	.	talon	.	.	.	.	.
d	.	Dillon	.	.	.	.	.	.	.
k	.	.	.	.	carline	Colin*	.	.	co‌
g	.	.	.	gallon	.	[gollan]	.	.	.
f	.	.	felon	phallin	.	.	fallen	.	.
v	.	villain*	.	.	.	.	.	.	.
θ	.	.	.	.	.	.	.	.	.
ð	.	.	.	.	.	.	.	.	.
s	.	.	.	.	.	.	.	.	.
z	.	.	.	.	.	.	.	.	.
ʃ	.	.	.	shallon	.	.	.	.	.
ʒ	.	.	.	.	.	.	.	.	.
h	.	.	Helen	.	hallan†	.	.	.	ch‌
tʃ	.	.	.	.	.	.	.	.	.
dʒ	.	.	.	.	.	.	.	.	.
m	.	.	melon	.	marline*	.	.	.	.
n	.	.	.	.	.	.	norlan'†	.	.
l	.	.	.	.	[lallan]	.	.	.	.
r	.	.	.	.	.	.	.	.	.
w	.	.	.	.	.	.	.	woollen	.
j	.	.	.	.	.	.	.	.	yu‌
pl	.	.	.	.	.	.	.	.	.
pr	.	.	.	.	.	.	.	.	.
bl	.	.	.	.	.	.	.	.	.
br	.	.	.	.	.	.	.	.	.
tr	.	.	.	.	.	.	.	.	.
tw	.	.	.	.	.	.	.	.	.
dr	.	.	.	.	.	.	.	.	.
kl	.	.	.	.	.	.	.	.	.
kr	.	.	.	.	.	.	.	.	.
kw	.	.	.	.	.	.	.	.	.
gl	.	.	.	.	.	.	.	.	.
gr	.	.	.	.	.	.	.	.	.
fl	.	.	.	.	.	.	.	.	.
fr	.	.	.	.	.	.	.	.	.
θr	.	.	.	.	.	.	.	.	.
sp	.	.	.	.	.	.	.	.	.
st	.	.	.	.	Stalin	.	.	.	.
sk	.	.	.	.	.	.	.	.	.
sm	.	.	.	.	.	.	.	.	.
sn	.	.	.	.	.	.	.	.	.
sl	.	.	.	.	.	.	.	.	.
sw	.	.	.	.	.	.	.	.	.
ʃr	.	.	.	.	.	.	.	.	.
spl	.	.	.	.	.	.	.	.	.
spr	.	.	.	.	.	.	.	.	.
str	.	.	.	.	.	.	.	.	.
skr	.	.	.	.	.	.	.	.	.
skw	.	.	.	.	.	.	.	.	.

* homophones—see page 225.
  Total number of words—46

ʌ	ɜ/r	eɪ	oʊ	aɪ	aʊ	ɔɪ	i/ə/r	ɛ/ə/r	ju
.	.	.	.	.	.	.	.	.	yulan
.	purlin	.	.	pylon	.	.	.	.	.
.	(berlin)	.	(bollen)†	.	.	.	.	.	.
.	.	.	.	.	.	.	.	.	.
Cullen	.	.	colon	kylin	.	.	.	.	.
.	.	Galen	.	.	.	.	.	.	.
.	.	.	.	.	.	.	.	.	.
.	.	.	.	.	.	.	.	.	.
.	.	.	.	.	.	.	.	.	.
sullen	.	.	Solen*	.	.	.	.	.	.
.	.	.	.	.	.	.	.	.	.
.	.	.	.	.	.	.	.	.	.
.	.	.	.	.	.	.	.	.	.
.	.	.	.	.	.	.	.	.	.
.	Merlin*	.	.	.	.	.	.	.	.
.	.	.	Nolan	nylon	.	.	.	.	.
.	.	.	.	.	.	.	.	.	.
.	.	.	.	.	.	.	.	.	.
.	.	.	.	.	.	.	.	.	.
.	.	.	.	.	.	.	.	.	.
.	.	.	.	.	.	.	.	.	.
Trullan	.	.	.	.	.	.	.	.	.
.	.	.	.	.	.	.	.	.	.
.	.	.	.	.	.	.	.	.	.
.	.	.	.	.	.	.	.	.	.
.	.	.	.	.	.	.	.	.	.
.	.	.	.	.	.	.	.	.	.
.	.	.	.	.	.	.	.	.	.
.	.	.	.	.	.	.	.	.	.
.	.	.	.	.	.	.	.	.	.
.	.	.	stolen*	.	.	.	.	.	.
.	.	.	.	.	.	.	.	.	.
.	smerlin†	.	.	.	.	.	.	.	.
.	.	.	.	.	.	.	.	.	.
.	.	.	swollen	.	.	.	.	.	.
.	.	.	.	.	.	.	.	.	.
.	.	.	.	.	.	.	.	.	.
.	.	.	.	.	.	.	.	.	.
.	.	.	.	.	.	.	.	.	.
.	.	.	.	.	.	.	.	.	.

Final—/lnz/ . For inflected forms add /z/ to appropriate words, e.g. gallons.

	i	ɪ	ɛ	æ	ɑ	ɒ(ɔ(ɑ	ɔ(oʊ	ʊ	ʊə
—	.	.	(Aaron)	.			.	.	
p	.	.	(perron)	.	.		.	.	
b	.	.	.	barren*	.	.	(boron)	.	
t	.	.	(pterin)	.	.		.	.	
d	.	.		Darren	.		.	.	
k	.	.		Carron*	(Karen)	.	.	.	
g	.	.	.	garron	.		.	.	
f	.	.	.	.	.	foreign	.	.	
v	.	.	.	varan	.		.	.	
θ	.	.	.	.	.	.	.	.	
ð	.	.	.	.	.	.	.	.	
s	.	.	serin	.	.	.	.	.	
z	.	.	.	.	.	.	.	.	
ʃ	.	.	.	Sharon	.	.	Shoran	.	.
ʒ	.	.	.	.	.	.	.	.	.
h	.	.	heron*	.	.	.	.	.	.
tʃ	.	.	.	.	.	.	.	.	.
dʒ	.	.	.	.	.	.	.	.	.
m	.	.	.	.	.	.	moron	.	.
n	.	.	.	.	.	.	.	(neurine)	.
l	.	.	.	.	.	.	.	.	.
r	.	.	.	.	.	.	.	.	.
w	.	.	.	.	.	warren*	.	.	.
j	.	.	.	.	.	.	.	(urine)	(ur
pl	.	.	.	.	.	.	.	(pleuron)	(pl
pr	.	.	.	.	.	.	.	.	.
bl	.	.	.	.	.	.	.	.	.
br	.	.	.	.	.	.	.	.	.
tr	.	.	.	.	.	.	.	.	.
tw	.	.	.	.	.	.	.	.	.
dr	.	.	.	.	.	.	.	.	.
kl	.	.	.	.	.	.	chlorin	.	.
kr	.	.	.	.	.	.	.	.	.
kw	.	.	.	.	.	.	.	.	.
gl	.	.	.	.	.	.	.	.	.
gr	.	.	.	.	.	.	.	.	.
fl	.	.	.	.	.	florin	.	.	.
fr	.	.	.	.	.	.	.	.	.
θr	.	.	.	.	.	.	.	.	.
sp	.	.	.	.	.	sporran	.	.	.
st	.	.	.	.	.	.	.	.	.
sk	.	.	.	.	.	.	.	.	.
sm	.	.	.	.	.	.	.	.	.
sn	.	.	.	.	.	.	.	.	.
sl	.	.	.	.	.	.	.	.	.
sw	.	.	.	.	.	.	.	.	.
ʃr	.	.	.	.	.	.	.	.	.
spl	.	.	.	.	.	.	.	.	.
spr	.	.	.	.	.	.	.	.	.
str	.	.	.	.	.	.	.	.	.
skr	.	.	.	.	.	.	.	.	.
skw	.	.	.	.	.	.	.	.	.

* homophones—see page 225.
Total number of words—40

ʌ	ɜ/r	eɪ	oʊ	aɪ	aʊ	ɔɪ	i/ə/r	ɛ/ə/r	jʊə
·	·	·	·	·	·	·	·	(Aaron)	(urine)
·	·	·	·	·	·	·	·	·	[purin]
·	·	·	·	Byron	·	·	·	·	(burin)
·	·	·	·	·	·	·	·	·	(Turin)
·	·	·	·	·	·	·	·	(Charon)	·
·	·	·	·	·	·	·	·	·	furan
·	·	·	·	·	·	·	·	·	·
·	·	·	·	·	·	·	·	·	·
·	·	·	·	siren*	·	·	·	·	·
·	·	·	·	·	·	·	·	·	·
·	·	·	·	·	·	·	·	·	·
·	·	·	·	·	·	·	·	·	Huron
·	·	·	·	·	·	·	·	·	·
·	·	·	·	gyron†	·	·	·	·	·
(murrain)	(murrain)	·	·	·	·	·	·	·	·
·	·	·	·	·	·	·	·	·	(neurine)
·	·	·	·	·	·	·	·	·	·
·	·	·	·	·	·	·	·	·	·
·	·	·	·	·	·	·	·	·	·
·	·	·	·	·	·	·	·	·	·
·	·	·	·	·	·	·	·	·	·
·	·	·	·	·	·	·	·	·	·
·	·	·	·	·	·	·	·	·	·
·	·	·	·	·	·	·	·	·	·
·	·	·	·	·	·	·	·	·	·
·	·	·	·	·	·	·	·	·	·
·	·	·	·	·	·	·	·	·	·
·	·	·	·	·	·	·	·	·	·
·	·	·	·	·	·	·	·	glairin	·
·	·	·	·	·	·	·	·	·	·
·	·	·	·	·	·	·	·	·	·
·	·	·	·	·	·	·	·	·	·
·	·	·	·	·	·	·	·	·	·
·	·	·	·	·	·	·	·	·	·
·	·	·	·	·	·	·	·	·	·
·	·	·	·	·	·	·	·	·	·
·	·	·	·	·	·	·	·	·	·
·	·	·	·	·	·	·	·	·	·
·	·	·	·	·	·	·	·	·	·
·	·	·	·	·	·	·	·	·	·

Final—/rnz/ . For inflected forms add /z/ to appropriate words, e.g. warrens.

	i	ɪ	ɛ	æ	ɑ	ɒ(ɑ	ɔ	ʊ	u
–	.	.	.	axon	.	oxen	auxin	.	.
p	.	.	.	.	.	.	.	.	.
b	.	.	.	.	.	boxen	.	.	.
t	.	.	Texan	.	.	toxin*	.	.	.
d	.	.	.	.	.	.	.	.	.
k	.	.	.	caxon	.	.	.	.	.
g	.	.	.	.	.	.	.	.	.
f	.	.	.	.	.	.	.	.	.
v	.	vixen	.	(vaccine)	.	.	.	.	.
θ	.	.	.	.	.	.	.	.	.
ð	.	.	.	.	.	.	.	.	.
s	.	.	.	Saxon	.	.	.	.	.
z	.	.	.	.	.	.	.	.	.
ʃ	.	.	.	.	.	.	.	.	.
ʒ	.	.	.	.	.	.	.	.	.
h	.	.	.	.	.	.	.	.	.
tʃ	.	.	.	.	.	.	.	.	.
dʒ	.	.	.	.	.	.	.	.	.
m	.	.	.	.	.	.	.	.	.
n	.	Nixon	.	.	.	.	.	.	.
l	.	.	.	.	.	.	.	.	.
r	.	.	.	.	.	.	.	.	.
w	.	.	.	waxen	.	[woxen]†	.	.	.
j	.	.	.	.	.	.	.	.	.
pl	.	.	.	.	.	.	.	.	.
pr	.	.	.	.	.	.	.	.	.
bl	.	.	.	.	.	.	.	.	.
br	.	.	.	.	.	.	.	.	.
tr	.	.	.	.	.	.	.	.	.
tw	.	.	.	.	.	.	.	.	.
dr	.	.	.	.	.	.	.	.	.
kl	.	.	.	klaxon	.	.	.	.	.
kr	.	.	.	.	.	.	.	.	.
kw	.	.	.	.	.	.	.	.	.
gl	.	.	.	.	.	.	.	.	.
gr	.	.	.	.	.	.	.	.	.
fl	.	.	.	flaxon	.	.	.	.	.
fr	.	.	.	.	.	.	.	.	.
θr	.	.	.	.	.	.	.	.	.
sp	.	.	.	.	.	.	.	.	.
st	.	.	.	.	.	.	.	.	.
sk	.	.	.	.	.	.	.	.	.
sm	.	.	.	.	.	..	.	.	.
sn	.	.	.	.	.	.	.	.	.
sl	.	.	.	.	.	.	.	.	.
sw	.	.	.	.	.	.	.	.	.
ʃr	.	.	.	.	.	.	.	.	.
spl	.	.	.	.	.	.	.	.	.
spr	.	.	.	.	.	.	.	.	.
str	.	.	.	.	.	.	.	.	.
skr	.	.	.	.	.	.	.	.	.
skw	.	.	.	.	.	.	.	.	.

* homophones—see page 225.
  Total number of words—15

162

ʌ	ɜ/r	eɪ	oʊ	aɪ	aʊ	ɔɪ	i/ə/r	ɛ/ə/r	ju
.	.	.	.	.	.	.	.	.	.
.	.	.	.	.	.	.	.	.	.
.	.	.	.	.	.	.	.	.	.
.	.	.	.	.	.	.	.	.	.
.	.	.	.	.	.	.	.	.	.
.	.	.	.	.	.	.	.	.	.
.	.	.	.	.	.	.	.	.	.
.	.	.	.	.	.	.	.	.	.
.	.	.	.	.	.	.	.	.	.
.	.	.	.	.	.	.	.	.	.
.	.	.	.	.	.	.	.	.	.
.	.	.	.	.	.	.	.	.	.
.	.	.	.	.	.	.	.	.	.
.	.	.	.	.	.	.	.	.	.
.	.	.	.	.	.	.	.	.	.
.	.	.	.	.	.	.	.	.	.
.	.	.	.	.	.	.	.	.	.
.	.	.	.	.	.	.	.	.	.
.	.	.	.	.	.	.	.	.	.
.	.	.	.	.	.	.	.	.	.

Final—/ksnz/ . For inflected forms add /z/ to appropriate words, e.g. Saxons.

163

	i	ɪ	ɛ	æ	ɑ	ɒ(ɑ	ɔ	ʊ	u
—	.	.	.	action	.	(auction)	(auction)	.	.
p	.	.	.	paction	.	.	.	.	.
b	.	.	.	.	.	.	.	.	.
t	.	.	.	.	.	.	.	.	.
d	.	diction	.	.	.	.	.	.	.
k	.	.	.	.	.	coction	.	.	.
g	.	.	.	.	.	.	.	.	.
f	.	fiction	.	faction	.	.	.	.	.
v	.	.	.	.	.	.	.	.	.
θ	.	.	.	.	.	.	.	.	.
ð	.	.	.	.	.	.	.	.	.
s	.	.	.	.	.	.	.	.	.
z	.	.	.	.	.	.	.	.	.
ʃ	.	.	.	.	.	.	.	.	.
ʒ	.	.	.	.	.	.	.	.	.
h	.	.	.	.	.	.	.	.	.
tʃ	.	.	.	.	.	.	.	.	.
dʒ	.	.	.	.	.	.	.	.	.
m	.	miction†	.	.	.	.	.	.	.
n	.	.	.	.	.	.	.	.	.
l	.	.	lection	.	.	.	.	.	.
r	.	.	rection†	.	.	.	.	.	.
w	.	.	.	.	.	.	.	.	.
j	.	.	.	.	.	.	.	.	.
pl	.	.	.	.	.	.	.	.	.
pr	.	.	.	.	.	.	.	.	.
bl	.	.	.	.	.	.	.	.	.
br	.	.	.	.	.	.	.	.	.
tr	.	.	.	traction	.	.	.	.	.
tw	.	.	.	.	.	.	.	.	.
dr	.	.	.	.	.	.	.	.	.
kl	.	.	.	.	.	.	.	.	.
kr	.	.	.	.	.	.	.	.	.
kw	.	.	.	.	.	.	.	.	.
gl	.	.	.	.	.	.	.	.	.
gr	.	.	.	.	.	.	.	.	.
fl	.	.	flexion	.	.	.	.	.	.
fr	.	.	.	fraction	.	.	.	.	.
θr	.	.	.	.	.	.	.	.	.
sp	.	.	.	.	.	.	.	.	.
st	.	.	.	.	.	.	.	.	.
sk	.	.	.	.	.	.	.	.	.
sm	.	.	.	.	.	.	.	.	.
sn	.	.	.	.	.	.	.	.	.
sl	.	.	.	.	.	.	.	.	.
sw	.	.	.	.	.	.	.	.	.
ʃr	.	.	.	.	.	.	.	.	.
spl	.	.	.	.	.	.	.	.	.
spr	.	.	.	.	.	.	.	.	.
str	.	.	.	.	.	.	.	.	.
skr	.	.	.	.	.	.	.	.	.
skw	.	.	.	.	.	.	.	.	.

Total number of words—17

164

ʌ	ɜ/r	eɪ	oʊ	aɪ	aʊ	ɔɪ	i/ə/r	ɛ/ə/r	ju
suction									
		—/kʃnd/							
		—/kʃnz/							
ruction†									
fluxion									

Final—/kʃnd/ . For inflected forms add /d/ to appropriate words, e.g. auctioned.
—/kʃnz/ . For inflected forms add /z/ to appropriate words, e.g. auctions.

	i	ɪ	ε	æ	ɑ/r	ɒ(ɑ	ɔ/r	ʊ	u
–	.	.	.	*apple*	.	.	.	.	.
p	people*	.	.	.	.	popple	.	.	.
b	.	.	.	.	.	.	.	.	.
t	.	tipple	.	.	.	topple	.	.	.
d	.	.	.	dapple	.	.	.	.	(d
k	.	.	.	.	carpel*	copple	.	.	.
g	.	.	.	.	.	.	.	.	.
f	.	fipple	.	.	.	.	.	.	.
v	.	.	.	.	.	.	vorpal	.	.
θ	.	.	.	.	.	.	.	.	.
ð	.	.	.	.	.	.	.	.	.
s	(sepal)	sipple	(sepal)	sapple	.	.	.	.	so
z	.	.	.	.	.	.	.	.	.
ʃ	.	.	.	.	.	.	.	.	.
ʒ	.	.	.	.	.	.	.	.	.
h	.	.	.	.	.	hopple	.	.	.
tʃ	.	.	.	chapel*	.	.	.	.	.
dʒ	.	.	.	.	.	.	.	.	.
m	.	.	.	.	.	.	.	.	.
n	.	nipple	.	.	.	.	.	.	.
l	.	.	.	.	.	.	.	.	.
r	.	ripple	.	.	.	.	.	.	.
w	wheeple	.	.	.	.	.	warple	.	.
j	.	.	.	.	.	.	.	.	.
pl	.	.	.	.	.	.	.	.	.
pr	.	.	.	.	.	.	.	.	.
bl	.	.	.	.	.	.	.	.	.
br	.	.	.	.	.	.	.	.	.
tr	.	triple*	.	.	.	.	.	.	.
tw	.	.	.	.	.	.	.	.	.
dr	.	.	.	.	.	.	.	.	.
kl	.	.	.	.	.	.	.	.	.
kr	.	cripple	.	[craple]†	.	.	.	.	.
kw	.	.	.	.	.	.	.	.	.
gl	.	.	.	.	.	.	.	.	.
gr	.	gripple	.	grapple	.	.	.	.	.
fl	.	.	.	.	.	.	.	.	.
fr	.	.	.	.	.	.	.	.	.
θr	.	.	.	.	[thrapple]†	[thropple]	.	.	.
sp	.	.	.	.	.	.	.	.	.
st	steeple	stipple	.	.	[stapple]†	[stopple]	.	.	.
sk	.	.	.	[scaple]	.	.	.	.	.
sm	.	.	.	.	.	.	.	.	.
sn	.	.	.	.	.	.	.	.	.
sl	.	.	.	.	.	.	.	.	.
sw	.	swipple	.	.	.	.	.	.	.
ʃr	.	.	.	.	.	.	.	.	.
spl	.	.	.	.	.	.	.	.	.
spr	.	.	.	.	.	.	.	.	.
str	.	.	.	.	.	.	.	.	.
skr	.	.	.	scrapple	.	.	.	.	scr
skw	.	.	.	.	.	.	.	.	.

* homophones—see page 225.
  Total number of words—54

ʌ	ɜ/r	eɪ	oʊ	aɪ	aʊ	ɔɪ	i/ə/r	ɛ/ə/r	ju
.	.	.	*opal*	.	.	.	.	.	.
.	*purple*	papal	.	.	.	.	.	.	pupil*
.	.	.	.	typal	.	.	.	.	.
.	.	.	.	.	.	.	.	.	(duple)
couple	[curpel]†	caple	copal	.	.	.	.	.	cupel
.	.	.	.	.	.	.	.	.	.
.	.	.	.	.	.	.	.	.	.
.	.	.	.	.	.	.	.	.	.
supple	.	.	.	.	.	.	.	.	.
.	.	.	.	.	.	.	.	.	.
.	.	.	.	.	.	.	.	.	.
.	hirple	.	.	.	.	.	.	.	.
.	.	.	.	.	.	.	.	.	.
.	.	maple	.	.	.	.	.	.	.
.	.	.	.	.	.	.	.	.	.
.	.	.	.	.	.	.	.	.	.
.	.	.	.	.	.	.	.	.	.
.	.	.	propyl	.	.	.	.	.	.
.	.	.	.	.	.	.	.	.	.
.	.	.	.	.	.	.	.	.	.
.	.	.	.	.	.	.	.	.	.
.	.	.	.	.	.	.	.	.	.
.	.	.	.	.	.	.	.	.	.
.	.	.	.	.	.	.	.	.	.
.	.	.	.	.	.	.	.	.	.
.	.	.	.	.	.	.	.	.	.
.	.	.	.	.	.	.	.	.	.
.	.	staple	.	stipel	.	.	.	.	.
.	.	.	.	.	.	.	.	.	.
.	.	.	.	.	.	.	.	.	.
.	.	.	.	.	.	.	.	.	.
.	.	.	.	.	.	.	.	.	.
.	.	.	.	.	.	.	.	.	.
.	.	.	.	.	.	.	.	.	.
.	.	.	.	.	.	.	.	.	.
.	.	.	.	.	.	.	.	.	.

Final—/pld/ . For inflected forms add /d/ to appropriate words, e.g. toppled.
—/plz/ . For inflected forms add /z/ to appropriate words, e.g. topples.

	i	ɪ	ɛ	æ	ɑ/r	ɒ(ɑ	ɔ/r	ʊ	u
−	·	·	·	·	·	obol	·	·	·
p	·	·	pebble	·	·	·	·	·	·
b	·	bibble	·	babble	barbel	bobble	bauble	·	·
t	·	·	·	·	·	·	·	·	(tu
d	·	dibble	·	dabble	·	·	·	·	·
k	·	kibble	·	cabble	·	cobble	corbel*	·	·
g	·	gibel	·	gabble	garble	gobble	·	·	·
f	feeble	·	faible	·	·	·	·	·	·
v	·	·	·	·	·	·	·	·	·
θ	·	(thible)	·	·	·	·	·	·	·
ð	·	·	·	·	·	·	·	·	·
s	·	[cibol]*	·	·	·	·	·	·	·
z	·	·	·	·	·	·	·	·	·
ʃ	·	·	·	shabble†	·	·	·	·	·
ʒ	·	·	·	·	·	·	·	·	·
h	·	·	·	·	·	hobble	·	·	·
tʃ	·	[chibol]	·	·	·	·	·	·	·
dʒ	·	·	·	jabble	·	·	·	·	·
m	·	·	·	·	marble	mobble	·	·	·
n	nebel	nibble	·	·	·	nobble*†	·	·	(n
l	·	·	·	·	·	·	·	·	·
r	·	·	rebel	rabble	·	·	·	·	ru
w	·	·	·	·	·	wobble	warble	·	·
j	·	·	·	·	·	·	·	·	·
pl	·	·	·	·	·	·	·	·	·
pr	·	[pribble]†	·	[prabble]	·	·	·	·	·
bl	·	·	·	·	·	·	·	·	·
br	·	·	·	brabble†	·	·	·	·	·
tr	·	tribble	treble	trabal	·	·	·	·	·
tw	·	·	·	·	·	·	·	·	·
dr	·	dribble	·	drabble	·	·	·	·	·
kl	·	·	·	·	·	·	·	·	·
kr	·	cribble	·	·	·	·	·	·	·
kw	·	quibble	·	·	·	·	·	·	·
gl	·	·	·	·	·	·	·	·	·
gr	·	·	·	[grabble]	·	·	·	·	·
fl	·	·	·	·	·	·	·	·	·
fr	·	fribble	·	·	·	·	·	·	·
θr	·	·	·	·	·	·	·	·	·
sp	·	·	·	·	·	·	·	·	·
st	·	stibble	·	·	·	·	·	·	·
sk	·	·	·	[scabble]	·	·	·	·	·
sm	·	·	·	·	·	·	·	·	·
sn	·	·	·	·	·	·	·	·	·
sl	·	·	·	·	·	·	·	·	·
sw	·	·	·	·	·	·	·	·	·
ʃr	·	·	·	·	·	·	·	·	·
spl	·	·	·	·	·	·	·	·	·
spr	·	·	·	·	·	·	·	·	·
str	·	·	·	·	·	·	·	·	·
skr	·	scribble	·	scrabble	·	·	·	·	·
skw	·	·	·	·	·	squabble	·	·	·

* homophones—see page 225.
  Total number of words—91

ʌ	ɜ/r	eɪ	oʊ	aɪ	aʊ	ɔɪ	i/ə/r	ɛ/ə/r	ju
.	.	able*	.	.	.	.	.	.	.
bubble	burble	Babel	.	Bible	.	.	.	.	bubel
.	.	*table*	.	.	.	.	.	.	(tubal)
double	.	.	.	.	.	.	.	.	.
.	.	cable	[coble]	.	.	.	.	.	.
.	.	gable	.	.	.	.	.	.	.
.	.	fable	.	.	.	foible	.	.	.
.	verbal	.	.	.	.	.	.	.	.
.	.	.	.	(thible)	.	.	.	.	.
.	.	sable*	.	.	.	.	.	.	.
.	.	.	.	.	.	.	.	.	.
.	.	.	.	.	.	.	.	.	.
hubble	herbal	hable	.	.	.	.	.	.	.
.	.	.	.	.	.	.	.	.	.
.	jirble†	.	.	.	.	.	.	.	.
.	.	Mabel	.	.	.	.	.	.	.
nubble*	.	.	noble	.	.	.	.	.	(nubile)
.	.	label	.	libel	.	.	.	.	.
rubble	.	.	.	.	.	.	.	.	.
.	.	.	.	.	.	.	.	.	.
.	.	.	.	.	.	.	.	.	.
.	.	.	.	.	.	.	.	.	.
.	.	.	.	.	.	.	.	.	.
trouble	.	.	.	tribal	.	.	.	.	.
.	.	.	.	.	.	.	.	.	.
.	.	.	.	.	.	.	.	.	.
.	.	.	.	.	.	.	.	.	.
.	.	.	global	.	.	.	.	.	.
[grubble].	.	.	.	.	.	.	.	.	.
.	.	.	.	.	.	.	.	.	.
.	(Fröbel)	(Fröbel)	.	.	.	.	.	.	.
.	.	.	.	.	.	.	.	.	.
stubble	.	stable	.	.	.	.	.	.	.
.	.	.	.	.	.	.	.	.	.
.	.	.	.	.	.	.	.	.	.
.	.	.	.	.	.	.	.	.	.
.	.	.	.	.	.	.	.	.	.
.	.	.	.	.	.	.	.	.	.
.	.	.	.	.	.	.	.	.	.
.	.	.	.	scribal	.	.	.	.	.
.	.	.	.	.	.	.	.	.	.

Final—/bld/ . For inflected forms add /d/ to appropriate words, e.g. bubbled.
—/blz/ . For inflected forms add /z/ to appropriate words, e.g. bubbles.

	i	ɪ	ɛ	æ	ɑ/r	ɒ(ɑ	ɔ(oʊ/r	ʊ	u
–			ettle†						
p	pightle		petal*		pattle†	pottle	portal		
b	*beetle**			battle*		*bottle*			
t		tittle		tattle					too
d						dottle†			
k		kittle	*kettle*	cattle	(cartel)		cautel†		cou
g									
f	foetal		fettle						foo
v		victual							
θ									
ð									
s	setal		settle						
z									
ʃ						[shottle]†			
ʒ									
h					(hartal)				
tʃ				chattel			chortle		
dʒ									
m			metal*		martel	mottle	mortal		
n		knittle†	nettle						
l	leetle†	little							
r				rattle	(Ratel)				roo
w		whittle*				wattle	[whortle]		
j									
pl									
pr				prattle					
bl									
br		brittle		brattle					bru
tr		trityl†							
tw						twottle			
dr									
kl									
kr						crottle			
kw		quittal†							
gl						glottal			
gr			Gretel						
fl									
fr									
θr						throttle			
sp		spittle*		spattle					
st					startle				
sk		skittle							
sm		smittle†							
sn									
sl									
sw									
ʃr									
spl									
spr				sprattle					
str									
skr				scrattle					
skw						squattle			

* homophones—see page 225.
  Total number of words—89

ʌ	ɜ/r	eɪ	oʊ	aɪ	aʊ	ɔɪ	i/ə/r	ɛ/ə/r	ju
.	.	.	.	.	.	.	.	.	.
.	.	.	.	.	.	.	.	.	.
.	*turtle*	.	total	title	.	.	.	.	.
.	.	.	dotal	dital	.	.	.	.	.
cuttle	kirtle*	.	.	.	.	.	.	.	.
guttle	.	.	.	.	.	.	.	.	.
.	(fertile)	fatal	.	.	.	.	.	.	.
.	.	.	.	vital	.	.	.	.	.
.	.	.	.	.	.	.	.	.	.
.	.	.	.	.	.	.	.	.	.
subtle*	.	.	.	cital	.	.	.	.	.
.	.	.	.	.	.	.	.	.	.
shuttle	.	.	.	.	.	.	.	.	.
.	.	.	.	.	.	.	.	.	.
.	hurtle	.	.	.	.	.	.	.	.
.	.	.	.	.	.	.	.	.	.
.	.	.	.	.	.	.	.	.	.
.	myrtle*	.	.	.	.	.	.	.	.
.	.	natal	notal	.	.	.	.	.	.
.	.	.	.	.	.	.	.	.	.
.	.	(Ratel)	.	.	.	.	.	.	.
.	[whirtle]	.	.	.	.	.	.	.	.
.	.	.	.	.	.	.	.	.	.
.	.	.	.	.	.	.	.	.	.
.	.	.	.	.	.	.	.	.	.
.	.	.	.	.	.	.	.	.	.
.	.	.	.	.	.	.	.	.	.
.	.	.	.	.	.	.	.	.	.
.	.	.	.	.	.	.	.	.	.
.	.	.	.	.	.	.	.	.	.
.	.	.	crotal	.	.	.	.	.	.
.	.	.	.	.	.	.	.	.	.
.	.	.	.	.	.	.	.	.	.
.	.	.	.	.	.	.	.	.	.
.	.	.	.	.	.	.	.	.	.
.	.	.	.	.	.	.	.	.	.
.	spurtle	.	.	.	.	.	.	.	.
.	.	statal	.	.	.	.	.	.	.
scuttle	.	.	.	.	.	.	.	.	scutal
.	.	.	.	.	.	.	.	.	.
.	snirtle	.	.	.	.	.	.	.	.
.	.	.	.	.	.	.	.	.	.
.	.	.	.	.	.	.	.	.	.
.	.	.	.	.	.	.	.	.	.
.	.	.	.	.	.	.	.	.	.
.	.	.	scrotal	.	.	.	.	.	.
.	.	.	.	.	.	.	.	.	.

Final—/tld/ . For inflected forms add /d/ to appropriate words, e.g. bottled.
—/tlz/ . For inflected forms add /z/ to appropriate words, e.g. bottles.

	i	ɪ	ɛ	æ	ɑ/r	ɒ(ɑ	ɔ/r	ʊ	u
–	.	(idyll)	.	addle	Ardil	.	.	.	.
p	.	piddle	pedal*	*paddle*	[padle]*†	.	.	.	*poo
b	beadle*	.	.	.	.	boddle	bordel†	.	boo
t	.	.	.	.	.	toddle	.	.	.
d	deadal	diddle	.	daddle†	.	.	dawdle	.	doo
k	.	kiddle	.	.	.	coddle	caudal*	.	.
g	.	.	.	Gadhẹl	.	.	.	.	.
f	.	fiddle	.	faddle	fardel	.	.	.	.
v	.	.	.	.	.	.	.	.	.
θ	.	.	.	.	.	.	.	.	.
ð	.	.	.	.	.	.	.	.	.
s	.	.	.	*saddle*	sardel	.	.	.	.
z	.	.	.	.	.	.	.	.	.
ʃ	.	.	.	.	.	.	.	.	.
ʒ	.	.	.	.	.	.	.	.	.
h	.	.	heddle	.	.	hoddle†	.	.	.
tʃ	.	.	.	.	.	.	.	.	.
dʒ	.	.	.	.	.	.	.	.	.
m	.	middle	*medal*	.	.	model	maudle†	.	.
n	*needle*	.	.	.	.	noddle	.	.	noo
l	.	.	.	.	.	.	.	.	.
r	.	riddle	[reddle]	[raddle]	.	.	.	.	.
w	wheedle	.	.	.	.	waddle	.	.	.
j	.	.	.	.	.	.	.	.	uda
pl	.	.	.	.	.	.	.	.	.
pr	.	.	.	.	.	.	.	.	.
bl	.	.	.	.	.	.	.	.	.
br	.	.	.	.	.	.	.	.	.
tr	.	.	tredle	.	.	.	.	.	.
tw	tweedle	twiddle	.	.	.	twaddle	.	.	.
dr	.	.	.	.	.	.	.	.	.
kl	.	.	.	.	.	.	.	.	.
kr	creedal	.	.	.	.	.	.	.	cro
kw	.	quiddle	.	.	.	.	.	.	.
gl	.	.	.	.	.	.	.	.	.
gr	.	griddle	.	.	.	.	.	.	.
fl	.	.	.	.	.	.	.	.	.
fr	.	.	.	.	.	.	.	.	.
θr	.	.	thredle	.	.	.	.	.	.
sp	.	.	.	.	.	.	.	.	.
st	.	.	.	staddle	.	.	.	.	.
sk	.	.	.	.	.	.	.	.	.
sm	.	.	.	.	.	.	.	.	.
sn	.	.	.	.	.	.	.	.	.
sl	.	.	.	.	.	.	.	.	.
sw	.	.	.	.	.	swaddle	.	.	.
ʃr	.	.	.	.	.	.	.	.	.
spl	.	.	.	.	.	.	.	.	.
spr	.	.	.	.	.	.	.	.	.
str	.	.	.	straddle	.	stroddle	.	.	.
skr	.	.	.	.	.	.	.	.	.
skw	.	.	.	.	.	.	.	.	.

* homophones—see page 226.
  Total number of words—88

ʌ	ɜ/r	eɪ	oʊ	aɪ	aʊ	ɔɪ	i/ə/r	ɛ/ə/r	ju
.	.	.	[odal]	idle*	.	.	.	.	udal†
puddle	.	[paidle]†	podal	.	.	.	.	.	.
buddle	.	.	bodal	.	.	.	.	.	.
.	.	.	.	tidal	.	.	.	.	.
.	.	daidle†	.	.	.	.	.	.	.
cuddle	curdle	.	.	.	.	.	.	.	.
guddle	girdle	.	.	.	.	Goidel	.	.	.
fuddle	.	.	.	.	.	.	.	.	feudal
.	.	.	.	.	.	.	.	.	.
.	.	.	.	.	.	.	.	.	.
.	.	.	.	.	.	.	.	.	.
.	.	.	.	sidle	.	.	.	.	.
.	.	.	.	.	.	.	.	.	.
.	.	.	.	.	.	.	.	.	.
.	.	.	.	.	.	.	.	.	.
huddle	hurdle	.	.	.	.	.	.	.	.
.	.	.	.	.	.	.	.	.	.
muddle	.	.	modal	.	.	.	.	.	.
.	.	.	nodal	nidal	.	.	.	.	.
.	.	*ladle*	.	.	.	.	.	.	.
[ruddle]	.	.	.	.	.	.	.	.	.
.	.	.	yodel	.	.	.	.	.	.
.	.	.	.	.	.	.	.	.	.
.	.	.	.	.	.	.	.	.	.
.	.	.	.	bridal*	.	.	.	.	.
.	.	.	.	.	.	.	.	.	.
.	.	.	.	.	.	.	.	.	.
.	.	.	.	.	.	.	.	.	.
cruddle†	.	*cradle*	.	.	.	.	.	.	.
.	.	.	.	.	.	.	.	.	.
.	.	.	.	.	.	.	.	.	.
.	.	.	.	.	.	.	.	.	.
.	.	.	.	.	.	.	.	.	.
.	.	.	.	.	.	.	.	.	.
spuddle	.	.	.	.	.	.	.	.	.
.	.	.	.	.	.	.	.	.	.
scuddle	.	.	.	.	.	.	.	.	.
.	.	.	.	.	.	.	.	.	.
.	.	.	.	.	.	.	.	.	.
.	.	.	.	.	.	.	.	.	.
.	.	.	.	.	.	.	.	.	.
.	.	.	.	.	.	.	.	.	.
struddle	.	.	.	.	.	.	.	.	.
.	.	.	.	.	.	.	.	.	.
.	.	.	.	.	.	.	.	.	.

Final—/dld/ . For inflected forms add /d/ to appropriate words, e.g. paddled.
—/dlz/ . For inflected forms add /z/ to appropriate words, e.g. paddles.

	i	ɪ	ɛ	æ	ɑ/r	ɒ(ɑ	ɔ/r	ʊ	u
—					(archil)				
p		pickle*							
b									
t		tickle*	teckel	tackle					
d			deckle		darkle				(duc
k			keckle	cackle		cockle*	corcle†		
g									
f	faecal	fickle					faucal		
v									
θ	thecal								
ð									
s	caecal	sickle*	seckel		sarcle	(socle)†			
z									
ʃ			shekel	shackle					
ʒ									
h			heckle	hackle		hockle			
tʃ		(chicle)							
dʒ									
m		[mickle]		mackle*					
n		nickel*							(nuc
l									
r		rickle					raucle†		
w									
j									
pl									
pr		prickle							
bl									
br		brickle*†							
tr	treacle	trickle							
tw									
dr									
kl									
kr				crackle					
kw				quackle					
gl		(glycol)							
gr				grackle					
fl									
fr			freckle						
θr									
sp			speckle		sparkle				
st		stickle							
sk									
sm									
sn							snorkel		
sl									
sw									
ʃr									
spl									
spr					[sprackle]†				
str		strickle							
skr									
skw									

* homophones—see page 226.

Total number of words—71

ʌ	ɜ/r	eɪ	oʊ	aɪ	aʊ	ɔɪ	i/ə/r	ɛ/ə/r	ju
·	·	·	·	·	·	·	·	·	·
buckle*	·	·	·	·	·	·	·	·	·
·	·	·	·	·	·	·	·	·	·
·	·	·	·	·	·	·	·	·	(ducal)
·	·	·	·	·	·	·	·	·	·
·	furcal	·	focal	·	·	·	·	·	·
·	·	·	vocal	·	·	·	(vehicle)	·	·
·	·	·	·	·	·	·	·	·	·
suckle	circle*	·	Sokel*	cycle	·	·	·	·	·
·	·	·	·	·	·	·	·	·	·
·	·	·	·	·	·	·	·	·	·
huckle	hurkle†	·	·	·	·	·	·	·	·
chuckle	·	·	·	·	·	·	·	·	·
[muckle]	·	·	·	Michael	·	·	·	·	·
knuckle	·	·	·	·	·	·	·	·	(nuchal)
·	·	·	local	·	·	·	·	·	·
ruckle	·	·	·	·	·	·	·	·	·
·	·	·	yokel*	·	·	·	·	·	·
·	·	·	·	·	·	·	·	·	·
·	·	·	·	·	·	·	·	·	·
·	·	·	·	·	·	·	·	·	·
truckle	·	·	·	·	·	·	·	·	·
·	·	·	·	·	·	·	·	·	·
·	·	·	·	·	·	·	·	·	·
·	·	·	·	·	·	·	·	·	·
·	·	·	·	·	·	·	·	·	·
·	·	·	·	(glycol)	·	·	·	·	·
·	·	·	·	·	·	·	·	·	·
·	·	·	·	·	·	·	·	·	·
·	·	·	·	·	·	·	·	·	·
·	·	·	·	·	·	·	·	·	·
·	·	·	·	·	·	·	·	·	·
·	·	·	·	·	·	·	·	·	·
·	·	·	·	·	·	·	·	·	·
·	·	·	·	·	·	·	·	·	·
·	·	[spraickle]†	·	·	·	·	·	·	·
·	·	·	·	·	·	·	·	·	·
·	·	·	·	·	·	·	·	·	·

Final—/kld/ . For inflected forms add /d/ to appropriate words, e.g. buckled.
—/klz/ . For inflected forms add /z/ to appropriate words, e.g. buckles.

	i	ɪ	ɛ	æ	ɑ/r	ɒ(ɑ	ɔ	ʊ	u
–	*eagle**	.	.	.	argal*†	.	.	.	.
p	.	.	.	.	.	.	.	.	.
b	beagle	biggle	.	.	.	boggle	.	.	.
t	teagle	.	.	taggle	.	toggle	.	.	.
d	.	.	.	daggle	dargle	.	.	.	Dou
k	.	.	.	.	.	coggle	.	.	.
g	.	giggle	.	gaggle	gargle*	goggle	.	.	goog
f	.	.	.	.	.	.	.	.	.
v	.	.	.	.	.	.	.	.	.
θ	.	.	.	.	.	.	.	.	.
ð	.	.	.	.	.	.	.	.	.
s	.	.	.	.	.	.	.	.	.
z	.	.	.	.	.	.	.	.	.
ʃ	.	.	.	.	.	shoggle†	.	.	.
ʒ	.	.	.	.	.	.	.	.	.
h	.	higgle	heggle	haggle	.	.	.	.	.
tʃ	.	.	.	.	.	.	.	.	.
dʒ	.	jiggle	.	.	.	joggle	.	.	juga
m	.	miggle†	.	.	.	.	.	.	.
n	.	niggle	.	.	.	.	.	.	.
l	legal	.	.	.	.	.	.	.	.
r	regal	wriggle*	.	raggle	.	.	.	.	.
w	.	wiggle	.	waggle	.	woggle	.	.	.
j	.	.	.	.	.	.	.	.	.
pl	.	.	.	.	.	.	.	.	.
pr	.	.	.	.	.	.	.	.	.
bl	.	.	.	.	.	.	.	.	.
br	.	.	.	.	.	broggle†	.	.	.
tr	.	.	.	.	.	.	.	.	.
tw	.	.	.	.	.	.	.	.	.
dr	.	.	.	draggle	.	.	.	.	.
kl	.	.	.	.	.	.	.	.	.
kr	.	.	.	.	.	.	.	.	.
kw	.	.	.	.	.	.	.	.	.
gl	.	.	.	.	.	.	.	.	.
gr	.	.	.	.	.	.	.	.	.
fl	.	.	.	.	.	.	.	.	flug
fr	.	.	.	.	.	.	.	.	frug
θr	.	.	.	.	.	.	.	.	.
sp	.	.	.	.	.	.	.	.	.
st	.	.	.	.	.	.	.	.	.
sk	.	.	.	.	.	.	.	.	.
sm	.	.	.	.	.	.	.	.	.
sn	.	sniggle	.	.	.	.	.	.	.
sl	.	.	.	.	.	.	.	.	.
sw	.	.	.	.	.	.	.	.	.
ʃr	.	.	.	.	.	.	.	.	.
spl	.	.	.	.	.	.	.	.	.
spr	.	.	.	.	.	.	.	.	.
str	.	striggle	.	straggle	.	.	.	.	.
skr	.	scriggle	.	.	.	.	.	.	.
skw	.	squiggle	.	.	.	.	.	.	.

* homophones—see page 226.
  Total number of words—61

ʌ	ɜ/r	eɪ	oʊ	aɪ	aʊ	ɔɪ	i/ə/r	ɛ/ə/r	ju
.	.	.	ogle	.	.	.	.	.	.
.	.	paigle	.	pygal	.	.	.	.	.
.	burgal*	.	bogle	.	.	.	.	.	bugle
.	tergal	taiglet†	.	.	.	.	.	.	.
.	.	.	.	.	.	.	.	.	.
guggle	gurgle	.	.	.	.	.	.	.	.
.	.	.	.	.	.	.	.	.	fugal
.	.	.	.	.	.	.	.	.	.
.	.	.	.	.	.	.	.	.	.
.	.	.	.	.	.	.	.	.	.
.	.	.	.	zygal	.	.	.	.	.
.	.	.	.	.	.	.	.	.	.
.	.	.	.	.	.	.	.	.	.
.	.	.	.	.	.	.	.	.	.
juggle	.	.	.	.	.	.	.	.	.
.	.	.	Mogul	.	.	.	.	.	.
.	.	.	.	.	.	.	.	.	.
.	.	.	.	(Rigel)	.	.	.	.	.
.	.	.	.	.	.	.	.	.	.
.	.	plagal	.	.	.	.	.	.	.
.	.	.	.	.	.	.	.	.	.
.	.	.	.	.	.	.	.	.	.
.	.	.	.	.	.	.	.	.	.
.	.	.	.	.	.	.	.	.	.
.	.	.	.	.	.	.	.	.	.
.	.	.	.	.	.	.	.	.	.
.	.	.	.	.	.	.	.	.	.
.	.	.	.	.	.	.	.	.	.
.	.	.	.	.	.	.	.	.	.
.	.	.	.	.	.	.	.	.	.
.	.	.	.	.	.	.	.	.	.
.	.	.	.	.	.	.	.	.	.
.	.	.	.	.	.	.	.	.	.
smuggle	.	.	.	.	.	.	.	.	.
snuggle	.	.	.	.	.	.	.	.	.
.	.	.	.	.	.	.	.	.	.
.	.	.	.	.	.	.	.	.	.
.	.	.	.	.	.	.	.	.	.
struggle	.	.	.	.	.	.	.	.	.
.	.	.	.	.	.	.	.	.	.
.	.	.	.	.	.	.	.	.	.

Final—/gl̩d/ . For inflected forms add /d/ to appropriate words, e.g. wriggled.
—/gl̩z/ . For inflected forms add /z/ to appropriate words, e.g. wriggles.

	i	ɪ	ɛ	æ	ɑ	ɒ(ɑ(ɔ)	ɔ	ʊ	u
—	.	.	.	.	.	offal	awful*	.	.
p	.	piffle	.	.	.	poffle	.	.	.
b	.	.	.	baffle	.	.	.	.	.
t	.	.	.	.	.	.	.	.	.
d	.	.	.	.	.	.	.	.	.
k	.	.	keffel	.	.	coffle	.	.	.
g	.	.	.	gaffle†	.	.	.	.	.
f	.	.	.	.	.	.	.	.	.
v	.	.	.	.	.	.	.	.	.
θ	.	.	.	.	.	.	.	.	.
ð	.	.	.	.	.	.	.	.	.
s	.	siffle	.	.	.	.	.	.	sou⟩
z	.	.	.	.	.	.	.	.	.
ʃ	.	.	.	shaffle†	.	.	.	.	.
ʒ	.	.	.	.	.	.	.	.	.
h	.	.	.	.	.	.	.	.	.
tʃ	.	.	.	.	.	.	.	.	.
dʒ	.	.	.	.	.	.	.	.	.
m	.	.	.	maffle†	.	.	.	.	.
n	.	.	.	.	.	.	.	.	.
l	.	.	.	.	.	.	lawful	.	.
r	.	riffle†	.	raffle	.	.	.	.	rue⟩
w	.	whiffle	.	.	.	waffle	.	.	.
j	.	.	.	yaffle	.	.	.	.	.
pl	.	.	.	.	.	.	.	.	.
pr	.	.	.	.	.	.	.	.	.
bl	.	.	.	.	.	.	.	.	.
br	.	.	.	.	.	.	.	.	.
tr	.	.	trefle	.	.	.	.	.	.
tw	.	.	.	.	.	.	.	.	.
dr	.	.	.	.	.	.	.	.	.
kl	.	.	.	.	.	.	.	.	.
kr	.	.	.	.	.	.	.	.	.
kw	.	.	.	.	.	.	.	.	.
gl	.	.	.	.	.	.	.	.	.
gr	.	.	.	.	.	.	.	.	.
fl	.	.	.	.	.	.	.	.	.
fr	.	.	.	.	.	.	.	.	.
θr	.	.	.	.	.	.	.	.	.
sp	.	.	.	.	.	.	.	.	.
st	.	.	.	.	.	.	.	.	.
sk	.	skiffle	.	.	.	.	.	.	.
sm	.	.	.	.	.	.	:	.	.
sn	.	sniffle	.	snaffle	.	.	.	.	.
sl	.	.	.	.	.	.	.	.	.
sw	.	.	.	.	.	.	.	.	.
ʃr	.	.	.	.	.	.	.	.	.
spl	.	.	.	.	.	.	.	.	.
spr	.	.	.	.	.	.	.	.	.
str	.	.	.	.	.	.	.	.	.
skr	.	.	.	.	.	.	.	.	.
skw	.	.	.	.	.	.	.	.	.

* homophones—see page 226.
  Total number of words—42

ʌ	ɜ/r	eɪ	oʊ	aɪ	ɑʊ	ɔɪ	i/ə/r	ɛ/ə/r	ju
.	.	.	.	.	.	.	.	.	.
.	purfle	.	.	.	.	.	.	.	.
.	.	.	.	.	.	.	.	.	.
tuffle†	.	.	.	.	.	.	.	.	.
duffel	.	.	.	.	.	.	.	.	.
cuffle	.	.	.	.	.	.	.	careful	.
.	.	.	.	.	.	.	.	.	.
.	.	.	.	.	.	.	fearful	.	.
.	.	.	.	.	.	.	.	.	.
.	.	.	.	.	.	.	.	.	.
.	.	.	.	.	.	.	.	.	.
.	.	.	.	.	.	.	.	.	.
shuffle	.	.	.	.	.	.	.	.	.
.	.	.	.	.	.	.	.	.	.
.	.	.	.	hyphal	.	.	.	.	.
.	.	.	.	.	.	.	cheerful	.	.
.	.	.	.	.	.	joyful	.	.	.
muffle	.	.	.	.	.	.	.	.	.
.	.	.	.	.	.	.	.	.	.
ruffle	.	.	.	rifle	.	.	.	.	.
.	.	.	woeful	.	.	.	.	.	.
.	.	.	.	.	.	.	.	.	.
.	.	.	.	.	.	.	.	.	.
.	.	.	.	.	.	.	.	.	.
truffle	.	.	.	trifle	.	.	.	.	.
.	.	.	.	.	.	.	.	.	.
.	.	.	.	.	.	.	.	.	.
.	.	.	.	.	.	.	.	.	.
.	.	.	.	.	.	.	.	.	.
.	.	.	.	.	.	.	.	.	.
.	.	.	.	.	.	.	.	.	.
.	.	.	.	.	.	.	.	.	.
.	.	.	.	stifle	.	.	.	.	.
scuffle	.	.	.	.	.	.	.	.	.
.	.	.	.	.	.	.	.	.	.
snuffle	.	.	.	.	.	.	.	.	.
.	.	.	.	.	.	.	.	.	.
.	.	.	.	.	.	.	.	.	.
.	.	.	.	.	.	.	.	.	.
.	.	.	.	.	.	.	.	.	.
.	.	.	.	.	.	.	.	.	.
.	.	.	.	.	.	.	.	.	.

Final—/fld/ . For inflected forms add /d/ to appropriate words, e.g. shuffled.
—/flz/ . For inflected forms add /z/ to appropriate words, e.g. shuffles.

	i	ɪ	ɛ	æ	ɑ/r	ɒ(ɑ	ɔ/r	ʊ	u
–	evil	.	.	.	arval*	.	orval†	.	.
p	.	.	.	.	.	.	.	.	.
b	.	.	bevel	.	.	.	.	.	.
t	.	.	.	.	.	.	.	.	.
d	.	.	devil*	.	.	.	.	.	.
k	.	.	kevel	cavil	carvel	.	.	.	.
g	.	.	.	gavel	.	.	.	.	.
f	.	.	.	.	.	.	.	.	.
v	.	.	.	.	varvel	.	.	.	.
θ	.	(thivel)	.	.	.	.	.	.	.
ð	.	.	.	.	.	.	.	.	.
s	.	civil	.	.	.	.	.	.	.
z	.	.	.	.	.	.	.	.	.
ʃ	.	.	.	.	.	.	.	.	.
ʒ	.	.	.	.	.	.	.	.	.
h	.	.	.	.	.	(hovel)	.	.	.
tʃ	.	.	.	.	.	.	.	.	.
dʒ	.	.	.	javel	.	.	.	.	.
m	.	.	.	.	marvel	.	.	.	.
n	.	.	nevel*†	.	.	novel	.	.	.
l	.	.	level	.	larval	.	.	.	.
r	.	.	revel	ravel	.	.	.	.	.
w	weevil	.	.	.	.	.	.	.	.
j	.	.	.	.	.	.	.	.	.
pl	.	.	.	.	.	.	.	.	.
pr	.	.	.	.	.	.	.	.	.
bl	.	.	.	.	.	.	.	.	.
br	.	.	.	.	.	.	.	.	.
tr	.	.	.	travel	.	.	.	.	.
tw	.	.	.	.	.	.	.	.	.
dr	.	drivel	drevill	.	.	.	.	.	.
kl	.	.	.	.	.	.	.	.	.
kr	.	.	.	.	.	.	.	.	.
kw	.	.	.	.	.	.	.	.	.
gl	.	.	.	.	.	.	.	.	.
gr	.	.	.	gravel	.	(grovel)	.	.	.
fl	.	.	.	.	.	.	.	.	.
fr	.	frivol	.	.	.	.	.	.	.
θr	.	.	.	.	.	.	.	.	.
sp	.	.	.	.	.	.	.	.	.
st	.	.	.	.	.	.	.	.	.
sk	.	.	.	.	.	.	.	.	.
ṣm	.	.	.	.	.	.	.	.	.
sn	.	snivel	.	.	.	.	.	.	.
sl	.	.	.	.	.	.	.	.	.
sw	.	swivel	.	.	.	.	.	.	.
ʃr	shrieval	shrivel	.	.	.	.	.	.	.
spl	.	.	.	.	.	.	.	.	.
spr	.	.	.	.	.	.	.	.	.
str	.	.	.	.	.	.	.	.	.
skr	.	.	.	.	.	.	.	.	.
skw	.	.	.	.	.	.	.	.	.

* homophones—see page 226.
  Total number of words—48

ʌ	ɜ/r	eɪ	oʊ	aɪ	aʊ	ɔɪ	i/ə/r	ɛ/ə/r	ju
.	.	aval	oval	.	.	.	.	.	.
.	.	.	.	.	.	.	.	.	.
.	.	.	.	.	.	.	.	.	.
.	.	.	.	.	.	.	.	.	.
.	.	cavel	.	.	.	.	.	.	.
.	.	[gavel]	.	.	.	.	.	.	.
.	vervel	.	.	.	.	.	.	.	.
.	.	.	.	(thivel)	.	.	.	.	.
.	.	.	.	.	.	.	.	.	.
.	serval	.	.	.	.	.	.	.	.
.	.	.	.	.	.	.	.	.	.
shovel	.	.	.	.	.	.	.	.	.
.	.	.	.	.	.	.	.	.	.
(hovel)	.	.	.	.	.	.	.	.	.
.	chervil	.	.	.	.	.	.	.	.
.	.	.	.	.	.	.	.	.	.
.	.	.	.	.	.	.	.	.	.
.	nerval	naval*	.	nival	.	.	.	.	.
.	.	.	.	.	.	.	.	.	.
.	.	.	.	rival	.	.	.	.	.
.	.	.	.	.	.	.	.	.	.
.	.	.	.	.	.	.	.	.	.
.	.	.	.	.	.	.	.	.	.
.	.	.	.	.	.	.	.	.	.
.	.	.	.	.	.	.	.	.	.
.	.	.	.	.	.	.	.	.	.
.	.	.	.	.	.	.	.	.	.
.	.	.	.	.	.	.	.	.	.
.	.	.	.	.	.	.	.	.	.
(grovel)	.	.	.	.	.	.	.	.	.
.	.	.	.	.	.	.	.	.	.
.	.	.	.	.	.	.	.	.	.
.	.	.	.	.	.	.	.	.	.
scovel	.	.	.	.	.	.	.	.	.
.	.	.	.	.	.	.	.	.	.
.	.	.	.	.	.	.	.	.	.
.	.	.	.	.	.	.	.	.	.
.	.	.	.	.	.	.	.	.	.
.	.	.	.	.	.	.	.	.	.
.	.	.	.	.	.	.	.	.	.
.	.	.	.	.	.	.	.	.	.
.	.	.	.	.	.	.	.	.	.

Final—/vld/ . For inflected forms add /d/ to appropriate words, e.g. levelled.
—/vlz/ . For inflected forms add /z/ to appropriate words, e.g. levels.

	i	ɪ	ɛ	æ	ɑ/r	ɒ(ɑ	ɔ/r	ʊ	u
–	eassel*†	.	.	.	.	.	.	.	.
p	.	.	pestle	.	*parcel*	pastel†	.	.	.
b	.	.	.	.	.	.	.	.	.
t	.	.	.	tassel	tarsal	tossel†	torsel*	.	.
d	.	.	(deasil)†	.	.	dossil*	dorsal*	.	.
k	.	.	.	(*castle*)	(*castle*)	.	.	.	.
g	.	.	.	.	.	.	.	.	.
f	.	fissle*†	.	.	.	fossil	.	.	.
v	.	.	vessel	vassal	varsal	.	.	.	.
θ	.	thistle	.	.	.	.	.	.	.
ð	.	.	.	.	.	.	.	.	.
s	(Cecil)	(sisal)*	(Cecil)	.	.	.	.	.	.
z	.	.	.	.	.	.	.	.	.
ʃ	.	.	.	.	.	.	.	.	.
ʒ	.	.	.	.	.	.	.	.	.
h	.	.	.	hassel†	.	.	.	.	.
tʃ	.	.	chessel	.	.	.	.	.	.
dʒ	.	.	.	.	.	jostle	.	.	.
m	.	missal*	.	.	.	.	morsel	.	.
n	.	.	nestle	.	.	.	.	.	.
l	.	.	.	.	.	.	.	.	.
r	.	.	wrestle	wrastle	.	.	.	.	.
w	.	*whistle*	.	(wassail)	[warsle]†	(wassail)	.	.	.
j	.	.	.	.	.	.	.	.	eus
pl	.	.	.	.	.	.	.	.	.
pr	.	.	.	.	.	.	.	.	.
bl	.	.	.	.	.	.	.	.	.
br	.	bristle	.	.	.	.	.	.	.
tr	.	.	trestle	.	.	.	.	.	.
tw	.	.	.	.	.	.	.	.	.
dr	.	.	.	.	.	.	.	.	.
kl	.	.	.	.	.	.	.	.	.
kr	cresol	.	.	.	.	.	.	.	.
kw	.	.	.	.	.	.	.	.	.
gl	.	.	.	.	.	glossal	.	.	.
gr	.	gristle	.	gracile	.	.	.	.	.
fl	.	.	.	.	.	.	.	.	.
θr	.	thrissel†	.	.	.	throstle	.	.	.
sp	.	.	.	.	.	.	.	.	.
st	.	.	.	.	.	.	.	.	.
sk	.	.	.	.	.	.	.	.	.
sm	.	.	.	.	.	.	.	.	.
sn	.	.	.	.	.	.	.	.	.
sl	.	.	.	.	.	.	.	.	.
sw	.	.	.	.	.	.	.	.	.
ʃr	.	.	.	.	.	.	.	.	.
spl	.	.	.	.	.	.	.	.	.
spr	.	.	.	.	.	.	.	.	.
str	.	.	.	.	.	.	.	.	.
skr	.	.	.	.	.	.	.	.	.
skw	.	.	.	.	.	.	.	.	.

* homophones—see page 226.
  Total number of words—67

ʌ	ɜ/r	eɪ	oʊ	aɪ	aʊ	ɔɪ	i/ə/r	ɛ/ə/r	ju
.	.	(eisel)†	.	(eisel)†	.	.	.	.	eusol
(pussel)	.	.	.	.	.	.	.	.	pucelle†
bustle	birsle†	basal	.	.	.	.	.	.	.
tussle	tercel	.	.	.	.	.	tiercel	.	.
.	.	.	.	.	.	.	.	.	.
.	cursal	.	.	.	.	.	.	.	.
.	.	.	.	.	.	.	.	.	.
.	versal	vasal	.	.	.	.	.	.	.
.	.	.	.	.	.	.	.	.	.
.	.	.	.	(sisal)	.	.	.	.	.
.	.	.	.	.	.	.	.	.	.
.	.	.	.	.	.	.	.	.	.
hustle	hirsel*	haysel†	.	.	.	.	.	.	.
.	.	.	.	.	.	.	.	.	.
[justle]	.	.	.	.	.	.	.	.	.
muscle*	.	.	.	.	.	.	.	.	.
.	noursle†	.	.	.	.	.	.	.	.
.	.	.	.	lysol	.	.	.	.	.
rustle*	.	.	.	.	.	.	.	.	.
.	.	.	.	.	.	.	.	.	.
.	.	.	.	.	.	.	.	.	.
.	.	.	.	.	.	.	.	.	.
.	.	.	.	.	.	.	.	.	.
brustle†	.	.	.	.	.	.	.	.	.
.	.	.	.	.	.	.	.	.	.

Final—/sl̩d/ . For inflected forms add /d/ to appropriate words, e.g. bustled.
—/sl̩z/ . For inflected forms add /z/ to appropriate words, e.g. bustles.

	i	ɪ	ɛ	æ	ɑ	ɒ(ɑ	ɔ	ʊ	u
–	easel	.	.	.	.	.	.	.	ouzel
p	.	pizzle	.	.	.	.	pausal	.	.
b	.	.	bezel*	basil*	[Basel]	.	.	.	.
t	teasel	.	.	.	.	.	.	.	.
d	diesel*	.	.	dazzle	.	.	.	.	.
k	.	.	.	.	.	.	causal	.	.
g	.	.	.	gazel	.	.	.	.	.
f	.	fizzle	.	.	.	.	.	.	foozle
v	.	(visile)	.	.	.	.	.	.	.
θ	.	.	.	.	.	.	.	.	.
ð	.	.	.	.	.	.	.	.	.
s	.	sizzle	.	.	.	sozzle	.	.	.
z	.	zizel	.	.	.	.	.	.	.
ʃ	.	.	.	.	.	.	.	.	.
ʒ	.	.	.	.	.	.	.	.	.
h	.	.	.	.	.	.	.	.	.
tʃ	.	chisel	chesil	.	.	.	.	.	.
dʒ	.	.	.	.	.	.	.	.	.
m	meazel	mizzle*	.	.	.	.	.	.	.
n	.	.	.	.	.	nozzle	.	.	.
l	.	.	.	.	.	.	.	.	(losel)
r	.	.	.	.	.	.	.	.	.
w	weasel	.	.	.	.	.	.	.	[woose
j	.	.	.	.	.	.	.	.	.
pl	.	.	.	.	.	.	.	.	.
pr	.	.	.	.	.	.	.	.	.
bl	.	.	.	.	.	.	.	.	.
br	.	.	.	.	.	.	.	.	.
tr	.	.	.	.	.	.	.	.	.
tw	.	.	.	.	.	.	.	.	.
dr	.	drizzle	.	.	drazel	.	.	.	.
kl	.	.	.	.	.	.	.	.	.
kr	.	crizzle	.	.	.	.	.	.	.
kw	.	.	.	.	.	.	.	.	.
gl	.	.	.	.	.	.	.	.	.
gr	.	grizzle	.	.	.	.	.	.	.
fl	.	.	.	.	.	.	.	.	.
fr	.	frizzle	.	frazzle	(frazil)	.	.	.	.
θr	.	.	.	.	.	.	.	.	.
sp	.	.	.	.	.	.	.	.	.
st	.	.	.	.	.	.	.	.	.
sk	.	.	.	.	.	.	.	.	.
sm	.	.	.	.	.	.	.	.	.
sn	.	.	.	.	.	.	.	.	snooz‌
sl	.	.	.	.	.	.	.	.	.
sw	.	swizzle	.	.	.	.	.	.	.
ʃr	.	.	.	.	.	.	.	.	.
spl	.	.	.	.	.	.	.	.	.
spr	.	.	.	.	.	.	.	.	.
str	.	.	.	.	.	.	.	.	.
skr	.	.	.	.	.	.	.	.	.
skw	.	.	.	.	.	.	.	.	.

* homophones—see pages 226–227.
  Total number of words—53

ʌ	ɜ/r	eɪ	oʊ	aɪ	aʊ	ɔɪ	i/ə/r	ɛ/ə/r	ju
.	.	aizle†	.	.	.	.	.	.	.
puzzle*	.	.	.	.	.	.	.	.	.
.	.	.	.	.	.	.	.	.	.
.	.	.	.	.	tousle	.	.	.	.
.	.	.	.	.	.	.	.	.	.
.	.	.	.	.	.	.	.	.	.
guzzle	.	.	.	.	.	.	.	.	.
fuzzle†	.	.	.	.	.	.	.	.	fusil
.	.	.	.	.	.	.	.	.	.
.	.	.	.	.	.	.	.	.	.
.	.	.	.	[sizel]	.	.	.	.	.
.	.	.	.	.	.	.	.	.	.
.	.	.	.	.	.	.	.	.	.
.	.	hazel*	.	.	housel	.	.	.	.
.	.	.	.	.	.	.	.	.	.
muzzle	.	.	.	.	.	.	.	.	.
nuzzle*	.	nasal	.	.	.	.	.	.	.
.	.	.	(losel)	.	.	.	.	.	.
wuzzle	.	whaizle†	.	.	.	.	.	.	.
.	.	.	.	.	.	.	.	.	.
.	.	.	.	.	.	.	.	.	.
.	.	.	.	.	.	.	.	.	.
.	.	.	.	.	.	.	.	.	.
.	.	.	.	.	.	.	.	.	.
.	.	.	.	.	.	.	.	.	.
.	.	.	.	.	.	.	.	.	.
.	.	.	.	.	.	.	.	.	.
.	.	.	.	.	.	.	.	.	.
.	.	.	.	.	.	.	.	.	.
.	.	(frazil)	.	.	.	.	.	.	.
.	.	.	.	.	.	.	.	.	.
.	.	.	.	.	spousal	.	.	.	.
.	.	.	.	.	.	.	.	.	.
.	.	.	.	.	.	.	.	.	.
snuzzle	.	.	.	.	.	.	.	.	.
.	.	.	.	.	.	.	.	.	.
.	.	.	.	.	.	.	.	.	.
.	.	.	.	.	.	.	.	.	.
.	.	.	.	.	.	.	.	.	.
.	.	.	.	.	.	.	.	.	.
.	.	.	.	.	.	.	.	.	.
.	.	.	.	.	.	.	.	.	.

Final—/zld/ . For inflected forms add /d/ to appropriate words, e.g. dazzled.
—/zlz/ . For inflected forms add /z/ to appropriate words, e.g. dazzles.

185

	i	ɪ	ɛ	æ	ɑ/r	ɒ	ɔ	ʊ	u
—	·	·	·	·		·	·	·	·
p	·	·	·	·	partial	·	·	·	·
b	·	·	·	·		·	·	bushel	·
t	·	·	·						
d	(deasil)†	·	(deasil)†	·	·	·	·	·	·
k	·	·							
g	·	·	·	·		·			
f	fetial	·	·	·	farcial	·	·	·	·
v	·	·	·	·	·	·	·	·	·
θ	·	·	·	·	·		·	·	·
ð	·	·	·	·	·	·	·	·	·
s	·	·	·	·	·	·	·	·	·
z	·	·	·	·	·	·	·	·	·
ʃ	·	·	·	·	·	·	·	·	·
ʒ	·	·	·	·	·	·	·	·	·
h	·	·	·	·	·	·	·	·	·
tʃ	·	·	·	·	·	·	·	·	·
dʒ	·	·	·	·	·	·	·	·	·
m	·	·	·	·	marshal*	·	·	·	·
n	·	·	·	·	·	·	·	·	·
l	·	·	·	·	·	·	·	·	·
r	·	·	·	·	·	·	·	·	·
w	·	·	·	·	·	·	·	·	·
j	·	·	·	·	·	·	·	·	·
pl	·	·	·	·	·	·	·	·	·
pr	·	·	·	·	·	·	·	·	·
bl	·	·	·	·	·	·	·	·	·
br	·	·	·	·	·	·	·	·	·
tr	·	·	·	·	·	·	·	·	truc
tw	·	·	·	·	·	·	·	·	·
dr	·	·	·	·	·	·	·	·	·
kl	·	·	·	·	·	·	·	·	·
kr	·	·	·	·	·	·	·	·	cru
kw	·	·	·	·	·	·	·	·	·
gl	·	·	·	·	·	·	·	·	·
gr	·	·	·	·	·	·	·	·	·
fl	·	·	·	·	·	·	·	·	·
fr	·	·	·	·	·	·	·	·	·
θr	·	·	threshel	·	·	·	·	·	·
sp	·	·	special	·	·	·	·	·	·
st	·	·	·	·	·	·	·	·	·
sk	·	·	·	·	·	·	·	·	·
sm	·	·	·	·	·	·	·	·	·
sn	·	·	·	·	·	·	·	·	·
sl	·	·	·	·	·	·	·	·	·
sw	·	·	·	·	·	·	·	·	·
ʃr	·	·	·	·	·	·	·	·	·
spl	·	·	·	·	·	·	·	·	·
spr	·	·	·	·	·	·	·	·	·
str	·	·	·	·	·	·	·	·	·
skr	·	·	·	·	·	·	·	·	·
skw	·	·	·	·	·	·	·	·	·

* homophones—see page 227.
  Total number of words—17

ʌ	ɜ/r	ɪə	oʊ	aɪ	aʊ	ɔɪ	i/ə/r	ɛ/ə/r	ju
	tertial								
		facial							
			social						
		racial							
		glacial							
		spatial							

Final—/ʃld/ . For inflected forms add /d/ to appropriate words, e.g. marshalled.
—/ʃlz/ . For inflected forms add /z/ to appropriate words, e.g. marshals.

187

	i	ɪ	ɛ	æ	ɑ/r	ɒ(ɑ	ɔ/r	ʊ	u
–	·	·	·	amyl	(aumil)	·	(aumil)	·	·
p	·	·	·	·	·	·	·	·	·
b	·	·	·	·	·	·	·	·	·
t	·	·	·	Tamil	·	·	·	·	·
d	·	·	·	·	·	·	·	·	·
k	·	(kümmel)	·	*camel*	Carmel	·	·	(kümmel)	·
g	·	·	·	·	·	·	·	·	·
f	·	·	·	·	·	·	formal*	·	·
v	·	·	·	·	·	·	·	·	·
θ	·	·	·	·	·	·	·	·	·
ð	·	·	·	·	·	·	·	·	·
s	·	·	·	samel	·	·	·	·	·
z	·	·	·	·	·	·	·	·	·
ʃ	·	schimmel	·	·	·	·	·	·	·
ʒ	·	·	·	·	·	·	·	·	(jume.
h	haemal	·	·	hamel†	·	·	·	·	·
tʃ	·	·	·	·	·	·	·	·	·
dʒ	·	gimmal	gemel	·	·	·	·	·	(jume
m	·	·	·	mammal	·	·	·	·	·
n	·	·	·	·	·	·	normal	·	·
l	·	·	·	lamel	·	·	·	·	·
r	·	·	·	·	·	·	·	·	·
w	·	·	[whemmle]†	·	·	[whommle]†	wormil	·	·
j	·	·	·	·	·	·	·	·	·
pl	·	·	·	·	·	·	·	·	·
pr	·	·	·	·	·	·	·	·	·
bl	·	·	·	·	·	·	·	·	·
br	·	·	·	·	·	·	·	·	brum
tr	·	·	·	trammel	·	trommel	·	·	·
tw	·	·	·	·	·	·	·	·	·
dr	·	·	·	·	·	·	·	·	·
kl	·	·	·	·	·	·	·	·	·
kr	·	·	·	·	·	·	·	·	·
kw	·	·	·	·	·	·	·	·	·
gl	·	·	·	·	·	·	·	·	·
gr	·	·	·	·	·	·	·	·	·
fl	·	·	·	·	·	·	·	·	·
fr	·	·	·	·	·	·	·	·	·
θr	·	·	·	·	·	·	·	·	·
sp	·	·	·	·	·	·	·	·	·
st	·	·	·	stammel	·	·	·	·	·
sk	·	·	·	scamel†	·	·	·	·	·
sm	·	·	·	·	·	·	·	·	·
sn	·	·	·	·	·	·	·	·	·
sl	·	·	·	·	·	·	·	·	·
sw	·	·	·	·	·	·	·	·	·
ʃr	·	·	·	·	·	·	·	·	·
spl	·	·	·	·	·	·	·	·	·
spr	·	·	·	·	·	·	·	·	·
str	·	·	·	[strammel]†	·	·	·	·	·
skr	·	·	·	·	·	·	·	·	·
skw	·	·	·	·	·	·	·	·	·

* homophones—see page 227.
  Total number of words—40

Λ	3/r	eɪ	oʊ	aɪ	aʊ	ɔɪ	i/ə/r	ɛ/ə/r	ju
pummel*.									
bummle†.									
	dermal	.	domal						
	(vermeil).								
	thermal	.							
hummel .									
[whummle]† .									
				primal					
			bromal						

[strummel]† .

Final—/mld/ . For inflected forms add /d/ to appropriate words, e.g. pummelled.
   —/mlz/ . For inflected forms add /z/ to appropriate words, e.g. pummels.

	i	ɪ	ε	æ	ɑ/r	ɒ)ɑ	ɔ/r	ʊ	u
−	.	.	.	annal*	.	.	.	.	.
p	penal	.	pennil	panel	.	.	.	.	.
b	.	.	.	(banal)	.	.	.	.	.
t	.	.	.	.	tarnal	[tonnell]†	.	.	.
d	.	dinnle†	.	.	darnel	.	.	.	.
k	.	.	kennel	cannel	carnal	.	cornel	.	.
g	.	.	.	.	.	.	.	.	.
f	phenol*	.	fennel*	fannel	.	.	faunal	.	.
v	venal	.	vennel†	.	.	.	.	.	.
θ	.	.	.	.	.	.	.	.	.
ð	.	.	.	.	.	.	.	.	.
s	.	.	.	.	.	.	.	.	.
z	.	.	.	.	.	.	.	.	.
ʃ	.	.	.	.	.	.	.	.	.
ʒ	.	.	.	.	.	.	.	.	.
h	.	.	.	.	.	.	.	.	.
tʃ	.	.	.	channel	charnel†	.	.	.	.
dʒ	genal	.	.	.	.	.	.	.	.
m	.	.	.	manille	.	.	.	.	.
n	.	.	.	.	.	.	.	.	.
l	.	.	.	.	.	.	.	.	.
r	renal	.	.	[rannel]†	.	.	.	.	.
w	.	[winnle]†	.	.	.	wanlet†	wornil	.	.
j	.	.	.	.	.	.	.	.	.
pl	.	.	.	.	.	.	.	.	.
pr	.	.	.	.	.	.	.	.	.
bl	.	.	.	.	.	.	.	.	.
br	.	.	.	branle	.	.	.	.	.
tr	.	.	.	.	.	.	.	.	.
tw	.	.	.	.	.	.	.	.	.
dr	.	.	.	.	.	.	.	.	.
kl	.	.	.	.	.	.	.	.	.
kr	.	.	crenel†	.	.	.	.	.	.
kw	.	quinol	.	.	.	.	.	.	.
gl	.	.	.	.	.	.	.	.	.
gr	.	.	.	.	.	.	.	.	.
fl	.	.	.	flannel	.	.	.	.	.
fr	.	.	.	.	.	.	.	.	.
θr	.	.	.	.	.	.	.	.	.
sp	.	spinel	.	.	.	.	.	.	.
st	.	.	.	[stannel]†	.	.	.	.	.
sk	.	.	.	.	.	.	.	.	.
sm	.	.	.	.	.	.	.	.	.
sn	.	.	.	.	.	.	.	.	.
sl	.	.	.	.	.	.	.	.	.
sw	.	.	.	.	.	.	.	.	.
ʃr	.	.	.	.	.	.	.	.	.
spl	.	.	.	.	.	.	.	.	.
spr	.	.	.	.	.	.	.	.	.
str	.	.	.	.	.	.	.	.	.
skr	.	.	.	scrannel	.	.	.	.	.
skw	.	.	.	.	.	.	.	.	.

* homophones—see page 227.
  Total number of words—61

ʌ	ɜ/r	eɪ	oʊ	aɪ	aʊ	ɔɪ	i/ə/r	ɛ/ə/r	ju
.	urnal	anal	.	.	.	.	.	.	.
.	.	.	.	.	.	.	.	.	.
.	.	(banal)	.	.	.	.	.	.	.
tunnel	ternal	.	tonal	.	.	.	.	.	.
.	.	.	.	.	.	.	.	.	.
.	colonel*	.	.	.	.	.	.	.	.
gunnel	girnel	.	.	.	.	.	.	.	.
funnel	.	fanal†	phonal	final	.	.	.	.	.
.	vernal	.	.	vinal*	.	.	.	.	.
.	.	.	.	.	.	.	.	.	.
.	.	.	.	.	.	.	.	.	.
.	.	.	zonal	.	.	.	.	.	.
.	.	.	.	.	.	.	.	.	.
.	.	.	.	.	.	.	.	.	.
.	.	.	.	.	.	.	.	.	.
.	journal	.	.	.	.	.	.	.	.
.	.	.	.	.	nounal	.	.	.	.
.	.	.	.	.	.	.	.	.	.
runnel	.	.	.	rhinal	.	.	.	.	.
.	.	.	.	.	.	.	.	.	.
.	.	.	.	.	.	.	.	.	.
.	.	.	.	.	.	.	.	.	.
.	.	.	.	.	.	.	.	.	.
trunnel	.	.	.	trinal	.	.	.	.	.
.	.	.	.	.	.	.	.	.	.
.	.	.	clonal	.	.	.	.	.	.
.	.	.	.	crinal	.	.	.	.	.
.	.	.	.	.	.	.	.	.	.
.	.	.	.	.	.	.	.	.	.
.	.	.	.	.	.	.	.	.	.
.	.	.	.	.	.	.	.	.	.
.	.	.	.	spinal	.	.	.	.	.
.	.	.	.	.	.	.	.	.	.
.	.	.	.	.	.	.	.	.	.
.	.	.	.	shrinal	.	.	.	.	.
.	.	.	.	.	.	.	.	.	.
.	.	.	.	.	.	.	.	.	.
.	.	.	.	.	.	.	.	.	.

Final—/nld/ . For inflected forms add /d/ to appropriate words, e.g. panelled.
—/nlz/ . For inflected forms add /z/ to appropriate words, e.g. panels.

	i	ɪ	ɛ	æ	ɑ	ɒ(ɔ(ɑ	ɔ(oʊ	ʊ	ʊə
–	·	·	Erroll	aril*	·	(oral)	(oral)*	·	·
p	·	·	peril	parrel	·	·	poral	·	·
b	·	·	Beryl*	*barrel*	(bharal)	·	borrel†	·	·
t	·	Tyrol*	·	·	·	·	·	·	·
d	·	·	·	·	·	·	·	·	·
k	·	·	·	carol*	·	coral*	(choral)	·	·
g	·	·	·	·	·	·	goral	·	·
f	·	·	·	·	·	forel	·	·	·
v	·	·	[verrel]	·	·	·	·	·	·
θ	·	·	·	·	·	·	·	·	·
ð	·	·	·	·	·	·	·	·	·
s	·	·	·	·	·	sorrel	saurel	·	·
z	·	·	·	·	·	zoril	·	·	·
ʃ	·	·	·	·	·	·	·	·	·
3	·	·	·	·	·	·	·	·	·
h	·	·	·	·	·	·	horal	·	·
tʃ	·	·	·	·	·	·	·	·	·
dʒ	·	·	·	·	·	·	·	(jural)	(jur
m	·	·	meril*	·	·	moral*	·	·	·
n	·	·	·	·	·	·	·	(neural)	·
l	·	·	·	·	·	(laurel)*	(laurel)	·	·
r	·	·	·	·	·	·	roral	(rural)	(rur
w	·	·	·	·	·	worral	·	·	·
j	·	·	·	·	·	·	·	(Ural)	(Ur
pl	·	·	·	·	·	·	·	(pleural)*	(plu
pr	·	·	·	·	·	·	·	·	·
bl	·	·	·	·	·	·	·	·	·
br	·	·	·	·	·	·	·	·	·
tr	·	·	·	·	·	·	·	·	·
tw	·	·	·	·	·	·	·	·	·
dr	·	·	·	·	·	·	·	·	·
kl	·	·	·	·	·	(chloral)	(chloral)	·	·
kr	·	·	·	·	·	·	·	(crural)	(cru
kw	·	·	·	·	·	quarrel	·	·	·
gl	·	·	·	·	·	·	·	·	·
gr	·	·	·	·	·	·	·	·	·
fl	·	·	·	·	·	·	·	·	·
fr	·	·	·	·	·	·	·	·	·
θr	·	·	·	·	·	·	·	·	·
sp	·	·	·	·	·	·	·	·	·
st	·	·	sterol*	·	·	·	·	·	·
sk	·	·	·	·	·	·	·	·	·
sm	·	·	·	·	·	·	·	·	·
sn	·	·	·	·	·	·	·	·	·
sl	·	·	·	·	·	·	·	·	·
sw	·	·	·	·	·	·	·	·	·
ʃr	·	·	·	·	·	·	·	·	·
spl	·	·	·	·	·	·	·	·	·
spr	·	·	·	·	·	·	·	·	·
str	·	·	·	·	·	·	·	·	·
skr	·	·	·	·	·	·	·	·	·
skw	·	*squirrel*	·	·	·	·	·	·	·

* homophones—see page 227.
  Total number of words—56

ʌ	ɜ/r	eɪ	oʊ	aɪ	aʊ	ɔɪ	i/ə/r	ɛ/ə/r	juə
.	.	.	.	.	.	.	.	.	(Ural)
.	.	.	.	pyral	.	.	.	.	.
burrel*	.	.	.	.	.	.	.	.	.
.	.	.	.	.	.	.	.	.	.
.	.	.	.	.	.	.	.	.	.
.	.	.	.	.	.	.	.	.	.
.	.	.	.	.	.	.	feral	.	furil
.	.	.	.	.	.	.	.	.	.
.	.	.	.	.	.	.	.	.	.
.	.	.	[sorel]*	.	.	.	.	.	sural
.	.	.	.	.	.	.	.	.	.
.	.	.	.	.	.	.	.	.	.
.	.	.	.	.	.	.	.	.	.
.	.	.	.	.	.	.	.	.	.
.	.	.	.	gyral	.	.	.	.	.
.	.	.	.	.	.	.	.	.	mural
.	.	.	.	.	.	.	.	.	(neural)
.	.	.	(loral)*	.	.	.	.	.	.
.	.	.	.	.	.	.	.	.	.
.	.	.	.	.	.	.	.	.	.
.	.	.	.	.	.	.	.	.	.
.	.	.	.	.	.	.	.	.	.
.	.	.	.	.	.	.	.	.	.
.	.	.	.	.	.	.	.	.	.
.	.	.	.	.	.	.	.	.	.
.	.	.	.	.	.	.	.	.	.
.	.	.	.	.	.	.	.	.	.
.	.	.	.	.	.	.	.	.	.
.	.	.	.	.	.	.	.	.	.
.	.	.	.	.	.	.	.	.	.
.	.	.	.	.	.	.	.	.	.
.	.	.	.	spiral	.	.	.	.	.
.	.	.	.	.	.	.	.	.	.
.	.	.	.	.	.	.	.	.	.
.	.	.	.	.	.	.	.	.	.
.	.	.	.	.	.	.	.	.	.
.	.	.	.	.	.	.	.	.	.
.	.	.	.	.	.	.	.	.	.
.	.	.	.	.	.	.	.	.	.
.	.	.	.	.	.	.	.	.	.
.	.	.	.	.	.	.	.	.	.
.	.	.	.	.	.	.	.	.	.

Final—/rld/ . For inflected forms add /d/ to appropriate words, e.g. spiralled.
—/rlz/ . For inflected forms add /z/ to appropriate words, e.g. spirals.

	i	ɪ	ɛ	æ	ɑ	ɒ	ɔ	ʊ	u
–	·	·	·	ample	·	·	·	·	·
p	·	pimple	·	·	·	·	·	·	·
b	·	·	·	·	·	·	·	·	·
t	·	·	temple	·	·	·	·	·	·
d	·	dimple	·	·	·	·	·	·	·
k	·	·	kemple†	·	·	·	·	·	·
g	·	·	·	·	·	·	·	·	·
f	·	·	·	·	·	·	·	·	·
v	·	·	·	·	·	·	·	·	·
θ	·	·	·	·	·	·	·	·	·
ð	·	·	·	·	·	·	·	·	·
s	·	simple	semple	(sample)	(sample)	·	·	·	·
z	·	·	·	·	·	·	·	·	·
ʃ	·	·	·	·	·	·	·	·	·
ʒ	·	·	·	·	·	·	·	·	·
h	·	·	·	·	·	·	·	·	·
tʃ	·	·	·	·	·	·	·	·	·
dʒ	·	·	·	·	·	·	·	·	·
m	·	·	·	·	·	·	·	·	·
n	·	·	·	·	·	·	·	·	·
l	·	·	·	·	·	·	·	·	·
r	·	rimple	·	·	·	·	·	·	·
w	·	wimple	·	·	(whample)†.	·	(whample)†.	·	·
j	·	·	·	·	·	·	·	·	·
pl	·	·	·	·	·	·	·	·	·
pr	·	·	·	·	·	·	·	·	·
bl	·	·	·	·	·	·	·	·	·
br	·	·	·	·	·	·	·	·	·
tr	·	·	·	trample	·	·	·	·	·
tw	·	·	·	·	·	·	·	·	·
dr	·	·	·	·	·	·	·	·	·
kl	·	·	·	·	·	·	·	·	·
kr	·	crimple	·	·	·	·	·	·	·
kw	·	·	·	·	·	·	·	·	·
gl	·	·	·	·	·	·	·	·	·
gr	·	·	·	·	·	·	·	·	·
fl	·	·	·	·	·	·	·	·	·
fr	·	·	·	·	·	·	·	·	·
θr	·	·	·	·	·	·	·	·	·
sp	·	·	·	·	·	·	·	·	·
st	·	·	stemple	·	·	·	·	·	·
sk	·	·	·	·	·	·	·	·	·
sm	·	·	·	·	·	·	·	·	·
sn	·	·	·	·	·	·	·	·	·
sl	·	·	·	·	·	·	·	·	·
sw	·	·	·	·	·	·	·	·	·
ʃr	·	·	·	·	·	·	·	·	·
spl	·	·	·	·	·	·	·	·	·
spr	·	·	·	·	·	·	·	·	·
str	·	·	·	·	·	·	·	·	·
skr	·	·	·	·	·	·	·	·	·
skw	·	·	·	·	·	·	·	·	·

Total number of words—19

194

ʌ	ɜ/r	eɪ	oʊ	aɪ	aʊ	ɔɪ	i/ə/r	ɛ/ə/r	ju
.	.	.	.	.	.	.	.	.	.
.	.	.	.	.	.	.	.	.	.
.	.	.	.	.	.	.	.	.	.
.	.	.	.	.	.	.	.	.	.
.	.	.	.	.	.	.	.	.	.
.	.	.	.	.	.	.	.	.	.
.	.	.	.	.	.	.	.	.	.
.	.	.	.	.	.	.	.	.	.
.	.	.	.	.	.	.	.	.	.
.	.	.	.	.	.	.	.	.	.
.	.	.	.	.	.	.	.	.	.
.	.	.	.	.	.	.	.	.	.
.	.	.	.	.	.	.	.	.	.
.	.	.	.	.	.	.	.	.	.
.	.	.	.	.	.	.	.	.	.
.	.	.	.	.	.	.	.	.	.
.	.	.	.	.	.	.	.	.	.
.	.	.	.	.	.	.	.	.	.
rumple	.	.	.	.	.	.	.	.	.
.	.	.	.	.	.	.	.	.	.
.	.	.	.	.	.	.	.	.	.
.	.	.	.	.	.	.	.	.	.
.	.	.	.	.	.	.	.	.	.
.	.	.	.	.	.	.	.	.	.
.	.	.	.	.	.	.	.	.	.
.	.	.	.	.	.	.	.	.	.
.	.	.	.	.	.	.	.	.	.
crumple	.	.	.	.	.	.	.	.	.
.	.	.	.	.	.	.	.	.	.
.	.	.	.	.	.	.	.	.	.
frumple	.	.	.	.	.	.	.	.	.
.	.	.	.	.	.	.	.	.	.
.	.	.	.	.	.	.	.	.	.
.	.	.	.	.	.	.	.	.	.
.	.	.	.	.	.	.	.	.	.
.	.	.	.	.	.	.	.	.	.
.	.	.	.	.	.	.	.	.	.
.	.	.	.	.	.	.	.	.	.
.	.	.	.	.	.	.	.	.	.
.	.	.	.	.	.	.	.	.	.
.	.	.	.	.	.	.	.	.	.

Final—/mpld/ . For inflected forms add /d/ to appropriate words, e.g. sampled.
—/mplz/ . For inflected forms add /z/ to appropriate words, e.g. samples.

	i	ɪ	ɛ	æ	ɑ	ɒ(ɑ	ɔ	ʊ	u
−	.	.	.	amble	.	.	.	.	.
p	.	.	.	.	.	.	.	.	.
b	.	.	.	.	.	.	.	.	.
t	.	tymbal†	.	.	.	.	.	.	.
d	.	dimble	.	.	.	.	.	.	.
k	.	.	.	.	.	.	.	.	.
g	.	.	.	gamble*	.	.	.	.	.
f	.	fimble	.	famble†	.	.	.	.	.
v	.	.	.	.	.	.	.	.	.
θ	.	*thimble*	.	.	.	.	.	.	.
ð	.	.	.	.	.	.	.	.	.
s	.	symbol*	semble	.	.	.	.	.	.
z	.	.	.	.	.	.	.	.	.
ʃ	.	.	.	shamble	.	.	.	.	.
ʒ	.	.	.	.	.	.	.	.	.
h	.	.	.	hamble	.	.	.	.	.
tʃ	.	.	.	.	.	.	.	.	.
dʒ	.	gimbal†	.	.	.	.	.	.	.
m	.	.	.	.	.	.	.	.	.
n	.	nimble	.	.	.	.	.	.	.
l	.	.	.	.	.	.	.	.	.
r	.	.	(remble)†	ramble	.	.	.	.	.
w	.	wimble	.	.	.	wamble	.	.	.
j	.	.	.	.	.	.	.	.	.
pl	.	.	.	.	.	.	.	.	.
pr	.	.	.	.	.	.	.	.	.
bl	.	.	.	.	.	.	.	.	.
br	.	.	.	bramble	.	.	.	.	.
tr	.	.	tremble	.	.	.	.	.	.
tw	.	.	.	.	.	.	.	.	.
dr	.	.	.	.	.	.	.	.	.
kl	.	.	.	.	.	.	.	.	.
kr	.	.	.	.	.	.	.	.	.
kw	.	.	.	.	.	.	.	.	.
gl	.	.	.	.	.	.	.	.	.
gr	.	.	.	.	.	.	.	.	.
fl	.	.	.	.	.	.	.	.	.
fr	.	.	.	.	.	.	.	.	.
θr	.	.	.	.	.	.	.	.	.
sp	.	.	.	.	.	.	.	.	.
st	.	.	.	.	.	.	.	.	.
sk	.	.	.	scamble†	.	.	.	.	.
sm	.	.	.	.	.	.	.	.	.
sn	.	.	.	.	.	.	.	.	.
sl	.	.	.	.	.	.	.	.	.
sw	.	.	.	.	.	.	.	.	.
ʃr	.	.	.	.	.	.	.	.	.
spl	.	.	.	.	.	.	.	.	.
spr	.	.	.	.	.	.	.	.	.
str	.	.	.	.	.	.	.	.	.
skr	.	.	.	scramble	.	.	.	.	.
skw	.	.	.	.	.	.	.	.	.

* homophones—see page 227.
  Total number of words—34

ʌ	ɜ/r	ɪə	oʊ	aɪ	aʊ	ɔɪ	i/ə/r	ɛ/ə/r	ju
umbel	.	.	.	.	.	.	.	.	.
.	.	.	.	.	.	.	.	.	.
bumble*	.	.	.	.	.	.	.	.	.
tumble	.	.	.	.	.	.	.	.	.
.	.	.	.	.	.	.	.	.	.
.	.	.	.	.	.	.	.	.	.
fumble	.	.	.	.	.	.	.	.	.
.	.	.	.	.	.	.	.	.	.
.	.	.	.	.	.	.	.	.	.
.	.	.	.	.	.	.	.	.	.
.	.	.	.	.	.	.	.	.	.
.	.	.	.	.	.	.	.	.	.
humble	.	.	.	.	.	.	.	.	.
jumble*	.	.	.	.	.	.	.	.	.
mumble	.	.	.	.	.	.	.	.	.
.	.	.	.	.	.	.	.	.	.
rumble	.	.	.	.	.	.	.	.	.
.	.	.	.	.	.	.	.	.	.
.	.	.	.	.	.	.	.	.	.
.	.	.	.	.	.	.	.	.	.
.	.	.	.	.	.	.	.	.	.
.	.	.	.	.	.	.	.	.	.
.	.	.	.	.	.	.	.	.	.
drumble	.	.	.	.	.	.	.	.	.
.	.	.	.	.	.	.	.	.	.
crumble	.	.	.	.	.	.	.	.	.
.	.	.	.	.	.	.	.	.	.
.	.	.	.	.	.	.	.	.	.
grumble	.	.	.	.	.	.	.	.	.
.	.	.	.	.	.	.	.	.	.
.	.	.	.	.	.	.	.	.	.
.	.	.	.	.	.	.	.	.	.
stumble	.	.	.	.	.	.	.	.	.
scumble	.	.	.	.	.	.	.	.	.
.	.	.	.	.	.	.	.	.	.
.	.	.	.	.	.	.	.	.	.
.	.	.	.	.	.	.	.	.	.
.	.	.	.	.	.	.	.	.	.
.	.	.	.	.	.	.	.	.	.
.	.	.	.	.	.	.	.	.	.
.	.	.	.	.	.	.	.	.	.
.	.	.	.	.	.	.	.	.	.

Final—/mbld/ . For inflected forms add /d/ to appropriate words, e.g. ambled.
—/mblz/ . For inflected forms add /z/ to appropriate words, e.g. ambles.

	i	ɪ	ɛ	æ	ɑ	ɒ(ɑ	ɔ/r	ʊ	u
–	·	·	·	·	·	·	·	·	·
p	·	*pistol**	·	pastel	·	postil	·	·	·
b	·	·	·	·	·	·	borstall*	·	·
t	·	·	·	·	·	·	·	·	·
d	·	distal	·	·	·	·	·	·	·
k	·	·	·	·	·	costal	·	·	·
g	·	·	·	·	·	·	·	·	·
f	·	·	festal	·	·	·	·	·	·
v	·	·	vestal	·	·	·	·	·	·
θ	·	·	·	·	·	·	·	·	·
ð	·	·	·	·	·	·	·	·	·
s	·	·	·	·	·	·	·	·	·
z	·	·	·	·	·	·	·	·	·
ʃ	·	·	·	·	·	·	·	·	·
ʒ	·	·	·	·	·	·	·	·	·
h	·	·	·	·	·	hostel*	·	·	·
tʃ	·	·	·	·	·	·	·	·	·
dʒ	·	·	·	·	·	·	·	·	·
m	·	·	·	·	·	·	·	·	·
n	·	·	·	·	·	·	·	·	·
l	·	listel	·	·	·	·	·	·	·
r	·	·	·	·	·	rostel	·	·	·
w	·	·	·	·	·	wastel†	·	·	·
j	·	·	·	·	·	·	·	·	·
pl	·	·	·	·	·	·	·	·	·
pr	·	·	·	·	·	·	·	·	·
bl	·	·	·	·	·	·	·	·	·
br	·	Bristol	·	·	·	·	·	·	·
tr	·	·	·	·	·	·	·	·	·
tw	·	·	·	·	·	·	·	·	·
dr	·	·	·	·	·	·	·	·	·
kl	·	·	·	·	·	·	·	·	·
kr	·	crystal	·	·	·	·	·	·	·
kw	·	·	·	·	·	·	·	·	·
gl	·	·	·	·	·	·	·	·	·
gr	·	·	·	·	·	·	·	·	·
fl	·	·	·	·	·	·	·	·	·
fr	·	·	·	·	·	·	·	·	·
θr	·	·	·	·	·	·	·	·	·
sp	·	·	·	·	·	·	·	·	·
st	·	·	·	·	·	·	·	·	·
sk	·	·	·	·	·	·	·	·	·
sm	·	·	·	·	·	·	·	·	·
sn	·	·	·	·	·	·	·	·	·
sl	·	·	·	·	·	·	·	·	·
sw	·	·	·	·	·	·	·	·	·
ʃr	·	·	·	·	·	·	·	·	·
spl	·	·	·	·	·	·	·	·	·
spr	·	·	·	·	·	·	·	·	·
str	·	·	·	·	·	·	·	·	·
skr	·	·	·	·	·	·	·	·	·
skw	·	·	·	·	·	·	·	·	·

* homophones—see page 227.
  Total number of words—16

ʌ	ɜ/r	eɪ	oʊ	aɪ	aʊ	ɔɪ	i/ə/r	ɛ/ə/r	ju
.	.	.	.	.	.	.	.	.	.
.	.	.	postal	.	.	.	.	.	.
.	.	.	.	.	.	.	.	.	.
.	.	.	.	.	.	.	.	.	.
.	.	.	coastal	.	.	.	.	.	.
.	.	.	.	.	.	.	.	.	.

Final—/stlz/ . For inflected forms add /z/ to appropriate words, e.g. pistols.

	i	ɪ	ɛ	æ	ɑ	ɒ(ɑ	ɔ	ʊ	u
—	.	.	.	.	.	.	.	.	.
p	.	pintle†	.	.	.	pontil	.	.	.
b	.	.	.	.	.	.	.	.	.
t	.	.	.	.	.	.	.	.	.
d	.	.	dental	.	.	.	.	.	.
k	.	.	[kentle]†	cantle	.	.	.	.	.
g	.	.	.	.	.	.	.	.	.
f	.	.	.	.	.	fontal	.	..	.
v	.	.	ventil	.	.	.	.	.	.
θ	.	.	.	.	.	.	.	.	.
ð	.	.	.	.	.	.	.	.	.
s	.	.	cental	santal	.	.	.	.	.
z	.	.	.	.	.	.	.	.	.
ʃ	.	.	.	.	.	.	.	.	.
ʒ	.	.	.	.	.	.	.	.	.
h	.	.	.	.	hantle†	.	.	.	.
tʃ	.	.	.	.	.	.	.	.	.
dʒ	.	.	gentle	.	.	.	.	.	.
m	.	.	mental	mantle*	.	.	.	.	.
n	.	.	.	.	.	.	.	.	.
l	.	lintel	lentil	.	.	.	.	.	.
r	.	.	rental	[rantle]	.	.	.	.	.
w	.	wintle†	.	.	.	.	.	.	.
j	.	.	.	.	.	.	.	.	.
pl	.	.	(plantal)	(plantal)	.	.	.	.	.
pr	.	.	.	.	.	.	.	.	.
bl	.	.	.	.	.	.	.	.	.
br	.	.	.	brantle	.	.	.	.	.
tr	.	.	trental	.	.	.	.	.	.
tw	.	.	.	.	.	.	.	.	.
dr	.	.	.	.	.	.	.	.	.
kl	.	.	.	.	.	.	.	.	.
kr	.	.	.	.	.	.	.	.	.
kw	.	quintal	.	.	.	.	.	.	.
gl	.	.	.	.	.	.	.	.	.
gr	.	.	.	.	.	.	.	.	.
fl	.	.	.	.	.	.	.	.	.
fr	.	.	.	.	.	.	.	.	.
θr	.	.	.	.	.	.	.	.	.
sp	.	.	.	.	.	.	.	.	.
st	.	.	.	.	.	.	.	.	.
sk	.	.	.	scantle	.	.	.	.	.
sm	.	.	.	.	.	.	.	.	.
sn	.	.	.	.	.	.	.	.	.
sl	.	.	.	.	.	.	.	.	.
sw	.	.	.	.	.	.	.	.	.
ʃr	.	.	.	.	.	.	.	.	.
spl	.	.	.	.	.	.	.	.	.
spr	.	.	.	.	.	.	.	.	.
str	.	.	.	.	.	.	.	.	.
skr	.	.	.	.	.	.	.	.	.
skw	.	.	.	.	.	.	.	.	.

* homophones—see page 227.
  Total number of words—26

ʌ	ɜ/r	eɪ	oʊ	aɪ	aʊ	ɔɪ	i/ə/r	ɛ/ə/r	ju
.	.	.	.	.	.	.	.	.	.
.	.	.	.	.	.	pointel	.	.	.
.	.	.	.	.	.	.	.	.	.
.	.	.	.	.	.	.	.	.	.
.	.	.	.	.	.	.	.	.	.
.	.	.	.	.	.	.	.	.	.
.	.	.	.	.	.	.	.	.	.
.	.	.	.	.	.	.	.	.	.
.	.	.	.	.	.	.	.	.	.
.	.	.	.	.	.	.	.	.	.
.	.	.	.	.	.	.	.	.	.
.	.	.	.	.	.	.	.	.	.
.	.	.	.	.	.	.	.	.	.
.	.	.	.	.	.	.	.	.	.
.	.	.	.	.	.	.	.	.	.
.	.	.	.	.	.	.	.	.	.
.	.	.	.	.	.	.	.	.	.
.	.	.	.	.	.	.	.	.	.
.	.	.	.	.	.	.	.	.	.
.	.	.	.	.	.	.	.	.	.
.	.	.	.	.	.	.	.	.	.
.	.	.	.	.	.	.	.	.	.
.	.	.	.	.	.	.	.	.	.
.	.	.	.	.	.	.	.	.	.
.	.	.	.	.	.	.	.	.	.
.	.	.	.	.	.	.	.	.	.
.	.	.	.	.	.	.	.	.	.
.	.	.	.	.	.	.	.	.	.
.	.	.	.	.	.	.	.	.	.
frontal .	.	.	.	.	.	.	.	.	.
.	.	.	.	.	.	.	.	.	.
.	.	.	.	.	.	.	.	.	.
.	.	.	.	.	.	.	.	.	.
.	.	.	.	.	.	.	.	.	.
.	.	.	.	.	.	.	.	.	.
.	.	.	.	.	.	.	.	.	.
.	.	.	.	.	.	.	.	.	.
.	.	.	.	.	.	.	.	.	.
.	.	.	.	.	.	.	.	.	.

Final—/ntld/ . For inflected forms add /d/ to appropriate words, e.g. mantled.
—/ntlz/ . For inflected forms add /z/ to appropriate words, e.g. mantles.

	i	ɪ	ɛ	æ	ɑ	ɒ(ɑ	ɔ	ʊ	u
–	·	·	·	·	·	·	·	·	·
p	·	·	·	·	·	·	·	·	·
b	·	·	·	·	·	·	·	·	·
t	·	tindal	·	·	·	·	·	·	·
d	·	[dindle]†	·	dandle	·	·	·	·	·
k	·	kindle	Kendal	*candle*	·	·	·	·	·
g	·	·	·	·	·	·	·	·	·
f	·	·	·	·	·	fondle	·	·	·
v	·	·	·	Vandal*	·	·	·	·	·
θ	·	·	·	·	·	·	·	·	·
ð	·	·	·	·	·	·	·	·	·
s	·	·	sendal	*sandal*	·	·	·	·	·
z	·	·	·	·	·	·	·	·	·
ʃ	·	·	·	·	·	·	·	·	·
ʒ	·	·	·	·	·	·	·	·	·
h	·	·	·	*handle**	·	·	·	·	·
tʃ	·	·	·	·	·	·	·	·	·
dʒ	·	·	·	·	·	·	·	·	·
m	·	Mindel†	·	·	·	·	·	·	·
n	·	·	·	·	·	·	·	·	·
l	·	·	·	·	·	·	·	·	·
r	·	[rindle]	·	[randle]	·	rondel	·	·	·
w	·	windle	·	·	·	wandle	·	·	·
j	·	·	·	·	·	·	·	·	·
pl	·	·	·	·	·	·	·	·	·
pr	·	·	·	·	·	·	·	·	·
bl	·	·	·	·	·	·	·	·	·
br	·	brindle	·	·	·	·	·	·	·
tr	·	trindle	·	·	·	·	·	·	·
tw	·	·	·	·	·	·	·	·	·
dr	·	·	·	·	·	·	·	·	·
kl	·	·	·	·	·	·	·	·	·
kr	·	·	·	·	·	·	·	·	·
kw	·	·	·	·	·	·	·	·	·
gl	·	·	·	·	·	·	·	·	·
gr	·	·	·	·	·	·	·	·	·
fl	·	·	·	·	·	·	·	·	·
fr	·	·	·	·	·	·	·	·	·
θr	·	·	·	·	·	·	·	·	·
sp	·	spindle	·	·	·	spondyl	·	·	·
st	·	·	·	·	·	·	·	·	·
sk	·	·	·	scandal	·	·	·	·	·
sm	·	·	·	·	·	·	·	·	·
sn	·	·	·	·	·	·	·	·	·
sl	·	·	·	·	·	·	·	·	·
sw	·	swindle	·	·	·	·	·	·	·
ʃr	·	·	·	·	·	·	·	·	·
spl	·	·	·	·	·	·	·	·	·
spr	·	·	·	·	·	·	·	·	·
str	·	·	·	·	·	·	·	·	·
skr	·	·	·	·	·	·	·	·	·
skw	·	·	·	·	·	·	·	·	·

* homophones—see page 228.
  Total number of words—28

ʌ	ɜ/r	eɪ	oʊ	aɪ	aʊ	ɔɪ	i/ə/r	ɛ/ə/r	ju
.	.	.	.	.	.	.	.	.	.
.	.	.	.	.	.	.	.	.	.
bundle	.	.	.	.	.	.	.	.	.
.	.	.	.	.	.	.	.	.	.
.	dirndl	.	.	.	.	.	.	.	.
.	.	.	.	.	.	.	.	.	.
.	.	.	.	.	.	.	.	.	.
.	.	.	.	.	.	.	.	.	.
.	.	.	.	.	.	.	.	.	.
.	.	.	.	.	.	.	.	.	.
.	.	.	.	.	.	.	.	.	.
.	.	.	.	.	.	.	.	.	.
.	.	.	.	.	.	.	.	.	.
.	.	.	.	.	.	.	.	.	.
.	.	.	.	.	.	.	.	.	.
.	.	.	.	.	.	.	.	.	.
.	.	.	.	.	.	.	.	.	.
.	.	.	.	.	.	.	.	.	.
.	.	.	.	.	.	.	.	.	.
[rundle]	.	.	.	.	roundel*	.	.	.	.
.	.	.	.	.	.	.	.	.	.
.	.	.	.	.	.	.	.	.	.
.	.	.	.	.	.	.	.	.	.
.	.	.	.	.	.	.	.	.	.
.	.	.	.	.	.	.	.	.	.
trundle	.	.	.	.	.	.	.	.	.
.	.	.	.	.	.	.	.	.	.
.	.	.	.	.	.	.	.	.	.
.	.	.	.	.	.	.	.	.	.
.	.	.	.	.	.	.	.	.	.
.	.	.	.	.	.	.	.	.	.
.	.	.	.	.	.	.	.	.	.
.	.	.	.	.	.	.	.	.	.
.	.	.	.	.	.	.	.	.	.
.	.	.	.	.	.	.	.	.	.
.	.	.	.	.	.	.	.	.	.
.	.	.	.	.	.	.	.	.	.
.	.	.	.	.	.	.	.	.	.
.	.	.	.	.	.	.	.	.	.
.	.	.	.	.	.	.	.	.	.
.	.	.	.	.	.	.	.	.	.
.	.	.	.	.	.	.	.	.	.
.	.	.	.	.	.	.	.	.	.

Final—/ndld/ . For inflected forms add /d/ to appropriate words, e.g. handled.
—/ndlz/ . For inflected forms add /z/ to appropriate words, e.g. handles.

	i	ɪ	ɛ	æ	ɑ	ɒ	ɔ	ʊ	u
–	.	inkle	.	ankle	.	.	.	.	.
p	.	.	.	.	.	.	.	.	.
b	.	.	.	.	.	.	.	.	.
t	.	tinkle*	.	.	.	.	.	.	.
d	.	.	.	.	.	.	.	.	.
k	.	kinkle	.	.	.	.	.	.	.
g	.	.	.	.	.	.	.	.	.
f	.	.	.	fankle	.	.	.	.	.
v	.	.	.	.	.	.	.	.	.
θ	.	.	.	.	.	.	.	.	.
ð	.	.	.	.	.	.	.	.	.
s	.	.	.	.	.	.	.	.	.
z	.	.	.	.	.	.	.	.	.
ʃ	.	.	.	.	.	.	.	.	.
ʒ	.	.	.	.	.	.	.	.	.
h	.	.	.	.	.	.	.	.	.
tʃ	.	.	.	.	.	.	.	.	.
dʒ	.	.	.	.	.	.	.	.	.
m	.	.	.	.	.	.	.	.	.
n	.	.	.	.	.	.	.	.	.
l	.	.	.	.	.	.	.	.	.
r	.	wrinkle	.	rankle	.	.	.	.	.
w	.	winkle	.	wankle	.	.	.	.	.
j	.	.	.	.	.	.	.	.	.
pl	.	.	.	.	.	.	.	.	.
pr	.	.	.	prankle	.	.	.	.	.
bl	.	.	.	.	.	.	.	.	.
br	.	.	.	.	.	.	.	.	.
tr	.	trinkle†	.	.	.	.	.	.	.
tw	.	twinkle	.	.	.	.	.	.	.
dr	.	.	.	.	.	.	.	.	.
kl	.	.	.	.	.	.	.	.	.
kr	.	crinkle	.	crankle	.	.	.	.	.
kw	.	.	.	.	.	.	.	.	.
gl	.	.	.	.	.	.	.	.	.
gr	.	.	.	.	.	.	.	.	.
fl	.	.	.	.	.	.	.	.	.
fr	.	.	.	.	.	.	.	.	.
θr	.	.	.	.	.	.	.	.	.
sp	.	.	.	.	.	.	.	.	.
st	.	.	.	.	.	.	.	.	.
sk	.	.	.	.	.	.	.	.	.
sm	.	.	.	.	.	.	.	.	.
sn	.	.	.	.	.	.	.	.	.
sl	.	.	.	.	.	.	.	.	.
sw	.	.	.	.	.	.	.	.	.
ʃr	.	.	.	.	.	.	.	.	.
spl	.	.	.	.	.	.	.	.	.
spr	.	sprinkle	.	.	.	.	.	.	.
str	.	strinkle	.	.	.	.	.	.	.
skr	.	.	.	.	.	.	.	.	.
skw	.	.	.	.	.	.	.	.	.

* homophones—see page 228.
  Total number of words—20

ʌ	ɜ/r	eɪ	oʊ	aɪ	aʊ	ɔɪ	i/ə/r	ɛ/ə/r	ju
uncle	·	·	·	·	·	·	·	·	·
·	·	·	·	·	·	·	·	·	·
·	·	·	·	·	·	·	·	·	·
·	·	·	·	·	·	·	·	·	·
·	·	·	·	·	·	·	·	·	·
·	·	·	·	·	·	·	·	·	·
·	·	·	·	·	·	·	·	·	·
·	·	·	·	·	·	·	·	·	·
·	·	·	·	·	·	·	·	·	·
·	·	·	·	·	·	·	·	·	·
·	·	·	·	·	·	·	·	·	·
·	·	·	·	·	·	·	·	·	·
·	·	·	·	·	·	·	·	·	·
·	·	·	·	·	·	·	·	·	·
·	·	·	·	·	·	·	·	·	·
·	·	·	·	·	·	·	·	·	·
·	·	·	·	·	·	·	·	·	·
·	·	·	·	·	·	·	·	·	·
nuncle	·	·	·	·	·	·	·	·	·
·	·	·	·	·	·	·	·	·	·
·	·	·	·	·	·	·	·	·	·
·	·	·	·	·	·	·	·	·	·
·	·	·	·	·	·	·	·	·	·
·	·	·	·	·	·	·	·	·	·
·	·	·	·	·	·	·	·	·	·
truncal	·	·	·	·	·	·	·	·	·
·	·	·	·	·	·	·	·	·	·
·	·	·	·	·	·	·	·	·	·
crunkle	·	·	·	·	·	·	·	·	·
·	·	·	·	·	·	·	·	·	·
·	·	·	·	·	·	·	·	·	·
·	·	·	·	·	·	·	·	·	·
·	·	·	·	·	·	·	·	·	·
·	·	·	·	·	·	·	·	·	·
·	·	·	·	·	·	·	·	·	·
·	·	·	·	·	·	·	·	·	·
·	·	·	·	·	·	·	·	·	·
·	·	·	·	·	·	·	·	·	·
·	·	·	·	·	·	·	·	·	·
·	·	·	·	·	·	·	·	·	·
·	·	·	·	·	·	·	·	·	·
·	·	·	·	·	·	·	·	·	·

Final—/ŋkld/ . For inflected forms add /d/ to appropriate words, e.g. wrinkled.
—/ŋklz/ . For inflected forms add /z/ to appropriate words, e.g. wrinkles.

	i	ɪ	ɛ	æ	ɑ	ɒ(a	ɔ	ʊ	u
—		ingle		angle*					
p		pinglet							
b				bangle					
t		tingle		tangle					
d		dingle		dangle					
k		kingle							
g									
f				fangle					
v									
θ									
ð									
s		single*							
z		zingel							
ʃ		shingle							
ʒ									
h									
tʃ									
dʒ		jingle		jangle					
m		mingle		mangle		Mongol			
n									
l		linglet							
r				wrangle					
w				wangle					
j									
pl									
pr		pringle							
bl									
br				branglet					
tr		tringle		trangle					
tw				twangle					
dr									
kl									
kr		cringle							
kw									
gl									
gr									
fl									
fr									
θr									
sp				spangle					
st					ɑ				u
sk									
sm									
sn									
sl									
sw		swingle							
ʃr									
spl									
spr		springle*		sprangle					
str				strangle					
skr									
skw									

* homophones—see page 228.
  Total number of words—34

ʌ	ɜ/r	eɪ	oʊ	aɪ	aʊ	ɔɪ	i/ə/r	ɛ/ə/r	ju
	.	.	.	.	.	.	.	.	.
bungle	.	.	.	.	.	.	.	.	.
.	.	.	.	.	.	.	.	.	.
.	.	.	.	.	.	.	.	.	.
.	.	.	.	.	.	.	.	.	.
.	.	.	.	.	.	.	.	.	.
.	.	.	.	.	.	.	.	.	.
.	.	.	.	.	.	.	.	.	.
.	.	.	.	.	.	.	.	.	.
.	.	.	.	.	.	.	.	.	.
.	.	.	.	.	.	.	.	.	.
.	.	.	.	.	.	.	.	.	.
.	.	.	.	.	.	.	.	.	.
.	.	.	.	.	.	.	.	.	.
jungle	.	.	.	.	.	.	.	.	.
.	.	.	.	.	.	.	.	.	.
.	.	.	.	.	.	.	.	.	.
.	.	.	.	.	.	.	.	.	.
.	.	.	.	.	.	.	.	.	.
.	.	.	.	.	.	.	.	.	.
.	.	.	.	.	.	.	.	.	.
.	.	.	.	.	.	.	.	.	.
.	.	.	.	.	.	.	.	.	.
.	.	.	.	.	.	.	.	.	.
.	.	.	.	.	.	.	.	.	.
.	.	.	.	.	.	.	.	.	.
.	.	.	.	.	.	.	.	.	.
.	.	.	.	.	.	.	.	.	.
.	.	.	.	.	.	.	.	.	.
.	.	.	.	.	.	.	.	.	.
.	.	.	.	.	.	.	.	.	.
.	.	.	.	.	.	.	.	.	.
.	.	.	.	.	.	.	.	.	.
.	.	.	.	.	.	.	.	.	.
.	.	.	.	.	.	.	.	.	.
.	.	.	.	.	.	.	.	.	.
.	.	.	.	.	.	.	.	.	.
.	.	.	.	.	.	.	.	.	.
.	.	.	.	.	.	.	.	.	.
.	.	.	.	.	.	.	.	.	.
.	.	.	.	.	.	.	.	.	.

Final—/ŋgld/ . For inflected forms add /d/ to appropriate words, e.g. tangled.
—/ŋglz/ . For inflected forms add /z/ to appropriate words, e.g. tangles.

	i	ɪ	ɛ	æ	ɑ	ɒ(ɑ	ɔ	ʊ	u
–	·	·	·	·	·	·	·	·	·
p	·	·	*pencil**	·	·	·	·	·	·
b	·	·	·	·	·	·	·	·	·
t	·	tinsel	(tensile)	·	·	tonsil	·	·	·
d	·	·	·	·	·	·	·	·	·
k	·	·	·	cancel	·	consul	·	·	·
g	·	·	·	·	·	·	·	·	·
f	·	·	·	·	·	·	·	·	·
v	·	·	·	·	·	·	·	·	·
θ	·	·	·	·	·	·	·	·	·
ð	·	·	·	·	·	·	·	·	·
s	·	·	·	·	·	·	·	·	·
z	·	·	·	·	·	·	·	·	·
ʃ	·	·	·	·	·	·	·	·	·
ʒ	·	·	·	·	·	·	·	·	·
h	·	·	(Hänsel)	hansel*	·	·	·	·	·
tʃ	·	·	·	(chancel)	(chancel)	·	·	·	·
dʒ	·	·	·	·	·	·	·	·	·
m	·	·	mensal	·	·	·	·	·	·
n	·	·	·	·	·	·	·	·	·
l	·	·	·	·	·	·	·	·	·
r	·	·	·	·	·	·	·	·	·
w	·	·	·	·	·	·	·	·	·
j	·	·	·	·	·	·	·	·	·
pl	·	·	·	·	·	·	·	·	·
pr	·	·	·	·	·	·	·	·	·
bl	·	·	·	·	·	·	·	·	·
br	·	·	·	bransle	·	·	·	·	·
tr	·	·	·	·	·	·	·	·	·
tw	·	·	·	·	·	·	·	·	·
dr	·	·	·	·	·	·	·	·	·
kl	·	·	·	·	·	·	·	·	·
kr	·	·	·	·	·	·	·	·	·
kw	·	·	·	·	·	·	·	·	·
gl	·	·	·	·	·	·	·	·	·
gr	·	·	·	·	·	·	·	·	·
fl	·	·	·	·	·	·	·	·	·
fr	·	·	·	·	·	·	·	·	·
θr	·	·	·	·	·	·	·	·	·
sp	·	·	·	spancel	·	sponsal	·	·	·
st	·	·	stencil	·	·	·	·	·	·
sk	·	·	·	·	·	·	·	·	·
sm	·	·	·	·	·	·	·	·	·
sn	·	·	·	·	·	·	·	·	·
sl	·	·	·	·	·	·	·	·	·
sw	·	·	·	·	·	·	·	·	·
ʃr	·	·	·	·	·	·	·	·	·
spl	·	·	·	·	·	·	·	·	·
spr	·	·	·	·	·	·	·	·	·
str	·	·	·	·	·	·	·	·	·
skr	·	·	·	·	·	·	·	·	·
skw	·	·	·	·	·	·	·	·	·

* homophones—see page 228.
  Total number of words—19

ʌ	ɜ/r	eɪ	oʊ	aɪ	aʊ	ɔɪ	i/ə/r	ɛ/ə/r	ju
·	·	·	·	·	·	·	·	·	·
·	·	·	·	·	·	·	·	·	·
·	·	·	·	·	·	·	·	·	·
·	·	·	·	·	·	·	·	·	·
·	·	·	·	·	council* ·		·	·	·
·	·	·	·	·	·	·	·	·	·
·	·	·	·	·	·	·	·	·	·
·	·	·	·	·	·	·	·	·	·
·	·	·	·	·	·	·	·	·	·
·	·	·	·	·	·	·	·	·	·
·	·	·	·	·	·	·	·	·	·
·	·	·	·	·	·	·	·	·	·
·	·	·	·	·	·	·	·	·	·
·	·	·	·	·	·	·	·	·	·
·	·	(mainsail).	·	·	·	·	·	·	·
·	·	nainsel	·	·	·	·	·	·	·
·	·	·	·	·	·	·	·	·	·
·	·	·	·	·	·	·	·	·	·
·	·	·	·	·	·	·	·	·	·
·	·	·	·	·	·	·	·	·	·
·	·	·	·	·	·	·	·	·	·
·	·	·	·	·	·	·	·	·	·
·	·	·	·	·	·	·	·	·	·
·	·	·	·	·	·	·	·	·	·
·	·	·	·	·	·	·	·	·	·
·	·	·	·	·	·	·	·	·	·
·	·	·	·	·	·	·	·	·	·
·	·	·	·	·	·	·	·	·	·
(stunsail).	·	·	·	·	·	·	·	·	·
·	·	·	·	·	·	·	·	·	·
·	·	·	·	·	·	·	·	·	·
·	·	·	·	·	·	·	·	·	·
·	·	·	·	·	·	·	·	·	·
·	·	·	·	·	·	·	·	·	·
·	·	·	·	·	·	·	·	·	·
·	·	·	·	·	·	·	·	·	·
·	·	·	·	·	·	·	·	·	·

Final—/nsld/ . For inflected forms add /d/ to appropriate words, e.g. pencilled.
—/nslz/ . For inflected forms add /z/ to appropriate words, e.g. pencils.

Homophones

— —	E (ea)† [ee]†; are R ah† (our); or oar ore awe (o'er) Orr; [ou]† [oo]† [oo']†; err ure†; A (ae)† eh† ay† aye a; O owe eau oh† o'†; eye I aye; air heir e'er† ere eyre Eyre Ayr; U you yew eye (yu);
p —	P pea pee (pi); par pah† [pa] parr; paw pore pour (poor); purr per pur†; pay peh pais; poh† Po Poe; pie (pi) pye† Pye; pier peer; pear pair pare [paire]† père;
b —	bee be B; bar baa bah†; boar bore bor (Boer) (Bohr); burr bur birr†; bay bey baye† (bez); bow beau bo† boh†; by buy bye; bough bow; boy buoy; beer bier bere bear; bear bare;
t —	tea tee T ti te; tar ta† tarre† (thar); tore tor taw; two to too; toe tow; tie Thai tye tai; tear tier teer Tyr; tare tear tahr;
d —	D dee ; door daw dorr dor†; do Doo [doo]† (due) (dew); day dey Day; doe Doe dough doh; die dye; dhow dow†; deer dear dere†; (dew) (due);
k —	key quay; car Carr carr ka (Kerr); core caw corp cor khor ca'†; coo coup; cur curr† (Kerr); K Kay kae† [cay] ka†; chi kye†; cow kow; queue cue Q;
g —	[ghee] gee† [gie]†; gore gaw†; goo† [gue]; gay [gae]†; guy Guy;
f —	fee (phi); far fa; four for fore faw (faugh)† [fa']†; fur fir; fay Fay (fey)†; fie† (phi); fear feer fere†; fair fare phare; few feu† phew†;
v —	vare vair;
θ —	thaw Thor;
ð —	thee (the); they thae†; though tho†; there their they're;
s —	sea see C si; saw sore soar soare†; (sue) sou Sue Sioux; sir serr; say [sae]†; sew sow so soh; sigh scye (psi) sye†; sow (sough)†; cere sear seer sere†;
ʃ —	she shea (ski); shore shaw Shaw pshaw†; shoe shoo (shew)†; shay Shea; sheer shear;
h —	haw hoar whore; who hoo†; her (Herr); hay hey (heigh)† [hae]†; hoe ho†; high hie (heigh)† hi†; how howe†; here hear; hair hare (Herr); hew hue Hugh whew†;
tʃ —	char charr; chore chaw; chirr churr; chai (chay); chow Chow†; chair [chare]†;
dʒ —	G gee jee†; jar Jah; jay J; joe† jo† Joe; joy Joy;
m —	me mi; mar [ma]† Meagher; more More (Moore) maw mhorr (moor) (moire); moo moue (mu); may May [mae]†; mow moe† mo†; mere mir meer†; mew meu (mu);
n —	knee (ne)†; knar gnar [na]† [narre]†; nor gnaw nor'; (gnu) (new) (knew); neigh nay née [nae]†; no know; nigh Nye; nare ne'er; (knew) (new) (gnu);
l —	lea lee Lee li Leigh; la† lah lar; law lore; loo Lou (lieu) (lew) [lo'e]†; lay ley (lei); low lowe† lo†; lie lye; leer Lear lear† lehr; lair (layer) [lare]†; (lieu) (lew);
r —	re ree; Ra [rah]†; raw roar ['rah]†; rue rew† roux; ray reh Ray re; row roe rho Roe; rye wry Rye;
w —	we wee; wore war waugh† waw† warre†; were whir; way weigh wey whey wae†; woe whoa†; why Y; whow† vau; weir we're wear†; wear where Ware ware;
j —	yarr yah; your yaw yore (you're); ewe you yew U (yu); yea (ae)†; [yowe]† yow†;
pl —	plough Plough;
pr —	pray prey;
bl —	blue blew; blay blae†;
br —	brew broo†; bray brae†; [breare]† [breer]†;

210

tr — tray (trait) trey; troy Troy;
tw — [tway]† (twa)†;
dr — dray drey;
kl — clue clew; (clough) [clow]†; cloy† cloye†;
kr — cree K'ri; crore craw; crew Kroo crewe;
kw — (quey)† (qua);
gl — glee (gley); glare glair;
gr — grew grue†; grey Gray;
fl — flee flea; floor flaw; flew flue 'flu; flow floe; flair flare;
θr — through threw; throw throe;
sp — spa spar; spore [spaw]†; spur sperre†; spay spae†; spear speir†;
st — star Starr starr; store [staw]†; sty (stey)† stye [stie]†; steer stere; stare stair;
sk — score skaw [scaur]†; sky Skye;
sl — slew slue (slough); sleigh slay sley [slae]†; slow sloe;
str — stray [strae]†;
skr — scray [scrae]†;

p — peep [peepe]†; pope Pope;
t — tope taupe;
k — kip kipp; cap Cap†; carp [cap]†; cop kop†; coop coupe; coup† cowp†;
s — soup soop†;
h — hip [hyp];
tʃ — cheap cheep;
n — nip Nip†; nap knap nappe† (nape); noop† (noup)†;
l — lap Lapp;
r — rip ripp†; repp rep†; wrap rap;
w — whop† wop†; warp whaup†;
j — yapp yap†;
tr — troop troupe;
dr — droop drupe;
kr — croup croupe; (crepe) crape;
gr — grip (grippe); grape graip†;
st — step steppe; stoop stoep† stoup (stupe);
sl — slipe slype;

b — bib bibb; barb barbe; bob Bob;
d — dab dabb;
k — cob kob cobb; curb kerb;
s — sorb Sorb;
tʃ — chub Chubb;
dʒ — jib (gib); Job jobe; jibe gybe;
m — Mab mab†;
n — nab knab; knob nob; knub nub†;
r — rob Rob;
w — web Webb;
sl — slub slubb;

— — ought aught; eight (ate) eyot [ait]†;

p — peat Pete; pit Pitt; pat Pat; part patte; port Porte (poort)†; putt put;

b — beat beet; bit bitt; bet bête; bat batt; bought bort; but butt; bait bate Bate; bite bight; bout bought; butte Bute beaut†;

t — tatt tat; tart tat; taut taught tort†; tait tate†; tight tite†; tout towt†;

d — dit† ditt†; daut† dort†; dight† dite†; doubt dout†;

k — cat (kat); cart carte (kat) quart; cot cott; court caught; cate Kate; coat cote; kite kyte† [keight]†;

g — girt Gert; gate gait;

f — feet feat; fit fytte; fort forte; fate fete;

s — sit cit†; sort sought [saut]†; (suit) soote†; syrt cert†; sate Seth; sight site cite cyte†;

ʃ — shoot chute;

h — heat [hete]†; heart hart; hate haet†; height hight†;

tʃ — chert chirt;

dʒ — jet jeat†;

m — meat meet mete; mat matt matte; mot† mott†; moat mote (mought)†; might mite;

n — knit nit; net nett†; gnat Nat; knot not nott; nought naught; night knight; knout nowt†;

l — leet leat† (lied); lit (luit); let Lett; loot (lute); light lyte† lite†; lout lowt†;

r — writ rit†; wrought raught†; root (route); wrote rote; right rite write Wright; (route) rout;

w — wheat [weete]† [weet]†; wit whit; wet whet; what watt [wot]† watt† [whot]†; wart watt†; wort whort wert†; wait weight; white wite† wight White;

j — yet yett†;

pl — (plait) plat; plate (plait);

bl — blight blite;

br — brute bruit brut;

tw — twite [twight]†;

kl — [clat]† clart†;

gr — great grate;

fl — flit flitt†; float flote†; flight flyte† Flite;

sk — scat† scatt†; skat scart† [skart]†; scot Scott; scout schout† skout†;

sm — [smout]† [smowt]†;

sl — slight sleight;

sw — sweet suite; swat swot;

sp — sprite spright;

str — straight strait;

— — add ad†; odd od†; ord† awed oared Ord Orde; aid aide; ode owed (od) ohed; eyed I'd ide;

p — poured pawed pored; paid payed; paired pared;

b — bead Bede; bad (bade); bard barred; board bored bawd baud†; booed boud†; bird burred burd† Byrd; (bade) bayed; bode bowed; buoyed Boyd;

t — teed tead†; ted Ted; tod Todd todde†; toad towed toed; tide tied;

d — deed [deid]†; [dad]† darred†; died dyed; dowd dowed†;

k — kid Kyd; cord chord cored cawed; cud khud; curd Kurd; cade [kade]; caird cared; cued† queued;

g — guard garred†; gaud† gored (gourd); guide guyed;

f — feed fee'd†; ford Ford; (fyrd) furred; fared faired;

s — seed cede; sard Sard; sword soared sawed sord; sewed sowed; side sighed [cide]†; seared cered;

z — (Z) (zed);
ʃ — sherd shirred;
h — heed he'd; hoard horde whored hoared [haud]†; herd heard Herd; hide hied;
tʃ — chard charred; chaired [chared]†;
dʒ — jarde jarred;
m — mead meed Mede Mead; maud Maud; mood mooed; maid made; mode mowed;
n — need knead kneed; nard knarred gnarred;
l — lead led; lord Lord laud lawed† (lewd) looed; laid lade; load lode lowed;
r — read reed Read rede†; red read reddt†; rude rued rood; rudd rud; raid rayed [rade]†; road rode rowed roed; reared [reird]†;
w — weed we'd weid†; wad wadd; ward warred; wood would; word whirred; wade weighed;
j — yard (yaud)†; (yaud)† yawed;
pr — preyed prayed; pride pried;
bl — blued [blude]†;
br — breed [brede]†; bread bred; brood brewed; braid brayed braide†;
kl — Claud clawed; Clyde clied†;
kw — quad† quod†;
gl — gleed [glede]; glowed glode†; glaired glared;
gr — grade greyed;
fl — flawed floored; flared flaired;
sp — sparred [spard]†; spade spayed [spayd]†; spode Spode;
st — staid stayed;
sl — slid 'slid†; slade slayed slaid†;
sw — Swede swede [sweed]†; suede swayed;
str — strode [strowed];

— — ark arc; auk orc; oke oak;
p — peak peek pique peke†; peck pec; pork pawk†; [pouke] pook†; Puck puck;
b — beck [becke]†; bark barque (Bach); bok bock; [birk]† burke Burke; bike† byke†;
t — tick tic; talk torque;
d — Dick dick†; dark [dak] dhak; dock doc†; dook† (douc) [duke]; dirk [dirke]†;
k — cock coque; cork calk caulk cauk;
f — fork falk†; fake faik†; fike† fyke†;
s — seek (Sikh); sick (Sikh) [sic]†; sack sac saque; Sark [sark]†; sock soc†; soak soke†;
ʃ — chic (sheikh); shock (shough); shake (sheikh);
h — hic† hick; hock hough; hike haik;
tʃ — chick tchick; cheque check Czech; chack† chark;
dʒ — jack Jack jak; juke† jouk†; jerk jerque;
m — Mac mack†; mark Mark marc marque† [mak]†; murk† merk; make [maik]; mike† Mike;
n — nick Nick; neck nek; knock nock;
l — leek leak; lack lac lakh; luke Luke; lake laik†;
r — reek wreak† reak† reke†; wrick rick; wreck reck; wrack† rack; rock roc; rake raik; [wroke]† roke;
w — weak week [weeke]†; whack Waac; walk [wark]†;
j — yolk yoke;
pl — (plack) (plaque);
bl — bloc block;
br — brock (brough); brook Brook; brake break;
kl — (clique) cleek†; click (clique); clack (claque); (claque) (clerk);
kr — (creek) creak; crick (creek);

213

fl	—	flock floc;
sp	—	speck spec†; spark [sparke]†;
st	—	stick stich; stalk stork; steak stake;
sn	—	snook [snoek];
str	—	streak streek†; strake† straik†;

final g

p	—	peg Peg;
b	—	big bigg; berg (burg) burgh;
d	—	dug Doug;
ʃ	—	shog (shough);
h	—	hag hagg†; hog hogg; Hague Haig;
dʒ	—	jag jagg;
m	—	mag [magg]†;
n	—	nag knag;
l	—	leg legge†;
r	—	rag ragg;
w	—	wig Whig whig†;
br	—	brag Bragg;
sk	—	skug† [scug]†;

final f

—	—	orfe auf; oof† [ouph]†;
t	—	tough (tuff) tuffe;
k	—	(calf) kaph; cough koff coff†;
g	—	gaff gaffe; goff† (golf);
f	—	fief (feoff); fife Phyfe;
s	—	surf serf;
h	—	(half) haaf†;
tʃ	—	chuff chough;
dʒ	—	jeff Geoff;
l	—	leaf lief†;
r	—	reef reif†; riff Riff; raff Raff†; rough ruff ruffe;
w	—	Waaf (waff)†; wharf (waff)†; waif waft†;
j	—	yaff† [yaf]†;
kl	—	cliff Cliff;
gl	—	glyph† gliff†;
gr	—	(graph) graff; graf (graph) [graff]†;
sk	—	scarf scaff†;

final v

—	—	eve Eve;
d	—	(div) deave†; dive (div);
k	—	carve calve; curve [kerve]†;
θ	—	thieve theave†;
h	—	have (halve);
dʒ	—	jive (gyve);
n	—	nave knave;
l	—	leave lieve†;
r	—	reeve [reave]†;
w	—	weave we've; wave waive;

214

kl	—	cleave cleve;
gr	—	grieve greave; grave Graves;
st	—	steeve stieve† Steve;
sl	—	sleeve sleave†;
skr	—	screeve scrieve†;

b	—	beth Beth; (bath) Bath barth; birth berth;
f	—	fourth forth; firth furth†;
s	—	saith† Seth; south sowth†;
r	—	(wroth) (wrath); ruth Ruth; (wroth) wroath;
w	—	(withe) (with); worth Worth;
sm	—	smith Smith;

s	—	scythe sythe† [sithe]†;
l	—	lithe lythe†;
w	—	with (withe);

—	—	S es; ass as; as arse†; Erse ers;
p	—	peace piece; (pass) (parse); purse perse [perce]†; pace [Pace]†;
b	—	Bess Bes; bass basse; boss Bos (bosch); bus buss; base bass;
t	—	tass tasse; terse terce†;
d	—	(Dis) diss; doucet† (deuce) (Douce); douse dowse;
k	—	cos Cos coss; course coarse [corse]†;
f	—	farce farse;
v	—	vice Vice;
s	—	cess [cesse]†; sass sasse†; sauce source; souse sous†;
h	—	horse hoarse [hawse]†; hearse herse†;
dʒ	—	jess Jess;
m	—	miss Miss mis†; mass Mass; morse Morse; moose mousse;
n	—	niece Nice; nis (nys)†; noose (nous); nice gneiss;
l	—	lease lis†; loose luce Luce; louse lowse†;
r	—	wrasse (rasse); Ross ross; race reis; rice reis†;
w	—	whiss [wis]†;
pl	—	place plaice;
br	—	(brass) brasse;
kr	—	crease Kris; cross crosse; crouse† (cruse);
gr	—	grease Greece [grece]†; grace Grace; grice gris†;
sp	—	spice speiss;
spr	—	spruce Spruce;

—	—	ease E's; (ours) R's; oars ores; ooze Ouse; owes O's; eyes ayes I's; heirs airs; use yews ewes U's (yus);
p	—	peas P's pees [peaze]†; pause pours pores paws; pays [peise]†; pize pies pyes; poise poys†; peers piers Piers; pairs pears pares;

215

b — bees B's bise; baas bars; bores boars; booze boos; burs burrs birrs†; baize bays beys (bez) bayes†; beaux bows; bows boughs (bowse) (bouse); buoys boys; biers beers beres; bares bears;

t — tease teas tees T's; tars tarres† (thars); tors taws tawse; tows toes toze; ties tyes Thais; toise toys; tiers tears teers; tears tares tahrs;

d — doors daws dorrs dors†; (dues) do's [doos]†; daze days; doze does; dyes dies; dowse dhows dows†; dears deers deres†;

k — quays keys; cars carrs; cause cores caws corps khors cors; coups coos; currs† curs; [cays] K's kaes† [kaies]†; cose coze; cues queues Q's;

g — gauze gores gaws†; guise guys;

f — feeze† fees; fizz phiz†; fours faws; furze furs firs; phase faze† fays feys; fears feers feres†; fares phares fairs; fuse feus†;

v — (vase) [vaes]; vise† vies; vairs vares;

s — seize sees seas C's seise†; soars sores saws; sirs serrs; sows sews; size sighs scyes syes†; sows (soughs)†; sears seers ceres seres†;

z — zuz zoos;

ʃ — sheas shes she's; shores pshaws†; shoos shoes (shews); shears sheers;

h — heeze† he's; his hizz†; hawse haws hoars whores; whose who's; haze hays heys; hose hoes; house how's howes† hows†; hares hairs; hues hews whews Hughes;

tʃ — cheese chese†; chars charrs; chores chaws; choose chews; churrs chirrs; Chows† chows; chairs [chares]†;

dʒ — gees G's jees†; jays J's; joes† jos† [dzos];

m — mease (mise)†; Mars mars; mores maws mhorrs (moors); maze maize; moze mows mose†; Muse muse mews;

n — neeze knees; gnars knars nas†; (noose) (news); naze neighs nays; nose knows; noise Noyes noys†; (news) (gnus);

l — lees leas lease leaze leese leeze lis; lores laws; lose loos; laze lays leys; lows lowes† lose; louse (lowse)† lehrs lears† leers; lairs [lares]† (layers);

r — ruse rues rews† roose†; raise raze rays; rose rows roes Rose; rouse rows;

w — wars waws†; weighs ways weys wase†; wise why's Y's; wiers wears†; wares wears;

j — yaws yours; yews use ewes U's (yus);

pl — please pleas;

pr — praise prays preys; prose pros; prize pries [prise]† pryse†;

bl — blaze blays blaes†; (blousé) blowze;

br — breeze brize brees; bruise brews (broose)† (broos)†; braze brays braes† braise braize (broose)† (broos)†; browse brows; [breers]† [breares]†;

tr — (traits) trays trez;

dr — druse Druz; dreys drays; dries drys;

kl — clause claws; clews clues; clays [claes]†; close (clothes); (cloughs) [clows]†; cloys† cloyes†;

kr — craws crores; cruise crews crewes† Kroos (cruse); croze crows;

gl — gloze glows; glairs glares;

gr — (grease) grees†; graze greys;

fl — fleas flees; flaws floors; flues flews; floes flows; flares flairs;

fr — freeze frieze frees; phrase frays fraise;

θr — throes throws;

sp — spars spas; spores [spaws]†; spurs sperres†; spays spaes†; spears speirs†;

st — stars starrs; stores [staws]†; stows† (stews); sties styes; steres steers; stairs stares;

sk — scores skaws [scaurs]†; skews 'scuse†;

sl — (sloughs) slues; slays sleys sleighs [slaes]†; sloes slows;

spr— sprees spreeze†;

skr— screws scruze†; scrays [scraes]†;

— —   ash aesc Ash;
b —   bosh boche (bosch)†;
k —   cash cache Cash;
n —   gnash Nash;
w —   wish whisht†;
fl —   flesh flèche;

— —   each eche† [eatche]†; itch [ich]†; H aitch;
b —   beach beech; batch bacht†;
d —   ditch dicht†; Dutch dutch†;
k —   cutch kutch;
m —   March march; much mutch†;
n —   (niche) knitch†;
l —   leech leach;
r —   reach [reech] (retch); wretch (retch);
w —   witch which;
br —   breach breech; brooch broach;
kw—   quitch [quich]†;
sk —   scotch Scotch;
skr—   scratch Scratch;

t —   targe taj;
g —   gauge gage;
s —   serge surge cerge;
m —   marge Marg;
fr —   frig† fridget†;
sw —   swage† [suage]†;

— —   M em; arm (aam); ohm om†;
p —   pam Pam;
b —   balm barm (bomb);
t —   team teem; tomb toom†; time thyme;
d —   dam damn; doom (doum); dime disme†;
k —   cam kam† [cham]†; calm [cam]†; corm [caum]†; coomb coom† combe; came kame kaim†;
g —   gam gamb†;
f —   form forme; firm ferm†;
s —   seem seam seame†; sam Sam; sum some (Somme); same [saim]†;
h —   hymn him; ham Ham; harm [halm]; hawn† [haulm]; home holm Holm heaume†;
dʒ —   Jim gym†; jam jamb jambe;
m —   malm [marm]† (ma'am)†; mum Mum;
n —   gnome nome Nome;
l —   limb limn [lym]†; lamb lam; lime [lyme]†;
r —   ream riem [reame]†; rom (rhomb); (room) rheum; rum rhumb; roam Rome; rhyme rime;
pl —   plum plumb;

217

br — bream bremet; brim (bream); (Brougham) Broome (broom); (broom) brume (brougham) (Brougham) Broome;
dr — dram drachm;
kl — claim [clambe]†; cloam [clomb]†; climb clime;
kr — chrome [crome];
gl — gloom glume;
gr — grim grimme Grimm; gramme gram; groom grume;
fl — fleam flemet; flam [flamm];
st — steam [steem]†;

final n

— — inn in; N en; an Ann annt; urn earn erne Erne; eigne aint;
p — peen pean; pan Pan panne; pern pirnt; pane pain; pine pynet; Paean paean paeon peon;
b — bean (been) benet beint; bin (been); ben Ben; ban Bant; born borne bawn (bourn); boon Boone [boun]; bone Beaune;
t — teen ctene teenet tenet; toon (tune); ton tun; turn tern terne; tine Tyne;
d — dean Deane [deen]† dene; Dan dant; Don don; (dune) Doon; done dun Doone; durnt dernt; deign Dane; dine dyne;
k — keen Keane; can cann; cont [conn] connet; kern kerne curnt; cane Cain Kane kain; coin quoin coign;
g — [gaun]† gawn; [gerne]† girnt; gain [gane]†;
f — fin Finn; phon font; fawn faun; fern firn; feign fain fane Fane; 'phone fonet;
v — vein vain vane;
s — seen scene (seine); sawn sornt; sun son sunn; cernet scernet; sane Seine (seine) saint [saine]† [sayne]†; sign sine synet;
ʃ — shin [shinne]†; Shan sharnt; shown (shone); shine sinht
h — [hern] Herne;
dʒ — gene Jean (jean); gin jinn; Jane (jean) (Jain) janet;
m — mean mien mesnet meanet; morn mourn morne (maun)†; [mun]† (maun)†; mane main Maine; moan mown;
n — Norn gnawn; nun none; known nownt;
l — lean lien; linn Lynne lint; lawn lornt; loon (lune); lane lain; loan lone; line lynet; [lown]† lount;
r — wren rennet; rain reign rein; roan Rhone ronet; Rhine [rine]†;
w — wean weent; win whin winnt; when wen; worn warn; one won; wane wain Wain Wayne; wine whine;
j — yearn yernt yernet;
pl — 'plane plain plane;
br — brent brennet;
kr — croon Kroon;
kw — queen quean;
gl — glen Glen;
gr — green greint; grain graine; groan grown; groin groyne;
θr — throne thrown;
sp — spurn spurnet; Spain spanet;
st — stain [stane]†;

final ŋ

b — bang bhang;
k — kang cangue;

218

g — gang gangue;
s — sing Synge;
m — ming Ming;
r — ring wring; wrong rong†; rung wrung;
w — whang wang†;
kl — clang klang†;
sw — swing Swing;

---

final l

— — eel eale†; L ell; all awl orle†; earl Earl; ale ail; aisle isle I'll; Yule you'll;
p — peel peal; Poll poll†; pall Paul pawl; pool poule; pearl Pearl purl; pail pale; pole poll Pole;
b — beal biel; bill Bill; bell bel belle bael; (Baal) (Basle); ball bawl; buhl boul†; burl birl† birle†; bail bale (Baal); bowl bole boll;
t — teal teil [teel]; till [til]; tool tulle; tail tale tael; toll tole†;
d — deal [deil]†; dalle dal Dahl; [dool]† (duel) (dual); dole dhole; (dual) (duel);
k — kill (kiln); carl Carl; col coll†; call caul; cool [cowl]†; kale kail; coal cole Cole kohl [cowl]; kyle Kyle chyle;
g — gill ghyll; gall Gaul; (ghoul) [gule]†; girl gurl†; gale Gael Gale; goal [ghole]†; gowl† (ghoul);
f — feel feal†; fill Phil; fail (faille); file phial (faille); fowl foul;
v — veal [vele]†; veil vale vail†; vile (vial) (viol);
θ — thowl thole;
s — seal seel sele ceil; sell cell sel† selle†; sal salle; sol Sol; sail sale; soul sole [sowle]†; soil soyle†;
ʃ — she'll [sheal]† shiel†; shawl schorl; shoal (shool)†;
h — heel heal he'll hele†; hell Hell Hel; hall haul; hail hale; hole whole;
dʒ — geal jeel†; jill gill Jill; gel jell; (joule) (jewel) (Joule); jowl (joule) (Joule);
m — mill mil (Milne); marl [marle]†; maul (Mall); merle Merle; mail male maile†; mole moll; moil moyle†; mule mewl;
n — kneel [neal]† Neil [neele]†; nil nill†; knell Nell; noll knoll;
r — real reel; rill rille; rail rayle†; role roll Rolle; roil (royal);
w — wheel wheal weal we'll weil weel; wall waul wawl†; whirl whorl; whale wail wale; while wile;
j — you'll Yule;
br — Braille brail;
tr — trail treille;
tw — tuille [tweel]†; twill 'twill; toile (twal)†;
gr — grill grille; grail grayle†
sp — spiel† speel† [speal]†; spall spawl;
st — steal steel steale†; style stile;
sk — school [schoole]†; skull scull [scul]†; scale skail†;

---

final ft

b — (baffed) (baft);
t — tift† tiffed;
d — (daffed) (daft);
k — coughed coft;
tʃ — (chaffed) (chaft);
l — left lefte†;
r — rift [rifte]†; ruffed roughed;

w	—	(waft) (waffed); (waft) (Wafd);
dr	—	(draft) (draught);
kl	—	[clift] cliffed; cleft klepht;
kr	—	(craft) kraft;
gr	—	(graphed) (graft);
sk	—	[scuft]† scuffed;

final st

p	—	(past) (passed); (passed) (past) (parsed); paste paced;
b	—	bust bussed; baste based bassed;
d	—	dust dost†; dowsed doused;
k	—	kissed kist†; cast caste; cost [coste]†;
g	—	guest guessed; gassed (ghast)†;
f	—	fust fussed;
v	—	verst versed;
s	—	cyst cist sist†; cest cessed;
h	—	hist† hissed; horst horsed (halsed)†; hurst hearsed†; host hoast†;
tʃ	—	chaste chased;
dʒ	—	jest gest geste jessed; (joust) juiced; just (joust);
m	—	mist missed; massed (mast); must mussed;
l	—	least leased; list Liszt;
r	—	reast reest† reist†; rest wrest; raced (rast)†;
w	—	whist wist†; waist waste;
pr	—	priest [preaced]†; pressed prest†;
bl	—	blest blessed;
br	—	breast Brest;
tr	—	tryst† trist†; trust trussed;
gr	—	(greased) grieced;

final nt

—	—	ant (aunt); (aunt) aren't an't†;
k	—	Kent kent†; cant (can't) Kant; count [compt]†;
g	—	[gant]† (gaunt);
f	—	faint feint;
s	—	scent cent sent;
m	—	meant [ment]†;
l	—	lent Lent leant;
w	—	want (wont); (wont) won't;
kw	—	quaint queint†;
gr	—	grant Grant; grunt Granth;

final lt

p	—	poult polt†;
b	—	bolt boult Boult;
k	—	kelt (Celt); (colt) Colt;
g	—	guilt gilt; gault Gault;
f	—	felt (veldt);
s	—	celt (Celt);
h	—	holt Holt;
m	—	moult [molt]†;

— — earned urned;
p — piend peened (point)†; pinned (point)†; pend penned; panned pand†; pained paned;
b — band banned; bond Bond;
t — teind teened† [teend]†; tinned [tind]†; tund tunned†; tined [tind]†;
k — [conned] kond†;
f — fond fonned†; find fined;
s — signed synd; sound [sownd]†;
tʃ — chynd† chined;
m — maund mourned [mauned]†; maned mained†; mind mined;
l — lind linned†;
r — reigned rained reined; rind rynd;
w — weaned weened†; wend Wend; wand wanned†; wind whined wined wynd†;
bl — blend blende; blonde blond;
st — (stownd)† (stound)†;

p — pealed peeled piel'd†; purled pearled; polled poled;
b — bield† bealed; build billed; bald balled bawled; birled† burled†; baled bailed; bold bowled bolled;
t — told tolled toled†;
k — called cauld†; cold coaled;
g — guild gild gilled;
f — field fealed†; fold foaled;
v — veiled vailed†;
s — ceiled sealed seeled; celled seld†; sold soled [sowled]†;
ʃ — shield [shealed]†;
h — healed heeled heled† [heald]; hauled [hauld]†; hailed haled; hold holed;
dʒ — gealed jeeled†; jelled gelled;
m — meld melled; mauled malled;
n — kneeled [neeld]†; knolled nould†;
w — wield weald Weald wheeled; weld welled; walled wauled wawled†; world whirled whorled; wailed waled whaled; wild wiled;
j — yeld† yelled; yawled [yauld]†;
sp — speeled† spieled†; spelled speld†; spauld† spawled spalled;
st — steeled [stealed]†;
sk — scald skald; scaled skailed†;

b — bisque bisk; Basque bask;
k — casque cask;
f — fisk† fisc;
m — masque mask;

b — bank banc;
k — conch conk;
s — sink cinque;
tʃ — chink Chink†;
r — rank ranke Rank;

j   —   yank Yank;
pr   —   prank pranck†;
fr   —   frank franc Frank;

w   —   [whilk]† [wilk]; whelk welk†;

d   —   delf delph;
w   —   wolf Wolfe;

—   —   arcs arks; orcs auks; oaks okes;
p   —   peeks peaks piques pekes†; pyx picks; pecs pecks; pax packs; pox pocks; pooks† [poukes];
b   —   becks [beckes]†; barques barks; box boks; burkes [birks]†; bykes† bikes†;
t   —   tics ticks; tax tacks; torques talks; tucks tux†;
d   —   dooks† (dukes) (doucs); dux ducks; [dirkes]† dirks;
k   —   kex kecks; cox cocks coques; calks corks caulks; coax cokes;
f   —   forks falks†; faikes fakes faiks† faix†; fykes† fikes†;
s   —   (Sikhs) seeks; six (Sikhs); sax Saxe sacks sacs sacques; [serks]† circs†; soaks sokes†;
ʃ   —   (shoughs) shocks; shakes (sheikhs);
h   —   hox† houghs hocks; hoax holks†; haiks hikes; hoicks† hoiks;
tʃ   —   chicks tchicks; checks cheques Czechs; charks chacks†;
dʒ   —   jaks jacks; jouks† jukes†; jerques jerks;
m   —   max† macks†; marques† marks Marx [maks]†; mux† mucks; makes [maiks]†;
n   —   nix nicks Nyx (Pnyx); neks necks; nocks knocks Knox Nox;
l   —   leaks leeks; lax lacks lakhs; lox locks; lux (luxe); lakes laiks†;
r   —   wreaks† reeks reaks† rekes†; ricks wricks; rex wrecks recks; racks rax†; rocs rocks; raiks rakes;
w   —   wax whacks Waacs; walks [warks]†;
j   —   yokes yolks;
pl   —   (plaques) (placks);
bl   —   blocks blocs;
br   —   brocks (broughs); breaks brakes;
kl   —   cleeks† (cliques); clicks (cliques); (clerks) claques;
kr   —   creaks (creeks); cricks (creeks); Crax cracks;
fl   —   flix flicks; flex flecks; Phlox flocks;
sp   —   specs† specks; sparks sparkes†;
st   —   Styx sticks; storks stalks; stakes steaks;
sn   —   [snoeks] snooks;
str —   streeks† streaks;

s   —   sense cense [sens]†;
h   —   Hanse (hance)† Hans;
l   —   (lance) (launce) Lance;

p — punch Punch;
l — lynch linch Lynch;
bl — Blanche blanch;

l — lunge longe;

t — tarpon tarpan;
r — Rippon Ripon;

b — (Bourbon) (bourbon);
g — gibbon Gibbon;
r — robin Robin; rubin Reuben;

— — eaten Eton Eaton;
p — pattern patten† paten;
b — bitten bittern; baton batten; Burton burton;
t — Titan tighten;
k — chitin chiton Chiton;
s — satin Saturn;
h — hearten hartin;
m — martin Martin marten;
l — (luiten)† litten†; Latin latten; Luton (luiten)† looten†;
r — ratton† ratten; rhyton righten;
w — wheaten [weeten]†;
pl — platen platan;
br — Briton Britain Britten; brighten Brighton;
kr — Cretan (cretin); (cretin) (cretonne);
kw — quartan quartern;
str — straighten straiten;

h — harden (hadden)†; hudden† (hadden)†;
m — madden Maddon;
l — leaden ledden†;
gl — gladden gladdon;

p — [perkin]† Perkin;
b — barken [barcon];
θ — thicken thickun†;
s — sicken (Sican) siccan†; soaken soken;
m — morkin malkin†;
l — liken lichen;
r — reckon reckan†;

223

— —	(argon) argan arghan;
h —	Hogan hogen†;
m —	Morgan morgen;
n —	noggin noggen†;
l —	logan Logan;
w —	wigan Wigan; waggon Wagon;
br —	brogan† Brogan;
tr —	trigon Trygon;
tr —	dragon Dragon;

— —	orphan (often);
r —	roughen ruffin†;
gr —	griffin griffon;

l —	leaven levin†;
st —	Steven steven†;

p —	person percen†;
f —	(fasten) farcin;
m —	(meson) messan†; mason Mason;
l —	lesson lessen; loosen (leucine);
gl —	glisten Glisson [glicin];

k —	cousin cozen;
s —	season seisin;
r —	rosen Rosen;
gr —	greisen (grison);

s —	session cession;

p —	pigeon pidgin;
l —	legion Legion;

t —	Timon timon†;
d —	demon daemon; Damon (daimen);
k —	Carmen Carman carmen;
g —	gammon (gamin);
h —	hymen Hymen Hyman;

dʒ — German german;
n — Norman norman; nomen gnomon;
l — lemon (leman)†;
br — Brahmen Brahmin;
kr — crumen crewmen;

---

final ln̩

p — pollen pollan;
k — Colin colin;
v — villain villein villan;
s — Solen solan Solon;
m — marline Marlin; Merlin merlon merlin murlain†;
st — stolen stolon;

---

final rn̩

b — barren baron;
k — Carron (Karen) (Charon);
s — siren Siren;
h — heron herren Heron;
w — warren Warren warrin;

---

final ksn̩

t — toxin tocsin;

---

final pl̩

p — people (pipal); pupil pupal;
k — carpel carpal;
tʃ — chapel Chappell;
tr — triple tripple†;

---

final bl̩

— — able [abeie] Abel;
k — corbel [corbeil];
s — [cibol] Sybil sibyl; sable Sabal;
n — nobble† [knobble] nubble [knubble];

---

final tl̩

p — petal pettle†;
b — beetle betel baetyl; battle battel;
k — kirtle curtal;
s — subtle suttle;
m — metal mettle; myrtle Myrtle;
w — whittle wittol;
sp — spittle spital†;

— — idle idol (idyll);
p — pedal peddle; [padle]† pardal;
b — beadle bedel†;
k — caudal caudle cordal;
m — medal meddle;
br — bridal bridle;

p — pickle picul;
b — buckle buccal;
t — tickle (tical);
k — cockle cockal;
s — sickle [Sikel]; circle cercal; Sokel (socle)†;
m — mackle macle;
n — nickel nicol;
j — yokel yokul;
br — bricklet (bricole);

— — eagle egal†; argal argol;
b — burgal burgle burghal;
g — gargle gargil;
r — wriggle rigol†;

— — awful (offal);

— — arval [arvel];
d — devil Devil devvel†;
n — nevel Neville; naval navel;

— — eassel† (eisel)†;
t — torsel torcel;
d — dossil dossel; dorsal [dorsel];
f — fissle (fissile);
s — (sisal) scissel (Sicel) (Cecil) sisel;
h — hirsel hirsle† hersall†;
m — missal (missel)† (missile); muscle mussel;
r — rustle russel Russel;

p — puzzle (pussel)†;
b — bezel bezzle†; basil Basil;

d — diesel (deasil)†;
h — hazel Hazel;
m — mizzle (missel)†;
n — nuzzle (nousle);

---

final ʃḷ

m — marshal Marshall martial;

---

final mḷ

p — pummel pommel†;
f — formal formel†;

---

final nḷ

— — annal anil;
k — colonel kernel;
f — phenol phenyl; fennel Fennell;
v — vinal vinyl;

---

final rḷ

— — aril aryl; oral aural;
b — Beryl beryl; burrel Burrell [bharal];
t — Tyrol Tyrrell Tirol;
k — carol Carol Carroll; coral (choral);
s — [sorel]† soral†;
m — meril Meryl; moral morel;
l — (laurel) (loral); (loral) [lorel]†;
pl — pleural plural;
st — sterol (sterile);

---

final mbḷ

b — bumble Bumble;
g — gamble gambol;
s — symbol cymbal;
dʒ — jumble jumbal;

---

final stḷ

p — pistol pistil;
b — borstall Borstal;
h — (hostile) (hostel);

---

final ntḷ

m — mantle mantel;

---

v — Vandal vandal;
h — handle Handel;
r — roundel rowndell†;

t — tinkle tincal (tinchel);

— — angle Angle;
s — single cingle;
sp — springle springal†;

p — pencil pensil (pensile);
k — council counsel;
h — hansel (Hänsel);

Appendix

INTRODUCTION

Listed in this Appendix are those words which have final consonantal combinations occurring too infrequently to justify their inclusion in a separate Table. Similarly, rare initial combinations are listed. Only those clusters which occur in at least four words are included; if they are to be found in more than twelve words they are recorded in tabular form, except /nz/ which would be primarily a repetition of the final /n/ Table.

The structure of the words selected for the Appendix is in keeping with that in the rest of the book, i.e. they are either monosyllables, or disyllables ending with a syllabic /m̩/ /n̩/ or /l̩/. Where one of these words begins with an unusual initial cluster (e.g. /ʃn̩/) it is included.

Homophones are recorded together, and include the inflected form of words which would not otherwise be listed.

Triphthongs

The four diphthongal glides ending with the weak /ə/, i.e. /aɪə/, /aʊə/, /eɪə/ and /oʊə/, which are sometimes considered as triphthongs but more usually form two syllables, are listed in this Appendix when they fall in words having no final consonant. No distinction is made between words with vowel glides transcribed (Jones; 1967) ai-ə and aiə as in *higher* and *hire*. For convenience, the /jʊə/ combination has also been included on this Table.

It has been pointed out by Gimson (1962) that these vowels may be reduced to two elements in rapid RP speech with the central sound being eclipsed, e.g. aʊə‡ > a:ə and aɪə > a:ə, producing new homophones such as *tyre-tower*. These variations are not included, nor are such rare combinations as /ɔɪə/.

Initial Consonants

In English there are a number of initial sound clusters, usually of foreign origin, for which fewer than four words are to be found: e.g. /ps/ in *psi*; /ts/ in (*tsar*); /kθ/ in *k'thibh*; /vl/ in *Vlach*; /vr/ in *vraic*; /pw/ in *puy*; /bw/ in *bwana*; /gw/ in *guan*; /θw/ in *thwart*; /zbl/ in *'sblood*. Such combinations are not listed.

‡ As symbolised in this book.

229

Final Consonants

Words listed in this section include the following:

1. Those with rare consonantal clusters, e.g. /lm/ as in *elm*.
2. Those which are generally used in their plural form only, e.g. *jeans*. When these occur as homonyms they are also listed, e.g. *hives* meaning 'a nettle rash and similar diseases . . .' (Chambers).
3. Those which have an uninflected form ending in a common cluster, e.g. *apt* with final /pt/ and *act* with final /kt/. These clusters are frequently found in certain regular verb forms, e.g. *hopped* and *packed* and for the formation of these combinations readers are referred to the /p/ and /k/ Tables.

Words enclosed in parentheses () indicate an alternate pronunciation but are not listed twice as in the Tables. Other markings are as indicated in the Key to Symbols on page xii.

References

CHAMBERS TWENTIETH CENTURY DICTIONARY (1952) Mid-Century Version (Ed. William Geddie), W. & R. Chambers, Edinburgh and London.
GIMSON, A. C. (1962) *An Introduction to the Pronunciation of English*, Edward Arnold, London.
JONES, D. (1967) *Everyman's English Pronouncing Dictionary*, (13th edn.) revised by A. C. Gimson, J. M. Dent & Sons, London.

TRIPHTHONGS

Initial	aɪə	aʊə	eɪə	oʊə	jʊə
— —	ire	hour, our	.	.	ewer, Ure, ure†, (you're)
p —	pyre	power, Power	payer	.	(pure)
b —	byre, buyer	bower	.	boa	.
t —	tyre, tire, tier	tower	.	tower	.
d —	dire, dyer, Dyer	dower	.	.	(dure)
k —	.	cower	.	.	(cure)
g —	.	gaur	.	Goa, goer	.
f —	fire	.	.	.	fewer
v —	via	.	.	.	viewer
s —	sire, sigher	sour	sayer	sower, sewer	(sewer)
ʃ —	shire, shyer	shower	.	shower	.
h —	hire, higher	.	.	hoer	hewer
dʒ —	gyre	.	.	.	.
m —	mire, Meyer	.	mayor, Mayor	mower	(Muir), (Mure), mure†
n —	.	.	.	knower, Noah	(newer)
l —	lyre, liar, lier	lour	layer	lower	(lure)
r —	.	.	.	rower	.
w —	wire	weigher	.	.	.
pl —	plier	plougher	player	.	.
pr —	prior, Prior, pryer	.	prayer	.	.
bl —	.	.	.	blower	.
br —	briar, brier	.	.	.	.
tr —	trier	.	.	.	.

Initial	aɪə	aʊə	eɪə	oʊə	jʊə
dr —	drier, dryer	.	.	.	.
kr —	crier	.	.	crower	.
kw —	choir, quire	.	.	.	.
gl —	.	glaur, glower	.	.	.
gr —	.	.	grayer	grower	.
fl —	flier	flour, flower	flayer	.	.
fr —	friar, fryer	.	.	.	.
θr —	.	.	.	thrower	.
sp —	spire	.	.	.	spewer
st —	.	.	stayer	.	stewer
sk —	skyre†	scour [scaur]†	.	.	skewer
sl —	slyer	.	slayer	slower	.
sw —	swire†	.	swayer	.	.
spr —	.	.	sprayer	.	.
str —	.	.	strayer	.	.
skw —	squire, Squire	.	.	.	.

INITIAL CONSONANTS

Initial sf	final
sphere;	—
sphene;	n
sphex;	ks
sphinx;	ŋks
sphacel;	sl
spheral;	rl

Initial dw	final
dwarf;	f
dwalm;	m
dwine;	n
dwang;	ŋ
dwell; dwale;	l
dwelt;	lt
dwindle;	ndl

FINAL CONSONANTS

Initial		final pt
—	—	apt/opt;
k	—	Copt copped†;
s	—	sept;
r	—	rapt wrapped;
w	—	wept;
kr	—	crypt/crept;
sl	—	slept;
sw	—	swept;
skr	—	script;

See pages 54–55 for regular verbs which have an inflected form ending in the /pt/ cluster (e.g. hopped). Add the letters p/ed to these words.

231

FINAL CONSONANTS (*cont.*)

Initial			final kt
—	—	act;	
p	—	Pict picked; pact packed;	
t	—	tact tacked;	
d	—	duct ducked;	
f	—	fact;	
s	—	sect;	
br	—	bract;	
tr	—	tract tracked;	
fr	—	fract†;	
str	—	strict;	

See pages 62–63 for regular verbs which have an inflected form ending in the /kt/ cluster (e.g. lacked). Add the letters *ed* to these words.

Initial			final m(p)t
t	—	tempt ['tempt]†;	
d	—	dempt†;	
k	—	kempt;	
n	—	nempt†;	
pr	—	prompt;	
dr	—	dreamt;	

Initial			final ʒ
b	—	beize;	
t	—	tige;	
v	—	vou(l)ge;	
l	—	(luge);	
r	—	rouge;	
gr	—	grège;	

Initial			final lv
d	—	delve;	
v	—	valve; volve†;	
s	—	(salve); solve;	
ʃ	—	shelve;	
h	—	helve;	
tw	—	twelve;	

Initial			final lθ
—	—	illth†;	
t	—	tilth;	
f	—	filth;	
h	—	health;	
w	—	wealth;	
sp	—	spilth;	
st	—	stealth;	

Initial			final ps
—	—	apse;	
s	—	seps Seps;	
ʃ	—	shaps†;	
l	—	lapse laps Lapps;	
tr	—	traipse;	

FINAL CONSONANTS *(cont.)*

θr — Thrips;
st — stirps;
sk — Scops;
ʃn — schnapps;

See pages 54–55 for nouns and regular verbs which have an inflected form ending in the /ps/ cluster (e.g. hops and apes). Add the letter *s* to these words.

Initial			final ts
—	—	it's its; Ats;	
f	—	fitz; fits;	
s	—	cits sitz sits;	
h	—	Harz harts hearts; hertz† Hertz hurts;	
bl	—	blitz;	
fr	—	Fritz;	
kw	—	quartz quarts;	
sp	—	spitz spits;	
sw	—	[swits]†; swats†;	

See pages 58–59 for nouns and regular verbs which have an inflected form ending with the /ts/ cluster (e.g. coats and eats). Add the letter *s* to these words.

Initial			final ls
—	—	else;	
p	—	pulse;	
b	—	bulse;	
d	—	dulse;	
f	—	(false);	
v	—	valse;	
s	—	salse;	
h	—	halse† hals†;	
w	—	(waltz);	
gr	—	grilse;	

Initial			final ŋks
dʒ	—	jinx† Jynx jinks†;	
m	—	minx minks;	
n	—	(Pnyx) nicks;	
l	—	lynx links/lanx†;	
j	—	[yunx];	
br	—	branks†;	

See pages 112–113 for nouns and regular verbs which have an inflected form ending with the /ŋks/ cluster (e.g. sinks and thanks). Add the letter *s* to these words.

Initial			final bz
θ	—	Thebes;	
n	—	nabs†;	
pl	—	plebs;	
sk	—	scobs;	

See pages 56–57 for nouns and regular verbs which have an inflected form ending with the /bz/ cluster (e.g. webs and sobs). Add the letter *s* to these words.

FINAL CONSONANTS (*cont.*)

			final dz
Initial			

— — adze adds; uds†; Ides;
g — gourds;
s — suds;
h — [hards]; [hurds];
l — Leeds leads; Lauds lords;
r — Rhodes roads;

See pages 60–61 for nouns and regular verbs which have an inflected form ending with the /dz/ cluster (e.g. beds and nods). Add the letter *s* to these words.

			final gz
Initial			

f — fegs†;
dʒ — (jougs); (jougs) jugs;
tr — troggs†;
dr — dregs;

See pages 64–65 for nouns and regular verbs which have an inflected form ending with the /gz/ cluster (e.g. bags and begs). Add the letter *s* to these words.

			final vz
Initial			

— — oaves;
f — fives;
v — vives;
θ — thieves;
h — halves; hives;
n — knives;
ʃ — sheaves;
l — loaves; lives;
kl — Cleaves cleaves cleves;
gr — [greaves] grieves; [graves] Graves;

See pages 68–69 for nouns and regular verbs which have an inflected form ending with the /vz/ cluster (e.g. caves and saves). Add the letter *s* to these words.

			final nz
Initial			

— — ens;
p — pons;
b — banns bans; bonze;
s — sans†;
h — Hans; harns†;
d — jeans genes; gens; Jones;
m — mains† manes;
n — Nones;
l — lens;
r — reins† reigns rains;
w — winze wins; wanze†;
br — bronze;
kl — cleanse;
kw — quinze quins†;

See pages 86–87 for nouns and regular verbs which have an inflected form ending with the /nz/ cluster (e.g. tins and tans). Add the letter *s* to these words.

FINAL CONSONANTS (*cont.*)

Initial			final lz
b	—	Bowles bowls bolls boles;	
k	—	Knowles knolls;	
g	—	gules†;	
v	—	vales;	
w	—	Wales wails;	

See pages 90–91 for nouns and regular verbs which have an inflected form ending with the /lz/ cluster (e.g. balls and fails). Add the letter *s* to these words.

Initial			final l(t)ʃ
p	—	pilch;	
b	—	belch;	
k	—	culch†;	
g	—	gulch†;	
f	—	filch;	
h	—	hilch†;	
m	—	milch; mulch;	
w	—	[welch];	
kw	—	quelch;	
skw	—	squelch;	

Initial			final lm
—	—	elm;	
k	—	culm Culm;	
f	—	film;	
h	—	helm;	
r	—	realm;	
w	—	whelm†;	
st	—	stulm;	
sk	—	schelm;	

Initial			final dm̩
—	—	Edam; Adam;	
b	—	boredom;	
d	—	dirdum;	
s	—	Sedum; czardom; Sodom;	
m	—	madam;	
l	—	Ledum;	
h	—	whoredom;	
kw	—	quidam;	
sm	—	[smeddum]†;	

Initial			final km̩
—	—	Occam; oakum; o'ercome†;	
k	—	kokum;	
s	—	caecum;	
h	—	hakim; hokum†;	
l	—	locum;	

FINAL CONSONANTS (*cont.*)

Initial		final ɡm̩
— —	[ogam]; [ogham];	
b —	begum;	
t —	(Targum); tergum;	
s —	Sorghum; sagum;	

Initial		final ðm̩
f —	fathom;	
z —	zythum;	
r —	rhythm;	
sm —	[smitham]†;	

Initial		final sm̩
p —	possum;	
b —	beesome†;	
t —	twosome;	
f —	foursome;	
n —	noisome;	
l —	lissom;	
w —	woesome; [waesome]†;	
bl —	blossom;	
ɡr —	grassum†;	
θr —	threesome;	

Initial		final zm̩
b —	(besom); bosom;	
k —	chasm;	
s —	seism;	
pl —	plasm;	
pr —	prism;	
kr —	chrism chrisom;	
sp —	spasm;	
sk —	schism;	

Initial		final nm̩
p —	paynim†;	
d —	denim;	
v —	venom;	
m —	minim;	
pl —	plenum;	
ɡr —	grannem†;	
st —	sternum;	

Initial		final ən
p —	(powan);	
ɡ —	gowan†;	
r —	(rowan) rowen; (rowan) (Rowan);	
j —	yewen†;	

Initial			final θņ
—	—	earthen;	
p	—	python Python;	
s	—	[cithern];	
br	—	Brython;	

Initial			final ðņ
b	—	[burthen]†;	
s	—	sithen†; southern;	
h	—	heathen;	
n	—	northern;	
r	—	wreathen†; writhen†;	

Initial			final ʒņ
—	—	(Asian);	
p	—	Persian;	
f	—	[fizzen]†; fusion;	
v	—	vision; version;	
s	—	(scission);	
l	—	lesion;	
pl	—	plosion;	
fr	—	Freisian;	
sw	—	suasion;	

Initial			final tʃņ
—	—	urchin;	
b	—	birchen;	
k	—	kitchen; Cochin;	
l	—	(lichen); larchen;	
sk	—	[scutcheon]†;	

Initial			final nņ
p	—	pennon;	
t	—	tenon; tannin;	
g	—	(guenon);	
k	—	canon cannon;	
f	—	finnan;	
z	—	(xenon);	
l	—	linen; linin;	
fl	—	[flannen]†;	
kr	—	kronen;	

Initial			final njņ
—	—	onion;	
b	—	bunion;	
k	—	canyon;	
r	—	runyon†;	

FINAL CONSONANTS (*cont.*)

Initial			final stṇ
—	—	Austin; Euston;	
p	—	piston; pastern†; postern;	
b	—	boston Boston;	
g	—	guesten†;	
s	—	cistern;	
w	—	western;	
j	—	[yestern]†;	

Initial			final nʃṇ
p	—	pension; pancheon; puncheon;	
t	—	tension;	
k	—	cantion†;	
m	—	mention; mansion;	
n	—	nuncheon;	
l	—	luncheon;	
tr	—	truncheon;	
sp	—	sponsion;	
st	—	stanchion;	
sk	—	scansion; [scontion]; [scuncheon];	

Initial			final əl
b	—	(bowel);	
t	—	(towel); tewel;	
d	—	(dowel) (Dowell); (dual) (duel);	
f	—	(fuel);	
v	—	(vowel);	
s	—	[sewel];	
ʃ	—	shewel (Shewell);	
dʒ	—	(jewel);	
n	—	knawel; (Nowell) (Noel);	
r	—	rowel (Rowell);	
kr	—	(crewel) (cruel);	

Initial			final θḷ
—	—	ethyl Ethel;	
b	—	bethel;	
l	—	lethal;	
m	—	methyl;	
br	—	brothel;	
st	—	stethal;	

Initial			final tʃḷ
—	—	(archil); [orchel];	
f	—	futchel;	
s	—	satchel;	
h	—	[hatchel];	
m	—	Mitchell;	
n	—	notchel;	
r	—	Rachel;	
dr	—	dratchell†;	
sw	—	switchel;	

FINAL CONSONANTS (*cont.*)

Initial			final dʒ
—	—	argil;	
p	—	pugil;	
k	—	cudgel;	
v	—	vigil; Virgil;	
s	—	sigil;	
n	—	Nigel;	
r	—	ridgel; (Rigel);	
str	—	strigil;	

Initial			final skl
p	—	(paschal) Pascal; (paschal);	
d	—	discal;	
f	—	fiscal; fo'c'sle;	
r	—	rascal;	

Initial			final ksl
—	—	axle;	
s	—	saxaul;	
n	—	noxal;	
r	—	wraxle†;	

Index to Tables and Homophones*

---

* Bold page numbers indicating Tables are followed by normal page numbers indicating the corresponding Homophones.

Index to Appendix

Subject Index